KARL KAUTSKY

1854–1938

KARL KAUTSKY
1854–1938

Marxism in the Classical Years

by Gary P. Steenson

UNIVERSITY OF PITTSBURGH PRESS

Publication of this book was assisted
by the American Council of Learned Societies
under a grant from the Andrew W. Mellon Foundation.

Published by the University of Pittsburgh Press, Pittsburgh, Pa., 15260
Copyright © 1978, University of Pittsburgh Press
Feffer and Simons, Inc., London
Manufactured in the United States of America

Library of Congress Cataloging in Publication Data

Steenson, Gary P., 1944–
  Karl Kautsky, 1854-1938.

  Bibliography: p. 291
  1. Kautsky, Karl, 1854–1938. 2. Socialism. 3. Socialists—Biography.
HX273.K34S7   335.4'092'4 [B]   78-3701
ISBN 0-8229-3377-2

To my mother and father,
Bernice L. and Leon P. Steenson

Contents

Illustrations

Acknowledgments

VALLERIE STEENSON PROVIDED ENCOURAGEMENT and guidance from beginning to end on this project. Her common sense and clear analytical abilities strengthened my work at many points. Her patience with interminable Kautsky anecdotes and monologues on obscure theoretical and historiographic points was astounding. My life and my work have gained immeasurably from our relationship.

As I have tried to argue in the case of Karl Kautsky, it is difficult to pinpoint specifically the intellectual influences of any person's life. In my own case, however, one person was of especial importance to my development as a historian. Albert Shirk Lindemann was my dissertation advisor and a teacher in the finest tradition. He taught me intellectual discipline, to eschew obfuscation, and to work hard at history. His detailed criticisms of my writing style improved it greatly. My debt to him is large and my gratitude sincere.

I was particularly fortunate to have access to invaluable sources of personal information about Karl Kautsky in the persons of Dr. and Mrs. Karl Kautsky, Jr. In many hours of conversation with these interested and interesting people, I was able to learn things about Kautsky and his milieu I could not have learned from any other source. The Kautskys also allowed me to borrow from their personal collection of photographs, many of which are included in this book. Finally, Dr. Kautsky read the completed manuscript and made several corrections of details.

Many of my friends were too often subjected to Karl Kautsky, but most of them bore up quite well. In fact, James McJannet Robertson was concerned enough about my inadequacies to read the manuscript very thoroughly and to comment extensively on matters of substance and detail both. His careful scholarship and wide knowledge of

German sources have been to my advantage. I thank him for his assistance. Sincere thanks are also due to Joe and Martha Bennett for support and encouragement.

The staffs of several libraries and archives deserve special recognition. I extend thanks to: Agnes Peterson and the Hoover Institution; the International Institute for Social History, Amsterdam; the interlibrary loan office at Indiana University–Purdue University, Fort Wayne; and the Green Library of Stanford University. Having been employed at the Green Library for almost two years, I have learned to appreciate more than ever the symbiotic relationship of scholars and librarians.

KARL KAUTSKY

1854–1938

Introduction

KARL KAUTSKY'S MAJOR OCCUPATION in life was translating
Marx's abstract theories and unsystematically presented political
precepts into the coherent doctrine of a mass party. From January
1880 to mid-1919, he devoted himself almost exclusively to the
socialist, working-class movement in Germany. In his capacity as unofficial theoretician of the Sozialdemokratische Partei Deutschlands
(SPD), Kautsky was the first person to attempt to coordinate systematically the activities of a significant mass movement with the theory of
Karl Marx. He did more to popularize Marxism in western Europe
than any other intellectual, with the possible exception of Friedrich
Engels. Moreover, Kautsky's works were translated into as many as
thirty languages in his own lifetime, a scope of potential influence not
achieved by Marx, Engels, and perhaps even Lenin until after their
deaths. Kautsky's initial popularization of Marx's economic doctrines
was probably the first full-length Marxian work translated into
Chinese. He corresponded with the leading figures of virtually every
socialist party in the world, from those of continental Europe to North
and South America, Asia, North Africa, and the Middle East. In book
after book, at one international congress after another, from 1895 to
1914, Karl Kautsky was the most important theorist of Marxism in the
world. Even today, after he has fallen into relative historical obscurity,
Kautsky's works are reissued in countries generally antagonistic to the
doctrine he espoused, like the United States and Taiwan, and in the
Soviet Union and its satellite nations of eastern Europe.[1]

Kautsky was a prolific writer; his works include histories, economic
treatises, political discussions, theoretical discourses, and party programs. But except for the last item, probably his most significant
contribution to the German and world Marxist movements was his

writing for and editing of the *Neue Zeit*, the major Marxian journal in Germany for almost four decades. Kautsky edited it from its founding in 1883 until 1917. His journal included articles by all the major Marxian theoreticians and politicians of the years before World War I. Its pages carried doctrinal debates, historical analysis, and contemporary political arguments. Although the journal never had a large circulation, it was very influential among socialist intellectuals in Germany and the rest of Europe.

For most of his years as the *Neue Zeit* editor, Kautsky and the political leaders of the SPD agreed on major issues. This was in large part due to Kautsky's dependence on August Bebel for guidance on political questions. Occasional disputes, as on the mass-strike issue in 1903–1906, were exceptions to the rule that the *Neue Zeit* was the theoretical arm of the party. But Kautsky did not by any means dominate SPD policy, and his Marxism was never accepted by the party without reservation. In theoretical terms the SPD began as, and remains to this day, a relatively harmonious but eclectic movement. But in 1914 the sometimes tenuous unity of the party was shattered by the outbreak of war, and Kautsky quickly moved away from the official SPD support for the German war effort. In 1917, he lost the *Neue Zeit* because his antiwar stand offended the party leadership. Kautsky never reestablished any regular connection with the SPD.

Unfortunately, Kautsky's character and theories are misunderstood and misrepresented by friend and foe alike. He has been neither well nor fairly treated by most historians and political scientists, let alone by doctrinaire political writers. Led by Lenin, communists have since 1918 vilified Kautsky as a turncoat and betrayer of the masses. The often equally dogmatic opponents of communism, especially in the Anglo-Saxon world, have criticized him for his radical rhetoric and rigid stands that prevented the SPD from developing into a broadly based democratic party. Although he has not been entirely without defenders, even some of these people have exaggerated and distorted to paint a sharper picture than the sometimes fuzzy reality justifies.[2]

Many authors have tried to deal with Kautsky's theory in more or less abstract terms, that is, by generalizing about the whole of his enormous corpus of work or by cataloging his theory according to certain sweeping concepts.[3] Still others have delved into particular aspects of Kautsky's activities or his relationships with particular people.[4] While many of these studies make important contributions, they all lack the sort of detailed look at Kautsky's personal life that reveals a different picture of him than does the more abstract or limited approach.

Until now only one major study of Kautsky's entire life has

appeared — Marek Waldenberg's *Wzlot i upadek Karola Kautsky' ego* (The rise and fall of Karl Kautsky). Because it was written in Polish and has not yet been translated, this work can reach only a very limited audience. Furthermore, Waldenberg devoted the overwhelming majority of his thirteen-hundred-odd pages to SPD and German politics, very few to the origins of Kautsky's thought, and even fewer to various personal events that are important to understanding Kautsky's interpretation of Marxism. Waldenberg does, however, make a surprisingly balanced and reasonable assessment of Kautsky.[5]

The present study is not a definitive biography; a great many personal matters are not discussed in detail. My particular concern is with the factors that brought Kautsky to develop his Marxism as he did; therefore I am more concerned with Kautsky-as-Marxist than with Kautsky in any other guise. I have emphasized those aspects of his life which were pertinent to his theoretical development and positions, and I have slighted those which had no direct or significant impact. I undertook this study as a preliminary to a more comprehensive investigation of pre-Leninist Marxism and the national movements associated with it. Many of the other figures from these years, including Luxemburg, Jaurès, Guesde, Plekhanov, and Lenin, for instance, have already been dealt with in biographies. I hope the present work fills a gap in the secondary literature.

The value of a more detailed and personal look at Kautsky's life will be demonstrated in the text that follows, but on four particularly important issues raised by other studies of Kautsky this approach yields new insights. First, Kautsky has a very widespread reputation as a dogmatist, an inflexible ideologue who rejected compromise and dealt harshly with intellectual and political opponents. However, a closer look at day-to-day activities shows that sometimes Engels and even more often Bebel stood behind Kautsky, pressing him on to more severe attacks. This happened in the case of Kautsky's criticism of Rodbertus in 1885, during the revisionism controversy of 1898–1903, and again in 1910 when the SPD Baden branch voted to support the state budget. Kautsky did frequently take firm stands, but often he had to be pushed to these positions by others.

Second, Kautsky's theory has been called Darwino-Marxism, and virtually all writers on the topic have agreed that he was heavily influenced by the evolutionary theory of Darwin and other naturalists. But as early as an obscure 1885 article, Kautsky specifically denied that natural laws could be applied to human society. He reaffirmed this position many times between 1885 and his last major theoretical work in 1928. In the latter he once again very pointedly rejected the evolutionary mode of development in human society. Only a detailed look at virtually all of Kautsky's writings uncovered this picture.

Third, many critics of Kautsky have claimed to see a break in his political thought sometime around 1910. While before that time he may have been revolutionary, so the argument goes, after about 1910 he became an out-and-out reformist. This position relies heavily on the Kautsky-Luxemburg debate and Kautsky's later rejection of Lenin's movement for evidence. A closer look at the whole of Kautsky's activity after 1910 reveals that he devoted more time to criticizing the reformist wing of the party than the more radical wing. During the Baden budget vote crisis, in defending the expulsion from the SPD of an extreme reformist, in rejecting the resurgent demands to include bourgeois liberals in the party, Kautsky continued his assault on the reformists. Even his support for election coalitions in the 1912 Reichstag campaign, far from representing an about-face for him, was simply the broadening of a position he had taken in 1893 with respect to Prussian Landtag elections.

Finally, Kautsky's most extreme and vociferous critics have been the communists, who have excoriated him as a renegade from the cause of revolution and for criticizing the Russian Revolution in particular. Of course he was a very severe critic of the Bolsheviks; he chastized them for excessive reliance on will and violence, for interfering in the socialist movements of other countries, and for attacks, both physical and verbal, on fellow socialists both inside and outside Russia. Most critics have found the source of Kautsky's critique of the Russian experience after 1917 in his overly strict interpretation of the Marxian paradigm of historical development. But a careful look at his wartime writings and correspondence reveals that he came to emphasize toleration of dissent and freedom of speech and expression within the party in reaction to the efforts of the majority prowar socialists to repress the minority antiwar socialists in Germany. When the Bolsheviks began riding roughshod over fellow socialists in Russia, Kautsky already had personal experience with this sort of repression. He had already seen it destroy the unity and strength of the German working-class movement. In addition to his theoretical objections to forcing backward Russia to socialism, Kautsky had the German model before his eyes.

Tracing Kautsky's intellectual growth reveals much about the appeal of Marxism, since many of the same variegated sources that influenced Marx's intellectual development also influenced Kautsky. Born thirty-six years after the founder of scientific socialism, Kautsky was as a young man also strongly influenced by romanticism, particularly by

George Sand, and even more caught up in the scientific rage of his time than was Marx. All of his adult life Kautsky retained an enthusiasm for Darwin's work, both its scientific content and its intellectually liberating impact. The question of the extent to which he was influenced by Darwin is the central one in analyzing his theory. In fact the larger question of to what extent he thought in scientific or deterministic terms is critical to evaluating the nature and quality of his interpretation of Marx; it is dealt with in greater detail later.

However much he was influenced by the intellectual movements of his time, Kautsky was neither naive nor simplistic in his acceptance of science. His comments on scientific matters are surprising in their sophistication and truly modern qualities. Even his earliest work contrasts sharply with the overdrawn pompousness of many of the scientists who influenced him. Moreover, Kautsky was always aware that the language and epistemology of science were fraught with debatable presuppositions, and he was particularly sensitive to the difficulties presented when these presuppositions were applied to humans and their societies. Thus in 1909, he commented on one of the fundamental techniques in science, the generalization from individuals to collectives: "In reality there are only individuals; their division into groups, classes [and] species exists merely in our heads, is merely a means for us to find our way about in the confusing totality of isolated phenomena."[6] Even when speaking most confidently about the supposed characteristics of this or that class, of the rulers, the oppressed, or any of the other collectives Marxists use so freely, Kautsky knew that the reality was the individual, not the faceless group. Yet at the same time, he fully accepted the necessity and validity of classification as a statistical construct.[7]

Evaluating the deterministic qualities of Kautsky's thought poses difficult problems, again because like all Marxists he used boldly deterministic language. Certainly Kautsky has been criticized more often for his supposed rigid determinism, even fatalism, than for any other error. The communists see this trait as a denial of Marx's unity of theory and practice, as a denial of the role of will as a shaping force in history. Of course similar criticism lies behind all accusations of Kautsky as dogmatic, whether made by communists or noncommunists. One of the major contentions of the present study is that Kautsky balanced between excessive emphasis on will and excessive emphasis on determinism; like Marx, he was ambiguous on this matter. But he was far from oblivious to the difficulties. Once, after having been endlessly accused by his reformist opponents of deterministic dogmatism, Kautsky confronted the issue directly: "If we speak of the necessity of the victory of the proletariat and of socialism that follows therefrom, we do not mean that victory is inevitable, or perhaps, as many of our critics perceive it, [that victory] must come of itself with fatalistic certainty, even if the revolutionary class does nothing. Here necessity is understood in the sense of the only possibility of further development." The ascension to power by the proletariat was a necessity, it was inevitable, according to Kautsky, only in the sense that without such progress, modern society would "stagnate and rot."[8]

Kautsky's determinism was also conditioned by his realization very early in his career as a socialist that the vital political issues of the day often took precedence over abstract, theoretical discussions. His first effort at a book-length publication was delayed for two years when the second assassination attempt on Kaiser Wilhelm in 1878 led to the outlawing of German social democracy. In a letter to Engels, he recognized that under the circumstances, with the party embattled and struggling to survive, abstract theorizing became "a problem of unlaid eggs."[9] Despite his own personal aversion to political involvement, much of Kautsky's theory and career were shaped by political developments. Until after the First World War, most of the eggs would remain unlaid for Karl Kautsky.

Eventually the constant intrusion of politics became much more than just an obstacle to Kautsky's desire to concentrate on the abstract. His interpretation of Marxism was shaped by the palpable fact that politics, though perhaps at base a reflection of economics, was the area in which the activities of the workers concentrated. In fact, so important did politics become for Kautsky that his perception of the nature of the class struggle, which all Marxists accept as the fundamental fact of capitalist society, was profoundly political, and he transferred the basic cause of revolution from the economic realm to politics. In so doing, he altered the relationship between political and socioeconomic revolution. He saw the goal of the socialist workers' movement as a political revolution, one that could be promoted by acts of will, that had to precede a social revolution. The latter was inevitable but could not be predicted, and it involved a change that could not be pinpointed in time. Although he explicitly made the distinction between social and political revolution only after the events of 1914, 1917, and 1918, it is implicit in most of his writing during the earlier years.

One of the most important sources of this interpretation is not hard to find—the ambiguous nature of Wilhelmine Germany. Though an Austrian by birth (actually a Czech since he was born in Prague, which in 1854 was part of the Austrian Empire), Kautsky made his mark in the history of socialism as the theoretician of the German party. By the late nineteenth and early twentieth centuries, in economic terms Germany fit the theoretical model of Marxism. It was heavily industrialized, largely urban, and had a large, socialist, working-class movement. With some exceptions in agriculture, Germany's economic sector was moving toward the increasing concentration predicted by Marx. But the Germany of the kaisers was still a long way from the political model Marxists postulated for a mature capitalist economy. Instead of having a bourgeois-dominated, republican form of government, or even a constitutional monarchy in which real power resided in a bourgeois-dominated government, as did England, Germany had a quasi-representative, quasi-constitutional monarchal state in which the kaiser and his Junker clique held most of the real power. The German financial-industrial-commercial bourgeoisie had influence in the government only to the extent that it was willing to compromise its supposed principles in an alliance with the reactionary, agrarian Prussian aristocracy which controlled the high offices of the government, civil service, and the military. Instead of being a mecca of free trade, as Marxists thought a mature capitalist society would be, Germany had high protective tariffs, initiated by agrarian interests but substantially backed by the bourgeois parties as well. Finally, the traditional bourgeois freedoms of speech, assembly, and press, under which Marxists could freely pursue their goal of a socialist future, were greatly restricted in Wilhelmine Germany.[10] Under these conditions, it is not surprising that Kautsky emphasized the need for the working-class movement in Germany to press for political modernization.

The emphasis he placed on politics, and the nature of the nonliberal political system he opposed, led Kautsky to espouse the cause of traditional liberal freedoms, while at the same time insisting that socialism and liberalism were not on a logical continuum—though he did acknowledge an intimate historical connection. He lived and wrote at a time and in a country in which the concept of political democracy was almost as offensive to proper society as was socialism. In fact many German circles made no distinction between socialism and democracy. Kautsky certainly saw no conflict between the two, but rather felt that true socialism could only be majoritarian and that true democracy could only be achieved under and through a socialist system. However, he seriously doubted that any typically liberal parliamentary system could result in democratic representation—elections were too widely spaced, the electorate too poorly educated, election campaigns too expensive, and so on. At the same time, he shared the general conviction of European socialists that their governmental ideal, at least prior to the achievement of socialism, was the democratic republic. He seems to have been convinced that under a democratic-republican form of government, a highly conscious, mass workers' party could achieve socialism peacefully, or with very little overt violence. But he was not so sanguine about the possibility of the peaceful victory of the necessary political forms in central and eastern Europe, and thus he postulated the necessity of revolution in those areas. Here again politics played a preeminent role in his theoretical considerations.

Marxism before the First World War, in what might be called the classical years of the doctrine, had not yet taken the dogmatic form that would later be associated with it. In a number of countries, bright, dedicated men and women were still trying to work out the practical implications of the rich, sometimes brilliant, sometimes obscure writings of Marx and Engels. Before Lenin and Russian communism came to power, the authoritarian, antiliberal implications of Marxism had not yet overwhelmed its equally powerful, but perhaps more subtle liberating and humanitarian implications. Many of the inherent contradictions of an apparently deterministic doctrine that called on its followers to organize and act so as to influence the course of history had not emerged before 1914. Furthermore, the people trying to interpret Marxism were working in markedly different environments, in different historical traditions, with different tools. Each individual Marxist intellectual had slightly different values, different interests, and different skills. Each obviously came up with different notions of Marxism.

Many of the intellectuals concerned with relating Marxian theory to the practical realm of the workers' lives were politically active within the movement or within the larger sphere of national politics; Kautsky was not. He was not a politician, a party or trade-union functionary, an organizer or agitator, and he only infrequently spoke at party congresses. Kautsky was a socialist writer and editor, but he had no other position of responsibility. He was an incredibly productive writer—a complete bibliography of his articles, books, translations, and pamphlets would include thousands of items. Thus despite the emphasis he placed on politics in his theoretical work, he did not involve himself in day-to-day struggles. This lack of practical activity sometimes made it difficult for him accurately to predict political developments and the mood of the masses in whose name he wrote.

Karl Kautsky was one of the most important and critically placed of those trying to make Marxism a workable social and political doctrine. His particular interpretation was obviously shaped by his personality, his intellectual training and experience, and the material he had to work with. Like most Marxists, Kautsky was attracted to the doctrine in the first place because of its essentially moral identification with the plight of the oppressed, and he stuck with Marxism because it offered an explanation of the nature of modern society that satisfied his highly rationalistic and scientific inclinations, bred in the intellectual climate of the late nineteenth century. But he failed in his effort to tie his brand of Marxism to a working-class movement that captured political power. This failure was in part due to his personal objection to some of the apparently necessary actions forced on Marxian revolutionaries if they are to achieve their espoused goals. When confronted with forces beyond his control, as in 1914, or when faced with the agonizing dilemma of choosing between consistency in ends or means, Kautsky generally chose fidelity to the humanistic means, perhaps at the expense of ever realizing the ends that had attracted him for so long.

A special point about Kautsky must be made here, since a surprising number of otherwise well-informed people think that he was a Jew. He was not. Just where this notion came from is unclear. In his memoirs, Kautsky referred to Nazi attacks on him as a Jew and postulated that his grandfather's owning of a house in the Jewish ghetto of Prague may have been the source of this myth. The very widespread association of Jews with socialism is another possible source of this misconception. Kautsky's second wife, Luise Ronsperger, was a Jew. After the Anschluss, two of Karl and Luise's sons were imprisoned by the Nazis, one for the duration of the war, and Luise herself eventually died in Auschwitz after a short internment. The confusion created by these persecutions possibly has led to the notion that Kautsky was a Jew also.[11]

Prague and Vienna
1854–1879

LITTLE IN KARL KAUTSKY'S FAMILY BACKGROUND and early life suggested that he would one day be the leading theoretician of a large Marxian working-class party. Born in Prague, 16 October 1854, Karl was the first child of seventeen-year-old Minna Jaich (1837–1912) and twenty-seven-year-old Johann Kautsky (1827–1896), both of whom were professionally associated with the Austrian theatrical world. In fact, Minna came from a family of actors and theatrical artists. Her father, Peter Anton Jaich, was a scene painter for theaters in Brünn, Prague, Vienna, and Klagenfurt, and also an actor. Johann Kautsky, though not of an artistic or theatrical family, had studied art in both Prague and Düsseldorf and made a life-long career of scene and stage design, serving a variety of theaters in Austria before setting up privately in 1871. On several occasions young Karl expanded his personal contacts with socialists outside of Austria while serving as a representative of his father's business.[1]

Despite Kautsky's efforts in his memoirs to establish a vague proletarian pedigree for himself, his immediate family was not proletarian by any stretch of the imagination. Though Johann and Minna were somewhat short of money in their first years of marriage, they had family connections to fall back on in times of great need. By the time Karl was six years old, his father was able to provide the family with a comfortable income which supported even the "oriental luxury" of at least two servants. Karl's birth was followed by three others: Minna, 26 January 1856; Fritz, 9 December 1857; and Johann, 29 February 1864. The Kautsky family was an amiable one, and its members retained congenial, if not intimate contacts even after Karl's socialist activities carried him down a much different path. Shortly after the death of his sister (who had married a successful architect), Kautsky wrote that he had not been close to his sister, even though they had not had disputes. Minna and Karl's second wife, Luise Ronsperger, had been good friends, and Minna had been very close to the Kautsky children, but Karl and his sister had had only limited, friendly contacts. Kautsky was upset by her death because she had been relatively young—only forty-eight— and active, but the death of Marx's daughter Eleanor, to say nothing of Engel's death, had affected him more strongly.[2]

Kautsky did retain intimate ties with his mother, who lived in Berlin near Karl and Luise from 1904 until her death in 1912. Karl and the elder Minna developed an interest in contemporary philosophy and natural science at about the same time. Freed from housewifely responsibilities by the family's heightened standard of living after 1860, and influenced by Karl's first tutor, Adolph Chlumsky, and by a close family friend, Wilhelm Kleinberger, Minna turned to intellectual pursuits. In 1874, when Karl received a copy of Ernst Haeckel's *The History of Creation* for Christmas, he and Minna studied it together. This book was very important in the development of Kautsky's thought. Eventually, when he began to write his first socialist pieces, he showed them to his mother for advice and approval. As an old man he recalled that his mother "of all the family members exercised the strongest influence on me."[3]

Though at first Minna only criticized her son's efforts from a literary point of view, she later became something of a socialist writer herself. Her rather romantic socialist fiction won her a minor reputation among international socialists before anything was known of her son's work. One of Kautsky's earliest letters from a leading figure of the German socialist movement concerned Minna's most recent novella, which appeared in the Leipzig party newspaper in early 1877. At the end of his first meeting with Kautsky, Marx seemed to think more highly of the mother than the son. Reporting on this meeting to his daughter Jenny, Marx wrote: "When this charmer first appeared at my place—I mean little Kauz ["queer fellow"]—the first which escaped me was: are you like your mother? Not in the very least, he assured me, and I silently congratulated his mother." On the other hand, when seeking to praise an early journalistic effort by Kautsky, Engels wrote: "Your pamphlet shows that you have inherited the novelistic talent of your mother. I like it better than all your earlier things." Kautsky at least gained some recognition from having his mother's reputation precede his own introduction into socialist circles.[4]

Education

Kautsky was an early and avid reader. By the age of six he had read a collection of children's Bible stories, another of animal stories, and a children's edition of Cooper's *Last of the Mohicans;* by eight he was particularly fond of geography. Because his parents were concerned about his health, he was tutored at home until he was nine. Beginning in 1864, he attended the old-fashioned and inferior Melk seminary, run by Benedictine monks. Then from 1866 to 1874, he attended the much more progressive Academic Gymnasium in Vienna. Kautsky remembered Melk as oppressive and stifling, the gymnasium as rigorous and boring. At the latter he studied religion, Latin, Greek, German, geography, history, mathematics, natural history, and, during the last two terms, philosophy. At Melk he had studied French as well as Latin, Greek, and German.[5]

Kautsky was a mediocre to poor student. At Melk his best year was his last, when he ranked eleventh in a class of twenty-one. At the gymnasium he fared little better, ranking around the middle of his class every year with two exceptions. In the 1866–1867 school year, a recurrence of a chronic illness toward the end of the term forced him to repeat the third form the following year. Passing out of the fifth form also required two tries. His performance in mathematics during the 1869–1870 term was so poor that it was judged unsatisfactory. Family complications prevented Kautsky from preparing for a special examination during the summer, and he had to repeat the fifth form the following year. He later offered a number of explanations for his rather poor performance at school. He recalled having been distrustful and suspicious of his teachers, though doubtless he shared these feelings with many of his fellow students. Second, since seating at the gymnasium was by rank, from front to back, Karl found himself at a disadvantage because of his poor vision; he was never near enough to the front of the class to follow closely what was happening. This was a particular disadvantage in mathematics, a subject for which he had little aptitude anyway. Finally, he suggested that sometimes his concern for extracurricular matters, as during the spring of 1871, when he followed the rise and fall of the Paris Commune, affected his studies adversely.[6]

At the end of his gymnasium career, Kautsky scored his highest marks in the history and philosophy examinations. In the fall of 1874, freed of any military obligation because of nearsightedness, he entered the university in Vienna with the intention of pursuing studies in "historical philosophy" to prepare for a career as a *Privatdozent* (a form of university lecturer) or a middle-school teacher. In his first term he took courses in psychology, general and municpal history, physical geography, and two literature courses, one on Schiller and Goethe, the other on old German literature. By the following term, he had decided to become a jurist, but another bout of illness forced him to give up this more rigorous course of study. He noted in his memoirs that this decision was also readily influenced by the fact "that the oratorical gift was denied me." This same illness also forced him to end his brief career as a private teacher of gymnastics by which he had earned a little money.

In his third term at the university, Kautsky returned to his original plan of study and took courses in Roman history and the history of the revolutionary period (c. 1785–1815), and a course concerned with a descriptive comparison of the major European countries, which proved to be another course in physical geography. He eventually attended a total of nine semesters at Vienna, but never took a degree. Though for a time he toyed with the idea of doing a dissertation on Thomas Jefferson as envoy to revolutionary France, and thereby completing the degree requirements, his socialist activities eventually won out and turned him away from academia.[7]

Evaluating the impact of Kautsky's university experience on the development of his thought is difficult. He himself observed that he had learned little at the university because he was always at odds with his professors. He also felt that to a great extent all socialists are autodidacts since there "is hardly a university chair for socialist science in a bourgeois state," and like all autodidacts his own knowledge of socialism was acquired in a disorderly manner. Certainly socialist leaders during Kautsky's first years in the movement tended to see his university training as a distinct disadvantage. Writing to August Bebel in 1885, Engels observed that both Kautsky and Eduard Bernstein were "real pearls" compared to the rest of "the terrible literary new blood" of the party. However, Engels noted that Kautsky had learned a "frightful mass of nonsense at the university," though he "takes pains to unlearn it again."[8]

In a later letter, Engels spelled out more clearly just what it was about Kautsky's university training that made it difficult for the young Austrian to be an effective Marxian propagandist. Agreeing with Bebel's evaluation of Kautsky's work as hasty and incomplete, Engels explained:

You have exactly hit upon Kautsky's decisive weakness. His youthful inclination towards hasty judgment has been still more intensified by the wretched method of teaching history in the universities—especially the Austrian ones. The students there are systematically taught to do historical work with materials they know to be inadequate, but which they are *supposed to treat as adequate,* that is, to write things which they themselves know to be false but which they are supposed to consider correct. That has naturally made Kautsky thoroughly cocky. Then the literary life—writing for pay and writing a lot. So that he has absolutely no idea what really scientific work means.

Engels added that though he sharply criticized Kautsky for these weaknesses, "I can comfort him with the fact that I did the same in my impudent youth."[9]

On the other hand, the sort of broad-ranging and rather disordered course of study Kautsky pursued at the university both reflected and molded his catholic intellectual tastes. Though he consistently considered himself a historian, his view of the discipline placed few limits on his scholarly activities. Strongly attracted by natural science, Kautsky was even more taken with efforts to apply the methods and conclusions of natural science, especially Darwinism, to the entire range of human history, including its social and economic aspects. Certainly this same inclination facilitated his conversion to Marxism, with all its comprehensive implications. The cockiness Engels referred to above became a sort of self-satisfied confidence as Kautsky matured, a trait which infuriated his ideological opponents immensely. And even his best historical works remained to the end marred by a willingness to claim conclusions with more assurance than his data allowed. At the same time, however, he retained throughout his life a willingness to learn, to study, to review and utilize the findings of others. In his first letter to Kautsky, Engels recognized the younger man's receptiveness and eagerness by observing, "You are one of the few of the younger generation who actually takes the trouble to learn something."[10] Finally, Kautsky's eclectic intellectual tastes perfectly suited him for his life-long work, popularizing Marxism on all fronts.

During his university years Kautsky was confronted with a universal problem, that of a career. As he became more involved with socialism, his chances of being both a servant of the state as a teacher and an opponent of the state as a socialist made this goal less reasonable. Quite naturally, given his immediate family background, Kautsky's inclination was to look to the arts and literature for an alternative. For a time he tried his luck as a muralist and painter. But discovering the difficulties of this career, and having been warned by a doctor that such work could cause permanent damage to his already weak eyes, he turned to literature (though how much easier on his eyes reading and writing would be is not clear). As early as his years at the Melk seminary, Kautsky had done some creative writing, but none of these efforts was ever published. In 1875–1876, Johann Kautsky enjoyed enormous success with a stage version of Jules Verne's *Around the World in Eighty Days,* and in response to this success, Karl, who had been encouraged by his father to write a play, produced a scientific fantasy in a similar mood. The play, the *Atlantic-Pacific Company,* was concerned with the construction of a Panama-Nicaragua canal, both as a scientific exploit and as a dramatic setting. The play met with only limited success; it played twenty times in Vienna in late 1877 and early 1878, had a short run in Graz and Berlin, and was sold to a London director, Edmund Gerson, for the impressive sum of five shillings. Kautsky followed the play to Berlin in 1879 and while there expanded his contacts with German socialists. Its failure to achieve major success, coupled with his increasing occupation with the socialist movement, led Karl to abandon his career as a playwright.[11]

Becoming a Socialist

Although both his father and maternal grandfather had played minor roles in the revolutionary events of 1848, Kautsky recalled in his memoirs that until his own involvement in the socialist movement, his immediate family was virtually apolitical. The closest thing to political consciousness in the family was a strong though sporadic Czech nationalism, a sympathy Kautsky shared for a time and one which was intensely felt by his first tutor, Adolph Chlumsky. The lack of political awareness and activity in the Kautsky family reflected several aspects of its existence. First, the theatrical environment is not one into which political developments regularly intrude. Second, after 1863, and several moves back and forth between Prague and Vienna, the Kautsky family settled in the latter city, where they were part of a small Czech minority in the midst of an overwhelming German majority. This minority status was not conducive to political activity, though it did reinforce Kautsky's Czech consciousness.[12]

The third reason for the Kautsky family's lack of political activism was the most important. For a number of years Johann Kautsky was either directly or indirectly dependent upon support from the state theaters of Vienna, and the possibility that oppositional political activity would endanger this support encouraged the family to remain apolitical. In his memoirs Karl passed this fact off as more of an irritant than an obstacle to his socialist activities. Yet, presumably, his father's dependence on state support was the reason he used pseudonyms on his earliest published work. Of the many names and initials so used — "K.," "K.K.," "St.," and others — "Symmachos," which means "comrade-in-arms," was the most common. And in a 1911 letter to his wife, Kautsky suggested that his father's relationship with the Austrian state was something more than an irritant, and he further revealed the family's reaction to his socialist proclivities. "Again and again," he wrote, referring to the years after 1874, "I had to hear that he [Johann] was employed at the Hoftheater, I would ruin him and the entire family if I involved myself with revolutionary elements." Even his mother, who was more sympathetic to socialism than was her husband, feared some horrible fate for her son. Kautsky noted that though his father's opposition was not especially harsh, in a way it was the more oppressive because it was not based on a conflict of ideals, "but sprang from fear."[13]

Where did Kautsky's socialist political consciousness come from? He was not of a working-class family, nor did he have extensive contacts with workers and their problems. His schooling was not the sort that yielded revolutionaries. He was not of a rebellious nature, and though perhaps he was not perfectly adjusted to the milieu of his youth, no particularly outstanding trauma marks the years immediately preceding his conversion to socialism.

Tracing the origins of Kautsky's socialist thought is made more difficult by the fact that at the age of eighty-two he began a memoir in which he discussed in considerable detail what he felt were the important intellectual influences of his early life. How much of this was the product of a perfectly natural effort to impose order on his intellectual development — perhaps more than had actually existed? How much was the product of faulty recollection? To ask these questions is not to suggest that Kautsky purposely distorted the account of his intellectual origins. Rather these questions implicitly challenge the notion that Kautsky's thought, or that of almost any other intellectual, developed systematically or linearly. With how much confidence can a historian say that Kautsky took a particular idea from a particular source and that he later added a particular refinement from another particular source?[14]

The temptation to be overly specific in identifying sources of thought must be resisted. For instance, most critics of Kautsky's thought have emphasized the influence of Darwin. That he read and was influenced by Darwin is indisputable — Kautsky himself recorded this in his memoirs, and even the most cursory review of his earliest published work will substantiate this influence. However, it is a major step from this assertion to the contention that Kautsky took his general outlook, or even many specific points, directly from Darwin. At about the same time he read Darwin, in the early 1870s, he also read and was influenced by Ernst Haeckel and Ludwig Büchner, and the latter had postulated biological evolution some years before the publication of Darwin's theory. Thus, if the historian is accurately to reproduce the conditions surrounding Kautsky's development, the problem is not just one of identifying specific sources, but also one of identifying and analyzing what others have called the "climate of the times."[15]

Thinking back after sixty-five years, Kautsky was able to pin down quite precisely the emergence of his political consciousness. In the summer of 1868, he paid a visit to an aunt and uncle who lived in a rural Bohemian village. Czech nationalist sentiments were running high that summer, as was peasant agitation. Kautsky remembered being profoundly impressed by this activity and recalled that after this visit he began to read the Viennese newspapers not only for "the theater and disasters," but also for "political correspondence and editorials." The sporadic Czech nationalism of the family surfaced in Kautsky for the next two years, and he considered himself "an outspoken Czech nationalist," with an infatuation with the great Italian spokesman of emerging nationalist movements, Garibaldi.[16]

A flirtation with Czech nationalist sentiments suited Kautsky's position very well during those years. To a young, intellectually curious boy living in an environment dominated by Czech artists and actors, but surrounded by the more mundane German burghers of Vienna, such sentiments offered an outlet for mild adolescent rebelliousness and also satisfied a theatrical need for the dramatic. Karl, like his siblings, had appeared on the stage, first playing in *Faust* at the age of six; his early inclination to write stories and plays is further evidence of a dramatic bent. His family's world was not necessarily one of make-believe, but it was one in which neither the blunt material demands of the working class nor the crass commercial exigencies of the petite bourgeoisie tied the emotions of youth to political and economic realities. The atmosphere of the Kautsky home was one of the "highest intellectual [or spiritual—the word *geistig* is more ambiguous than its English translation] activity," in which "energetic idealism" aroused in young Karl a "thirst for knowledge."[17]

Because Kautsky derived his Czech nationalism from rather insubstantial, though none the less real, sources, it was not a long-lived emotion. The sort of constant reinforcement such youthful passion usually requires was not present in Vienna, where his schoolmates were mostly Austrian Germans and where his father dealt professionally, if not personally, with a predominantly German world. Though many of the family friends were Czechs, they were not the anti-Austrian peasants of rural Bohemia but a much more cosmopolitan and culturally integrated artistic elite. Karl had learned both Czech and German as a small child, but his mother was never very comfortable with Czech, and German was generally spoken at home. The most regular source of news for the family was not Czech nationalist or peasant journals, but the German-language, bourgeois press of the Austrian capital. In this environment Kautsky's Czech nationalism could hardly survive for long, and it did not.[18]

The most immediate source of Kautsky's conversion to a more radical political awareness was the content of the ideology prevalent among intellectual Czech nationalists during the late 1860s and the 1870s. The outstanding figure during this period was the historian Frantisek Palacky (1789–1876). In addition to being a romantic Czech nationalist who glorified Bohemia's past in service of its future, Palacky was also a political liberal, strongly influenced by the principles of 1789. Despite the implications of 1848, especially in Germany, that the earlier identity of radical politics and nationalism was drawing to an end, in the reactionary, multinational Austrian Empire of the last half of the nineteenth century this equation still carried a great deal of weight. That Kautsky could come to what he called "French-republican radicalism" by way of Czech nationalism was entirely consistent with the close interrelation of the two ideologies at the time.[19]

Two events powerfully reinforced the radical political content of Kautsky's Czech nationalism in early 1871. First of all, in the spring of that year, in the wake of the German victory in the Franco-Prussian War, Paris rose in rebellion against the invading forces and the rest of France to found the famous and infamous Commune. Between the great French Revolution and the Russian Revolution of our own century, few events provoked more extreme ideological splits in Europe than did the rise and fall of the Commune. At the time, and for years after, it was the model of the future for the working-class-oriented left of the political spectrum and the symbol of the horrors and extremism of lower-class political power for the peasant-bourgeois forces of the center and right. Kautsky's romantic radicalism ensured that his sympathies would be with the Communards, and these sympathies then pushed his political radicalism to identification with the socialism presumably characterized by the Commune.[20]

The second major influence on Kautsky in 1871 was his reading of George Sand's romantic novel *The Sin of M. Antoine.* In his memoirs he recalled that the Commune roused in him an interest in socialism and sympathy for the workers, but that these sentiments had only an ethical and not a rational content, and that though "ethical necessity is the starting point of all socialist striving and thought," without a basis in "economic and historical knowledge" such sentiments are a dead end. Presumably Sand's novel offered him an introduction to the knowledge necessary to give socialism a firm basis. In his memoirs he strongly emphasized the impact of *The Sin of M. Antoine,* but only in the sense that it showed him the need for study and that the coming of socialism would require a long process of development.[21]

However, another source reveals a much different role for Sand's work in Kautsky's life. As already noted, Karl's family, especially his father, were greatly concerned about the politically dangerous consequences of socialist activities and opinions. Furthermore, Kautsky found himself isolated: "None of my relations, no friends of the family, none of my fellow students could tell me what socialism was," he recalled. In the midst of this isolation, and even hostility, Karl found comfort and support in reading and rereading *The Sin of M. Antoine.* Many years later he wrote to his wife: "In this situation I accidently found the book of George Sand. It filled me with jubilant delight. It gave me certainty and courage. It did not show me my way . . . but it smoothed the way for me, let me scorn all objections and condemnation, all ridicule and ruin. . . . Ever since I held onto the book like an old friend who helped me through a hard time—perhaps the hardest, because I was still so young and growing up in respectful awe of my parents." This letter clearly shows that the novel, far from providing Kautsky with guidelines for the rational pursuit of socialism, offered powerful emotional support to a romantic young man who felt himself besieged from all sides.[22]

To the reader today, *The Sin of M. Antoine,* or *Le péché de M. Antoine* (1846), seems a hopelessly romantic tale of trials and heroics. Emile, the communistically inclined son of the ultimate bourgeois, M. Cardonnet, falls in love with Gilberte, daughter of Antoine, Comte de Chateaubrun, a fallen-from-riches, but still honorable, aristocratic landowner. M. Cardonnet, who has long been concerned with his son's rejection of the material world of business and his attraction to intellectual pursuits, strikes a bargain with Emile. He will approve his marriage to Gilberte if Emile agrees to abandon his chimerical dreams of human harmony and devote himself to the family business. In the end Gilberte is revealed to have been the product of an adulterous relationship between M. Antoine and the long-dead wife of the fabulously wealthy communist, M. le Marquis de Boisguilbault—this was the sin of M. Antoine. Through the good offices of Jean

Jappeloup, the all-good, freedom-loving petty artisan, M. Antoine and M. le Marquis are finally reconciled, whereupon the latter leaves his fortune and estate to Gilberte and Emile. He exhorts them to turn their inheritance to the service of communism, but only after mature reflection and study. M. Cardonnet reconciles himself to Emile's new wealth, and everyone lives happily ever after.

The characters in *M. Antoine* are overdrawn and overly simplistic. M. Cardonnet is harsh, cunning, antiintellectual, and rejects his wife. Jean Jappeloup rebels against the coming of the factory system and becomes an outlaw while trying to serve his fellow humans. Gilberte, beautiful of course, bears the burdens of the fall from riches with true nobility. The situation is a little silly, with the supposedly hard-headed, practical Cardonnet obstinately constructing his factory on a stream for which both science, in the form of his son's geological and hydromechanical study, and native intelligence, in the person of Jean, predict periodic and disastrous flooding. But with such material, Sand was able to make her point clearly: the conflict between the bourgeois world of industrial capitalism and the finer world of intellectual, spiritual freedom under communism. The "entire absence of idealism" in M. Cardonnet is revealed in his criticism of Emile's failure to acquire practical skills at the university: "and I tell you all this fine philosophico-metaphysico-politico-economical learning is of all things the vainest, the falsest, the most chimerical and the most ridiculous, not to say the most dangerous, for a young man." On the other hand, Emile's rejection of his father's material acquisitiveness and glorification of capitalist competition is no less dogmatic:

> No, father, never! . . . for that is not the road for mankind to follow. There is in it no trace of love or pity or gentleness. Man was not born to know naught but suffering and to extend his conquests over matter only. The conquests of the intellect in the domain of ideas, the pleasures and refinements of the heart, which, according to your plan, should be carefully regulated accessories of the workingman's life, will always be the noblest and sweetest aspiration of every normally constituted man. . . . O father, instead of fighting with the strong against the weak, let us fight with the weak against the strong.[23]

As a full-grown Marxist, Kautsky would later deny many of the notions in *M. Antoine*—the implicit antiindustrialism, the supposed virtues of petit bourgeois artisans, and the reliance on inherited aristocratic wealth for the founding of the communist society, for instance. But in 1871, the romantic drama of Emile's situation made a strong impression. Here was support for his own sympathies for the underdog, for his own aversion to "the brutal arrogance of the victors" over the Commune. Here, too, was evidence that he was not alone, that socialism and the cause of humanity had already won far-flung support. Many themes in Sand's novel were to be persistent concerns of Kautsky's for the rest of his life. The inherent, but often unperceived, conflict between the workers and the owners in industry, the need to base socialism on education and knowledge, and perhaps the view of the coming of socialism as a product of intellectual activity (though this last point will require much closer analysis before it can be accepted) are all themes which the writings of the mature Kautsky share with *The Sin of M. Antoine*.

By late 1871, Kautsky's Czech nationalism had become a vaguely socialist, democratic radicalism characterized by romantic sympathies for the lower classes and a sense that knowledge and study would show the way of the future. In 1873 and 1874, he wrote a series of articles and short stories, none of which ever reached the press, in which he sought to reconcile capital and labor by means of "equality, freedom, improved and general education, elimination of idleness, and gradual elevation of the workers into capitalists." Politically, Kautsky felt that these ends could be achieved through the establishment of a federal republic with unconditional freedom of speech, press, and assembly, general and equal franchise for both sexes, and free education through high school with additional aid for poor students. This radical republican state was to overcome worker-owner conflicts by gradually buying up factories and turning them over to the workers to be run as cooperatives.[24]

With the exception of this last point, the political notions Kautsky held at this time were rather standard fare for the radical democratic left throughout Europe. Furthermore, the elimination of conflict through the establishment of worker-run cooperative industry not only was central to Lassalle's plan for Germany, but had earlier been proposed by French socialists, particularly by Louis Blanc in the 1840s. Long afterward Kautsky denied any familiarity with either of these two sources at the time, but the ideas of the French social thinkers had appeared in the Czech nationalist press and even in Vienna's liberal bourgeois press, and by 1864, Lassalle and his plans had been covered by these papers. At any rate, Kautsky's attitudes at this time were not based on a *Weltanschauung* at odds with that of the leftist opposition in

Europe through most of the first three-quarters of the nineteenth century. Radical democracy and ethical socialism were both consistent with the dominant Christian world view.[25]

At about this same time, Kautsky began to come under the influence of what was probably the most significant intellectual development of the last half of the nineteenth century, the rise of positivism and materialism and the decline of religion. During the eighteenth and early nineteenth centuries, the inability of traditional society to cope with the changes produced by the rise of capitalism and industry, plus the specific demands of industry itself, initiated a twofold change in intellectual activity that dramatically affected the dominant world view of Western society. On the one hand, there was an increasing emphasis on rational analysis and a collateral rejection of traditional authority. On the other hand, the demands for improved technology for industry led to an ever more detailed and rigorous analysis of the makeup of the material world. An extreme example of the first of these tendencies was the rational and historical critique of Christian dogma undertaken in Germany by the Young Hegelians. Beginning with David Strauss's *Life of Jesus* (1835), this movement culminated in Ludwig Feuerbach's anthropological atheism and his somewhat crass materialism. The tendency to ever increasing analysis of the material world came to a climax, as far as notions of human uniqueness were concerned, with the validation of organic evolutionary theory offered by Darwin in 1859 and 1871. In the hands of other scientific analysts, or natural philosophers as they continued to be called until the end of the nineteenth century, the social and philosophical implications of Darwinism were often carried to the same conclusions as those reached by Feuerbach: atheism and materialism. The second of these tendencies had the greater influence on Kautsky, serving as the basis of a new *Weltanschauung* which was at odds with that of radical democracy and ethical socialism.[26]

Buckle, Haeckel, and Büchner

The major sources of Kautsky's contact with natural-scientific and materialist thought during the early and mid-seventies were Henry Thomas Buckle, *The History of Civilization in England* (first translated into German in 1859 and 1861), which Kautsky read during the summer of 1874; Ernst Haeckel, *The History of Creation* (1868), which Kautsky received as a Christmas gift in 1874; Ludwig Büchner, *Force and Matter* (1855); and, of course, Darwin's two major works, *The Origin of Species* (1859) and *The Descent of Man* (1871). Kautsky felt that

Darwin's works were the most important influence on his own views of nature and, to the limited extent Darwin dealt with social animals and the origin of society, of society also. But he was even more impressed with Haeckel's attempts to apply the observations of natural science to human society, and found Büchner's much more daring, almost socialistic, conclusions the most attractive of all. Darwin's work requires no summation here, and the full impact of Darwin on Kautsky, as mediated by Engels, will be dealt with in the next chapter. But in order to get a feeling for Kautsky's intellectual milieu during the mid-1870s, a brief review of Darwin and longer summaries of Buckle, Haeckel, and Büchner will be useful.[27]

Darwin did not, of course, introduce evolutionary theory; Lamarck and Goethe became famous for similar theories many years before Darwin, and Ludwig Büchner asserted a theory of descent from one or a very few primary forms in his 1855 work. Darwin was, however, the first to provide a convincing theoretical model for a mechanism of evolution, natural selection, and thus invested evolutionary theory with the kind of scientific legitimacy it had previously lacked. What most impressed Kautsky was the extent to which Darwin was able to eliminate references to a deity from explanations of the origins of living organisms and by this suggest that perhaps the Christian God was not a necessary reference for comprehension of the nature of the world. Like most young radicals of his time, Kautsky saw the various forms of organized Christianity as obstacles to both practical social progress and the intellectual emancipation that accompanied this progress. The strength of reactionary clerical parties in Vienna during the 1860s and 1870s gave substance to the first of these objections, while Karl's years at Melk, which he had found extremely oppressive and stultifying intellectually, gave him personal experience with the second. Thus Darwin's impact on Kautsky at this time not only was personally liberating, in that it paved the way for his natural-scientific and materialist *Weltanschauung,* but also provided potential weapons for an attack on the political and social structure he was beginning to turn against.

Kautsky recalled long after the fact that the major impact that the works of Haeckel and Büchner had on him came from their efforts to apply natural-scientific observations to human society. That Kautsky could have drawn much from the social criticism of Ernst Haeckel is doubtful. Haeckel, who became Germany's leading proponent and popularizer of social Darwinism in its most blatant forms, emphasized heredity and almost totally excluded environment as a causative agent when discussing human behavior. Thus he objected to advances in medical science because they allowed the weak and sickly to survive and propagate; he opposed the move to abolish capital punishment because this would perpetuate the class of criminals, which Haeckel saw as an almost exclusively hereditary group. This sort of anti-humanitarian, anti-lower-class analysis could not have struck a responsive chord in the young Kautsky, so recently inspired by Sand's picture of the nobility and misfortune of the lower classes.[28]

Haeckel was also extremely ethnocentric and decidedly unhistorical and unsophisticated in his defense of the white European tribes, as he called them. His laws of increasing perfection and differentiation in human evolution, coupled with a staggering lack of cultural awareness, allowed him to write nonsense like the following: "Among the lowest tribes of nations, most of the individuals resemble one another so much that European travelers often cannot distinguish them at all. With increasing civilization the physiognomy of individuals becomes differentiated, and finally among the most highly civilized nations, the English and Germans, the divergence in the characters of the face is so great that we rarely mistake one face for another." Haeckel used pseudo-scientific arguments of natural tribal and even specific superiority to justify the extermination of American Indians and European imperialism in general. Even in his very earliest writings, Kautsky was entirely free of Haeckel's strong sense of racial and cultural superiority.[29]

On the other hand, some aspects of Haeckel's work reinforced Kautsky's budding socialist and natural-scientific, materialist position. When very early in the *History* Haeckel asserted that "the highest triumph of the human mind, the true knowledge of the most general laws of nature, ought not to remain the private possession of a privileged class of savans [sic], but ought to become the common property of all mankind," Kautsky must have nodded heartily in agreement. Kautsky was also attracted by Haeckel's boldness and his confidence in natural science. Haeckel contended that the origin of species by natural selection was "a *mathematical necessity* of nature which needs no further proof" and that "the actual value and invincible strength of the Theory of Descent does not lie in its explaining this or that single phenomenon, but in the fact that it explains *all* biological phenomena." As a representative of positivism, Haeckel gave expression to its extreme rationalism by formulating law upon law which supposedly attested to the regularity and order, and therefore the material foundations, of the world. Finally, Kautsky's growing materialist and anti-Christian posture received powerful support from Haeckel's dogmatic contention that "the soul of man, just as the soul of animals, is a purely mechanical activity . . . that . . . is transmitted by inheritance, . . . just as every other quality of the body is materially transmitted by propagation."[30]

Kautsky's contact with Haeckel did not end with his reading of *The History of Creation*. In 1882, encouraged by his Viennese friend Heinrich Braun, and with a letter of introduction from Victor Adler, Kautsky approached the university in Jena, where Marx had got his doctorate by correspondence, with hopes of getting his recently completed study of the family and marriage accepted as a doctoral dissertation. Kautsky introduced himself and his study in a long letter to Haeckel, who at the time occupied a chair at Jena. Though Haeckel seems to have been impressed with the study, Kautsky never received the degree because Haeckel could only examine in zoology, and the Jena authorities determined that, in the absence of a university position in ethnology, Kautsky's study most closely fit into philology. In the fall of 1882, Kautsky abandoned his efforts after having traveled to Jena to try to settle the matter. Eventually his study of the family and marriage was published by the Stuttgart journal *Kosmos*. Haeckel was closely associated with this journal, which later became one of the main sources by which his "monism" was popularized, and he may have arranged for the publication of Kautsky's study.[31]

Like that of Haeckel, Büchner's work was characterized by an almost incredible confidence and a powerful sense of finality, of having discovered truth, or at least the way to truth. In the preface to his first edition (1855), he wrote: "*It is part of the very nature of philosophy to be intellectually the joint property of all,*" a sentiment later echoed by Haeckel. The two men were similar in other ways as well. Büchner's work went through at least fifteen revised German editions, and in the later editions he quoted copiously from Haeckel and commented favorably on much of Haeckel's work. Both insisted on a monistic, as opposed to a dualistic, view of the world that was based on the assertion that all things were subject to natural, mechanical laws and forces. Both argued that the only differences between the organic and the inorganic were of degree, not kind. Both asserted the identity of the brain and mind, body and soul. Both accepted a hierarchical conception of the world of organisms, with perfection increasing from plants to animals and, within the animal phyla, to humans. Both rejected the Christian God and all forms of deism, and both gave free will an extremely limited range of action. If anything, Büchner was even more racist and ethnocentric than Haeckel, arguing that Europeans and the "negroes of Eastern Africa" had almost nothing in common: "Their reason is not like ours. . . . Compassion, uprightness, gratitude, prudence, family affection, modesty, conscientiousness, and remorse are unknown things. . . . [They have] no history, no traditions, no poetry, no morality, no imagination, no memory."[32]

In contrast to Haeckel, however, Büchner much more directly took up the philosophical implications of his work. He rejected materialism, idealism, spiritualism, and in fact all systems. "Science," he wrote, "is not idealistic, nor spiritualistic, not materialistic, but simply natural; she seeks to learn everywhere facts and their logical corollaries, without doing homage in advance to a system in this or that direction." Büchner saw science as merely rationalistic and empirical. Also unlike Haeckel, he did not view the human species as an end, but rather saw it as a transcendent phase in the ongoing process of evolution. He also admitted that much remained to be explained in nature, but argued that "we ought not to hold Nature responsible for this, but only the imperfection of our knowledge."[33]

All this clearly points up the difficulties of precisely indicating sources for Kautsky's thought. The intellectual climate of the times was virtually permeated with bold and confident proponents of a natural-scientific, naturalist-materialist world view. Though almost all such writers paid homage to the achievements of Darwin, many of those who influenced Kautsky went far beyond Darwin's cautious observations on the social realm to make radical and strikingly modern, but also often naive and unfounded, assertions. In his memoirs and many of his early and late writings, Kautsky indicated that much of his thought was taken from Darwin, but he used this name as a shorthand symbol for a much more complex group of influences.

For instance, Kautsky claimed that Darwin was the source of his own conviction that the so-called social instinct, far from being of divine origin, was natural.[34] But the following passage from Büchner reveals a possible alternate source for this observation:

Now seeing that man is essentially a social being, and can, without society, either not exist at all or only be thought of as a predatory animal, it becomes easy to understand that his living in social communion with others must have saddled him with duties of reciprocity which in the course of time developed into definite moral axioms. The beginnings of this are to be found in family life, which in the sequel developed into tribal and national life. Morality is therefore much older than religion, the latter being only a requirement of the individual, while the former is a requirement of society and had its germ in the earliest beginnings of social co-existence.[35]

In other words, morality, or the "ethical impulse," was the product of the natural social condition of humans, not of divine intervention or religion. The conclusion, then, was not exclusive to Darwin, though validation by reference to lower animals may have been. For Kautsky the critical point was the naturalness, that is, the nondivinity, of the ethical impulse, something which Büchner asserted no less plainly than did Darwin. In his first presentation of his own views of the origin of social instincts in humans, Kautsky referred to both the social organization of lower forms of life and the natural necessity of the ethical impulse in human society.[36]

Finally, Kautsky claimed to have been much impressed with Büchner's near socialist positions. Here Büchner was very much in conflict with Haeckel and Buckle with whom he otherwise shared so much. Kautsky was much taken with passages like this: "Society must be so organized that the welfare of one shall no longer be conducive to the detriment of others, as is now too often the case; everyone ought to find his own interest indissolubly connected with that of all, and on the other hand the welfare of the community should be like a mathematical function of the welfare of the individual." Strikingly lacking in class awareness, phrased in moral rather than determinist terms, this passage nonetheless represents better than anything in Haeckel, Buckle, or Darwin, the position toward which Kautsky was moving in the mid-seventies.[37]

The impact of the fourth major intellectual influence of the presocialist years, Buckle, was of a much different sort than that of Darwin, Haeckel, and Büchner. Though Buckle claimed to be writing a natural-scientific history of man, he was far less concerned with biological and physical phenomena than with intellectual factors in the shaping of human society. His science consisted of maintaining that all human actions were motivated by antecedent conditions and stimuli "and that, therefore, if we were acquainted with the whole of the antecedents, and with all the laws of their movements, we could with unerring certainty predict the whole of their immediate results." Buckle was not certain that he could identify all the antecedents of human action, but his confidence that all could be known, and that accurate prediction could derive from that knowledge, was an ideal that Kautsky shared for most of his life. This attitude was a further reflection of the confidence inspired by scientific advances during the last half of the nineteenth century.[38]

Buckle's *History of Civilization in England* was a curious work that began by denying that previous historians, concerned as they were with politics, diplomacy, and courts, had done anything of value. Buckle then asserted in pseudo-materialistic terms that climate, food, soil, and something he called "the General Aspect of Nature" were the most important physical agents influencing human development. He also contended that in countries in which a capricious nature prevailed, the inhabitants developed the imaginative faculties of the mind at the expense of the reasoning ones, and as a consequence such countries remained culturally and intellectually backward. And finally, in what seems a clear enough statement, Buckle wrote that "the history of the human mind can only be understood by connecting with it the history and aspects of the material universe."³⁹

But from this point on the *History of Civilization* took a much different turn. Buckle held that civilization was the triumph of the mind over external agents and that therefore mental laws were more important than physical ones, and he argued that "the growth of European civilization is solely due to the progress of knowledge." He then proceeded to explain the French Revolution as the exclusive result of the impact of English intellectual notions on prominent Frenchmen, with no reference at all to material conditions in France. Buckle further undermined the earlier intimations of a materialist outlook by declaring that "the real history of the human race is the history of tendencies which are perceived by the mind, and not events which are discerned by the senses." Finally he concluded the journey from pseudo-materialism to idealism with the observation that "in every great epoch there is one idea at work which is more powerful than any other, and which shapes the events of the time and determines their ultimate issue." Many of these oddly contradictory notions were to be treated in a different and more consistent manner by the young Kautsky.⁴⁰

First Publications

Kautsky's earliest work was published primarily in two journals of German socialism, the *Volksstaat,* which appeared in Leipzig and was replaced on 1 October 1876 by the *Vorwärts*; and secondarily in the Austrian socialist press—the *Gleichheit,* which was published in the Neustadt suburb of Vienna, and *Der Sozialist,* which originated in Vienna proper. Though he joined the tiny Austrian party in January 1875, almost two-thirds of his writing from then through 1878 appeared in the Leipzig journals, in part because the German press was much more prosperous, in part because the Austrian press was harassed by censorship and forced shutdowns. The majority of more than seventy-five articles written in his first four years as a socialist fell into two categories: those dealing with natural-scientific matters and their relationship to socialism, and those dealing more reportorially with political and socialist developments in Austria. Only one article from this period, "The Physiognomy of Today's Society," *Vorwärts*, 31 March 1878, dealt directly with economic questions, and few articles show any particular Marxian influence. Though Kautsky mentioned Marx several times, and even published a translation of a portion of Marx's *Poverty of Philosophy* in the *Gleichheit* in September 1875, little overt sign of his growing Marxism appeared in print until 1878.[41]

One of Kautsky's major preoccupations during the early years was to bring natural science, especially Darwinism and related theories, to the service of socialism. During the seventies and eighties, the great majority of German writers who tried to apply aspects of Darwinian theory to the human realm were anything but socialists. The concepts of struggle and survival of the fittest seemed to offer a solid scientific basis and rationalization for the acquisitive, competitive capitalism of early industrialization. Socialism, which evoked the brotherhood of man and noncompetition as ideals of social organization, appeared unscientific in its rejection of conflict and competition. Kautsky's efforts, therefore, often took the form of criticizing writers who argued against socialism because it was contrary to the prevalent natural-scientific concepts. This was the format for his two-part article entitled "Socialism and the Struggle for Existence," which appeared in the *Volksstaat* in early 1876.[42]

This article began by reviewing some of the many attacks directed against socialism by its opponents, who contended it was immoral, traitorous, based on thievery, antiscientific, and so on. Kautsky accepted the assertion that socialists were the enemies of capitalism, but staunchly denied that they were the enemies of science. Science, he wrote, offered socialism help in its fight against "the old world" and gave it "its best support." Therefore, he continued, socialists cannot be still when attacked as antiscientific, otherwise confusion would result in the ranks of socialism and the enemy would be strengthened, albeit only temporarily. More specifically, Kautsky directed his attention to three works: *Die Darwinische Theorie* by Georg Seidlitz, *Der Kampf ums Dasein* by Robert Byr, and *Culturgeschichte* by Friedrich v. Hellwald. These men variously argued that the rejection of private property would of necessity lead to the decline of humanity (Seidlitz), that constant struggle among humans was a natural law (Byr), and that if the socialists were to win, it would only be the result of might over right, since the domination of one part of mankind over another was natural law also (Hellwald).

Kautsky admitted that the struggle for survival was an organic law to which all beings were subject, but he contended that the very means by which this struggle was carried on were subject to development and that for some organisms, like bees and ants, groups formed the basic unit of the struggle, not individuals. Because the conditions under which some animals live dictate the "solidarity of its members," the herd or family prevails over the individual. Kautsky argued that such was the case for humans, among whom "instinctive solidarity rules as a weapon in the struggle for existence in society." Among certain humans, namely the bourgeoisie, industrialists and speculators, in "the salons of Paris and the anterooms of the Winter Palace," the struggle of all against all went on; bourgeois science established this conflict as a basic principle of social organization, claiming Darwinism as natural-scientific justification for the "purest egoism" of social life.[43]

What this picture of human life overlooked, according to Kautsky, was that humans are often motivated by ideals, by an instinctive solidarity that has brought people to die for tradition, for monarchs they have never seen, for the tribe, and even for the state, "which often has taken their last penny from them." In the second part of the article, Kautsky expanded on the notion that abstract ideals serve as foci of solidarity, and that group, rather than individual, struggle prevails among humans. What was instinctive solidarity in lower animals became moral duty in humans; groups came to focus around the state or nation, race, and church, all abstract ideals. But under the economics of capitalism, all such ideals are gradually undermined, and rapacious individual competition destroys solidarity and returns humanity to the more primitive form of one against one. Kautsky concluded that only socialism could overcome the divisive aspects of bourgeois society, and that socialism was "the higher step of the normal historical development of the struggle for survival." Finally, Kautsky claimed that all zoological, anthropological, and historical evidence demonstrated that the strongest social instincts prevailed in the absence of private property, and that therefore the proletariat of modern society, those without property, would form organizations of the greatest solidarity to ensure the victory of socialism.[44]

Evidence of the influence of Darwin and, to a lesser extent, Büchner abounds in this article. Kautsky attempted to use the master and his discipline against the opponents of socialism and to imply that Darwinism was being misused as a defense of the bourgeois order. His critique of the bourgeois proponents of Darwinism in the social realm was valid in that they did miss the collective or social aspects of human life; his efforts to tie social instincts in humans to naturalistic rather than divine origins gave at least a semiscientific substance to this critique. But the influence of Buckle is also apparent. Darwin presented social solidarity as a response to pressing and persistent demands of the environment and as a form of behavior which became instinctual with time. Kautsky's substitution of moral duty, of abstract ideals, for instinctual behavior represented a leap from naturalism to romantic idealism that held socialism to be a moral duty without linking this duty to material conditions in the lives of the working class. Just as Buckle moved from a position that held the mind to be causally related to the material universe to one in which ideas had independent qualities, Kautsky moved from naturalistic arguments for social instinct to viewing socialism as a moral but not a material imperative.

Finally, this article demonstrates the extent to which Kautsky remained under romantic influences in 1876, which helps explain the inconsistencies of his theoretical analysis. In imagery and style, "Socialism and the Struggle for Existence" represents some of his most effective writing. In later years, as he got more "scientific," his style became heavy and pedantic. But more importantly, several passages reveal the intensity and passion of his belief in socialism: "Were socialism not a fight for natural right against the most revolting injustice, were it not a doctrine of brotherly love which binds all workers and will unite all of humanity, and if in socialist society the higher development of all personal qualities were impossible, only then would the proclamation of socialism make no sense."[45] George Sand had scored heavily with young Karl, and the science was still a rationalization for, or an attempt to give validity to, an essentially moral commitment. In many ways the rest of his career, especially his adoption of Marxism, can best be understood as a continuing effort to provide the scientific support the times demanded for the cause to which he gave sixty years of his life.

In his memoirs, Kautsky reported that he first read *Capital* in 1875 and that under its influence he spent much time in the years that followed studying economics and economists. However, though his published work in the years 1875–1879 contains several references to Marx, there is little evidence that the Marxian analysis of history and society made much of an impact on the young Austrian until the end of March 1878. As late as 8 March 1878, in an article entitled "History and Socialism," Kautsky identified geography, geology, physiology, and the natural sciences in general as concerns of future historians who had freed themselves from the domination of Christian idealism. Surely his failure to mention economics in this context shows that Kautsky was less influenced by Marx during these years than he later suggested. In fact, as far as its historiographical outlook is concerned, this article did little more than paraphrase Buckle.[46]

Kautsky was so far from being under the influence of Marx's conceptions during the early years that Engels singled out some of his work for criticism. At the time Engels did not know the identity of the author of the pseudonymous articles that disturbed him. In a letter to August Bebel, Engels commented on the state of theory among the younger writers of the movement:

> But it seems to be impossible for our people, at least a number of them, to confine themselves in their articles to what they have really comprehended. In proof take the endless columns theoretically socialist in content which have been penned by Ky, Symmachos and all the rest of that crowd, whose economic blunders, erroneous views, and ignorance of socialist literature furnishes the best means of thoroughly destroying the theoretical superiority of the German movement up to now.[47]

Kautsky later observed that it was no wonder Engels complained about the quality of the work which appeared in the *Volksstaat*, since it really had been bad. But, Kautsky added, much of the blame for the poor quality had to go to the editors of the journal, who should have given guidance to their young contributors. Specifically, Kautsky blamed not the official editors, Wilhelm Hasenclever and Wilhelm Liebknecht, but the latter's son-in-law, Bruno Geiser, who frequently served as de facto editor when the other two men were occupied with their official duties as socialist representatives in the Reichstag. The fact that Geiser and Kautsky became outspoken enemies after 1883 must be considered when assessing Kautsky's criticism of the *Volksstaat* editorial staff. But it is true that during the four years Kautsky contributed articles to the *Volksstaat* and the *Vorwärts* only one editorial note was attached to his work commenting on the accuracy of his facts and interpretation. Certainly the brash young autodidact could have benefited from more active guidance on the part of the editorial staff. In later years, when he became an editor himself, Kautsky tried to provide such guidance to his younger co-workers.[48]

At the same time that many of Kautsky's articles were appearing in the *Vorwärts*, a long series of articles by Friedrich Engels was also being carried by the journal. Published in many parts beginning on 3 January 1877 and running through 7 July 1878, this series was collected into book form and published in October 1878 under the title *Herr Eugen*

Dühring's Revolution in Science. It soon was called simply *Anti-Dühring.* This book was probably the most influential single work in winning young German socialists to the cause of Marxism. Certainly it was instrumental in the conversion of Kautsky and of Eduard Bernstein, onetime closest friend and later revisionist anatgonist of Kautsky. Bernstein said of *Anti-Dühring:* "It converted me to Marxism." Kautsky felt that "no book had done so much for the understanding of Marxism as this one."[49]

Even though Kautsky did not thoroughly study the complete *Anti-Dühring* until the winter of 1879–1880, some effects of his reading of the articles began to appear in his writing by the spring of 1878. On 31 March, Kautsky's first article primarily concerned with economics was published, and in it Kautsky referred to "economic relations" as "the basis of society." This assertion differed markedly from his 8 March evaluation of the subjects important for future historians, and it reflected his emerging Marxian orientation. Two weeks later, he further indicated the direction in which he was inclining by observing in another article that labor and capital are not opposites in and of themselves, but only to the extent that these concepts represent social relations of production.[50] Kautsky certainly did not become a Marxist between 8 and 31 March 1878, but by the latter date he was beginning to change his views somewhat, moving from an obsession with natural-scientific explanations of the origins of humans and their society to an increasing awareness of the importance of economic matters. Several more years of diligent study with Bernstein and careful guidance from Engels would be required before Kautsky would consider himself a consistent Marxist.

Austrian Socialism

The party with which Kautsky was associated for his first five years as a socialist could not begin to satisfy the young intellectual's rather grandiose visions of the future of the movement. Founded in April 1874, the Austrian Social Democratic Workers' Party suffered from several major weaknesses that kept it small and politically insignificant for a long time. By the late 1870s the Austrian Empire was far from being a major industrial nation. Though it had experienced some industrial growth since 1850, especially in railroad construction, by 1870 the industrial working class comprised on 12 percent of the total population, and by 1880 still only 27 percent. Moreover, the largest concentration of industrial workers was in Bohemia, where other factors worked against close ties with the Austrian party. To further complicate things for the socialists of the Hapsburg empire, Austria was entering a period of severe economic depression at the time the party was founded. Taking 1873 levels as 100, by 1875 production in the coal-mining industry had fallen to 89, in iron ore to 76, in beer and brewing to 56, and in brick-making to 25; obviously employment suffered proportionately. In correspondence to the *Vorwärts* from Vienna, dated 26 May 1877, Kautsky reported that since 1 January there had been only nine new construction starts in the entire city, and workers had flocked to each one willing to work for any wage. High unemployment and migration out of depressed areas reduced party and trade-union membership and undermined the spirit of those in the movement. Even among artisans and handicraftsmen, typically the most fruitful recruiting grounds for young socialist parties, the mid-seventies were hard times. In 1873, the Vienna shoemakers' union had 962 members, by 1876, only 186; during that same period the Graz woodworkers' union membership fell from 600 to 150.[51]

Austrian socialism was also rent by internal disunity from the very beginning. Not surprisingly, a party based on the multinational con-glomeration that was Austria reflected many of the problems generated by the clash of nationalities. These problems are too complex to deal with here, other than to indicate that the German portions of the Austrian Empire, especially Vienna, played a disproportionately large role in the movement and thereby irritated the other national groups. One historian of Austrian socialism concluded: "One serious hindrance to the further development of the Austrian workers' movement was the deficient understanding of a part of the German-speaking workers' leaders for the national needs of the non-German-speaking [*anderssprechenden*] workers."[52]

During the early years of the Austrian Social Democratic Workers' Party, a far more frequent and devisive internal conflict than that of the nationalities was one based on differences in tactics and conceptions of the nature of the party. In part because the immediate predecessor of the party, the Arbeiterbildungsverein (Workers' Educational League), was born during that brief springtime of liberalism which followed the Austrian defeat in the 1866 war with Prussia, the Austrian movement was from the beginning split between those who sought to ally the workers with the bourgeois forces for change and those who argued that the workers had to be independent from, and indeed opposed to, bourgeois liberalism. The former group was encouraged by J. B. Schweitzer, Lassalle's successor as president of the Allgemein deutsche Arbeiterverein, to support the Austrian liberals against the reactionaries, a position which, given the strong

German nationalism of Austria's liberals, exacerbated relations with non-German groups within the working-class movement. Supporters of this view in the Austrian party were headed by Heinrich Oberwinder and were generally referred to as the moderates. Those who wanted to maintain the complete independence of the workers and form them into a separate political party were headed by the Scheu brothers (Andreas, Heinrich, and Josef), Johann Most, Emil Kaler-Reinthal, and others, and were generally known as the radicals.[53]

With the establishment of the social democratic party in the spring of 1874, the radicals won out over the moderates, but at virtually the same time a new tactical split began to develop which would once again divide the party into two, and then three, groups. In 1876, reunion with some of Oberwinder's former supporters reopened the old moderate-radical split. In August of that same year, Kaler-Reinthal's effort to lessen governmental persecution by adoption of a more moderate program fed this split. However, in the following years an even more disruptive internal division emerged when many Austrian socialists, especially Most and Andreas Scheu, turned toward a form of anarchism inspired by the famous Russian, Mikhail Bakunin. By 1880-1881, the party had developed three factions—one that argued in favor of legality and cooperation at all cost, one that was increasingly inclined toward illegality and even violence, and a third which sought cooperation with, but independence from, other groups within the empire opposed to the reactionary government. This latter group emphasized education; their program included democratic and state-supported cooperative planks which reflected the strong Lassallean influence at work in Austria.[54]

Internally divided and weakly based as it was, the Austrian party was an easy and constant prey for the Austrian government. The franchise was limited to less than one-third of the adult male population and was based on a three-class system of voting that favored the wealthy and elected a Reichsrat with very few powers. The imperial government was adept at other forms of harassment and oppression as well. Many socialist leaders were prosecuted for treason and lesser antistate activities; socialist meetings were frequently forbidden or disrupted even when they met the stringent requirements of state laws; and journals were constantly censored or banned for printing or attempting to print articles offensive to the state. The Austrian police were particularly good at bribing or blackmailing socialist leaders into serving as agents—Dr. Hippolyte Tauschinsky, a prominent early leader of the movement, was revealed as a police agent in 1874 after having been under suspicion for years, and even Kaler-Reinthal eventually served in the same capacity. All in all, the government that learned its oppressive techniques from a master, Prince Metternich, was able to hamper severely but never quite eliminate the socialist movement.[55]

When Karl Kautsky joined the Austrian party in January 1875, the dominant split was between Oberwinder's moderates and the Vienna-centered radicals led by the Scheu brothers and, following Andreas Scheu's emigration to London in July 1874, by Johann Schwarzinger. Kautsky allied himself with the radicals because they seemed to be opposing the "corruption and cowardly opportunism" of the moderates. Despite his absence, Andreas Scheu continued to influence the Austrian movement, and shortly after Kautsky joined the party he began a correspondence with Scheu which molded the younger man's political and party attitudes for the next four or five years. Scheu's influence was the first example of something that characterized most of Kautsky's career as an active socialist. Though he often developed theoretical positions on his own, he never felt comfortable in practical political matters unless he could receive close counsel from someone whose political acumen he trusted and respected above his own. Scheu was followed by Bernstein and Engels in this role, and then Bebel. Scheu's influence on Kautsky was of considerable importance, and the former's gradual conversion to anarchism elicited a similar temporary development in Kautsky, just as many years later Kautsky would become the theoretician of SPD "centrism" under the influence of Bebel's practical politics.[56]

Kautsky's role in the Austrian party was a model for all his later participation in the German and international socialist movements. He took no part in administration or organization, either of the party or the trade unions; he neither held nor ran for public or party offices; he was exclusively a propagandist, teacher, and very occasional speaker. Though he frequently attended meetings of the party leadership, listening with interest to what went on and learning from it, he very rarely contributed. In fact, as a lecturer to trade unions and workers' educational leagues, Kautsky probably had more direct contact with workers and rank-and-file party members in the first years in Austria than at any other time during his more than six decades as a socialist. He lectured mostly in history, especially on Rome, the sixteenth century in Germany (concentrating on the peasant wars, on which topic he later wrote a book), and eighteenth-century French intellectual history as the ideological background to the French Revolution. In his memoirs Kautsky noted that the governmental observer, a required guest at all working-class gatherings, usually brought the history of the eighteenth century to an end in May 1789—before the outbreak of revolution.[57]

Having aligned himself from the beginning with Scheu's radicalism, Kautsky followed when this radicalism began to turn into anarchism. Besides Scheu's influence, the conversion to anarchist sympathies also reflected his frustration with the small size and impotence of the Austrian party. In his role as correspondent from Austria to the *Vorwärts,* Kautsky repeatedly emphasized the ineffectiveness of the party and its persecution by the state. His first report opened with this observation: "There is certainly nothing more thankless than being correspondent from Austria for a social democratic paper. There is not a political life here for the working class, [not] even a scanty one, what the laws graciously grant is reduced by unheard of interpretations." Kautsky excused long gaps in his correspondence by contending that nothing was going on in the Austrian movement. Given the revolutionary inclinations of a young romantic, this stagnancy could only arouse enthusiasm for "propaganda of the deed." If nothing was happening in Austria, socialists had to take steps to stimulate activity.[58]

By late 1877, Kautsky's radicalism had developed to the point of support for Lassalle's conception of "one reactionary mass," the if-you-are-not-with-us-you-are-against-us view of nonsocialists which Marx complained about when it cropped up in the 1875 Gotha program of the German movement and against which Kautsky himself was later to campaign vigorously. In a lead article for the *Vorwärts,* Kautsky coupled this notion with a critique of German bourgeois science: "The unification of all parties into a single reactionary mass against the socialists always increases; it always becomes more difficult for a friend of true freedom to belong to any other party than the social democratic. This phenomenon is revealed not only in the political and social realms, but also in the scientific." The prominent German scientist Rudolf Virchow had made the mistake of denying that theories of descent as applied to humans were as yet sufficiently proven to be taught as scientific fact, while arguing that religion should continue to be part of the school curriculum. Kautsky attacked Virchow both for his blindness in refusing to accept descent theories and for his absurd support for religious education, as though religion were fact. This article closed with an impassioned description of the world as divided into the defenders of limited science, militarism, the church, and suppression on the one hand, and the defenders of the general franchise, press and organizational freedom, the abolition of the standing army, labor, and democratic science on the other. Kautsky saw no third possibility; whoever would be consistent and defend any one position from either group must favor all others of that group. This article clearly reveals the tendency of the young Kautsky to couple science and democratic socialism into a comprehensive *Weltanschauung*.[59]

A series of events in 1878 acted on Kautsky's radical inclinations to move him even closer to anarchist sympathies. Early in that year, revolutionary activities in Russia, especially Vera Zasulich's attempt on the life of a government official, prompted Kautsky to write an article in which he called upon his Austrian comrades to take the courage and self-sacrifice of their Russian counterparts as an example. Of course such sentiments could not get by the censors and into print. This episode marked one of the very few times Kautsky came into personal conflict with the law, for not only was the article suppressed, but Kautsky was summoned to court to face possible criminal prosecution. On the advice of a sympathetic lawyer, he simply said nothing in court, and since the article had been written under a pseudonym the charge against him was dropped. Later in 1878, the famous assassination attempts on the German kaiser occurred. Kautsky's response was to point out that even though the Austrian government did not have the comfortable excuse of an assassin, it none the less oppressed the working-class movement. He implied that Austrian socialism did not have much to lose by assassination attempts, since rights that did not exist could not be suspended. Finally, late in 1878, the German government responded to the attempts on the kaiser's life by outlawing social democracy. The German party and its press capitulated rather quietly, and when this was contrasted with the high level of Russian revolutionary activity at about the same time, the German passivity did not come off well with many of the fiery young men of the Austrian movement. When Johann Most, who had moved from Austria to Germany and then to London, began to publish his anarchistically oriented *Die Freiheit,* the breach left by the virtual disappearance of the less radical German socialist press was partially filled. For a few months in 1879, Kautsky served *Die Freiheit* as correspondent from Austria, and he recalled many years later that even after he had begun to contribute to the exiled German social democratic press, he had "certainly moved away from Most, but . . . still had not broken with him completely."[60]

For a number of reasons the young Austrian's flirtation with anarchism was brief. By late 1877, Kautsky had already developed an elaborate natural-scientific, socialistic world view and had begun to give expression to his strongly theoretical inclination in articles contributed to both the Austrian and German socialist presses. Though at this time his work was still frequently marked with romantic overtones, he was moving rapidly toward a more rationalistic, less passionate analysis of human society and away from the youthful obsession with vigorous, and perhaps fruitless, action. The theoretical content of the anarchism of Most and his Austrian followers was less than impressive; it could hardly occupy the full time and attention of Kautsky's eclectic and ambitious intellect. Moreover, by the end of the seventies he had not yet decided on a career. Having given up law, convinced that a socialist would not be tolerated as a teacher in the state-controlled schools of Austria, he had nearly decided to use a recent inheritance from his grandfather to set himself up as a bookseller, with supplemental income to be derived from writing. However, the socialist press of Austria was not nearly large enough to allow Kautsky to support himself with his pen; to make a living as a writer he would have to find a richer field to work in than the tiny and oppressed Austrian movement. Finally, just as he was deciding to become a bookseller, he was offered a subsidized position among the exiled German socialists in Zurich. In accepting this offer, he was assured of a market for his socialist work, but only if he completely abandoned his quasi-anarchist sympathies. His move to Zurich also took him out of the environment of Austrian socialism which was becoming increasingly dominated by Most's brand of anarchism. The combination of his developing *Weltanschauung*, his desire to make a living as a socialist, and his removal from Austrian influences ended Kautsky's anarchism forever.[61]

The offer of financial support came from Karl Höchberg, a wealthy German socialist. In 1879 Höchberg founded a new journal, *Jahrbuch für Sozialwissenschaft und Sozialpolitik,* which appeared in Zurich. One feature of the *Jahrbuch* was to be reports on the progress of socialist movements in various countries, but Höchberg knew no one from Austria to call upon for this duty, so he asked Wilhelm Liebknecht for a recommendation. Liebknecht, who had been personally involved in the Austrian movement since at least 1869, suggested Kautsky, whom he had met in Leipzig in 1877 when Karl was representing his father's business consortium. During 1879, Höchberg and Kautsky established a correspondence; Höchberg was also the first to pay Kautsky for a piece of socialist writing; and on 8 October 1879, Höchberg put up 400 gulden to help finance the publication of Kautsky's first book. In addition to giving indirect financial support to young socialist intellectuals, Höchberg also provided direct subsidies, as in 1879 when he brought Eduard Bernstein to Zurich to serve as his personal secretary. Höchberg was sufficiently impressed with Kautsky's potential to write to him on 17 January 1880, offering to pay his passage to Zurich and to support him while he devoted himself to serious scholarship and socialist literature. By four o'clock on the afternoon of 23 January 1880, Kautsky had arrived in Zurich, thus beginning forty-five years of virtually unbroken devotion to German socialism.[62]

The Peripatetic Decade
1880–1890

BOTH PERSONALLY AND INTELLECTUALLY the decade of the eighties was the most important in Kautsky's life. In these years he was married twice and divorced once; his second marriage lasted almost fifty years. He lived for nearly equal periods in Zurich (1880–1882, 1884), Vienna (1882–1883, 1888–1889), and London (1885–1888), and for a short time in the isolated German city of Stuttgart (1883) before settling there in late 1890. During the 1880s, he also established virtually all the major friendships of his life—with Engels, Bebel, Bernstein, Adler, Eleanor Marx, and a variety of Russians, Frenchmen, and other non-Germans. In 1883, the founding of *Die Neue Zeit* as the German organ of Marxism gave Kautsky a job (he was primary editor from 1883 to 1917), a regular source of income, and a means through which he could develop and promote his own brand of Marxism. Studying closely with Bernstein in Zurich, under the personal guidance of Engels in London, and through extensive correspondence with both men when separated, Kautsky developed during the eighties from a brash natural-scientific, romantic socialist into a consistent Engelian-Marxist with highly catholic intellectual tastes. Although he was virtually unknown to most socialists outside Austria when he arrived in Zurich in January 1880, by 1890 he was one of the two most prominent presumed heirs to Marx and Engels, and in 1891 he wrote the theoretical portion of the official program of the world's largest socialist workers' party, the SPD.

Zurich

The move from Vienna to Zurich changed Kautsky's living conditions in many significant ways. For the first time in his life, at age twenty-six, he was on his own, independent of his immediate family. Höchberg had promised financial support, and Kautsky reported to his parents shortly after his arrival in Zurich that his income would be at least 3,000 marks per year. This more than comfortable sum allowed him to enjoy some of the amenities of cosmopolitan Zurich. One old family friend, writing in rather awkward English, responded to Kautsky's early letters from the Swiss city by observing: "I hear of Spanish wines, and dainties of all countries, which you enjoy, and ladies of all countries with whom you have intercourse. Is this our well-behaved and sober Charles that was?" During the Zurich years Kautsky acquired the nickname "Baron Juchzer," or "Baron Shout of Joy." The first part stuck with him the rest of his life, apparently derived from the somewhat fastidious dress which distinguished him from many of the more slovenly emigrés. The second part of the nickname referred to Kautsky's exuberance and optimism. Bernstein recalled that many times at the weekly meetings of the Moorish Club, the regular gathering of the German socialist emigrés in Zurich, "Karl Kautsky, a nimble and extremely inventive person, delighted us, when our mood was more than usually extravagant, by irresistibly amusing imitations of acrobats, or as a fantastic dancer."[1]

Zurich was a hotbed of socialist emigrés during the eighties, mostly Germans and Russians. Very few of the exiles had any contact with the Swiss workers, and they tended to form closed, inner-directed groups with their fellow countrymen. In contrast to his experience in Vienna Kautsky spent most of the time in Zurich in association with non-proletarians. Furthermore, his contacts were usually limited to the intellectuals of the German movement since the politically active, like Bebel, Liebknecht, and others, were protected in Germany by their status as Reichstag representatives and did not have to live in exile. They frequently visited Zurich, however, and as an Austrian, Kautsky was fairly free to travel in Germany and visit the politicians. As a result, given that Austria had no socialists in its parliament until after the turn of the century, Kautsky certainly had more contact with politically active socialists in Zurich than he had had in Vienna. Nevertheless, most of his time was spent in the company of intellectuals who were not active in politics.[2]

Höchberg and Bernstein were the men with whom Kautsky spent the most time. In addition to giving extensive financial support, Höchberg influenced Kautsky in two ways. First, he was the first good editor Kautsky worked with; in contrast to the editors of the *Vorwärts* and the *Volksstaat*, Höchberg conscientiously read and criticized the young Austrian's articles, offering guidance and stimulation for intellectual development. The brash young Kautsky not only needed such tutoring, he also appreciated it. Second, Höchberg expanded Kautsky's intellectual horizons by introducing him to Herbert Spencer's work and by encouraging him to study practical economics, especially protective tariffs and international labor legislation. Kautsky did write on labor legislation and in 1881 he attended a congress of the International Association for Reform and Codification of National Law in Zurich, hoping to advance the cause of international labor legislation. But a special study of protective tariffs, which Höchberg encouraged Kautsky to undertake in the spring of 1881, was displaced by another topic suggested by Engels: the origins of the family and marriage. In a striking example of his inclinations at the time, he abandoned the study of pressing, extremely practical problems to devote himself to a question of historical and anthropological importance, but of little immediate relevance to the working-class movement. During his first stay in Zurich, Kautsky was not particularly active in emigré discussion groups, though he sometimes gave historical presentations on Ireland and once discussed Socrates. He was much more interested in pursuing intellectual research, and when in early 1881 Liebknecht suggested that Kautsky might be more useful to the movement back in Austria, Karl wrote to Engels that he had "no desire to waste common blows as an agitator."[3]

Of even greater importance than Höchberg to Kautsky's theoretical development during the Zurich years was his very close personal relationship with Eduard Bernstein. Five years Kautsky's senior, and long active in the German movement, he had come to Zurich as Höchberg's private secretary in 1879. Kautsky and Bernstein became friends almost immediately. In a very short time the two were constant companions who worked and studied together, wrote joint letters to Engels, and relaxed and enjoyed themselves together. Having preceded Kautsky to Zurich, Bernstein was able to introduce the younger man to the various groups of emigrés, especially the Russians and the French. And from his participation in party affairs, Bernstein was able to enlighten Kautsky about the finer points and inner workings of the German movement; his experience and personal inclinations made him far superior to Kautsky in political matters. With Bernstein, Kautsky undertook the intense study of Engels' *Anti-Dühring* that finally converted them both to Marxism. What began in Zurich was not simply an association of like-minded individuals, but what Bernstein called "a very close friendship relation and a kind of fighting comradeship," a relationship which led Kautsky to observe that they "became so much of one heart and one soul that we were considered as a sort of red Orestes and Pylades." Though Kautsky was later to assert in his memoirs that he had learned little of theoretical importance from Bernstein, in fact their development into Marxists was simultaneous and mutual, and the intensity of their personal relationship was precisely what made their break at the turn of the century such a powerful and disturbing event in Kautsky's life.[4]

One of the major activities of the German socialist exiles in Zurich was the publication of the official party newspaper, the *Sozialdemokrat*. Founded late in 1879, after the antisocialist law had all but eliminated the domestic party press, the *Sozialdemokrat* was edited by Georg von Vollmar until his resignation in January 1881. For a time Kautsky was on the verge of being catapulted into prominence in the German movement when he was briefly considered as a potential successor to Vollmar. The task of naming a new editor was Bebel's, and his first inclination was to have Liebknecht take over primary control, writing the lead articles and the political review, with Kautsky handling the correspondence and the technical aspects of editing. By December 1880, however, Bebel had abandoned this plan, and he took Bernstein to London in part to get approval from Marx and Engels of Bernstein's appointment as Vollmar's replacement. Kautsky was not given this prestigious appointment for a variety of reasons, but primarily because Bebel and Engels were not certain that he was altogether to be trusted with such a critical position. Both the older men felt that he lacked sufficient knowledge of German affairs, that he was not particularly adept in his political judgments, and that he was better suited for more theoretical work than was appropriate for the official party newspaper. Engels was unhappy with the "doctrinaire" tone of some of Kautsky's contributions to the *Sozialdemokrat*, and even as late as 1886, he felt that Bernstein was a better political polemicist because he was not a "university man," but a "businessman and, what is not least, [a] Jew. . . . One learns warfare only in wars." Kautsky had also given Bebel the impression that even if offered the editorship he would accept it only temporarily since he hoped to leave Zurich for London and closer study with Marx and Engels. However, Kautsky did give Bernstein a great deal of assistance with the editorial chores, and Kautsky and Liebknecht edited numbers 30–36 of the *Sozialdemokrat* in the late summer of 1881.[5]

Despite his reservations about Kautsky's abilities as a political analyst, Engels recognized that he was an eager and promising disciple. From their very first contact, Engels adopted an attitude toward him that was both encouraging and critical. When Bernstein and Bebel went to London in December 1880, Kautsky sent along with them a copy of his study, *The Influence of Population Increase on the Progress of Society,* which had just been published in Vienna. Kautsky was seeking the approval of Marx and Engels and also hoped to be recognized as a proponent of the materialist conception of history which he and Bernstein had recently adopted. In a cover letter he professed to Engels, "I wish nothing more than to learn from you." In his reply, Engels was doubtful about the importance of the population study, but responded to Kautsky's expressed desire to come to London for further study: "You are quite right to come here. . . . it has become very necessary for you to come away from the uncritical atmosphere in which the entire . current German-produced historical and economic literature decays." This advice—to concentrate even more on abstract historical studies— strongly reinforced Kautsky's personal inclination.[6]

Late in March 1881, Kautsky arrived in England for his first visit to Marx and Engels and the British Museum; he stayed until late June. Though encouraged by Engels' response to his first letter, he was somewhat apprehensive about how he would be received in London since Liebknecht had reported that "the two old ones [Marx and Engels] had not spoken well of" Kautsky. In fact Kautsky and Liebknecht disagreed about the value of visiting London. Bebel thought it useful, but Liebknecht felt that the time would be better spent in Germany in closer contact with the day-to-day movement. Kautsky concluded that Liebknecht did not care much about theoretical development. Despite these slight misgivings, the visit to the old ones was a success. He met mostly with Engels, often for long theoretical discussions, and was invited to attend the Sunday afternoon gatherings at his home. Karl also did some research at the British Museum, just enough to tantalize the source-hungry historian in him and to convince him of the need to spend a longer period in London. He made a second visit in 1884, before settling there for over three years beginning in 1885.[7]

Kautsky saw little of Marx during his first visit, and did not make a very good impression on him. Marx wrote this evaluation shortly after their first meeting: "Engels too has taken a much milder view of this Kauz since he proved himself a very talented drinker. . . . He is a mediocrity with a small-minded outlook, superwise (only 26), very conceited, industrious in a certain sort of way, he busies himself a lot with statistics but does not read anything very clever out of them, belongs by nature to the tribe of the philistines but is otherwise a decent fellow in his own way. I turn him over to friend E[ngels] as much as possible." Marx died before Kautsky's second visit, and the two men never got to know one another very well. On the other hand, Kautsky's relationship with Engels became much closer in the next decade, at least in part because they both enjoyed tippling. On his second trip to London, Kautsky arrived on Engels' birthday and proceeded to overdo the celebration with champagne, only to awake next day to a hangover and a postcard from Engels asking if Kautsky had managed to make it safely back to his hotel.[8]

Engels' evaluation of Kautsky after their first meeting was not as harsh as Marx's, but Engels realized that Kautsky was not well suited to be a political writer and continued to feel that he needed a great deal more experience before he could become a major intellectual figure in the Marxian movement. In a letter written while Kautsky was still in London, Engels complimented Bernstein on the tone adopted by the *Sozialdemokrat* and added that Bernstein should not feel himself ill equipped for the editorship because of his lack of formal education. Engels argued that the proper tone for a political journal is not that of "erudition," but of being able to grasp the essence of a situation quickly. "That, for example, Kautsky would not be able to do," Engels continued, "he always has too many secondary points of view. Certainly that is good for longer review articles, but on a newspaper where one must make up one's mind quickly, often one cannot see the forest for the trees, and that must not happen in a party organ." A few months later, Engels observed to Bebel that though Kautsky was "an extremely good fellow," he was also "a born pedant and hair-splitter in whose hands the complicated questions do not become simple, but the simple complicated."[9] By 1883, Engels was still pessimistic about the younger generation of Marxian theoreticians: "In the theoretical work I still as yet do not see who will replace me and M[arx]. What the young [ones] have tried is worth little, mostly even less than nothing. Kautsky, the only one who studies industriously, must write in order to live, and can therefore certainly produce nothing."[10]

The need to write in order to live began to bear down on Kautsky again shortly after his return from London in 1881. In mid-November, Höchberg suffered personal financial difficulties which forced a reduction in support for Kautsky. The two men had already begun to move apart theoretically; as early as 1880, Höchberg was uncomfortable with the Marxism of both Kautsky and Bernstein, and by 1881 Kautsky and Höchberg specifically disagreed on the question of whether or not Germany should establish colonies. Kautsky argued against colonies, Höchberg in favor of them. But despite these differences, Höchberg had remained generous to the young Marxists, paying for trips to London, financing book publication, and providing regular support. In his memoirs Kautsky paid high tribute to

Höchberg for his generous and selfless support. By April 1882, however, Kautsky felt that he had to leave Zurich: Höchberg was withdrawing support not only from him personally, but also from the *Sozialdemokrat* and most of the other literary projects he had helped finance.[11]

The Founding of *Die neue Zeit*

Having decided to leave Switzerland, Kautsky once again faced the necessity of making a living, and this necessity dictated where he would go. His fondest wish was to move to London, but first consideration had to be given to the matter of money, so he returned to Vienna, thinking his chances of gaining a regular income there were better than in London. Things had not improved in the socialist movement during his absence. State repression was as extensive as ever, the anarchists with whom he had so recently flirted had grown much stronger, and the number of socialists working for an organized, politically oriented movement had shrunk to a minimum. Because of his association with the *Sozialdemokrat* in Zurich, Kautsky returned to Vienna with considerably more prestige, or notoriety, than he had had earlier. He frequently found himself pushed into positions of leadership among those who favored the German type of party and close ties with the German movement. After an uncharacteristically modest recognition of the need to orient himself on recent developments before writing on them, Kautsky entered the fray on the side of those urging organization for political ends. He reacted very sharply to the anarchists' rejection of demands for a general franchise, arguing that "one can hardly push nonsense further," and harshly condemned anarchist violence, which he felt only aided the opponents of the workers' movement. In contrast to his less certain position on political questions when he left Vienna in 1880, Kautsky now justified political organization as the only way to give future direction to the movement. In October 1882, he attended a socialist party congress in Brünn, where he was called upon to draft a new party program on very short notice. Drawing from his memory of the program Marx had drafted for the Frenchman Jules Guesde in 1880, Kautsky wrote out brief proposals that called for struggle by all means that recognized the rights of the people, that is, excluding terrorism. This program later served as the basis of the Hainfeld program of 1888, which finally united Austrian socialism under Victor Adler's leadership.[12]

Despite his increased activity and importance in the Austrian party, Kautsky was not happy in Vienna. The movement was still tiny and harassed, and he had experienced the excitement of the much larger, more interesting, though no less harassed, German party. He had also acquired a taste for historical research and for close contacts with Marxian intellectuals. Vienna seemed far from the action, and oppressive. He received his letters at a cover address and had to use the same subterfuge in writing to Engels, lest their correspondence be confiscated by the imperial police. His isolation from intellectually stimulating comrades led him to write long, involved letters to Engels on a variety of theoretical and political subjects. When Engels could not find time to respond in kind, Kautsky was stung by what he felt was rejection by his chosen mentor. Only intercession by Bernstein and reassurances from Engels that the problem was simply lack of time stilled Kautsky's discomfort. Furthermore, he had not found employment. The Austrian socialist press could not provide sufficient support, so he had to look elsewhere.[13]

As early as June 1882, Kautsky began negotiations to establish the world's first scholarly journal devoted to the explication and propagation of Marxism. Working closely with Liebknecht and the German socialist editor J. H. W. Dietz, to whom he was introduced by Bernstein, he hoped to found a journal that was not subsidized by the party and was free to promote Marxism within the rapidly growing German movement. Dietz was essential to the project because a publisher was needed who was ideologically inclined to take the financial and political risks involved in publishing such a journal in Germany under the antisocialist law. Correspondence with Dietz did not begin until August, but by September negotiations had advanced far enough to necessitate a personal meeting. In October, Dietz, Bebel, Liebknecht, Kautsky, and, much to Kautsky's irritation, Liebknecht's son-in-law, Bruno Geiser, met in Salzburg to conclude the arrangements. Kautsky contributed 2,000 marks to the venture as did his Viennese friend, Heinrich Braun, with Dietz assuming financial responsibility for the remainder. *Die neue Zeit*, the name agreed upon for the new journal, was to be of moderate length, to cost fifty pfennig, and to appear monthly beginning 1 January 1883. Officially it was not a party publication, though the presence of Bebel and Liebknecht at this founding meeting meant that the *Neue Zeit* would be closely tied to an important segment of the party. Liebknecht was designated a permanent contributor, and Dietz, Liebknecht, and Kautsky comprised the editorial board. Kautsky was clearly to assume primary responsibility for the regular editorial tasks and receive a salary for his work; the *Neue Zeit* was his journal.[14]

At the time of the establishment of the *Neue Zeit*, the German socialist movement was dividing into two groups, the moderates and the radicals. Such an internal division had existed since the founding of the party and would continue until after World War I, but under the antisocialist law tensions between the two groups were particularly acute. The moderates were led by most of the Social Democratic *Fraktion* of the Reichstag, which had assumed de facto leadership of the party immediately after the beginning of the antisocialist law and was officially endorsed in this capacity by the party's 1880 Wyden congress. They tended to play down the class nature of the movement, tried to avoid antagonizing the hostile government by avoiding revolutionary rhetoric, and emphasized piecemeal reform, social and political inte-gration of their followers, and the need to recognize the strength of their opposition. Though disgusted by the injustices perpetrated on the lower classes in Germany and uncomfortable with Bismarck's autocratic state, the moderates in the party *Fraktion* concentrated on working within the system and expanding the party's appeal to sectors of the population other than the industrial working class. To the limited extent that they were theoretical, the moderates were eclectic and Lassallean; they represented the petit bourgeois, democratic roots of German socialism. The radicals, who were represented in the *Fraktion* only by Bebel, an often unreliable Liebknecht, and, until 1884, by Vollmar, emphasized the class nature of both the German state and their own party. They seemed at times to relish the pariah status of socialists and spoke more boldly of the need for fundamental change and vaguely of some sort of impending revolution. The major strength of the radicals lay in the intellectuals of the movement, headed by the exiled *Sozialdemokrat* and those surrounding it, especially Vollmar, Bernstein, Kautsky, and Bebel. These men all identified themselves in varying degrees as followers of Marx and Engels, though in fact none but Bernstein and Kautsky had very clear notions of what constituted Marxism.[15]

Much of the debate between the radicals and moderates centered on the material published in the *Sozialdemokrat*. Quite sensibly the moderates of the *Fraktion* argued that if they were going to be held accountable for what appeared in the official party journal, they should have some say over its contents. On the other hand, the radicals felt that the moderates of the *Fraktion* were not necessarily representa-tive of the majority of the party since they were elected by their Reichstag constituencies and were not the elected leaders of the party. The radicals doggedly fought against efforts to muzzle the rhetoric of the *Sozialdemokrat*. Kautsky had participated in this dispute while in Zurich, and after the establishment of the *Neue Zeit* he found himself even more embroiled in what was a long and at times extremely acrimonious fight.

Kautsky's intentions concerning the *Neue Zeit* were clear from the beginning—it was to be a journal of scientific socialism, of Marxism. In 1883, Liebknecht was closely identified with the old ones in London. Kautsky recalled much later that at that time in the party many held that "Marx [was] Allah and Liebknecht his prophet." Liebknecht's participation in the *Neue Zeit* announced its Marxist orientation in a way that Kautsky's name as yet could not. When Bernstein hinted that Engels might contribute an article on Darwin to the first number, Kautsky was ecstatic: "I could think of no better introductory article for a popular monthly than one on Darwin. The name alone is already a program." Though in the end Engels did not do this article, Kautsky devoted much of the space in the first year of the *Neue Zeit* to discussion of evolutionary theory and the development of social instincts in humans. Marx and Darwin were to be the twin pillars on which the *Neue Zeit* rested, and Kautsky obviously saw the two as a natural pair. He outlined his hopes for the new journal as follows: "We want to handle all science as well as art and anything of public interest. Only daily politics should be excluded. . . . We want to popularize knowledge, to enlighten the workers." While this plan may sound insipid enough in a political sense, he felt that his new journal would strengthen the hand of the radicals in their dispute with the moderates. In fact, despite his disinclination to participate actively in the politics of the socialist movement, he constantly felt compelled to engage in the polemics of the political disputes because he felt that his theoretical critique would help combat the moderate faction during the 1880s.[16]

Because he was an intellectual, Kautsky interpreted the moderate-radical split in theoretical terms. He argued that the moderates were representatives of petit bourgeois socialism—their doctrines were "Dühring–Louis Blancist philistinism." Within the *Fraktion* the Marxists were effectively represented only by Bebel; Geiser was the leader of the petit bourgeois tendency (and thus Kautsky's distress at having Geiser present at the *Neue Zeit* organizational meeting); Wilhelm Blos was a personal opponent of Marx; Vollmar, though a radical, was unclear theoretically; and the rest of the *Fraktion* was composed of good men, but not Marxists. Kautsky urged Engels to attack these petit bourgeois socialists, fearing that their activities, if not countered, would make a split inevitable. What particularly incensed him about conditions in the German movement was that party leadership devolved upon the *Fraktion* which was dominated by the so-called educated. The moderate Reichstag deputies of the party,

Geiser, Blos, Frohme, and others, were not the ones the party members would elect to the central committee if they were free to vote. Kautsky insisted that these petit bourgeois, educated moderates had no influence among the party rank-and-file and no mass support among the workers. Nonetheless, they had to be combated because they could mislead the workers and eventually provoke a split. In outlining to Engels his objections to the petit bourgeois socialists in the party, Kautsky tied political and theoretical positions together: "It is peculiar that almost all the educated of the party belong to this tendency, even if they are not in contact with one another; *unconsciously* they arrive at the same ideas. They are all enthusiastic about colonies, the national idea, further revival of German antiquity, complete trust of cooperation with the government, replacement of the class struggle through the power of 'justice,' denial of materialism and the materialist conception of history—Marxist dogma, as they call it—and raving insults to Manchesterism, which is already long dead."[17]

For the first year the *Neue Zeit* avoided entering directly into party disputes, concentrating instead on scientific and historical topics. But during this year, several changes took place in Kautsky's living conditions that eventually brought him directly into the conflict. First, shortly after the initial number of the *Neue Zeit* appeared, Dietz began to pressure Kautsky to move from Vienna to Stuttgart, where Dietz's publishing facilities were located, in order to ease the task of editing the new journal. Though Kautsky had not expected to leave Vienna at that time, he did move to Stuttgart in April 1883, shortly after his marriage to Louise Strasser. But Stuttgart was provincial and isolated, and Kautsky was very unhappy with its lack of research resources and its distance from the centers of socialist activity. He reported to Engels that a brief visit to Bernstein in Zurich was like going to an oasis in the midst of a desert, and that Bebel's brief stays in Stuttgart were likewise invigorating. "I went to Germany to get to know the German movement," he complained, "but in Swabia, at least, I only find many philistines." Second, Kautsky quickly discovered that the income from editing the *Neue Zeit* was not sufficient to live on, especially for two people. The original agreement with Dietz provided Kautsky with 250 marks per month (equal to the 3,000 marks Höchberg had provided in 1880–1881), but in order to ease the financial squeeze of the first year, Kautsky would only accept 150 marks. From this he had to pay editorial costs such as postage, subscriptions, and office supplies, which amounted to about 30 marks per month, leaving Karl and Louise only 30 marks per week to live on. In order to supplement his income, Kautsky went to Zurich to try to get a position as a regular contributor to the *Zurich Post*. But on his return, the Stuttgart police suggested that, as a foreigner, he must expect to be deported if he continued to make suspicious trips to Zurich and Vienna. He then decided to leave Stuttgart, and, though he would have preferred to go to London permanently, he settled for a brief visit there before moving once again to Zurich in January 1884.[18]

The move satisfied Kautsky's desire to be closer to the center of socialist activity, but it also endangered his control over the *Neue Zeit* and plunged him deep into the moderate-radical dispute. When he left Stuttgart, Dietz needed someone on the spot to tend to the mundane, day-to-day tasks of editing. Unfortunately, he chose Blos and Geiser. The choice could not have been worse had it been calculated to offend, and eventually Kautsky very reluctantly concluded that perhaps Blos and Geiser had been chosen to give offense. The problem began in May 1884 and centered on Blos's political review column for that month. Kautsky was infuriated, not only by the content of the piece, which included praise for the Austrian government's position on the "normal work day" without pointing out the autocratic character of that government, but even more by the assault on the major premise of the *Neue Zeit* that such an article represented. Kautsky contended that from the very beginning the "anti-Marxist gentlemen in Germany" had been after the *Neue Zeit* "because it is in fact the only socialist newspaper in Germany that stands on Marxian grounds." He felt that the moderates had worked through, and even with, Dietz to take over the journal: "Now the results of this intrigue are becoming evident. The imposition of the political review by Blos was merely the first stage. Now Dietz goes further and demands that Blos should become a *responsible editor* of the *Neue Zeit*." To Dietz, Kautsky wrote that he would gladly work with or under Liebknecht, but never with Blos. He demanded an end to Blos's influence on the *Neue Zeit* and threatened to withdraw from the journal rather than see it made into "an organ of Geiser's clique. . . . It is better that the *NZ* should go under honorably than fall into the hands of the Geiserists."[19]

The resolution of this conflict is very interesting because it marks the emergence of the alliance between the theory of Kautsky and the politics of Bebel. When he first protested to Dietz, Kautsky was not especially hopeful that the matter would be resolved in his favor. Since he and Dietz obviously disagreed, the decision would rest with Liebknecht as the third member of the editorial board. Kautsky feared that if Dietz brought Geiser to the conference on Blos's role on the *Neue Zeit*, Geiser would influence Liebknecht to side with Blos and Dietz. During the first week of June, Bebel also entered into the dispute by protesting to Dietz about the inclusion of the work of Geiser and Blos in the *Neue Zeit*. Backed by Bebel, and as a result of Bebel's intervention, by Liebknecht also, in late June Kautsky was able to announce an almost complete victory to Engels. Dietz agreed to drop the political review and claimed that Blos would no longer have any influence on the journal. Liebknecht was also supporting Kautsky's continued demand for a retraction of the position espoused by Blos.[20]

Bebel had decided that Kautsky's theoretical opposition to the moderates would help in the political struggle against them. One part of Kautsky's assault was an article that sharply attacked Rodbertus, a German economist and favorite of the moderates. While Rodbertus was a harsh critic of capitalism, he was also intensely loyal to the Bismarckian Reich. Bebel recognized the importance of attacking the moderates on this ground, and he suggested to Dietz that Kautsky's article be reprinted as a separate pamphlet. Bebel also felt that he was being unfairly attacked in the *Neue Welt*, which was edited by Geiser and published by Dietz. To Kautsky, Bebel explained that he had told Dietz "that the two tendencies of the party are quite precisely expressed in the *Neue Welt* and in the *Neue Zeit*, and just for that reason the *Neue Zeit* cannot be dropped." Bebel clearly identified himself with the tendency associated with the *Neue Zeit*.[21]

Following Bebel's lead, Kautsky also saw two tendencies in the party, those for the *Neue Zeit* and those against it. Of the latter he said: "Marxism, the conception of our party as the organization of the proletariat fighting the class struggle, is in these circles everywhere hated or at least not understood." He also realized that the preservation of his own position with the *Neue Zeit*, as well as Bernstein's job with the *Sozialdemokrat*, depended on Bebel's support. Kautsky and Bebel were to operate in tandem—the one in theory, the other in politics and party affairs—for many years in the future.[22]

Bebel's support won the battle but not the war, at least not yet. Only three days after announcing victory to Engels, Kautsky reported that Dietz was beginning to make noises about impending bankruptcy and the impossibility of supporting the chronic deficit of the *Neue Zeit*. Bernstein agreed with Kautsky that this was a political decision on Dietz's part, because the *Neue Welt*, which had an even greater deficit than the *Neue Zeit*, was not going to be dropped. Bernstein also suggested that in this matter Dietz was being influenced by Geiser, who was supported by Liebknecht. Engels' response to the announcement of the possible end of the *Neue Zeit* must have come as quite a shock to Kautsky and the rest of the radicals: "That the *Neue Zeit* should end is no catastrophe for the party." Engels argued that under the antisocialist law there was little the journal could do about the intraparty conflict, because under the law the moderates "can speak out entirely unhindered, [while] we are restrained by what gives them cover."[23]

The original plan of the *Neue Zeit* had been to deal theoretically and historically with everything but daily politics so as to avoid prosecution under the antisocialist law while advancing the cause of scientific socialism. But even on this level the Marxists sometimes found it difficult to toe the line. In April 1884, Engels and Kautsky had agreed that a proper critique of Lewis Morgan's *Ancient Society* (1877) could not appear in the *Neue Zeit* because Morgan's concluding chapter on private property as the source of class conflicts could not be discussed in a manner compatible with the law. As the *Neue Zeit* became more involved in party disputes, Kautsky too began to feel restrained, particularly when he wanted to write on things like the colonial question and the "right to work" concept. But he was not willing to give up his journal because he felt it was the "only newspaper in Germany which stands fully and completely on Marxist ground." Bebel agreed and convinced Dietz to continue publication. He also got Dietz to stop talking about a further reduction in Kautsky's pay for editing the *Neue Zeit* and to assume postal costs for the journal.[24]

By June 1884, Kautsky had decided to leave Zurich for London in order to pursue his historical studies, to renew personal contacts with Engels, and to supplement his still too meager income by contributing to English journals and serving as English correspondent for continental socialist papers. The Blos-Geiser controversy delayed announcement of this decision, but reinforced his desire to leave. By October, even before the fate of the *Neue Zeit* had been decided for certain, he announced to Bebel his determination to go to London. Bebel and Dietz gave their approval, though the latter doubted that Kautsky would be any happier in London than he was in Zurich. Liebknecht was not so eager to agree, arguing that Kautsky would be lost for Germany if he moved to London. Kautsky argued back: "But what does it mean to lose touch with Germany? To be moved away from the party troubles and petty fights in order to win a viewpoint from which one can perceive the development of Germany not from the condition of one or another electoral district, but in relationship to the total development of modern humanity. And to capture this viewpoint is in my opinion the task of the *Neue Zeit*."[25]

The withdrawal to London ended for almost five years Kautsky's personal involvement with the infighting of the German party, reflecting his feeling that "I am more skillful with my pen than with my mouth." Kautsky saw his task as one of propaganda, of advancing the cause of scientific socialism. He dedicated the *Neue Zeit* to bringing "people to consciousness of what Marxism is and what it is not." He rebutted the attacks of the moderates by declaring that such a position was "not narrow-minded dogmatism, . . . but clarity and consciousness of direction as opposed to the uncritical opportunist eclecticism which today is the fashion in the party." Kautsky felt that he was best equipped to be a propagandist from a distance, not a political activist and an organizer. But he did not see that by drawing away from the political arena he lost touch, not just with Germany, but with the pressures and problems that confronted the day-to-day movement. In his desire to serve theory better, he lost touch with practice. After a brief visit to Vienna and a stop in Berlin, Karl and Louise arrived in London in late January 1885.[26]

London

The London years yielded much of the work that established Kautsky as a leading Marxist theoretician. In close contact with Engels and the magnificent resources of the British Museum, and freed from the time-consuming squabbles of the German movement, he concentrated on history and economics. Thanks to the generosity of a wealthy supporter and to his own capacity for work, he was able to live fairly comfortably in London, even though expenses were greater there than in Stuttgart or Vienna. The wealthy backer this time was Heinrich Spiegler, brother-in-law of Karl's Viennese friend Heinrich Braun. From shortly after his arrival in London until his final return to Germany in 1890, Kautsky received the equivalent of about 100 marks (£5 sterling) per month from Spiegler. This income, plus the 150 marks from the *Neue Zeit* and the honoraria collected from contributions to other journals, allowed the Kautskys to enjoy England. The honoraria were sometimes quite handsome, as in March 1887, when he received 55 marks for an article which appeared in Adler's *Die Gleichheit* in Vienna. Though on at least one occasion he was forced to ask Engels for a loan when the regular monthly payments were disrupted, by 1885 the problem of a regular and sufficient income had largely been solved. In addition to his literary work, Kautsky also served as agent for his father's efforts to sell original stage designs to English theater architects. Apparently he was not especially attentive in this work. The Kautsky archives in Amsterdam contain seventeen letters to Karl, covering just under a year, from one Walter Emden, architect, and Emden's secretary, which are requests, rerequests, and demands for responses to letters, for translations of stage designs, and other matters of business.[27]

Although much more detached from party problems than before, Kautsky did not entirely escape intraparty disputes by moving to London. One particular problem, which plagued him for a long time, concerned his co-workers on the *Neue Zeit*. Having successfully turned back one effort by the moderates to establish Blos on the regular staff and a suggestion by Dietz that still another moderate Reichstag representative, Louis Viereck, work on the journal, Kautsky tried to find someone he trusted theoretically to take on some of the work. He was perfectly willing to give space to non-Marxian writers, but objected to having any but the doctrinally safe do editorial jobs. Ironically, the first person Kautsky suggested as acceptable to him was Georg von Vollmar. Although at the time Vollmar was still considered a radical, he was beginning to move away from the rest of the radicals and soon became one of the most outspoken proponents of peasant-based reformism in the SPD. Vollmar and Kautsky eventually engaged in long polemics over the questions of state socialism and appealing to the peasantry. Fortunately for the journal's radical, Marxist reputation, Kautsky's suggestion that Vollmar contribute regularly as German correspondent was vetoed by Dietz. Bebel, too, had been lukewarm on Vollmar's appointment.[28]

The problem of an acceptable co-worker became even more acute during the spring of 1885, when the moderates of the *Fraktion* supported the government's bill authorizing subsidies for German steamships operating in African and Asian waters. The radicals, led by Bebel in Germany and Bernstein and the *Sozialdemokrat* among the exiled intellectuals, vigorously condemned this explicit support for the hated capitalist system and Bismarck's government. When the *Fraktion* moderates demanded control over what Bernstein printed in the *Sozialdemokrat*, a split within the party seemed certain for a time. In this conflict, Kautsky followed Engels' lead in arguing that the issue was not sufficient cause for the radicals to force a break, that Liebknecht, not Bernstein should answer the moderates' attacks on the *Sozialdemokrat*, and that above all Bernstein should not give up the paper. His reasoning on this last point reflected his convictions about the nature of the German party and its press and their relationship to the political representatives elected as Social Democrats. Kautsky wrote to Bernstein: "Just because you do not have the trust of the *Fraktion*, you must remain. You are not the *Vertrauensmann* of the *Fraktion*, but the *Vertrauensmann* of the party." Engels also advised Bebel to hold onto the *Sozialdemokrat* and the *Neue Zeit*, the only journals that the radicals (or "we," as Engels wrote) held.[29]

Engels and Bebel were both very willing to recognize Kautsky as an ally in political matters by the mid-1880s, but both still harbored reservations about the younger man. Engels was sometimes not certain that, "as an Austrian," Kautsky was capable of fully understanding the subtle nuances of German politics. Bebel still felt in 1885 that Kautsky had a tendency to judge situations too quickly, without careful reflection. Significantly, when in late December of that year he felt the need for another attack against pro-Rodbertus, pro-Lassalle forces in the party, especially against Louis Viereck, Bebel's first choice to lead the attack was Bernstein. If not Bernstein, then he hoped that Kautsky would take on the task with Engels' assistance. In fact, neither Bernstein nor Kautsky wrote the article. Bernstein was too busy, and Kautsky felt too restrained by the antisocialist law. He thought that he could safely print such an article only if it was limited to a theoretical discussion, which, while "more innocuous," was also "more difficult, [and] for the masses more uninteresting." Despite the difficulties and reservations, Engels, Bebel, and Kautsky were fundamentally in agreement on social democratic politics in the 1880s. When Bebel was imprisoned in 1886 for having attended the illegal Copenhagen party congress of 1883, Kautsky feared that his absence left no one to protect "the gentlemen of the *Fraktion* from making fools of themselves." And Engels and Bebel both fully agreed with Kautsky's view of Blos and the other moderates. In the spring of 1890, Engels and Kautsky jointly protested to Bebel about unauthorized changes Blos had made in a *Neue Zeit* article by Engels on Russian foreign policy. In his reply to Engels, Bebel called Blos "*ein Schwachmatiker und ein Waschlappen*" ("an ignoramus and a sissy"), thus fully endorsing Kautsky's own aversion to Blos.[30]

On 14 June 1888, to the surprise, and eventually shock, of almost all their acquaintances, Karl and Louise Kautsky, accompanied by Karl's brother Hans, left London. Though ostensibly on their way to St. Gilgen, Switzerland, for a summer vacation, in fact Karl and Louise went to Vienna to get a divorce. When news of the real purpose of the trip reached London, Germany, and Zurich, condemnation of Kautsky was almost universal. Adler, Bebel, the Liebknechts, Tussy (Eleanor) Marx, and others, all but Bernstein, who had been closest to the Kautskys, were very severe in their judgment. Of all of Kautsky's friends, Engels was by far the most strongly affected; he had developed a sincere affection for Louise and felt that Karl was treating her very shabbily. In his first letter to Kautsky following news of the impending divorce, Engels was bewildered and very surprised. He cautioned Kautsky to consider how much harder on the woman than the man divorce was. To Bebel, Engels wrote: "The history of the Kautskys has astonished us all. Louise has conducted herself with unusual heroism in the entire thing. K was in a drunken frenzy, . . . I have written to [him] that it was the stupidest trick of his life."[31]

The divorce created hard feelings and a measure of personal bitterness on both sides. Not surprisingly, Kautsky staunchly defended his own innocence in the matter, but generally he was not eager to discuss the details with most of his correspondents. To Bebel, Kautsky wrote that he regretted that he had not controlled himself better upon first meeting Louise, because he finally realized that he had never loved her. Though unhappy about the divorce, Kautsky claimed that he did not feel guilty. He also contended that the split was not so sudden, that he was not so fickle or irresponsible as Bebel might think. "What has taken place so astonishingly quickly," Karl wrote, "has developed for more than a year, and others, such as Ede [Bernstein], are in no way so unexpectedly affected as you." Much later Kautsky felt that most of his friends, except Engels, eventually recognized that Louise was not as blameless as many had assumed in 1888–1889; Tussy Marx especially learned to hate Louise passionately. In a footnote to a letter from Engels that predicted Karl would one day regret the split with Louise, Kautsky commented, "This day never occurred."[32]

Divorce was a long process in Vienna, and Kautsky was not able to return to London until October 1889. During that time Engels tried diligently to bring about a reconciliation between Karl and Louise. He also continued to correspond with Kautsky on theoretical and party matters, but frequently had a difficult time keeping his personal disappointment with Kautsky from influencing their intellectual relationship. For his part, Kautsky was at times less than frank with Engels about the possibility of a reconciliation. In late January 1889, Engels proposed that Kautsky prepare, "with the help of your wife," the fourth volume of Marx's *Capital* for publication. He offered payment of £50 per year, asserting that Kautsky could prepare the 750 pages in about two years by "dictating to your wife." Though Kautsky was pleased with the offer, he hedged on accepting and suggested that perhaps both he and Bernstein should work on the project. He explained that his return to London would have to be delayed as he was not well, that he wished to remain in touch with Austrian party activities for a few months, and in addition, Louise was taking a midwifery course that would not be completed for a time. Kautsky did not mention that the divorce proceedings required his presence in Vienna; in fact he implied that he may have changed his mind about the divorce and that he and Louise would return to London together. Eventually Engels reluctantly accepted the divorce, and in 1890 he offered Louise a position in his home as housekeeper-secretary, a move Karl approved and encouraged.[33]

Engels and Kautsky never reestablished the close relationship that had prevailed before the divorce. Although the two men met often between 1890 and Engels' death and remained in frequent correspondence, sharing news and gossip as of old, Engels' affection for Louise and his distress with Karl's actions prevented a return to the previous warm friendship. In 1892, they had a very long and at times bitter feud when Kautsky asked Engels to get Louise to sign her literary productions Strasser-Kautsky, or in some other manner than just Louise Kautsky. Although he was probably influenced by his mother, Kautsky's request was simple enough and probably quite innocent of any ulterior intent, but sensitivity and mistrust on the part of the aging Engels converted the simple request into a cause. His first response was to side openly with Louise, calling her "my own child," and implying that the divorce had been Kautsky's doing, so Kautsky would just have to live with the consequences. Kautsky defended his original request and denied that he had intended Louise any ill will, but Engels would not hear of it. In a very nasty letter, Engels mocked the pretensions that made Kautsky think every female who published under the name Kautsky must be his wife or mother and concluded, "By your unreasonable demand you hurt Louise deeply, I fear more deeply than you can again put right." Kautsky continued to profess his innocence of offense to Louise, but also persisted in his request for the name change. In the end Louise did not change her name until 1894, when she married Ludwig Freyberger, a Viennese doctor. But Kautsky's relationship with Engels had been further undermined by this episode.[34]

Following Engels' death in 1895, Kautsky was very much surprised to find that he had not been named an executor of Engels' literary remains. Engels had complained bitterly in his last letter to Kautsky about not being included in Kautsky and Bernstein's *History of Socialism* project, but the protest had a false ring and probably had little to do with Kautsky's exclusion as an executor. The project was begun in 1886, and though neither Kautsky nor Bernstein had ever directly asked Engels to participate—according to Kautsky because they assumed he was too busy with the third volume of *Capital*—that Engels could have failed to even hear about the *History* for over eight years was impossible. Almost certainly in the last years of his life Engels turned against Kautsky because of bitterness over Karl's supposed mistreatment of Louise. Quite likely Louise also played a more direct role in the disposition of Engels' will. Adler and Bebel combined forces to try to get Louise to influence Engels to leave Marx's literary remains, which were in Engels' possession, to the German party rather than to Marx's children. This rather devious plan was only partially successful, but Louise could well have urged Engels to prevent Kautsky from having access to things as well. Engels would have been receptive to such suggestions, and the results strongly suggest this possibility.[35]

Kautsky returned to London after his divorce, but stayed only a brief time. Late in 1889, he learned from Dietz of the latter's intention to convert the *Neue Zeit* from a monthly into a weekly with the lapsing of the antisocialist law. Dietz insisted that the increased work load demanded Kautsky's constant presence in Stuttgart, and rather than taking a chance on losing "the most capable, intelligent, and decent" of publishers, Kautsky agreed to return to Stuttgart. In part he was encouraged by Dietz's offer to raise the salary for editing the journal to 3,000 marks per year. In March 1890, he left London for Vienna. While there, he married for the second and last time. His new bride was Luise Ronsperger, a young friend of his mother's whom Kautsky had met in 1888, and to whom he was closely attached by the summer of 1889. Kautsky declared his love and proposed marriage to Luise in December of that year: "I live by my pen and stand in the opposition. . . . I am no agitator, but a private scholar, and I am in the pleasant position of being able to say that the most difficult time, the beginning, lies behind me. Today I have a name, if not in Austria then in Germany, where my public lives; my works are not merely read, but, what is far more important from the standpoint of a household, bought also." On 9 April, after delaying to the last moment, Kautsky announced his impending marriage in a letter to Engels. He defended Luise by explaining that "after almost 10 years as a manager of a confectioner's shop, [she] has certainly gained experience with real life, but has not become a philistine." Kautsky was certain that he and Luise would be compatible since "she knows and shares my views, and a comprehensive general education makes it possible for her to acquire an understanding of my work." A few days later, the two were married, and in late August they moved to Germany, where they remained until 1924.[36]

Literary Works of the 1880s

When Kautsky arrived in Zurich in January 1880, he was still primarily a romantic, natural-scientific socialist. By the time he moved to London, almost exactly five years later, he was a convinced Marxist of the Engelian vein, and by his return to Germany in 1890, he was probably the leading theoretician of the SPD. The process of conversion was long and marked by theoretical and analytical inconsistencies at many points. Kautsky's brand of Marxism always bore traces of his earlier natural-scientific bent, though to a great extent by 1885 overt appeals to biological or naturalistic explanations were replaced by an emphasis on historical, social, and economic determinants. The persistent natural-scientific qualities of Kautsky's Marxism were not just the product of his earlier inclinations, but resulted from an interaction of these inclinations with the views expressed in Engels' *Anti-Dühring*. A *Weltanschauung* derived from the works of Haeckel, Büchner, Buckle, and Darwin made Kautsky particularly receptive to Engels' expansion of Marx's more specific historical and economic analysis of capitalist society into a comprehensive world view.[37]

Like so much of the work of Marxists, *Anti-Dühring* began as a critique of a non-Marxist. In the preface to the second edition, Engels contended that he would not have undertaken such an enormous task, that is, presenting a comprehensive world view, had not Eugen Dühring pretended (in his *Course of Philosophy* and other works) to be able to explain the origins of chemistry, nature, society, and the universe in one fell swoop. Engels also contended that pure criticism was not enough; a counterexplanation, a positive presentation, had to be given. In this way, what began as an attack on a fuzzy-thinking, socialist pretender became an elaborate presentation of Marxism or, to use Engels' own words, "a conception of nature which is dialectical and at the same time materialist." Though he denied that in presenting this comprehensive world view he was outlining a fixed system, the net effect of *Anti-Dühring* was to provide Kautsky and others caught up in the Darwinian, positivist tenor of the times with an all-embracing, "scientific" theory that favored the deterministic over the voluntaristic implications of Marx's writing.[38]

Carried to an extreme, the deterministic implications of Engels' dialectical materialism could result in quietism. If the entire universe and all of human knowledge and experience could be explained by a comprehensive system based on Marxian principles, then the "scientific" prediction of the inevitable collapse of the capitalist system due to internal contradictions and the equally inevitable rise of the classless, postrevolutionary society reduced human activity to triviality. Of course, Marx's own writings were characterized by both a confident assertion of the inevitable collapse of bourgeois society and a powerful and pressing call for action, and therefore were ambiguous at best. The danger of Engels' extrapolation was that its very comprehensiveness would swing the balance to determinism. However, Engels himself certainly did not carry his own analysis to this extreme. He continued to insist upon the need to develop working-class consciousness of the historical role of the proletariat through organization and political activity. As will be shown below, Kautsky, too, did not succumb to quietism, though his own lack of personal involvement in party and political activities and his strong humanitarian sympathies led him to put a good deal of weight on the deterministic aspects of Marxism. The extent to which he was influenced by his own natural-scientific inclinations and the importance of this for his interpretation of the nature and tactics of the SPD form the central issues in the debate over Kautsky's historical significance.[39]

Much of Kautsky's writing during the early eighties was aimed at integrating Marxism-according-to-Engels and Darwinism-according-to-Kautsky. In various articles in the *Sozialdemokrat* he discussed Darwin's work as a liberating force in the struggle against the "medieval-monarchist" world view, emphasized the natural origin of the human social instinct, and identified the origins of social and political organization with the social impulse of humans, rejecting the contract theory in the process. During the first three years of the *Neue Zeit*, he devoted a great deal of space to discussion of social instincts in animals and humans and attacked the Herbert Spencer school of Darwinian sociologists and its anarchist fellow travelers (as Kautsky saw them) for their insistence that the primitive human condition was individualistic and anarchistic. He argued that the earliest organization of humans, primitive communism, was based on equality and discipline backed by a powerful sense of collective solidarity. This line of argument reached a climax in a three-part article entitled "The Indian Question," which appeared in the *Neue Zeit* in 1885. Here Kautsky investigated the impact of the arrival of white Europeans on the native population of North America. After describing in rather idyllic terms the equality, security, and sometimes harsh discipline of the Indians' primitive-communistic society, he concluded that it was the rapacious greed of the individualistic whites that led them to devastate the land and murder the Indians. To the extent that it concentrated on these themes, Kautsky's work during the early eighties was a continuation of that of the middle and late seventies.[40]

But at the same time he was laboring to establish the natural-scientific validity of socialism, Kautsky was also using Marxian concepts and vocabulary more and more often. For instance, in "The Indian Question," Kautsky explained the defeat of the North American natives by white Europeans in terms of technological superiority: "Not the better, stronger, more intelligent people wins, but the higher means of production." His political analysis was also increasingly couched in terms of class conflict and the class nature of the state; this tendency was particularly striking in a number of articles which appeared in the *Sozialdemokrat* in 1881. Unfortunately his efforts to integrate Darwin and Marx sometimes resulted in a curious muddle of apparent contradiction.[41]

In the first year of the *Neue Zeit*, Kautsky specifically linked the work of Marx and Darwin. In an article entitled "A Materialist Historian," he argued that some years before Darwin's theory emerged, Marx had placed history on a firmer basis by establishing "the development of the struggle for existence as the driving impulse [of history]." This was not, of course, the individualistic struggle which the Manchester school tried to pass off as natural law, but rather "the struggle of man as a social animal in the social community, in a word: the class struggle." Kautsky then went on to argue, with special reference to Buckle, that Marx had also dealt a death blow to the so-called materialist historians of the Enlightenment tradition. Marx had shown that ideas were not the motive force of history because ideas were only the result of conflicting class interests. Though "the momentarily prevailing intellectual tendencies" are as automatically the result of the class struggle as animal instincts are the result of the struggle for survival, human intellectual ideals change because class interests change with economic conditions. The Enlightenment materialist historians had sought for material causes in nature. When confronted with the historical phenomenon of change, these writers were forced to explain it in terms of ideals, since nature is relatively permanent in comparison with historical development. Kautsky concluded that only when Marx tied his materialist explanation to something that changed, to the means of production, was history given a useful and accurate materialist basis.[42]

Thus while trying to argue that social instincts are natural in humans, and that Marx's notion of class struggle was comparable to Darwin's notion of the struggle of species, Kautsky was also trying to make class struggle the result of the historically specific means of production—he wanted to have his cake and eat it too. If the social instincts of humans are "natural," and rapacious individualism only a perversion brought on by bourgeois capitalism, then these instincts cannot be historically specific also. In fact, Kautsky pointedly rejected the idea that relatively unchanging nature could explain the dynamics of history, while only slightly loosening his grip on Darwin. He could have overcome the contradiction of his analysis simply by arguing, as he was later to do, that the social solidarity of the proletariat and the individualism of the bourgeoisie were both products of different aspects of capitalist production. This would have required that he abandon the natural-scientific basis of socialism he had worked so hard to establish. Instead, in 1883, he juxtaposed the contradictory views without reconciling them.

Beginning in late 1883, an ever increasing amount of Kautsky's time was devoted to Marx and an ever decreasing amount to natural-scientific topics. His writings on Marx had two aspects: simply to present Marx's work in shortened and popularized form, and to counter the arguments of Marx's critics and of those authors whom Engels and Kautsky perceived as competitors of Marx in socialist theory. The first aspect is best represented by two works: the German edition of Marx's *Poverty of Philosophy* (Marx wrote it originally in French), translated by Kautsky and Bernstein and published in 1885; and Kautsky's *Economic Doctrines of Karl Marx*, which first appeared in 1887. The latter was one of the most important works in establishing Kautsky's reputation as a leading Marxian theorist. Within four years of its initial publication, it had been translated into Russian, Serbo-Croatian, Swedish, Polish, and Czech, and since has been translated into at least eighteen languages, many several times. *Economic Doctrines* originated as a response to Gabriel Deville's abridged and popularized edition of *Capital* which was first published in France in 1883. At first Kautsky and Bernstein set out to prepare a German translation of Deville's book. But they soon abandoned this project, in order to concentrate more fully on *Poverty of Philosophy,* and because Kautsky, encouraged by Engels, had decided to write his own exposition of Marx's economic thought. Kautsky wrote *Economic Doctrines* in London with regular and important assistance from Engels. No work more clearly demonstrates the close cooperation of Kautsky and Engels than this one.[43]

In *The Economic Doctrines of Karl Marx,* Kautsky attempted to summarize the most significant economic features of Marx's "Contribution to the Critique of Political Economy," "Wage Labor and Capital," *Capital,* and *Poverty of Philosophy. Economic Doctrines* did not present new statistical evidence nor did it discuss economic literature. While keeping formulae to a minimum, Kautsky carefully and straightforwardly defined critical terms like *commodity, profit, surplus value, socially necessary labor,* and *constant* and *variable capital. Economic Doctrines* began with a very brief historical review of the development of capitalism and then described the process of capitalist production and the effects of capitalism on labor. Kautsky strongly emphasized the historical specificity of capitalism as an instrument of historical development. This work was a lucid and fairly comprehensive summary, though not an imaginative extension, of Marx's economic analysis. The large number of translations and editions of *Economic Doctrines* attests to its widespread influence.[44]

The second aspect of Kautsky's work on Marx during the middle and late eighties was the criticism of non-Marxist writers, which was almost always coupled with at least some positive presentation of Marx. Encouraged by Engels, he took up the attack in Marx's name, battling all pretenders to the title of scientific socialist. One curious side to the criticism was that while both Kautsky and Engels privately insisted that the men they were attacking did not constitute serious threats to the unity and strength of the working-class party, both men nonetheless expended a great deal of energy in their attacks. In part such attacks served as cover for political criticism of the Bismarckian state; in part they were the product of the insecurity of German Marxists, who realized that theoretically the party was still extremely eclectic; in part they were simply excuses to promote the cause of Marxism. Kautsky tended to use two tactics in these criticisms; the most common was to accuse opponents of misunderstanding Marx. Often this criticism was justified, as when Albert Schäffle, a university professor and Austrian government minister, took Marx's value theory to be the basis for an assault on capitalist society, rather than a descriptive analysis of the nature of capitalism. The other tactic was to identify opponents as idealists who ignored or did not understand the true nature of modern society. Finally, Kautsky usually implied that those who disagreed with Marx were at best opportunists and at worst lackeys of the ruling class.[45]

Kautsky did not merely conduct one-sided criticisms; the *Neue Zeit* was the site of give-and-take between proponents of various theories. The first major theoretical dispute, in 1884–1885, began with an assault by Kautsky on the ideas of Karl Johann Rodbertus-Jagetzow (1805–1875). As with much of his writing from this period, Kautsky was guided in detail by Engels. The draft articles were sent to London and returned with manuscript comments and letters of criticism. The purpose of these articles, and the reason Engels took such an active interest in them, was to counter the seductive appeal of the Rodbertus brand of socialism that postulated a major role for the German state as protector of the true interests of the workers. Beginning with Ferdinand Lassalle, those who claimed to speak for the toilers of the nation had frequently included strong nationalistic appeals and calls for state aid. Although both Engels and Kautsky claimed in public and private that Rodbertus and his followers posed little immediate threat within the German party, the vigor with which the attack was undertaken revealed the bravado of these claims. At the same time, this series of articles was as much a presentation of Marxian theory as it was an attack on Rodbertus and as such forms an integral part of Kautsky's program of propagating Marxism among German socialists. Because of the restraints imposed by the antisocialist law, Kautsky felt compelled to limit his specific political attacks on Rodbertus's theories. He was, however, able to discuss politics, albeit indirectly and not in terms of immediate issues. This debate reveals the extent to which Kautsky was concerned with political matters as well as with more abstract theoretical discussion.[46]

Carl August Schramm, an academic follower of Rodbertus, was Kautsky's antagonist. The discussion began with a two-part article by Kautsky that ostensibly reviewed Rodbertus's posthumously published work, *Capital: Four Social Letters to v. Kirchmann* (1884). Schramm responded with a critique, to which Kautsky replied, which in turn prompted an answer from Schramm, and finally the series ended with Kautsky's article, "Final Word."[47] Victory for Kautsky was a foregone conclusion, since the journal was his and he had the power to cut off debate whenever he chose. On the other hand, he was in no way required to give Schramm space for response; he did so in order to fulfill the original intention of allowing appropriate response to polemical articles in the *Neue Zeit* itself, that is, of providing a forum of rational theoretical discussion. Kautsky was undoubtedly further encouraged to publish Schramm's articles once the paucity of their content became evident.

Though both men engaged in nit-picking and *ad hominem* arguments, only Kautsky also offered substantive criticism. His first contention was that Marx was a materialist and Rodbertus a philosophical idealist who tried to explain social reality by "eternal" concepts. Methodologically, Kautsky contended, Rodbertus converted the abstraction necessary for good scientific analysis into construction of artificial concepts, like "national income" and "national capital," rather than concepts that were firmly rooted in the real world. This idealist fabrication led Rodbertus to conclude that organization of the working class and limitations on the work day would not alleviate the disadvantages of the workers; state action was needed to limit the exploitation of the proletariat by capitalism while preserving private property. Kautsky felt this revealed a silly disregard for the necessities of capitalist production. His major political objection was that

Rodbertus stood "on monarchist and nationalist grounds," that is, he accepted the authoritarian, Junker-dominated state of Germany and sought only to reform it. With what for him was the clinching argument, Kautsky concluded that Rodbertus, far from being the founder of scientific socialism as his followers claimed, was a "conservative utopian" interested only in winning the support of the workers for the large landowners' struggle with the modern industrial bourgeoisie.

Opening his first response with "people who live in glass houses should not throw stones," Schramm refused to defend Rodbertus against Kautsky's specific criticisms, but rather argued that Marx and Rodbertus were not all that different. He contended that both Marx and Rodbertus sought socialism and based their critiques of contemporary society on abstractions like the primitive, isolated producer. Both men were brilliant political economists and social critics, so why not accept both, just as one appreciates two good poets of different styles. Schramm held that Kautsky was warped by dogmatic Marxism and implied that he had purposely misinterpreted Rodbertus to exaggerate his case. The only argument Schramm put forth that was even marginally substantive was his rejection of the Marxian conception of the mode of production as the fundamental determinant of the social and political superstructure of society. He argued that other, broader, though undefined, material and ideal determinants were also important. In the end Schramm's defense consisted of a series of unsubstantiated assertions; he did not attempt the sort of economic analysis Kautsky offered. Kautsky countered his opponent's contention that both Marx and Rodbertus could be honored by reminding Schramm that in poetry beauty, not scientific truth, was at stake. If two scientists defend opposing interpretations of the same phenomenon, both cannot be right.

Kautsky's presentation included a review of Marx's discussion of modern society and history. When Schramm equated Marx with Rodbertus, Kautsky strongly emphasized the historical quality of Marx's definitions and critique. He flatly and convincingly rejected Schramm's contention that Marx started his economic analysis from consideration of the abstract, isolated individual. According to Kautsky, Marx recognized as no analyst before him that there were no "eternal" considerations, that the human world was a dynamic one in which "eternal" qualities were totally lacking. This emphasis on historicity and relativity indicated that by this time Kautsky had come to view development in modern capitalist society in terms contrary to rigid "natural necessity." The picture he drew here was not analogous to the Darwinian conception of biological development. Rather Kautsky emphasized the historical specificity of the Marxian analysis and also its methodological utility. Early in 1885, in a review of an anonymous book entitled *The Aristocracy of Intellect as a Solution to the Social Question,* Kautsky very specifically rejected the notion that laws of the organic realm could be applied to the realm of human social activity:

> It is a scientific axiom that laws which are found for one area of human knowledge cannot without further ado be carried over to other areas. It seems that each is entirely independent, that laws which are characteristic of organic nature, for example those of heredity, natural selection, and so forth, may not be used in chemistry or astronomy. Strangely, it is today in some circles not only considered acceptable, but as true science if one applies the laws of organic nature to explanations of social conditions. Thus is society considered as an organism, like the family or a cell, thus are social phenomena, which only belong to a specific historical epoch, placed on a level with natural phenomena, as for example when the Manchester school is connected with natural selection.[48]

By 1885, Kautsky had clearly broken with the school, as represented by Büchner, Haeckel, and Spencer, which contended that human society was merely an extension of the animal world and similarly dominated by natural law. Though he still held that humans were "naturally" social, and that this inclination was reinforced in the proletariat under the specific social conditions that prevailed in a capitalist society, he felt that the laws governing human society were distinct from those operating in the organic, animal realm. That Kautsky perceived the workings of human society in terms of laws at all is a reflection of his commitment to a rationalistic, materialist world view, but he was not simply expanding Darwinian biological concepts to apply them to human activity, and he specifically denied that such an expansion was justifiable. He had moved away from his implicit position of the seventies and early eighties.

Earlier Kautsky had tended to view socioeconomic developments as something that disrupted natural human instincts. Thus the extreme competitiveness and individualism of the capitalist system destroyed the social instincts of humans and created among the bourgeoisie, the petite bourgeoisie, and the peasantry the struggle of all against all. This view is reminiscent of that of Rousseau and the late Enlightenment and many of the romanticists that "natural man" had somehow been perverted by the emergence of organized society and the state; it is also a view frequently held by anarchists. During his early years as a socialist writer, Kautsky had been influenced by both romantic and anarchist notions, and his conception of the relationship between human nature and society reflected these influences. By the mid-1880s, he had converted to a materialist view that did not see social organization as a perversion of nature, but simply explained human action in terms of social conditions, without any particular reference to the mythical primeval character of humans. Under the influence of Marxism, he assumed that immediate social conditions take precedence over any supposed natural attributes people may have, thus rendering superfluous his earlier contention of the naturalness of the social instinct. Certainly he continued to feel that somehow the proletariat was more natural, and therefore, given his natural-scientific prejudices, better than other classes because of its social instincts. But this line of argument virtually disappeared from his writings as he concentrated more and more on economic and political topics.[49]

Following the debate with Schramm, Kautsky began to pursue a much more consistent Marxian course. In an 1886 article, he discussed Chinese village communism in terms very similar to those employed in the earlier article on the North American Indians. But in this article he concluded by pointing out three characteristics of this social form: it prevented the emergence of a proletariat, it gave rise to an unbelievably strong conservatism, and it was "the firmest basis of oriental despotism." The lingering romantic idealism evidenced in "The Indian Question" was gone, and the Chinese village social organization of the late nineteenth century was dealt with as an historical construct. Finally, in an 1887 article, Kautsky argued that the failure of Cabetian communes in the United States did not prove that communism was hopeless. Rather, he continued, the petit bourgeois handicraftsmen who made up these communes had not been conditioned by their means of existence to accept the high degree of discipline and cooperation required to make such an experience succeed. He concluded that "the mode of production . . . influences all of humanity." From the mid-1880s to the years after the First World War and the Russian Revolution, he emphasized this sort of Marxian analysis at the expense of his earlier natural-scientific bent.[50]

Kautsky perceived himself as primarily a popularizer and defender of Marxism and not a creative or innovative thinker in economics and general theory. Any evaluation of him must be based on an awareness that when he began espousing Marxism, it was still novel and little known. Certainly Kautsky did not add significantly to Marxism, either as a socioeconomic theorist or as a revolutionary ideologist. But he did form an essential link between the theoretical works of Marx and Engels and twentieth-century revolutionary movements by popularizing and establishing the validity of Marx's analysis of bourgeois capitalism. In literally hundreds of books and articles from the 1880s on, Kautsky labored to explain what Marx had written and to show that the Marxian analysis was correct. Later, and often more imaginative, Marxian theorists were indebted to Kautsky as the man who assured them an audience by arousing widespread interest in Marxism and, in the *Neue Zeit,* providing the world's first journal devoted to the propagation of Marxism.

In addition to his *Economic Doctrines* and his theoretical polemics, Kautsky promoted acceptance of Marxism by German socialists through his economic articles in the *Neue Zeit.* In these articles he presented a variety of statistics from official sources to show that economic concentration, overproduction, periodic crisis, and the immiserization and proletarianization of the working classes were occurring. In 1883 he demonstrated from official statistics that both mortality and disability rates were increasing among Prussia's miners; that in the German state of Saxony the percentage of the populace receiving an income of less than 800 marks per year was steadily increasing; and that productivity, production, and mechanization were increasing in the German sugar and the American iron and steel industries. In 1885, by a careful and sophisticated reading of the 1880 United States census, Kautsky disproved Albert Schäffle's assertion that the number of small agrarian holdings was on the increase in America. And in several articles from 1887 through 1889, he argued vigorously that industrial capitalism was killing itself because "the greater the overproduction, the greater the competition, [and] the stronger is every impulse which goads greater productivity and economy within the factories." As a whole, these articles constitute an extensive indictment of capitalism as seen by a Marxian intellectual, and they were exactly the sort of propaganda that impressed the sympathetic but uncommitted readers of the *Neue Zeit.*[51]

The one area of economics in which Kautsky made an original contribution during the 1880s was the discussion of colonialism (he did not use the word *imperialism* until after 1890). In his first article on colonialism, which appeared in one of Karl Höchberg's journals in 1880, he identified two classes of colonies: exploitative colonies and work colonies. The former he condemned without reservation because their only purpose was to plunder natural resources, and their effect was usually to devastate the native population for the advantage of a very few entrepreneurs and traders. He gave conditional approval to work colonies, those intended to be permanently settled and worked by citizens of the colonizing country, but the conditions he imposed (social-democratic political freedoms and economic prosperity for all settlers) were prohibitive. These conditions were not realized in the colonizing countries themselves, as Kautsky well knew. In an 1882 letter to Engels, he suggested that under certain conditions, as when the colonizing power was industrially and politically advanced and the colony backward, perhaps colonization could be progressive if it brought capitalism with it. But this was the only time during the eighties that he even suggested that something good could come from colonies. In a number of *Neue Zeit* articles he developed a careful, enlightened, and consistently hostile critique of nineteenth-century European colonial expansion.[52]

While Kautsky recognized that colonies had been a necessary source of original capital accumulation during the fifteenth through the seventeenth centuries, he felt that the other important aspect of colonies, as markets for contemporary capitalism, was quickly being exhausted. In the *Neue Zeit* articles of the eighties, he expanded on his original distinction between work colonies and exploitative colonies and condemned both on the basis of German economic self-interest and on humanitarian grounds. He now rejected work colonies without qualification for four reasons. First, he did not feel they were necessary to relieve overpopulation, since Germany was not overpopulated. Besides, by careful and imaginative analysis of population, election, and emigration statistics, he showed that in fact heaviest emigration originated in areas of low population. He also demonstrated that, with few exceptions, emigration was not a safety valve for discontent since it was highest in areas that voted most heavily for progovernment parties and lowest where the major opposition party, the SPD, was strongest. Second, Kautsky argued that work colonies would not advance the cause of German nationalism since they either failed or, when successful, the settlers developed new national loyalties. Third, most areas of the world suitable for the establishment of work colonies, that is, areas with moderate climates, were already taken. Therefore, for Germany to settle such lands would require either a major war of conquest or a tremendous number of German immigrants. And finally, Kautsky quite sensibly pointed out that even if work colonies could now be founded, there was no guarantee that they would trade exclusively with Germany.[53]

Kautsky saved his harshest criticism for exploitative colonies. In vivid terms he argued that these colonies, which were usually based on slave or near-slave labor, brutalized both the colonizers and the native population and often led to the extermination of the latter. This brutalization was the result of several things. For one, living conditions were so harsh in exploitative colonies that only the most brutal and uncultured of the white Europeans went there. Kautsky was particularly appalled by the exploitative and inhumane relationships between the white male colonizers and their purchased native concubines. He quoted with approval the eighteenth-century French expression, "La canaille de l'Europe, c'est l'aristocratie des Indes." He also argued that by their very nature exploitative colonies encouraged the white Europeans to seek the greatest possible profit in the shortest possible time without regard to long-term developments. The fact that such colonies were profitable for only a very few merely drove those who failed to greater ruthlessness and inhumanity. But perhaps Kautsky's most perceptive critique of both types of colonies was based on what we would today call a conflict of cultures and values. Though he did not use the terminology of present-day sociologists and historians, he nonetheless discussed the confrontation between white Europeans from industrially advanced countries and less advanced Africans and North American Indians in a strikingly modern way. He pointed out that in all the debates over colonization, one thing was never mentioned, namely the rights of the native population. What to Europeans seemed sparsely populated or even empty land was often as heavily populated as hunting land can be. North American Indians, for instance, had no concept of landownership that allowed them to understand what Europeans were doing in the New World. With arguments like these, Kautsky revealed his strong humanitarianism and his own sensitive awareness of cultural specificity. He recognized the right of the native populations not to be westernized, Christianized, and modernized, though his discussion was also marked by a feeling that colonization was inevitable.[54]

As with other issues discussed in the *Neue Zeit*, Kautsky did not completely ignore the political implications of the colonial issue. In fact, the distinction he made between work and exploitative colonies grew out of a need to combat German colonial enthusiasts who were clamoring for funds and military support from the state to further the cause of the German Empire. Many of Kautsky's articles appeared at times when colonialism was a hot political issue. For instance, his analysis of German emigration appeared in the spring of 1885, at the same time that the bill for state subsidization of German steamship lines was being considered in the Reichstag. One of Kautsky's points was that the procolonialists confused the benefits of the two kinds of colonies (such as getting rich and emigration by the lower classes), while they failed to mention the disadvantages (such as brutalization and failure). From his analysis of colonialism, he drew two political conclusions that continue to be echoed in fact and theory in the twentieth century. First, he predicted that the all-too-gradual modernization of the colonized countries would eventually yield native rebellion against domination by the Europeans. Second, arguing that they faced a common exploiter in the capitalist class, he discussed the common interests of, and a possible coalition between, the industrial proletariat of the European nations and the natives of the colonies.[55]

Politics had a persistent way of intruding into most of Kautsky's writing of the 1880s. Powerful personal disinclination, the original design for the *Neue Zeit*, and caution demanded by the antisocialist law combined to keep him from concentrating on political matters, and yet he constantly felt compelled to discuss politics and considered politics a fundamental part of the working-class movement. Furthermore, he was convinced that political issues were too important to be left to the politicians alone, because they tended to overemphasize practical, day-to-day matters at the expense of long-range theoretical consid- erations. He argued that theory was vitally important to politics be- cause it allowed a party to perceive future trends in society and economics and to mold its policies to conform to these trends. Kautsky also felt that one of the major strengths of the international socialist movement was its theoretical ability; he was especially scornful of English socialists whom he saw as purely empirical and thus much inferior to the Marxists. Finally, though like most Marxists he held that the trade unions were schools for socialists, he was the first to identify the tendency of trade unions to ignore larger political issues while concentrating on more immediate and narrower economic matters. In an 1884 letter to Engels, Kautsky deplored the lack of theoretical concern within German socialist circles despite continued trade-union activity. Anticipating almost exactly Lenin's later and more famous dictum, Kautsky wrote: "And not all questions can be decided by class instinct alone, so much the more as the trade-union movement turns increasingly into trade-unionist ruts." In other words, without theoretical guidance, practical activity does not yield socialist consciousness. Engels responded that he felt Kautsky was too harsh in his judgment of the German masses.[56]

Much of what Kautsky wrote on politics during the first year in Zurich was directed against the anarchists and was therefore moderate in tone. But he soon found himself on the side of the radicals in opposition to the moderates of the German party, so his political writing once again assumed the radical tone of, though a different content from, his pre-Zurich flirtation with anarchism. On the other hand, with the possible exception of those articles devoted to speculation about the nature of postrevolutionary society, Kautsky's political writings of the eighties tended to be very realistic and, on occasion, surprisingly practical. Balancing this realism, however, was a strong inclination to optimism about the coming of the revolution and about the political power of the socialists vis-à-vis the German state. In the spring of 1884, Kautsky predicted in a letter to Engels that the upcoming election would be a good one for the SPD, which it was. But he also felt that there was some chance of getting the antisocialist law moderated or even dropped, which did not happen until 1890. Kautsky added, "however I must mention that Ede [Bernstein] considers me an optimist." A further measure of this optimism was his prediction three weeks later that even with the antisocialist law, the rising tide of public support for the socialists would make the German government think twice about prohibiting the publication of a new book by Engels. Engels himself was less sanguine about the prospect of publication.[57]

At times during the 1880s Kautsky's political views were very simple and even dogmatic. Politics for him was the class struggle, and all states were class states which ruled for the dominant economic class. Although he recognized that when confronted with regional, quasi-feudal forces, the proletariat was oriented toward the national whole, he insisted that nationalism was an essentially modern, bourgeois phenomenon. Only when nationalism was a revolutionary force was the proletariat nationalistic; once national particularism became a fetter on further development, the proletariat became internationalist and the national state its enemy. This line of reasoning led Kautsky to a blanket rejection of nationalization, or state socialism as bourgeois critics then called it. His opposition was summarized in the following syllogism: "State socialism is socialism by the state and for the state. It is socialism by the government and for the government. It is therefore socialism by the ruling class and for the ruling class." He was especially direct and vehement in his opposition to the German state. He wrote to Bebel that "opposition to Bismarck's representative system is an essential element of our movement." The Prussian Junkers who dominated the German government, he contended, were motivated by "petty vindictiveness" and pursued "guttersnipe politics." He also had the pseudorepresentative governments of Austria and Germany in mind when he referred to parliamentarism as a "comical farce."[58]

On the other hand, Kautsky was also capable of subtler and more careful political analysis. For instance, he was one of the first Marxists to contend explicitly that the ideal government for most of Europe's bourgeoisie was not a republic but a constitutional monarchy. Marx himself had tended to posit French republican forms as the purest form of bourgeois political domination. Kautsky held that notions such as the general franchise, universal (male) military obligation, and cumpulsory education were not ideals of the greater part of the European bourgeoisie, but imports via France from "the great North American republic." He also appreciated that after the proletarian, socialist revolution the state could not immediately be discarded. Some form of state would have to be used by the proletariat to complete the revolution. The abolition of the state would be the last, not the first act of the proletarian regime. Furthermore, he was undogmatic enough to realize that though the classical form of the modern state might be the bourgeois national state, "the classical form exists only as a tendency, it seldom develops completely purely."[59]

The subtleties of Kautsky's political writing derived from his basic awareness of the complexities of modern society. While he recognized a general tendency toward increasing bifurcation into a massive proletariat and a tiny bourgeoisie, he consistently argued that it was only a tendency, that in fact capitalist society consisted of a great variety of interests. And the variety was not incidental, rather "the capitalist mode of production rests on the opposition of the different classes; on the opposition of tendencies within the same class; on the opposition of the different industrial states." He was also fully aware of the intricacies and internal conflicts of state governments: "In a government . . . by no means a single will rules, and its actions are by no means completely thought out, deliberately applied, and directed to one particular end. Different influences and tendencies make themselves felt in varying strengths, and often disrupt the unity of will of the government in the severest way. And the application of these desires through the bureaucracy does not always conform entirely with the intentions of the government. Every bureaucratic body has its own life, its own traditions, which often prove more powerful than the will of the government."[60]

During 1881, in the midst of the debate within German socialism between the radicals and the moderates, Kautsky formulated his conception of the nature and function of the party, a conception he was to hold to for the rest of his life with very little alteration. The climate of the dispute caused him to adopt a tone of exaggerated militancy that he was to drop in later, less tense, discussions. But essentially only the tone changed, not the fundamental analysis. Most of his contributions to the on-going debate appeared in the official party paper, the *Sozialdemokrat*, where they often elicited lively responses from the moderates.

Kautsky began by defining social democracy as a revolutionary party, not because it relied on violence, but because it held that "the social question" could not be solved within existing society. He went on to define revolution as an event so elemental that it could not be decreed. He named three essential conditions for revolution: a general and profound discontent engendered by economic and political pressures; a catalytic event, such as famine or war; and the inability of existing states to cope with the revolutionary situation. The role of a social democratic party, once these conditions existed, was to lead the revolution, preventing unnecessary chaos and ensuring victory for the workers. Therefore, the function of the party was "not to organize the revolution, but to organize for the revolution; not to make the revolution, but to use it." Kautsky cited three means by which the party could organize for the revolution: participation in elections, not because socialism could be achieved through parliaments, but because of the propaganda and agitation value of elections; promotion of good labor legislation, to prove the goodwill of the party and to increase the sense of solidarity and strength among the workers; and support for trade-union organization and strikes.[61]

Largely to combat moderate tendencies within the party that still hoped to tie the workers' movement to the oppositional bourgeoisie, and also to counter governmental and conservative propaganda, Kautsky specifically denied that a bourgeois-dominated republic was the first step to socialism. The bourgeoisie, he argued, had never really been republican and certainly was not now republican in Germany; rather it supported a military monarchy. He rejected the idea that social democracy was an extension of bourgeois democracy, though both called for freedom and they had fought together in 1848. But then the German bourgeoisie had been revolutionary, he continued, and now it was reactionary. Though both parties still called for freedom, social democracy sought freedom from the domination of one class or one person, while the bourgeoisie sought absolute individual freedom. Kautsky argued that the latter was in fact anarchy, an unnatural condition for humans and a farce given the technical conditions of production. The bourgeoisie really sought only the freedom of entrepreneurs and landowners to exploit the lower classes. Obviously Kautsky had put the cart before the horse here. In Germany the socialists were not allowed to speak, meet, or write freely. Rejecting the value of these traditional, bourgeois, individual freedoms meant rejecting not only the function of the party as he himself had defined it, but also his own role as party propagandist. Robert Seidel, a moderate socialist, took Kautsky to task for having implicitly rejected the traditional liberal freedoms.[62]

The defense Kautsky offered following Seidel's critique was somewhat feeble. First he claimed he had neglected the traditional freedoms because they were so fundamental to the socialist program that mentioning them was unnecessary; then he offered arguments that were at the same time too extreme and too highly qualified to be convincing. His emphasis was on the collective, as represented by the party, as opposed to the individual: "Vis-à-vis the totality, the individual has no rights, only duties." He then identified the party with the organized and conscious part of the working class, the class interests of the workers with the interests of the party, and concluded that committed individuals owed the party all, the party owed nothing to the individuals in it. Now this was all rather fearsome and totalitarian sounding, and taken alone certainly suggested a rather extreme conception of the party and the role of individuals. However, Kautsky continued his discussion by saying that the only limit to the subjugation of the individual to the whole was equality: "the totality may demand no more from any single individual than from all the others." He also added that reason was "obviously" also a limiting factor, and discussed restrictions on speech, press, assembly, and even religion as unreasonable and violations of the precept of equality.[63] In the end Kautsky backed down, while trying to preserve face with sharp words. He was forced to admit, in effect, that to a certain extent social democracy was both the logical and the historical consequence of bourgeois democracy. The more moderate content of his contribution to this debate was a truer reflection of his long-term political views than was the extreme language. But the extreme language also reflected an inclination on his part that persisted through most of his long association with the SPD. In public defense of his positions, Kautsky tended to exaggerate his real feelings for the sake of propaganda and dramatic effect. This tendency became even more marked in the years from 1890 to 1914, when he clearly viewed himself as the defender of Marxian orthodoxy against deviations to the right and to the left.

That Kautsky's extreme language in the debate over the nature and function of the party was more the result of the circumstances of the argument than of his rational analysis of the issues is further attested by another persistent strain in most of his works in the 1880s, namely a strong humanitarianism. In his earliest work, Kautsky identified the victory of socialism with the victory of humanity. In 1880, he wrote effusively of the working class as "the pioneer of a new age . . . which establishes the 'kingdom of God' on earth and which will make all people into humans!" His powerful condemnation of the violence of Austrian anarchists was accompanied by this caution: "Social Democracy is a party of human love, and it must always remain conscious of its character even in the midst of the most frenzied political fights." His humanitarian strain was most evident in works in which he analyzed social problems. For instance, after a careful review of statistics on the mortality rates of indigent and orphaned children cared for in institutions, he concluded that the care of such children was inhumane because it did not provide love. Why not, he asked, support indigent mothers so they will not have to give up their children? Why not finance foster parents? Kautsky also railed against the so-called Christian morality that shamed unwed mothers into giving up their children. In a plaintive plea for greater humanity, he called for tolerance in such situations. Indeed, Kautsky was always very sensitive to human suffering, which he blamed largely on the capitalist system, and saw socialism as a potential force for humanizing the world. This humanitarian sympathy accounted for his strong attachment to the works of George Sand and later caused him to balk in the face of the apparent necessity of revolutionary violence. While strong humanitarianism may have made him a less effective revolutionary, it also rendered his writing sometimes startlingly modern in tone.[64]

Finally, something must be said of Kautsky's historical writings during the 1880s. If in politics he identified Marxism with the class struggle, in a more general sense he identified it with the materialist conception of history. He generally considered himself a historian first and foremost, and as an old man he felt that his historical works were "much more original and theoretically significant" than his economic works. His major histories of the period were *Thomas More and His Utopia* (1888) and *Class Struggles in the Age of the French Revolution* (1889), both of which were based largely on research done at the British Museum and written under Engels' tutelage. Kautsky also wrote several articles that later served as a basis for his studies of the origins of Christianity and the Reformation in Central Europe. These articles included "The Origins of Biblical Prehistory," "On the Luther Jubilee," "The Origins of Christianity," and "The Miners and the Peasant Wars." A very early and forgettable effort yielded *Ireland: An Historical Sketch* (1880), which was little more than a summation of the work of others.[65]

Thomas More seems a curious work today. Why Kautsky chose this preeminently Catholic and elitist thinker and statesman as one of the two most important precursors of modern socialism (Thomas Müntzer was the other) is not entirely clear. In this work Kautsky discussed the age of humanism and the Reformation in terms of the developing conflict between nascent mercantile capitalism and feudalism dominated by the pope. He then presented More's background—a classical scholar, a long-time representative of the London merchants in the English court, and an opponent of absolutism who sought to restrain the king without appealing to the populace. But the major aim of the book was to present More's *Utopia* as the first socialist work to foresee the demise of capitalism and speculate about the nature of the postcapitalist society. With an impressive disregard for More's dramatic historical legacy, Kautsky argued that had More not written *Utopia,* he would have quickly lapsed into obscurity. By crediting to More's genius all the things he liked in *Utopia* and passing over all the things he did not like as regrettable consequences of the age, he managed to eulogize a man who condoned slavery, flogging, and the burning of heretics, who denied the right of the general populace to have a say in government, and who viewed the world through traditional Catholic eyes.[66] The book is still interesting because Kautsky went beyond the theological discussions that usually dominated biographies of More at that time, but it failed to make a very convincing case for him as a precursor of modern socialism.

Class Struggles was an effort to analyze the enormously complicated events of the French Revolution from 1788 to the ascension of Napoleon. Unlike *Thomas More,* this book dealt with issues vital to the workers' movement and for this reason was more widely read and influential than Kautsky's first effort at biography. Furthermore, *Class Struggles* was written in late 1888 and early 1889, in the midst of Kautsky's divorce and the cooling of relations with Engels. The latter read *Class Struggles* in manuscript form and sent Kautsky a very sharply worded critique. Kautsky incorporated almost all of the detailed criticisms into the final draft, and Engels' sharp tone elicited humble and grateful responses, from Kautsky, who clearly realized why the critique was so harsh.[67]

In *Class Struggles,* Kautsky offered a very careful and reasonable analysis of the economic interests that motivated the various classes and groups in French society during the Revolution. He claimed, in the 1908 preface to a new edition, that the work was intended to prove that "dogmatic Marxism" was capable of subtle arguments, and in fact that the Marxists, recognizing the economic complexities of society, could write much more accurate history than those historians who only looked at surface events. Kautsky showed that the nobility was split into those who supported the court, those who opposed it, and those who went over to the side of the Third Estate. He discussed the many layers of the Third Estate and emphasized the importance of peasant and street-rabble uprisings in sustaining and advancing the revolution. Though his sympathies were obviously with the *sans-culottes,* he viewed the sequence of events in the Revolution as the inevitable results of the immature development of the French bourgeoisie and as a necessary step in the progression toward modern capitalist society. *Class Struggles* was a convincing example of the utility of the materialist conception of history and its potential as a weapon in the orthodox struggle against both those who would merge the workers' movement with the bourgeoisie and those who argued that the workers should have nothing to do with any other group. It was a fitting last work for this decade in which Kautsky prepared for the role of international arbiter of Marxism that would be his after he returned to Stuttgart in 1890.[68]

Challenge from the Right
1890–1904

KAUTSKY AND HIS NEW WIFE settled in Stuttgart in late 1890, shortly before the expiration of the antisocialist law. In the next quarter century the SPD grew into a massive party, and Kautsky's reputation grew with it. During these years he became an important figure in the international movement as well as the leading theorist of the SPD. His international prestige was largely a product of his relationship with the German party, and his place in the SPD derived from his alliance with Bebel, his skill as a polemicist, his control of the *Neue Zeit*, and his role as editor of the Marx *Nachlass* ("literary estate"), especially volume four of *Capital*. Kautsky drafted much of the official program the SPD adopted in 1891, aided the Austrian and Hungarian parties with their programs, and corresponded with the leading figures of virtually every socialist party in the world. At congresses of the Second International and in his private correspondence and public writing, he was frequently called upon to arbitrate theoretical disputes, to hand down authoritative judgments as the successor to Marx and Engels. According to one prominent historian of Marxism, during these years Kautsky "helped turn Marxism from an esoteric system into the doctrine of a gigantic political movement."[1]

Under the antisocialist law, the electoral fortunes of the SPD had increased steadily. This trend reached a climax on 20 February 1890, when the SPD became the largest party in the Reich, receiving over 1.4 million votes. With the lapse of the law the party continued to grow, surpassing 2 million votes in 1898, 3 million in 1903, and 4 million in 1912. At the same time, party and trade-union membership increased enormously, as did the bureaucracies of both organizations. But the euphoria induced by this growth did not completely mask the malaise and discontent within the party before 1914. Electoral success and bureaucratic growth increasingly threatened the supposed revolutionary posture of the party as integration into the prevailing system replaced intransigent opposition. Greater size endangered the unitary nature of the party as the south German socialists increasingly pursued independent policies. Despite its status as a social and political pariah and its negligible political power, the SPD was a focal point in the politics of the Wilhelmian Reich. The antisocialist law, the "new course" of Wilhelm II, the election of 1907, and Chancellor Bethmann Hollweg's concern with the party all attest to the SPD's importance in the formulation of official and unofficial policy. But this negative role did not satisfy those within the party who hoped to make it an effective political force. The increase in votes did not yield a comparable increase in mandates; not until 1912 did the party have the largest Reichstag delegation, 110, barely a quarter of the total. Even an absolute majority would have meant little in the pseudorepresentative Reich. Moreover, by 1912–1913, the SPD's steady growth was slowing up; the party had apparently reached a saturation point, beyond which lay stagnation.[2]

Party developments after 1890 intensified the moderate-radical differences that had characterized German socialism since its beginnings. Electoral success, a rising standard of living, and the conservatizing influence of bureaucratization strengthened the moderate forces, while the persistent ostracism of the SPD, the periodic violence of labor disputes, frustration with lack of power, and, after the turn of the century, the debate over imperialism, all fed the so-called radical fraction. During the years before the First World War, the moderates constituted the right wing of the party; the radicals were the left wing. Until the emergence of revisionism in the late nineties, right and left most often indicated attitudes toward party tactics and views of the nature and goals of the party. The right wing tended to concentrate exclusively on parliamentary activity, gradual reform, and the expansion of the party's appeal, especially to the peasantry. The left wing, while not rejecting parliamentary activity, tended to call for extraparliamentary action as well, drastic political reforms to alter the nature of the Reich, and preservation of the exclusively working-class character of the party. From 1890 to 1904, Kautsky devoted most of his time to fighting what he considered the pernicious tendencies of the right. These tendencies included support for state socialism, appeals to the peasantry, and overemphasis on the efficacy of parliamentary reform. After the mid-nineties, Kautsky also struggled against Bernstein's revisionism, the first and only theoretical attempt to justify the right wing of the SPD. Not until after the 1905 Russian revolution did an SPD left wing begin to emerge as distinct from Kautsky's position, and not until then did he feel compelled to distinguish his own position as centrist, between the traditional deviations to the right and the new deviations to the left.

Editing the *Neue Zeit*

From his return to Germany in 1890 until he lost the journal in 1917, a great deal of Kautsky's time was devoted to editing the *Neue Zeit*. This job entailed a staggering amount of work. In 1892, he reviewed nearly five hundred unsolicited article manuscripts, over three hundred of which were returned. These unsolicited articles often required sharply worded responses in order to clarify positions of the SPD. Even articles Kautsky solicited did not always work out as expected. In late 1893, he rejected as unacceptable an article about Lessing from Paul Ernst, a dramatist-critic associated with the left wing of the Berlin party. Kautsky had expected an article based on the materialist conception of history, but found that Ernst was not of that school of thought. Such incidents made him suspicious of those intellectuals who were not full-time adherents to the cause. Kautsky's editorial responsibilities also included an enormous amount of correspondence; in 1895 he estimated that he wrote approximately one thousand letters per year, and in September 1896 he was writing about twelve letters every day. Kautsky also received a large number of inquiries from people he identified as "bourgeois and students," who asked about such things as value theory, "our relation to ethics," and other matters. These inquiries often required article-length answers and sometimes consumed more time than either editorial or private correspondence. Their great number also led Kautsky to admit reluctantly that the majority of readers of the *Neue Zeit* were bourgeois, not workers as he had hoped.[3]

During most of his years at the head of the *Neue Zeit*, Kautsky complained periodically of being overburdened with work. Though he always had co-workers to assist him, not until 1899 did he have coeditors whom he felt he could entrust with editorial responsibilities. Again and again he complained that he was prevented by the burdens of the *Neue Zeit* from pursuing his own theoretical development. Especially during the first three or four years after the return to Germany, he felt that he wasted time with routine work, with reading "bad manuscripts, bad brochures, and bad newspapers," and that such work was causing him to decay theoretically. However, his capacity for work usually was more than a match for the demands made on him. At one point in 1896, he was working on seven different projects—two books, two articles, two revisions of previous works, and a translation of a series of articles from the Marx *Nachlass*—as well as keeping up his editorial work. This capacity for hard work once led Adler to exclaim: "You are simply a human demon! If I had your strength, or even a tenth of it!"[4]

Not just the work of editing a weekly bothered Kautsky; he was even more upset with having to live in Stuttgart. He had agreed to move back to Germany with the expiration of the antisocialist law in part because he recognized that, as far as socialism was concerned, Germany was where the action was. He soon discovered, however, as he had during his earlier residence, that Stuttgart did not share in much of the action of German socialism. In the 1890s, it was an isolated, backward city on the edge of the rural splendor of the Black Forest region in southern Germany. It had neither a vigorous socialist circle nor sufficient research facilities, the only things that would have made living there palatable to Kautsky. London had Engels and the British Museum; Vienna had family and friends; Berlin was the center of German socialist activity. Kautsky would have preferred any of these three great cities to Stuttgart, but several factors worked to keep him and his family there until 1897.[5]

Kautsky was dependent on the *Neue Zeit* for a regular income. Dietz had made the departure from London more attractive by guaranteeing Kautsky 3,000 marks per year, and on 1 October 1891, this figure was raised to 5,000 marks. The increase was most welcome as the Kautsky family was growing rather swiftly. In February 1891, the first of three children, all boys, was born, and on 13 January 1892, the second, Karl Kautsky, Jr., made his appearance while his father was in London for a brief visit. The proximity of the two births led Karl, Sr., to exclaim in a letter to Engels: "Holy Malthus, pray for me!" The responsibilities of a family made him more cautious about abandoning Stuttgart and the *Neue Zeit* than he might otherwise have been.[6]

Both Dietz and Kautsky agreed that editing the *Neue Zeit* as a weekly required the editor's presence in Stuttgart, and this further limited Kautsky's ability to get away from provincial Swabia. He could leave Stuttgart for extended visits to London and Berlin only if he could find a coeditor whom he trusted. For a time in 1892, Kautsky and Engels thought they had found such a man in Conrad Schmidt. But Schmidt (1863–1932), once identified with the left wing of the Berlin party organization, could not be pursuaded to give up plans to move to Zurich and be a *Privatdozent*. After Schmidt, several men were considered, including Bruno Schoenlank, Heinrich Braun, Franz Mehring, and Max Schippel, but all were found wanting for one reason or another. Though Kautsky would have gladly accepted Bernstein as a coeditor at any time before 1897, he was under indictment for *lèse-majesté* and not free to return to Germany until 1901.[7]

Three other options existed for Kautsky which would have allowed him to leave Stuttgart and have more time for his own theoretical work. One was to change the *Neue Zeit* back into a monthly; another was to move the journal's headquarters to Berlin; and the third was simply to give up publication. The first of these options received a great deal of attention from Kautsky not only because it would have freed him of burdens, but also because he and Dietz differed on how to solve another problem, namely overcoming the *Neue Zeit*'s chronic deficit. Both men recognized, as did virtually everyone associated with the journal, that it was neither read by workers nor subscribed to sufficiently to be self-supporting. One critic suggested that the *Neue Zeit* could just as well be published in Kamchatka for all the foreigners who wrote for it, and Bebel complained that the journal was not topical enough. But Kautsky contended that when he called on these critics to contribute articles that would overcome these weaknesses, none was forthcoming.[8]

Since the *Neue Zeit* was not an official party organ, its losses were underwritten not by the party, but by Dietz privately. Dietz's solution to the deficit was to change the content of the journal, to appeal to a greater number of subscribers by running short articles concerned with subjects of more immediate interest. Kautsky agreed that this would probably increase circulation, but he had two objections. First of all, he argued, in order to become more topical the *Neue Zeit* would have to be published in Berlin where its editor could keep on top of current developments. Second, while Kautsky wanted to move to Berlin, both he and Engels felt that popularizing the journal could only be done by sacrificing the best part of the *Neue Zeit*, and its *raison d'être*, the theoretical articles. Kautsky suggested that the monthly format be restored, and each issue enlarged, so that more space could be devoted to serious theoretical topics. He argued that this would streamline costs while preserving the journal's true value. If Dietz and Bebel felt a new weekly was needed, then a new one should be started without destroying the *Neue Zeit*.[9]

Abandoning his journal completely was the most extreme solution to Kautsky's discomfort with Stuttgart. But by late 1893, he had become so frustrated with the isolation of the town that he announced that he was moving to Vienna in April 1894, whether or not a suitable replacement had been found, and whether or not it would mean the end of the *Neue Zeit*. In fact, of course, he did not go to Vienna and did not give up his journal. Although his frustration and sense of isolation were real, his commitment to the cause of advancing and strengthening Marxism was even stronger. He was acutely aware that Marxism did not dominate the German party and that among the party and trade-union rank and file, and particularly among the unorganized workers, no theory carried much weight. His conviction that the *Neue Zeit* was the only Marxian journal in Germany convinced him that to give it up would be a death blow to Marxism there. However much he wanted to leave Stuttgart, and he sincerely detested living there, his sense of duty to the workers and to Marxism prevented him from taking the final step of departure. In a letter to Adler announcing his decision not to come to Austria, Kautsky explained that he had come to the realization that the only way he could leave Stuttgart was to give up the *Neue Zeit*. That he could not do, he wrote, because "I am too much [a] church father."[10]

Not only was the *Neue Zeit* the sole organ of Marxism in Germany, it also provided many of the party's leading intellectuals with the lion's share of their income. In addition to Kautsky, Bernstein, Schippel, Mehring, and Bebel were also largely dependent upon it. This was one of the major reasons Dietz continued to carry the journal's substantial yearly deficit, and it was apparently the decisive reason for the changes made in the journal in August 1895. After almost five years of steady hounding from Kautsky to change things, after nearly as many years of dissatisfaction with the sales and appeal, though not the quality, of the *Neue Zeit*, on 2 August, Dietz, Bebel, and Kautsky met to discuss three proposals: (1) shifting the journal to Berlin; (2) converting it into a monthly; and (3) reorganizing payment for articles and raising the price per issue. Point one was rejected quickly because all three men agreed that the move would mean an increase in costs that neither Dietz nor the party was willing to shoulder at that time. Kautsky argued vigorously in favor of point two, but Dietz and Bebel would not hear of it. Rather Kautsky got a long lecture from Bebel about not letting personal wishes overrule the fact that as a weekly the *Neue Zeit* supported important party intellectuals, especially Bernstein, Mehring, and Schippel.[11]

Agreement was reached on point three—the price was raised from 20 to 25 pfennig, which would give Dietz an increase of 1.5 marks profit per yearly subscription. Figuring the present circulation at forty-five hundred, subtracting from five hundred to one thousand subscribers who would balk at the price increase, but adding five hundred new readers who would come over to the *Neue Zeit* with the end of Bernstein's *Sozialdemokrat,* Kautsky calculated that Dietz would

Cover of *Die neue Zeit,* 14 July 1900

net an increase of about 6,000 marks per year. In addition Bernstein and Mehring would each take a cut in pay of 100 marks per month for their work on the *Neue Zeit*, bringing their yearly stipends to 3,600 marks each. Bernstein would make up the loss by receiving an additional 100 marks a month from the official party journal, *Vorwärts*, and Mehring would receive a similar amount from the *Wahre Jacob*, another party journal published by Dietz. Finally, Schippel's honorarium from the *Neue Zeit* would be increased by 75 marks per month. These changes would save Dietz 1,500 marks per year, which, when added to the 6,000 marks increase in income, amounted to a potential net increase of 7,500 marks per year. Kautsky expressed the hope that this amount "may cover the deficit" of the *Neue Zeit*. Although he was greatly disappointed that he and his family would have to spend at least another year in "Stukkert," he was grateful that his own salary was not reduced. The intricacies of this settlement reveal the extent to which the *Neue Zeit*, though a private undertaking, was tied to party affairs. Furthermore, the journal was obviously important as a means of support for party intellectuals. The 1894 SPD congress had debated the issue of the level of pay for party intellectuals, with the party leadership successfully defeating the minority proposal to limit salaries to 3,000 or 4,000 marks per year. Kautsky's 5,000 marks was a comfortable income, though not high. Editors who oversaw dailies earned at least 5,500 marks, and Liebknecht got 7,200 for his work on the *Vorwärts*.[12]

Less than a week after this complicated agreement was reached, Tussy Marx threw a wrench into the works by asking Kautsky to assume primary responsibility for editing the Marx *Nachlass,* of which she had recently assumed control following Engels' death. Though Kautsky had agreed to accept the August settlement for at least a year, Tussy's offer changed matters considerably, and from late August through the spring of 1896, he vacillated between going to London and staying in Germany with the *Neue Zeit.* By February, Tussy was growing annoyed with his indecision, which resulted from his perennial money difficulties and his need to measure the relative importance of the *Nachlass* work against that of the *Neue Zeit.* The money issue centered on three things: how much the eventual publisher of the fourth volume of *Capital* would be willing to pay Kautsky for editing it; whether additional guaranteed sources of income could be found; and whether Dietz would continue the *Neue Zeit* after Kautsky's departure and pay him 150 to 200 marks per month as a permanent contributor. The matter of a publisher was not settled until long after Kautsky had decided not to go to London. Adler offered him 100 marks per month to be London correspondent for the *Arbeiterzeitung*, but other potential sources of income remained too indefinite to allow him to commit himself fully. The decisive factor was Dietz's attitude toward the *Neue Zeit*, and he threatened to end the journal if Kautsky went to London. Karl felt that the *Nachlass* work was very important and prestigious, but his own journal was even more critical to the cause of Marxism in Germany.[13]

Though Kautsky announced at least twice during the spring of 1896 that he definitely was moving to London, regardless of the fate of the Neue Zeit, he never made the move. For a time Dietz strongly hinted that he would be willing to convert the journal back into a monthly, keeping Kautsky as editor in absentia. Then he gave in to Kautsky's earlier demand and announced in early May that the *Neue Zeit* headquarters would be transferred to Berlin beginning 1 October 1896. Kautsky and his family did not move until 1897, but the chance to get out of Stuttgart permanently, coupled with the uncertainty of income in England, turned him against going to London. The 1895 party congress debate on the agrarian question had further reinforced his belief that the *Neue Zeit* had to be preserved, and when Dietz threw in Berlin as additional bait, Karl began to make plans to try to edit the *Nachlass* during brief visits to London while keeping up with full-time obligations to the *Neue Zeit*.[14]

Kautsky's conception of the nature and function of the *Neue Zeit* and of party intellectuals was constantly reinforced by party developments during the period 1890 to 1904. Debates on the party program and the agrarian question, the increasingly complex problems of tactics for the rapidly growing socialist movement, and above all, the revisionism crisis of the late nineties, served to strengthen his conviction that the only function of socialist intellectuals was to provide clarification for the workers in matters of theory. This view was predicated on two assumptions. First, "the class condition of the proletariat produces socialist *inclinations*, but not socialist knowledge." Second, without theory the German movement would "come to an English conception of things which only concerns itself with the tangible, the obvious, the practical, to the conception of the old unionism." Kautsky felt that one of the major problems in the German movement was that "this conception lies very near many of our people, namely the determined trade unionists; we must do everything to root it out because it is the grave of revolutionary thinking." He was willing to tolerate a good deal of theoretical inconsistency among the workers, but not among party intellectuals. The workers, because of their class instincts, were at least predisposed to the correct course, but "the confused intellectual has no such compass, he gropes helplessly in the dark." He felt that good-hearted but wrong-headed intellectuals did damage to the socialist cause. Thus when his close friend, Heinrich Braun, founded a journal that boasted of its eclectic theoretical basis, Kautsky sharply condemned the undertaking for extolling "characterlessness as a special virtue." For ten years the *Neue Zeit* had labored "to cram the people with Marxism and to bring an end to coquetting with Messieurs Rodbertus, Dühring, Schäffle, etc." Braun had founded a journal that would "ruin the laboriously gained, not altogether fixed clarity and . . . make our work futile." Kautsky trusted to objective conditions to generate energy and motion among the workers, but he clearly thought that the workers were to be channeled into proper courses by the theoretical dikes erected by socialist intellectuals. His view obviously demanded that intellectuals associated with the movement should espouse consistent, and preferably Marxian, positions.[15]

With the exception of the years of the revisionist debates (1898–1899, 1901–1903), Kautsky rarely spoke at party congresses. Just prior to the 1895 congress, where the agrarian question was argued at length, Karl reported to Luise that he was apprehensive because party comrades "think I have come with a big speech in my belly, [and] that is not agreeable." He was quite pleased that this speech came off as well as it did and surprised when a 1902 congress speech was well received. He was never part of the official party or congress leadership, though he did serve on various committees. Nor did he ever run for a Reichstag seat. When in 1890 Dietz proposed that he might become a German citizen and get elected as a representative from Stuttgart, Kautsky was cool to the idea. Three years later this suggestion was made again, and in rejecting it again he offered a very perceptive self-evaluation: "You do not need me in *parliament*. I am no speaker and even less a debater. The good thoughts always come to me *after* a debate. I am also no politician, neither a jurist nor an organizer. . . . I could only be a follower in parliament, and would play a mournful role, because one would expect something of me. It would go even more poorly with me than with [Paul] Lafargue, and I would, like him, forfeit my scientific efficiency under parliamentarism without exchanging it for something better." Though he toyed with the idea several times, Kautsky did not become a German citizen until after the fall of the Wilhelmine state. Until then his status as a foreigner ensured that he could not be politically active.[16]

The combination of Kautsky's conception of the function of the *Neue Zeit* and his aversion to personal, active participation in grass-roots politics reveals something about his attitude toward one of the fundamental issues of Marxism, the relationship between theory and practice. While his view of the role of the *Neue Zeit* presupposed intimate cooperation between theory and practice, his attitude toward his own involvement in practice meant that he did not perceive the two as inseparably interdependent. Though he was aware that his theory suffered when he was isolated from the centers of action, he was never convinced that the perspective of distance and detachment was less important than the familiarity of immediate experience. He repeatedly emphasized that politicians and trade-union leaders got bogged down in day-to-day details at the expense of the larger overview. But as with many other conservatizing factors in the SPD after 1890, Kautsky only made perceptive observations about the increasing influence of Reichstag representatives and trade unionists; he did not suggest ways to counter this influence. As most of his more politically astute associates pointed out on many occasions, he was an inveterate optimist who thought all would go right in time. He demanded constant and careful attention to theory and did not argue that revolution would occur come what may. But he also failed to perceive that criticism without action would not stem the antirevolutionary tendencies within the party. In large part he did not see the latter because he was not an activist himself.[17]

The Party Program

At the last exile congress of the German socialist party before the expiration of the antisocialist law, held in St. Gall, Switzerland, in 1887, Ignaz Auer, Bebel, and Liebknecht were charged with drafting a new party program. The majority of delegates at this congress concluded that conditions in Germany and the party had changed sufficiently since the 1875 party program was adopted to require a new program. This commission was supposed to fulfill its charge by the following congress. But at that gathering in Halle in 1890, Liebknecht explained the failure to fulfill the charge in terms of preoccupation with survival and also the need to rethink things entirely with the end of the antisocialist law. Liebknecht's resolution calling for a new program vaguely mentioned that the Gotha program was out of date and promised that the party leadership would propose a new program at the 1891 congress. The discussion that came between the Halle congress and the adoption of a new program at Erfurt opened the door for Kautsky's emergence as the leading theorist of the party.[18]

Debate preceeding Erfurt included a thorough airing of old programs, criticizing them in light of contemporary conditions, and then proposing new program drafts which in turn would be criticized in the party press. All of the party journals and most of its intellectuals took part in this process, but none was more active than Kautsky in the *Neue Zeit*. His original plan, suggested by Dietz, was to run a series of articles by several different people, including Auer, Bebel, Bernstein, and Engels, which would discuss various aspects of the program. But when asked by Kautsky for a contribution, Engels replied that he was too busy with Marx's *Nachlass* to write a new article. Instead he sent the manuscript of a letter and comments Marx had written after the 1875 German party program was proposed. This work, now known as the *Critique of the Gotha Program*, had been circulated privately in 1875 among leaders of German socialism and was first published in the *Neue Zeit* in January 1891. Knowing full well that it was a potential bombshell, because the *Critique* harshly criticized the Gotha program and included disparaging remarks about Lassalle and some of the party leadership, Engels suggested in his cover letter that if Kautsky felt he could not print it, it should be sent to Adler to be published in Austria. But he concluded, "it is far better if it appears in Germany itself, and in the party organ especially founded for such things, the *Neue Zeit*." Though Kautsky was somewhat apprehensive about the possible impact of this document, he was also eager to make known Marx's attitude toward the old program.[19]

Isolated in Stuttgart, Kautsky was confronted on 8 January 1891 with a very important decision. Should the harsh criticism of the Gotha program be published in the *Neue Zeit* or not? On that day Kautsky wrote to Bernstein: "Hardly ever have I so painfully felt my isolation, and especially the separation from you, as today." He was certain that the *Critique* would help to win the majority of the party to his own position, but added that "one does not happily undertake such important action without having discussed it with a trusted friend or comrade." In a postscript to his letter, Kautsky alluded to Bernstein's continuing exile in London, and to the similar position he found himself in, by writing: "You yourself know best what it means to be isolated in a responsible position." Clearly he would have preferred to have his own decision to publish, which was apparently made immediately, reinforced by Bernstein, Bebel, and others. He explained to Bernstein that the *Neue Zeit* would carry the *Critique* for three reasons. First, Engels was willing to accept ultimate responsibility for publication. Second, Kautsky felt that "it would be deplorable if Engels were forced to publish a piece of the Marx *Nachlass*" in Austria through Adler. Third, Kautsky assumed that since the original letter had been intended for Auer, Bebel, and Liebknecht, as well as others, Engels must have already notified Bebel of the imminent publication. Kautsky knew that some old Lassalleans would be offended, but the *Critique's* value outweighed such considerations.[20]

Kautsky also wrote to Engels on 8 January, explaining that he was delighted with the *Critique* and would publish it. He asked if Engels had notified Bebel and Liebknecht and added that only some sharply sarcastic remarks about the program's authors would be edited out, for the sake of party peace. A few days later he sent Engels a further defense of the deletions. He also commented that Dietz had seen the proofs and had not been enraged by the article, much to Kautsky's relief. In his response to these two letters, Engels gave general approval to the sorts of deletions Kautsky proposed and added that he had just written to Bebel about publishing the letter. Because Liebknecht had made distorted reference to the contents of Marx's letter during the program commission report of the Halle congress, Engels felt that notifying Bebel beforehand of the publication of the *Critique* would have put him in an awkward position. Bebel, Engels contended, would have had to decide whether or not to consult Liebknecht, and the latter "would have moved heaven and hell to prevent the printing." With this letter, dated 15 January, Kautsky first discovered for certain what he had suspected for the past week: Bebel too was going to be surprised by the publication of the Gotha program criticism.[21]

What followed was a bizarre series of events that made the publication of Marx's criticisms far more disruptive for Kautsky than it should have been. Sometime between 15 and 25 January, Kautsky informed Bebel by letter that Marx's work would be printed, and Bebel responded that he was not familiar with the material. Then on 25 January, Kautsky sent the article proofs to Bebel in Berlin, and Dietz went to Berlin also. Only after meeting with Bebel did Dietz realize the full implications of publishing the *Critique*. However, though the two men apparently discussed the article on the twenty-fifth or twenty-sixth, not until the afternoon of 28 January did Dietz wire Kautsky to stop distribution of the issue carrying the article. By that time it was too late, and Kautsky knew that Dietz and Liebknecht, and maybe Bebel also, would be furious about not being consulted beforehand. To Bernstein, Kautsky commented that as a result of this affair, "perhaps I will come to London sooner than I thought."[22]

A brief, but intense storm broke in SPD circles over the publication of the *Critique of the Gotha Program*. Although Engels steadfastly claimed responsibility, the majority of the SPD Reichstag *Fraktion,* including above all Dietz and Liebknecht, harshly chastized Kautsky as the villain. In the *Vorwärts,* the *Fraktion* denounced Kautsky for deception and further assaulted him both by letter and verbally. Most of the rest of the party remained strangely silent, but the *Fraktion*'s attack was severe. Kautsky asserted that he did not "care a straw for the *Fraktion*," but consented to write a conciliatory article anyway, for the sake of party unity. Privately he excused the *Fraktion* for what he called "*one* sound reason: their grandiose ignorance." Bebel's reaction upset Kautsky a good deal, especially since he had notified the party leader before the publication date that the article would appear.[23]

Kautsky responded most vehemently to Liebknecht's attack. In a letter to Engels, he directly accused Liebknecht of having deliberately kept the original 1875 letter from Bebel. Though Liebknecht claimed that Bebel had been in prison when the letter from Marx arrived, Kautsky pointed out that Bebel had been released from prison in late April, and the letter was dated 5 May. Kautsky and Liebknecht had long been at odds, largely because Kautsky resented Liebknecht's unearned reputation as a theorist and Liebknecht resented Kautsky as a non-German upstart. But when Liebknecht upbraided Karl for indiscretion in not notifying Bebel in advance, Kautsky rejoined: "If Bebel did not know what was in the letter, for that I was not responsible, but the one who suppressed the letter from him. It will be seen if and what the old sinner [Liebknecht] will answer to that. This time he has trapped himself in his own failures." The Kautsky-Liebknecht relationship went downhill from this point on.[24]

After this storm of protest quieted down, the party's preparation for the adoption of a new program proceeded quite calmly. Liebknecht drafted a proposal that appeared in the *Vorwärts*, but Kautsky thought it a very poor effort, designed only to avoid the disgrace of once again coming up with nothing. Since Liebknecht no longer had Marx's letters to plagiarize, Kautsky argued, his "vulgar socialism . . . [was] dull and absurd." By late September 1891, less than three weeks before the Erfurt congress, Karl was beginning to feel sorry for Liebknecht and his efforts to draft a new program. He reported to Engels that he had asked Bebel to speak to Liebknecht about these efforts, since someone "must save the old one from himself." And in the *Neue Zeit*, Kautsky subjected Liebknecht's proposal and others to a reasoned critique, discussing the origins and fallacies of state socialism and terroristic anarchism, the conservative potential of direct legislation, the economic and scientific basis of modern socialism (Marxism), the class nature of the state, the fallacy of the "one reactionary mass" slogan, and the major weakness of program proposals other than his own—they were overly long. He closed by insisting that in fact theoretical unity prevailed within the party since most of the differences in the proposed programs concerned emphasis, not principles. Publicly Kautsky tried to play a conciliatory role in the weeks before the Erfurt congress, confident that his proposal, backed by Engels and the prestige of Marx, would win.[25]

One particularly interesting aspect of Kautsky's discussion of the program proposals was his refutation of fatalism as one of the dangers of Marxism. This was one of the few times he directly confronted the determinist-voluntarist ambiguities of Marx's work. His major point was that while Marx taught that the direction of social development was not established arbitrarily, but out of necessity, he also taught that the motive force of development was "the struggle of opposites, the class struggle." Kautsky argued that these two positions constituted the dialectical core of Marx's theory and that the implicit voluntarism of the latter was as essential as the determinism of the former. Immediately after rejecting fatalism in Marx, he baldly asserted that "the final victory of the proletariat is inevitable," because the economics of modern capitalism made it so. However, he tied determinism in economics to voluntarism in politics by arguing that economically determined class struggles also have a political aspect:

> Every class struggle is a political struggle. The proletariat cannot fight its economic struggles without political rights; it constantly encounters state power when it fights the exploiter. Gaining and using political rights [and] making state power subject to its interests are absolute necessities for the proletariat. It must therefore organize itself as an independent party to which falls the task of maintaining its interests in political life, which must devote itself to the end of conquering the state, this most powerful and only adequate lever to bring about the transfer of the means of production to the possession of all.[26]

This argument rejected all fatalistic dependence on inevitable historical development. Kautsky also used this reasoning to refute the notion held by some "revolutionary enthusiasts" that better is worse, that is, that if their living conditions improve, workers will become less revolutionary. He argued that the success of positive work, or reform in the present society, would only teach the workers the value of organization. He contended this was so because class conflict, not poverty, was the root of the struggle for the workers' emancipation. By blending voluntarism and determinism in this manner, by asserting in effect that the workers must work for their own inevitable conquest of the state and political power, Kautsky preserved the ambiguous and elusive quality of Marx's own work.

The Erfurt Congress

The 1891 party congress was held in Erfurt from 14 through 20 October. When the 230 delegates assembled in the Kaiser Hall, they found it draped with two banners, one saying Workers of the World Unite! and the other, The Workers Are the Rocks on Which the Church of the Future Will Be Built! The religious allusions were probably conscious: SPD congresses had an aura of spiritual renewal about them, and the host party organization often got carried away with enthusiasm. This gathering in the ancient Saxon city so closely associated with Luther was to be the congress at which the party ratified the scriptures of the movement. Kautsky captured the camaraderie of these annual gatherings when he wrote to Luise on the second day of the congress: "I am sorry not to be able to show you our comrades, a body of splendid fellows, as [they] are assembled here." Karl was amused by the fact that in a way he was attending the congress as the representative of the recently retired Bismarck. His mandate was from Lauenberg where the former chancellor's retirement estate was located. Karl Frohme, a long-time SPD Reichstag representative, had yielded his mandate to Kautsky so that the party's theoretician could be a voting participant in the congress.[27]

Though much of the congress was spent in debate over the so-called *Jungen* revolt which centered in Berlin, the major task was the acceptance of a new party program. Paul Singer, the congress cochairman, opened the first session by declaring that just as the Halle congress had provided the party with new organization, so this one was to provide a new program "which scientifically and indisputably expresses our demands in clear and generally understandable form, and like the previous program will be a polestar for us in the struggles, a guide to victory." To accomplish this grandiose goal, a twenty-one-member commission, including Kautsky, Bebel, Liebknecht, and Vollmar, was elected on 18 October. Its job was to choose from the many proposals that had been offered and discussed in the party press before the congress. Of the four complete proposals seriously considered, the choice quickly narrowed down to Kautsky's draft presented in the *Neue Zeit* or the central committee's draft which had been written and defended by Liebknecht, but to which Bebel, Auer, and others had also contributed. The two drafts did not differ markedly in content, but

Kautsky's was much the shorter. At the commission's first meeting, a vote to accept one of these two drafts as a working basis resulted in a seventeen to four victory for Kautsky. Liebknecht was again offended by this vote and had to suffer the additional blow to his ego of reporting the commission's results to the entire congress. On the whole Liebknecht's presentation was judicious, though he only reluctantly credited the *Neue Zeit* draft for its brevity and clarity. The program was accepted by a very large majority on the last day of the congress after an extremely brief discussion. The general theme of unity and harmony, so laboriously maintained at most SPD party congresses, prevailed again.[28]

In its final form the Erfurt program combined a theoretical section written mostly by Kautsky and a tactical section written mostly by Bernstein and Bebel. The theoretical portion was short, only two pages, and defined economic and political developments in what by then were orthodox Marxian terms. Engels had read Kautsky's final proposal, but of the four or five changes in wording he suggested, only one was incorporated into the program. Where Kautsky had referred to "the growth of the yield of human labor," Engels recommended substituting the more precise *products* for *yield,* and the program commission agreed. Kautsky reported to Engels after the congress that though acceptance of the *Neue Zeit* draft as a basis was a foregone conclusion once Bebel had thrown his influence behind it, hammering out the end product was not so easy, ironically because of Bebel's obstinacy on some points. Engels, Bernstein, and Kautsky had all protested when Bebel added the phrase "one reactionary mass" to the *Neue Zeit* proposal published in the *Vorwärts* prior to the congress, and Kautsky led an almost unanimous opposition to Bebel's effort to get the program commission to include this phrase in the final draft. Though Kautsky won on this point, he lost when he opposed Bebel over inclusion of a demand for the "free administration of justice." Thus though Bebel's support carried the day for Kautsky's program, the two men were not in complete agreement on specifics. The only major changes in the theoretical portion were the addition of two paragraphs, one emphasizing recurrent crisis in capitalist society, and the other accentuating references to the class struggle. The commission entrusted Kautsky with the duty of adding these sections. The theoretical portion in its final form pleased both Engels and Kautsky, though Engels found the practical demands "philistine."[29]

After Erfurt, Kautsky was called upon by the party central committee to write a pamphlet that explained and amplified the program. This pamphlet turned into a book, *Das Erfurter Programm* (1892), which became Kautsky's most famous and most translated work.

In the introduction to a 1971 reissue of W. E. Bohn's 1910 English translation, Robert Tucker called this book "one of the minor classics of Marxist thought." It was also the first major work Kautsky published without receiving Engels' comments on the manuscript, and to this extent it constitutes the first work in which Kautsky presented his own Marxism without tutoring from Engels. However, *Das Erfurter Programm* did not, because of that, mark a turning point of any sort in Kautsky's theory. After eleven years of close guidance, Kautsky's Marxism did not differ from Engels' on any essential points.[30]

Das Erfurter Programm had five sections. The first three described the origins and nature of the modern productive system and was a condensation of Kautsky's earlier treatment of this topic in *The Economic Doctrines of Karl Marx*. As in the earlier work, Kautsky defined terms and described the process of the development of capitalism. Part four, "The Commonwealth of the Future," discussed the role of human action in history and the possible forms of the future state. Kautsky was definite on the former: "When we speak of the irresistible and inevitable nature of social revolution, we presuppose that men are men and not puppets; that they are beings endowed with certain wants and impulses, with certain physical and mental powers which they will seek to use in their own interest." But on the second subject he was more reluctant to commit himself. He argued that because social development was so complex as to preclude specific prediction and replication, "sketching plans for the future social state is about as rational as writing in advance the history of the next war." Nonetheless, because so many opponents of socialism demanded a model of the future society, he made certain suggestions about the decay of the family under capitalism and its disappearance under socialism, confiscation by the workers of the means of production (though not the property of small artisans and peasants), the tendency toward equalization of wages, and "not the freedom of labor, but the *freedom from labor*."[31]

Part five of *Das Erfurter Programm* discussed the nature of class relations and the tactics and channels of activity open to the workers. Kautsky emphasized the potential of labor organization, education, reform, and participation in parliament. But, he cautioned repeatedly, no one should "imagine that such [things] could delay the social revolution." His belief that this revolution did not necessarily have to be accomplished with "violence and bloodshed" was accompanied by the observation that "never yet was any revolution accomplished without vigorous action on the part of those who suffered most under existing conditions." Though he argued here that the proletariat was constantly growing in number and strength, he also strongly implied that it was tending to greater isolation and increasingly confronted with a united and hostile opposition. Close reading of this portion of *Das Erfurter Programm* reveals the moderating impact of internal party and external governmental pressures on Kautsky. Here, as in so much of his other work, he tried to placate the right wing of the party without abandoning the revolutionary commitment of Marxism. In so doing he may well have laid the foundation for later charges of cryptorevisionism and antirevolutionary mentality, but in the context of the times, *Das Erfurter Programm* was a document that most party members and all bourgeois critics took to be revolutionary in implication and intent.[32]

The Peasant Question

Most of Kautsky's time after 1890 was devoted to the *Neue Zeit* and the SPD, but another task undertaken in 1895 also demanded a great deal of his attention, namely editing the Marx *Nachlass*. In 1888, Engels had set Kautsky to work editing Marx's notes that would eventually constitute the fourth volume of *Capital*. However, the disputes over Kautsky's divorce had led Engels to suspend Kautsky's work on this manuscript. After Engels' death, possession of the Marx *Nachlass* passed to Tussy Marx and Laura Marx-Lafargue. Since Tussy lived in London where the *Nachlass* was, she assumed primary responsibility for organizing and publishing it. One of her first acts was to ask Kautsky to resume his work on volume four of *Capital*, and she eventually gave him first right of refusal on all the material in the *Nachlass* that was to be published. In addition to complicating Kautsky's living conditions, the editing added to his already enormous work load. He took it on gladly, however, because it was extremely prestigious and because he perceived it to be part of his responsibility as intellectual heir to Marx and Engels.[33]

Difficulties in getting a publisher for the fourth volume contributed to Kautsky's final decision to stay in Germany rather than move to London. Tussy's hope was that Dietz could publish the work because of his close association with a strong working-class movement and because Dietz and Kautsky could work together. But once she began to investigate matters, she discovered that Otto Meissner, the original German publisher of *Capital*, had contractual rights to successive volumes of that work. The terms of the contract with Meissner were not generous enough to provide Kautsky with the income he needed in order to move to London. Tussy and Kautsky briefly tried a ploy to convince Meissner that what Kautsky was working on was not volume four of *Capital,* but a discrete work. This failed when Meissner agreed to provide funding that would allow Kautsky to visit London for a few weeks every year in order to work on the manuscript. In the end Tussy admitted that though she would have preferred to have Dietz publish the work, she felt morally bound to let Meissner have it, since at the time the first volume of *Capital* was issued, he "was the only publisher in Germany who [would] even look at—let alone publish—[Marx's] work." After Tussy's tragic, early death, Laura reaffirmed Kautsky's position as editor. Ironically, the work was eventually published by Dietz in 1904–1910 as *Theories of Surplus Value.*[34]

Party tactics, the nature and limits of activities a Marxian working-class party could pursue, and the development of theory were Kautsky's major intellectual concerns during the period 1890–1904. The tactical questions that demanded the most attention were the party's relationship to the agrarian population, the matter of cooperation with the bourgeoisie, and franchise reform. In this same period Kautsky engaged in a polemical exchange with the English socialist Ernest Belfort-Bax, in which the materialist conception of history was scrutinized. But the major theoretical event of these years was the conflict over Eduard Bernstein's revisionism. Kautsky's defense against, and attack on, Bernstein's new theory dominated the years from 1898 to 1903. This debate ended for a long time the very close personal relationship between the two men and forced Kautsky to clarify and strengthen his own theory. During these years his position as theorist of the party solidified, and, often prodded by Bebel, he repeatedly chastized the opponents of the official party line. Nearly all of the tactical and theoretical considerations pitted him against the right wing of the party, which tended to give his work a radical flavor that at times belied the moderation of his true position. This apparent radicalism was also reinforced by the peculiar nature of the German state and society in the years before World War I.

The peasant question was an old concern in German socialist circles. Before his conversion to socialism, Liebknecht was associated with the largely peasant Saxon People's Party, and the delegation he led to the 1869 Basel congress of the First International voted against an anti-private-property resolution because peasant influences were so powerful among early German socialists. The problem of the relationship between socialism and the peasantry has rather obvious and natural roots. The workers employed in the factories of fledgling industrial societies were often drawn from the peasant population. Rapidly growing industrial centers frequently were merely worker-inhabited islands in a sea of rural agrarian villages. The powerlessness and poverty of both workers and peasants made them seem natural allies to early socialists still preoccupied with French revolutionary images of the people struggling against the oppressors of the old order. This image persisted for a long time in Germany, where even after the arrival of the industrial age, the quasi-feudal Junkers of Prussia dominated national politics.[35]

Kautsky's concern with agrarian matters began early in his socialist career. At the time he entered the Austrian movement, peasant agitation and opposition to the government were characteristic of many areas of the Austrian Empire, especially his native Bohemia. Many Austrian socialists thought the party had a chance to win followers among the peasantry as well as the working class, but Kautsky did not belong to this group. Although he made specific suggestions about appeals that might be directed at the peasantry, in the late 1870s his estimation of social democratic prospects among the rural population was already low, and it declined steadily thereafter. He felt that the major problems were the peasants' obsession with private property and a limitless egoism that prevented them from being attracted by collective or futuristic aspects of the socialist program. His specific ideas at this time included a call for the state to provide cheap credit, something he would later scoff at when suggested by others. He also envisioned "agrarian trade unions or farmers' leagues" that might serve as transitional institutions between private ownership and collectivization. He advised socialist agitators in the countryside to avoid attacks on religion or on child and female labor, but he felt that socialists should also consider using religious books as covers for their propaganda, arguing that "good aims justify any means that are not contradictory [to the ends]." At best Kautsky thought that the socialists, through hard work and serious propaganda, might neutralize the antisocialist prejudices among the peasants and maybe win an occasional passive supporter. But he was convinced that the hostilities between the city and the countryside could not be overcome easily.[36]

Very quickly Kautsky abandoned even these halfhearted efforts to find ways to appeal for peasant support. Though he was sympathetic to the misery and hopelessness of the peasantry, he was convinced that it was doomed to disappear under capitalism and appalled by its apparent ignorance and conservatism. In an address to the "agrarian population," which appeared in the *Sozialdemokrat in* 1880, he called upon the peasants to recognize their own misery; he argued that they shared common enemies with the workers and therefore should make common cause with them. Employers, state officials, and the Reichstag

104 · KARL KAUTSKY

lawyers were the enemies of urban and rural workers alike, but the large landowners, whom the peasants looked upon as friends, were in fact their special enemies. The landowners told the peasants that the socialists wanted to burn, murder, and pillage, when in fact the socialists wanted to return to the peasants what the large landowners had taken away—the forests, the good land, the commons. Kautsky had earlier confessed to Engels that writing a good peasant pamphlet was very difficult because "one should make 'positive' proposals, for the peasants are not satisfied with general principles, but at the same time one should be neither utopian nor petit bourgeois." And by 1880 Kautsky felt that the positive proposals socialists could make honestly were extremely limited. The fact of the matter was that as an emerging proponent of industrially oriented, progressive Marxism, Kautsky saw the peasantry as an archaic remnant of a dying economic order that was destined to disappear. The tremendous effort necessary to win a few peasants to socialism could better be spent organizing urban workers and fighting the bourgeoisie.[37]

During the period of the antisocialist law, the SPD was too preoccupied with survival in the cities to spend much time worrying about appeals to the peasantry. But after 1890, the restoration of freedom to propagandize, coupled with the party's growing electoral success, once again brought the agrarian question to the fore. Socialist politicians, especially in south Germany, began to see the large peasant population as potential voters, and, led by Georg von Vollmar of Bavaria, they tried to woo the peasantry by supporting provincial agrarian reforms. Interest in the agrarian question was heightened in the early nineties when for the first time in German history an association of farmers, the Bund der Landwirte, was formed. This association, dominated by the large landowners of the East Elbe region, proposed to unite small and large farmers into an interest group that worked through politics to the advantage of agriculture. By 1894 the SPD forces that advocated appeals to the peasantry had gained sufficient backing to demand that the party adopt an agrarian policy to be grafted onto the Erfurt program. The passage at the 1894 Frankfurt party congress of a resolution calling for such action launched an extremely long, acrimonious, and eventually fruitless debate. The issues were the most fundamental ones of the nature of the party (popular democratic or working-class, federated or centralized), tactics (reform or revolution), nature of the state (potential tool or enemy of the party), and the relationship between theory and practice. Kautsky played a key role in this dispute.[38]

Bruno Schoenlank and Georg von Vollmar set the tone for the entire debate in the speeches they gave in defense of their resolution at Frankfurt. Schoenlank referred to the need to "complete and expand" the Erfurt program by adding an agrarian plank. He argued for plain language that would provide guidelines for practical agitation, not the vague theory which he implied characterized the rest of the party program. He also emphasized that the Berliners, who dominated the party, could not properly understand the peasant problem, that it had to be handled on a local level. Vollmar reinforced these regional and antitheoretical positions. He, too, strongly emphasized that the peasants were there to be won by the SPD, but not by the methods and people of the cities and not by theory. He proposed that the party had become so large that it needed a division of labor—one part concentrating on industrial workers, another on theory and literature, and a third on the agrarian question and agrarian agitation. Though Vollmar tried to give his position theoretical legitimacy by denying that the same laws of development applied to both agriculture and industry, his primary concern was clearly to win peasant votes and thus increase party strength. The Schoenlank-Vollmar resolution calling for the formation of a fifteen-member committee to draft an agrarian program passed with only thirty dissenting votes. The strongly practical bias of the committee was accentuated by the inclusion of eight Reichstag representatives and one member of the lower house of Saxony.[39]

Kautsky's response to the call for an agrarian program came quickly, and he immediately identified what was for him the critical issue. Vollmar, as the leader of the south German, propeasant forces in the party, was trying to undermine both the working-class and the revolutionary character of the party. To Bernstein, Kautsky wrote:

> Our party is actually the only serious oppositional party in the Reich; all the discontented flock to us, swelling our vote, but only a part of them become socialists. This situation cannot last much longer. It is necessary, if this situation is not to dissolve our basic character, that beneath [the SPD] rises a party of energetic discontents who, without being revolutionary, still make a more determined opposition than the bankrupt bourgeois democrats. And just in the south, where the class struggle is still not very harsh, where the workers stand very near the peasants and the petite bourgeoisie, such a party has good chances in the future. If we let Joerg [Vollmar] build such a party, for which he will be an idol, and if we do not try to stop him from doing it, then our party will approach his ideal.

Kautsky told both Bernstein and Engels that a split with Vollmar's peasant reformists would be better than a "brittle peace." He argued that if the issue was not forced to a split immediately, then the same battle would have to be fought again, perhaps in two years or less. In that time the opposition would probably grow stronger, because "Vollmar is a great peasant catcher."[40]

A rather curious interlude interrupted Kautsky at the very beginning of what was to be a long, serious polemic against the right wing of the party. A bourgeois journalist turned socialist, Georg Ledebour (1850–1947), writing in the *Fränkische Tagespost* and the *Vorwärts*, claimed that Kautsky was "a hundred miles further right" than either Schoenlank or Vollmar, because the Erfurt program had claimed that the workers were not interested in seizing the small peasants' holdings after the revolution. Ledebour claimed that the two south Germans sought only to relieve the problems of the peasantry under capitalism, while Kautsky contended that small peasant holdings would persist under socialism, too. Thus Kautsky's theory gave cover to Vollmar's tactics. This criticism anticipated the later cryptorevisionist analysis of Kautsky's work. It also forced Kautsky to protect his left flank while attacking on the right, something that became common after 1905. In his rebuttal he pointed out that the Erfurt program did not claim that the small holdings of peasants had a future under socialism, but simply that the proletariat would have no need to seize these holdings because they would not long survive under maturing capitalism or socialism. The polemic eventually got very sharp, with Ledebour accusing Kautsky of acting like a priest and trying to be the pope of socialist theory. Kautsky ended the exchange because it had descended into personal attack and because he did not want to provoke a fight between the *Vorwärts* and the *Neue Zeit*.[41]

In his major assault on Vollmar and the right wing of the party, Kautsky felt hampered by three things. Once again he was keenly aware of the isolation of Stuttgart and wrote to Engels: "One is truly completely isolated here. . . . it is bad if one knows only his own opinion on a question." Second, he agreed with Paul Singer's observation that the SPD Reichstag *Fraktion* was more "Vollmarized" than the party as a whole. He objected to the prestige and influence of men who he felt did not reflect the will of the party membership. But above all else, Kautsky was angered by the Bebel-inspired effort of the *Vorwärts* to pretend that there was no disturbance in the party, calling this *Straussenpolitik* ("ostrich politics") that only played into Vollmar's hands. He felt that Bebel was adopting "an especially reformist attitude" in the matter, that "August sits this time with the Bavarians; he is the 'representative' of the 'peasant king' of Bavaria, Joerg [Vollmar]." Such problems did not prevent Kautsky from vigorously fighting what he perceived to be destructive tendencies within the party.[42]

Just as before the party program congress at Erfurt, so before the agrarian program congress at Breslau in 1895, the party prepared itself with analysis and criticism in the party press. Kautsky began his part in this debate by discussing the nature of the peasantry and landholding. Drawing from the official occupational census of 1882, he observed that while more than half of Germany's total of over 45 million people still lived outside the cities, only a little over 19 million engaged in agrarian undertakings, and almost 11 million of this latter group were agrarian wage laborers and their families. This meant that less than 8.5 million people could even begin to qualify as landed peasants and families, less than 20 percent of the total population. From this he concluded that the task of socialists in the countryside was simply one of raising the consciousness of the majority of the population that was really a rural proletariat. He also argued vigorously that the size of the rural proletariat would continue to increase while the number of landed peasants would decline as capitalism matured. Second, Kautsky contended, as he had for years, that among even the most depressed portions of the rural population, sentiments opposing socialism and favoring private property were so strong that the truth would not alter them. And third, he argued that since land was the most important means of production, in fact, the basis of all production, a socialist society without socialized landholding would be an absurdity. The land, like all other means of production, had to be held collectively after the revolution.[43]

Once the program proposal was published in July, Kautsky turned his attention to specific criticism of that document. His first objection was that the proposed drastic changes in the tactical portion of the party program, including calls for democratization and social improvements couched in the language of bourgeois democrats and bourgeois social reformers, contradicted the most fundamental theoretical precept of the SPD, namely that it was the party of the class struggle and the proletariat. He argued that the Erfurt program had demanded two kinds of reform: those to the advantage of all citizens and those to the special advantage of the workers. But the new proposals would single out the peasants for special treatment. By including such clauses in its program, the party would deny its class nature; it would become indistinguishable from many other parties that appealed for general support. He rejected an implicit equation of democracy and the dictatorship of the proletariat and contended that

Switzerland and the United States showed that a democratic state was not necessarily a proletarian state. The decisive interests of a class in political terms, Kautsky argued, were not those it shared as consumers and citizens with all other classes, but those which were peculiar to it alone. Social democracy had nothing of importance to offer the special interests of the peasantry in the present state form and social order. The agrarian commission's proposed program called for state socialism, the nationalization of forests, commons, water power, mortgages, and other things. Kautsky objected that this presupposed that the state was not a class state, that these steps would not simply increase the power of a capitalist-dominated tool. State-supported agrarian cooperatives were also part of the new proposals, but the party had already rejected the demands for state-supported workers' cooperatives that had been in the old Gotha program. In some ways Kautsky found the program superfluous, as when it called for special laws to protect agrarian workers. He argued that the Erfurt program demanded such laws for all workers, agrarian and industrial, and to the extent that the new clauses would protect the peasants as holders of private property, they contradicted the socialist ideals of the party.[44]

With what he described to Luise as an effort to be conciliatory, Kautsky emphasized that the task confronting the agrarian commission quite probably was an impossible one. The amount of material it had to deal with was enormous; the commission, like the party as a whole, was not united on the peasant question; and even if the commission majority came up with a program, the party majority might not accept it. Kautsky contended that the commission had been asked to square a circle, to reconcile irreconcilables: "A social democratic agrarian program for the capitalist mode of production is an impossibility." He urged that the party agitate among the peasantry, but without promising things that could not be delivered. The peasants must be told that they were doomed, that they could not compete with large-scale, capitalist farms. He realized that this line was not very "practical," that it would not win many peasant votes, but argued that the time was not ripe for appeals that would win thousands of voters. He concluded: "We have to go to the country at first not in order to reap, but to sow."[45]

Needless to say, Kautsky's arguments did not still the debate. The Breslau congress, which met from 6 through 12 October 1895, spent more than half its business sessions discussing the matter. Vollmar was ill at the time and did not attend the congress, but the commission's arguments were ably and prestigiously presented by Schoenlank, Bebel, Liebknecht, and others. Dr. Max Quarck formally presented the agrarian commission report. In his speech, much of which was directed at Kautsky's precongress criticisms, Quarck claimed that what was at stake was not "a few hundred thousand votes," but the future of humanity, which to a certain extent depended on the future of agriculture. He further argued that since the socialist parties of many other countries had agrarian programs, the principles of the international movement were not at stake on this issue. The only people upset by the proposed program, claimed Quarck, were "the agrarian Manchesterian comrades" of the German party, who had yet to realize that "nothing is accomplished by radicalism in words alone." After Quarck finished, Kautsky offered his own resolution calling for the rejection of the commission's proposal; it was signed by twenty-four other party members, including one member of the agrarian commission, Schippel, seven of the eighteen Reichstag representatives at the congress, and Paul Singer, a congress cochairman. Kautsky was pleased to report to Luise that seventeen people claimed the right to speak against his resolution and forty in favor of it.[46]

Schippel delivered the major speech in defense of Kautsky's resolution, and in Vollmar's absence, Bebel delivered the major attack. Schippel denounced the agrarian program as unoriginal and contrary to the party's principles. He identified its origins with the younger party organizers who worked among the small peasants and wanted "to drive out the devil of the anti-Semitic agrarian movement with the Beelzebub of our own agrarian demands." Bebel began his speech by denouncing Schippel as a party newcomer and criticizing him for cooperating with the commission and then turning against it. His major substantive points were that realization of the entire agrarian program would not alter the course of economic development, but only relieve the suffering of the peasantry; that the program did not contradict party principles; and that it would not cost the workers anything. If, as Kautsky claimed, many of the proposals in the program would only strengthen the capitalist state, asked Bebel, why has the state not already taken such steps? Many things were already nationalized, like social insurance and the railroads, and the workers benefited from them; why should the peasants not also get some help from the state? Bebel concluded his speech with a warning to the party: If it expected to bring an end to the agrarian question by accepting Kautsky's resolution, the members would be disappointed, because it was an immediate and pressing problem that would persist until dealt with practically. Kautsky followed Bebel and primarily reiterated most of the arguments presented before the congress convened. Besides pointing out that Bebel had failed to mention that workers in nationalized industries were not allowed to organize, Kautsky made two new points. First, the party was going at the whole thing backward. A declaration of principle was accepted at Frankfurt, and now the party was to decide on an agrarian program at Breslau; afterward, according to Bebel, the matter would be subjected to further study. Kautsky suggested that it would be more rational to study the matter thoroughly before making a decision on it. Second, Kautsky closed his speech by admitting that an agrarian program would win the SPD votes in the countryside, but argued that "at the decisive moment" the peasants would desert the party. In a rousing reassertion of the revolutionary roots of the party, he concluded: "We face great and difficult battles and must train comrades-in-arms who are resolved to share everything with us and to fight the great fight to the end."[47]

Despite Bebel's prestige and persuasive speech, Kautsky's resolution passed by a vote of 158 to 63; it was one of very few party votes Bebel ever lost. The proportion of Reichstag members who voted against Kautsky's resolution was four times higher than those who voted for it, but only two of the twelve members of the party leadership opposed it. Most party members who had been or were to be associated with the right wing voted against the resolution, but many did not, including Blos and Geiser, Kautsky's old antagonists. Karl was immensely pleased with the congress because it had reaffirmed the party's class character and stopped the invasion of nonsocialist oppositional elements. Bebel, on the other hand, saw Breslau as a victory for dogmatism and a certain source of future divisiveness. Both men were wrong in part, and both erred in their evaluations of the party and the issue. Kautsky mistakenly assumed that the proponents of the agrarian program intended to abandon the party's commitment to the proletariat, when in fact most of them only sought to exploit other sources of discontent within the Reich. Only an enormously successful campaign among the peasantry could have changed the working-class nature of the party membership and leadership. Not even Vollmar had such illusions about how much support the SPD could win from the peasants even with an agrarian program. Even if appeals to the peasantry were successful, according to Kautsky's own theory the number of peasants would continue to decrease and the number of workers continue to increase. Kautsky also assumed that his distinction between electoral campaign appeals to the peasants and exclusion of peasant planks from the party program was one that rank-and-file members would perceive. But on this, as on many other issues, Kautsky was being far too subtle. Most of the congressional delegates supported the Kautsky resolution because their cultural and emotional prejudices made them see the peasants as part of the backward-looking, archaic forces that kept workers and their party isolated and scorned. This was where Bebel made his mistake also. What he saw as dogmatism was in fact the powerful emotional identification of the delegates with the good cause of the industrial workers. The very institution of the annual congress served to reinforce powerfully the prevalent feeling among party members that they were comrades serving a just purpose. Kautsky's major error was his failure to recognize that theoretical condemnation would not retard the growth of antirevolutionary elements in the party. He could not follow up his victory in theory with organizational reforms or expulsions that would have "purified" the party membership. Vollmar and his south German reformist forces may have lost the battle, but they soon realized that they were still winning the war.[48]

Bebel had predicted that the agrarian question would persist, and it did. Less than a year after Breslau, the party's propeasant elements received a tremendous new stimulus when the results of the official 1895 occupational census were published. Between 1882 and 1895 the number of middle-sized agrarian holdings (12.5 to 50 acres) had increased, both absolutely and relatively, and the south Germans made much of it. In 1899 Kautsky published *The Agrarian Question,* in which he emphasized the intensity of exploitation of the land, rather than the size of the holding, as critical to the question of survival under capitalism; technical inferiority would doom independent peasants even if the size of their holdings increased slightly. Eduard David, one of the leaders of the SPD propeasant forces, rebutted Kautsky's book in 1903 with his own *Socialism and Agriculture,* which Kautsky, in turn, criticized in a long series in the *Neue Zeit.* But even then the issue did not die. Though the SPD never made great gains among the peasantry, especially in the Catholic-dominated regions of the south, Vollmar and his followers continued after 1895 to direct their energies toward winning peasant converts. In later years, the south Germans became nearly a separate party, pursuing reformism and compromise quite in contradiction of official party policy. Kautsky had said before Breslau that a split at that time was necessary if the party were to avoid becoming an indistinguishable mass of discontents. But having won his point in theory, he was content to let practice take care of itself. In the years after Breslau, he continued to man the barricades of theory while the reformists ignored the party program and solidified their regional power base.[49]

Tactical Issues and the Paris Congress

The proper conduct of a socialist party in a hostile political system was the major tactical question confronting German and international socialism in the years before the First World War. In Germany before 1905, the major problems included in this category were, in addition to the agrarian question, whether or not the party should participate in elections under Prussia's three-class franchise, and the propriety of entering into election compromises with left-bourgeois parties in Reichstag elections. On the international level the particularly thorny problem of if and when a socialist could accept a ministry in a bourgeois government was added to this list. It was a major issue at the 1900 Paris congress of the Second International. Two years earlier a French socialist, Alexandre Millerand, had accepted Premier Waldeck-Rousseau's offer of the ministry of commerce, thus becoming the first European socialist to accept a governmental post under nonrevolutionary conditions and forcing to the fore the issue of the extent to which socialists could cooperate with a nonproletarian government. Those within the French movement who objected to Millerand's action sought to have the International condemn participation. Kautsky's positions on these matters revealed his flexibility on political issues, but were also further examples of his failure to perceive the interaction of theory and practice and his tendency to make overly subtle distinctions.

All of Kautsky's judgments on political questions were predicated on several assumptions. First, he assumed that an independent, socialist, working-class party was a necessity, given the modern class struggle. Second, he rejected as absurd the view represented by the phrase "one reactionary mass" and argued that at times socialists had to support bad liberal candidates against worse reactionary or conservative candidates — the socialists had to use the disunity of the opposition to their own advantage. Third, he was convinced that bad theory was far more dangerous than bad practice and was willing to accept a good deal of practical compromise as long as its justification did not involve deviation from acceptable theory. Fourth, he trusted to the inevitable development of capitalist economics to ensure that the conflicting class interests of the proletariat and the bourgeoisie would always prevent the formation of any but the most transient coalitions between the two. And finally, he felt that certain political forms, namely the traditional bourgeois freedoms and republican government, were of such importance to the workers that the need to defend them could temporarily take precedence over the bourgeois-proletarian class struggle. According to Kautsky, a staunchly independent, theoretically sound workers' party could use elections and parliamentary activity to advance its own cause by entering into agreements with nonproletarian parties and by siding on certain issues with liberal opponents of the workers against reactionary opponents of the workers.

The 1893 party congress passed a resolution proposed by Bebel rejecting participation in the Prussian Landtag elections because of the three-class franchise system which prevailed there. Under this system the wealthy were favored by a weighted voting system that effectively reduced the possibility of the election of a working-class candidate. Though Kautsky, still in Stuttgart at the time, was cautious about passing definitive judgment from a distance, he was inclined to agree with Bernstein's opposition to the congressional decision. In fact, he soon elaborated this vague position into a strong stand in favor of active involvement in just such situations. In a letter to Adler, he condemned the English Social Democrats, and most of the SPD, for accepting the notion of "one reactionary mass" and not considering the advantages of cooperation with nonproletarian, left-bourgeois parties. He argued that in England and in Germany the socialists were not strong enough to rule, but they were strong enough to influence "the struggles of the old parties with one another and to give them the direction which our interests require." Kautsky felt that it was mostly the youth of the German party for whom opposition to compromise was like "atheistic fanaticism," but he also held that "our leaders blow the same horn," especially Liebknecht.[50]

By 1897 conditions in Prussia and the Prussian Landtag had changed in such a way that various groups in the SPD began to call for reconsideration of the 1893 resolution against participation. The Junkers of Prussia seemed to be gaining strength on the *Land* level, and as regionalism limited the ability of the Reichstag to act, the *Land* representative bodies started taking on more importance. When in early 1897 the Prussian Landtag only narrowly rejected a bill proposed by the Junkers to further restrict assembly and coalition rights, an outcry went up in the SPD for greater involvement in Prussian Landtag elections in order to try to stave off Junker oppression. Kautsky was in full sympathy with this position, and in two *Neue Zeit* articles that appeared before the 1897 party congress, he argued in favor of participation in the Prussian elections. Though he emphasized that the most efficacious kind of electoral agitation was still that aimed at electing SPD representatives, he argued that the Prussian situation offered the party a chance to weaken the Junkers, expand its sphere of activity, intensify the fight for a general franchise in Prussia, and perhaps even elect some candidates of its own. He pointed out that for years the party had informally followed the policy of voting for left-liberal candidates in Reichstag runoff elections without demanding reciprocity, "not to render those gentlemen a favor, but because it serves the interests of liberal development and the proletariat to let none of the great bourgeois parties get too powerful and the opposition too weak." If this policy was acceptable on the national level, it made even more sense in opposition to the Prussian Junkers. At this time (1897), he also argued that "one reactionary mass" was clearly not prevailing in Prussia, that even the most narrow-minded liberal opponents of the workers had to realize that the Junkers were more dangerous than the socialists.[51] His only caution was this:

> As long as we preserve our proletarian character, corruption from cooperation with other parties is not to be feared, even if occasional mistakes, which can nowhere be entirely avoided, should appear. On the other hand, if we give up [our] proletarian character, we lose the firmest ground under our feet and become a ball of the most contradictory interests, like the anti-Semites. Compromises in action are not dangerous, but those in program are.[52]

Kautsky suggested that the specifics of participation had to be worked out on the local level, and both he and Bebel considered the whole project experimental. At the 1897 Hamburg congress, the main speaker in favor of repealing the 1893 resolution, Ignaz Auer, expressed his own and the party's agreement with Kautsky's sentiments. The resolution in favor of participation in the Prussian Landtag elections passed by 145 votes to 64.[53]

Two years after the Hamburg congress Kautsky both reinforced and qualified the general position he espoused during the discussion of the Prussian Landtag election issue. The occasion this time was the Dreyfus affair in France. What began as the obscure persecution of a Jewish army officer accused of treason became one of the greatest political causes of the French Third Republic. After the publication in January 1898 of Emile Zola's *J'Accuse*, in which the duplicity and suspiciousness of the charges against Dreyfus were dramatically revealed, the affair quickly developed into a life-and-death struggle between the defenders of the Republic on one side, mainly liberal and socialist politicians and intellectuals, and the enemies of the Republic on the other, mainly the church and the army. Though many French socialists argued that the entire affair was none of their concern, a purely bourgeois matter, several leading figures of the French movement became convinced that the affair did pose questions of vital importance to socialists, namely the preservation of evenhanded justice, limitations on the power of the army, and the survival of the Republic. Led by the most impressive of their politicians, Jean Jaurès, the French socialists by early 1899 had generally made Dreyfus's cause their own.[54]

Earlier in the Dreyfus affair, in June 1898, Millerand had accepted the ministerial post offered by the Radical leader Waldeck-Rousseau. Both the affair and Millerand's action prompted response from Kautsky. He had high praise and great admiration for Jaurès's stand and argued that nothing could be more disastrous than for a "fighting class" like the proletariat to assume neutrality in a crisis that affected the welfare of the entire nation. It was not only the right, but also the duty of social democrats everywhere to take part in differences between bourgeois parties "in the interests of freedom and humanity." He advised vigorous action on the part of French socialists because the advanced workers would instinctively realize the importance of the affair, and therefore the socialists must take the lead or lose out to the liberal bourgeoisie. Furthermore, he saw the Dreyfus affair as part of what he called "the great reactionary movement" of Europe which was characterized by the advance of militarism and the bankruptcy of liberalism. On the other hand, Kautsky condemned Millerand's action for two reasons. First, the inclusion in the cabinet of General Gallifet, the bloody suppressor of the Paris Commune, made it shameful for any socialist to take part in that government. But more significantly in the long run, Kautsky felt that Millerand had made a serious tactical error, that the Dreyfus affair demanded only that the socialists stand behind the bourgeois ministry in its fight against the military. Though he insisted that the issue was tactical, not theoretical, Kautsky argued that under the circumstances Millerand had unnecessarily exposed himself and the French movement to the dangers of major compromise with the forces of the bourgeoisie.[55]

At the 1900 Paris congress of the Second International, the issues raised by the Dreyfus and Millerand affairs were the center of attention. Kautsky found himself in a curious position at this congress: His resolution, which opposed entering into electoral alliances with bourgeois parties but approved socialist entry into bourgeois governments under extraordinary conditions and with prior party approval, was opposed by the section of the multifaceted French movement that he supported. The Parti ouvrier francais (POF), headed by Jules Guesde, was generally considered the Marxist wing of French socialism, and of the several socialist parties in France, it had the most in common with the SPD. But Guesde and the Italian socialist Enrico Ferri proposed their own resolution which condemned participation by socialists in a bourgeois government under any conditions. Kautsky objected to this as too restrictive, because conditions could not be anticipated sufficiently to know what might happen in the future. In tactical matters he felt strongly that socialists had to preserve "the necessary elasticity for the unfathomable future." To defend his position, he offered two examples of when the German socialists might conceivably enter a government of the left-wing parties: to wage a "people's war" against a Russian invasion, or if "fundamental democratic institutions" were in danger and could be saved in no other way. Kautsky's arguments carried the day. After the Paris congress, he took pains to reassert his support for the Guesdists, but he continued to insist that in this case they had erred.[56]

Revisionism

While the debates over participation, defense of republican institutions, and ministerialism were going on, another and ultimately more disruptive crisis was slowly emerging within the ranks of German socialism. This was the theoretical dispute centering on Eduard Bernstein's revisionism. Bernstein began to develop his new views in a series of articles that appeared the *Neue Zeit*. The series, entitled "Problems of Socialism," ran in eight parts from November 1896 through the summer of 1898, but the active debate raged until 1903 and smoldered long after that. The controversy provoked by these articles eventually came very close to splitting the party, and it destroyed the intimate friendship of Bernstein and Kautsky. It spilled over into the international socialist arena and even today remains one of the most intriguing of the many doctrinal disputes marking the history of socialism. No event in Kautsky's life up to 1914 caused him so much anguish as his split with Bernstein, and nothing forced him to defend his Marxism so carefully and strongly as the confrontation with revisionism.[57]

Ironically, Bernstein's articles appeared in numbers of the *Neue Zeit* containing a polemic between Kautsky and an English socialist, Ernest Belfort-Bax, concerning the nature and limits of the materialist conception of history. The irony was that Bax criticized Bernstein while Kautsky defended his long-time friend. The polemic itself was not particularly imaginative, and as usual in the *Neue Zeit*, it was weighted in Kautsky's favor from the start by virtue of his control of the journal. Kautsky criticized Bax as a false friend who claimed to be a Marxist but was in fact an idealist. Bax countered with attacks on Kautsky for nit-picking and dogmatism, but was unable to refute Kautsky's points effectively. Karl pointed out that though Bax claimed agreement on three-quarters of the issues involved, the last quarter, the extent to which Bax claimed ideas have independent determinative qualities in history, was what made Bax's position that of a "sentimental utopian." On several occasions during the exchange, Kautsky referred to himself and Bernstein as major proponents of true Marxism. At the end of one article, Kautsky belittled Bax's contention that Bernstein had "unconsciously ceased to be a social democrat" in accepting as inevitable the expansion of capitalism into the Armenian region of Turkey. Before too long, Kautsky would condemn Bernstein for a conscious and dastardly desertion of Marxism in terms that made Bax's criticism seem mild indeed.[58]

Revisionism has already been dealt with in other sources, though its importance has usually been misinterpreted and the depth and substance of its theoretical content exaggerated by American and English scholars. Bernstein's major point was that the SPD should stop talking like a revolutionary Marxian party because it acted like a reformist party willing to work within the existing system. He underpinned this demand with theoretical revisions which rejected the Hegelian, dialectical materialist roots of Marxism and sought to establish a Kantian, ethical socialism as the doctrine of the SPD. Bernstein also denied the validity of the Marxian notions of value theory, recurrent crisis, the prevalence of class struggle, and the need for a purely proletarian political party. His famous dictim emphasizing the importance of the movement itself and the insignificance of its socialist and revolutionary aims ("the goal is nothing, the movement everything") was in fact a clear statement of the theoretical paucity of his position. Bernstein was not a subtle thinker, but an eclectic autodidact. While his revisionist writings may have accurately outlined the position of a certain faction of the SPD, they did not capture the spirit prevalent among the ordinary party members, who shared an intense conviction of the uniqueness of the proletariat and the reality in imperial Germany of the class struggle of orthodox theory. However, those Social Democrats who had long been trying to expand the party's appeal beyond the working class greeted Bernstein's theoretical support for their practical actions with open arms. Men like Vollmar, David, and others welcomed Bernstein's theory as a weapon to be used against the consistent Marxists of the party, at whose head Kautsky stood.[59]

Tremendous amounts of time and energy were squandered on the revisionist controversy in the SPD press and at party congresses. Bernstein's theory was officially renounced at the 1899 Hanover congress by a vote of 216 to 21, and again at the 1903 Dresden congress by a vote of 288 to 11. At Hanover, the party specifically rejected its own conversion into "a democratic-socialist reform party," and at Dresden it specifically denied that the class struggle was weakening. Despite the virtual unanimity of opposition to Bernstein, he was still able to stir up controversy because he brought into the theoretical arena the persistent but often covert conflict within the SPD between the moderates and the radicals. The opposing positions had been debated, with Bernstein on the radical side, during the antisocialist law period when the *Sozialdemokrat* and the Reichstag *Fraktion* disagreed on tactics; radicals and moderates had battled over state socialism in the early nineties; they engaged in an ongoing conflict concerning the party's relationship to the agrarian population; and they would dispute many other questions after the revisionism crisis faded away. But in each of these cases, the radical or "orthodox" position represented best by Karl Kautsky won official approval without altering or demanding alteration of party actions that perpetuated the moderate-radical division. The apparent paradox of this situation can only be reconciled if the function of theory in the German socialist movement and in Kautsky's perception of that movement is understood.[60]

Many contemporary observers felt that Bernstein merely brought the party's theory into touch with the political realities of Germany, and most historians have agreed with this evaluation. But in fact this was not so. With the exception of the preservation of the exclusively proletarian character of the party, Bernstein and Kautsky disagreed on very few questions of tactics. Their voluminous debate in party journals and newspapers was almost solely concerned with theory, specifically whether certain Marxian assumptions—value theory, recurrent crisis, concentration, immiserization, and others—fit the available facts or not. And yet the central issue of the revisionism debate was not really the content of the theory but its function in the life of the party. Kautsky recognized this at the 1898 party congress, the first time he made any public statement on Bernstein's new theory. He expressed his astonishment that Bernstein felt compelled to emphasize certain points on which there was in fact no disagreement within the party—that legal activities were more favorable than illegal ones; that the more successful the party was, the more its opponents would be forced into illegal actions; and that the major tasks of the party were democratic and economic reforms and promoting the organization of the proletariat. The disagreement came, according to Kautsky, on the issue of what all this meant. Bernstein, judging from his observations of England, concluded that through democracy the proletariat could achieve political power, and Kautsky agreed that this was so in England. But in Germany things were different; in Germany no forces for democracy besides the workers existed, so the victory of democracy depended on the victory of the proletariat. Because of this, Kautsky argued, the way recommended by Bernstein would spell disaster in his native country. Instead of urging the workers to cooperate with an undemocratic bourgeoisie, as Bernstein was, in effect, suggesting, official party theory provided the workers with self-confidence, with the certainty of victory. Theory thus became practice for Kautsky; one of the tactics of the party was to teach the workers the reality of the German condition by emphasizing the uniqueness of the proletariat. The rest of the debate between Kautsky and Bernstein revolved around this central point. Both men agreed that cooperation with nonproletarian democratic groups for the peaceful conversion of capitalism into socialism would be ideal, but Kautsky claimed that this path could not be followed in Germany. Conditions there made the radical implications of Marxism valid, and thus he argued vigorously that the Marxian analysis was correct in Germany.[61]

This question of whether revisionism or Kautsky's Marxism was more in touch with the realities of the party and Germany is one of the most important in the historiographical literature on the SPD. A great many historians have contended that Bernstein was simply recognizing the nature of the party and rejecting Kautsky's revolutionary language as fantasy. But neither these historians nor Bernstein himself realized that no matter how much the SPD said it wanted to cooperate with bourgeois liberals, two sides are required for cooperation, and most German liberals simply would not join into coalitions with the "unpatriotic," antireligious socialists. Furthermore, Bernstein never confronted the question of what would happen if the socialists won an overwhelming majority of the seats in the Reichstag. The highest representative body in Wilhelmine Germany could not have opposed the wishes of the kaiser and his court clique even if it had wanted to. As Kaiser Wilhelm II delighted in pointing out, if he ordered the army to shoot all the Reichstag representatives, it would. Even though the SPD may have been a central focus of politics in the Second Reich, and even though the kaiser and his men worried about the attitudes of both the Reichstag and the SPD, there really was never any practical hope that either the Reichstag or the socialists would simply grow into power. On the other hand, the situation of a unanimously oppositional Reichstag would have been critical, and the tension created by this situation would certainly have brought major upheaval to Germany. If this is so, then Kautsky's view of pursuing growth and election as preparation for revolution was eminently realistic, while Bernstein's assumption that revolution could be avoided by gradual growth and compromise was naive.

All this is not to suggest, of course, that theory was incidental to the revisionism crisis or that the long theoretical disputes were sterile intellectual game-playing. Kautsky's view of the function of theory in the working-class movement ensured that he would stoutly defend his "orthodoxy" against Bernstein's assault. For Kautsky, Bernstein's emphasis on the immediate, day-to-day aspects of the movement spelled disaster for the SPD. Without systematic theoretical guidance, the workers would flounder in the morass of petty politics and narrowly focused economic demands. Therefore Kautsky was convinced that defending the theoretical framework which he had laboriously erected for the SPD was vitally important to the survival of the movement.

Kautsky also had a deep personal commitment to Marxism. For almost twenty years he had devoted himself exclusively to the task of studying, clarifying, and popularizing Marx's work. This deduction both reflected and intensified his psychological investment in Marxism, which made the defense against revisionism necessary in personal terms. He revealed this aspect of his response to revisionism when he wrote to Bernstein: "Should sometime the materialist conception of history and the conception of the proletariat as the motive force of the coming social revolution be vanquished, then I would certainly have to confess I would be finished, then my life would have no more meaning."[62] He was signaling to his friend the depth of his commitment.

The theoretical disputes during the revisionism crisis eventually covered virtually every aspect of Marxism from the materialist conception of history to value theory to the intensity of the class struggle. One particular part of the debate deserves special attention here because of what it revealed about the importance of politics to Kautsky's interpretation of Marxism. This was his discussion of the phenomenon called *Verelendung,* which is somewhat awkwardly translated into English as "immiserization."

Marx had argued that one of the inevitable consequences of capitalist production was the increasing depth and breadth of poverty among the proletariat. He held that this increasing immiserization would lead to increasing social tension in the form of the class struggle, which in turn would yield the revolution that would introduce socialism. But by the early twentieth century it was clear that in most mature capitalist systems the industrial proletariat was in fact enjoying a rising standard of living. Eduard Bernstein, among others, took this as a sign that Marx's predictions were wrong, and in fact this view was a major precept of revisionism.

Kautsky developed his own mature view of *Verelendung* in response to Bernstein's argument. In so doing he reinforced his contention that class cooperation on a major and long-term scale was not possible in Wilhelmine Germany. He also made politics more important than economics by arguing that the ever increasing class struggle was not the product of "the actual immiserization of the mass of the people," but of the continual social and political assault on the working class made by the ruling classes.[63] This may seem a major deviation from Marx's own writings, which fairly clearly and unambiguously asserted that, on the whole, capitalism as an economic system demands the increasing exploitation of the workers in the form of getting more work for less pay. But Marx, too, emphasized politics a good deal, especially in his histories. Furthermore, Kautsky's theory was a response to the realities of German society, where large numbers of organized workers were increasing their real wages, and where increasing political tensions with the growth of the SPD reached new levels by the 1907 Reichstag campaign. These apparently contradictory developments were in large part the basis of the theoretical disputes of revisionism against orthodoxy.

The revisionism crisis was far more than just another doctrinal dispute for Kautsky; it was a serious personal matter that forced him into agonizing reappraisal of his almost twenty-year relationship with Bernstein. The two had been inseparable companions during the Zurich years and while both were in London, and they had maintained a regular correspondence after Kautsky returned to Germany. Besides defending Bernstein against Bax's attacks, Kautsky had long been considering Ede, as close friends called Bernstein, as a possible coeditor of the *Neue Zeit*. Undoubtedly this close personal relationship was the major cause of Kautsky's long delay in attacking revisionism. Though as early as 12 November 1896 he was complaining mildly to Adler about some of Bernstein's minor lapses, not until late 1897 did he directly confront Ede himself, and not until March 1899 did he launch a major attack in print. Other Marxian theoreticians, especially Rosa Luxemburg and Georgi Plekhanov, attacked Bernstein's deviations much more quickly. But not just his close friendship with

Bernstein delayed Kautsky's criticism, he was also receiving contradictory signals from his two main advisors on political matters, August Bebel and Victor Adler.[64]

Once it became clear to Kautsky that Bernstein was falling away from the Marxian fold, he turned to Adler for counsel. Early in March 1898, Karl wrote to Luise: "I do not know what I should think of Ede. What does Adler say about it?" What Adler said was that he did not understand what Kautsky was so upset about. He argued that Bernstein's writings were useful and timely reminders of the need to rethink old positions which may have simply become slogans. But by the spring of 1898, Kautsky had begun to worry about Ede. Tussy Marx reported from London that Bernstein had grown irritable and difficult to live with. She advised Kautsky that Bernstein should be removed from England and brought back into contact with Kautsky and the German movement in order to overcome "Ede's present unhappy sceptical pessimism." In her last letter to Kautsky, Tussy wrote: "You alone can make Ede our own Ede again. It hurts me more than I can say to write this. . . . Ede is so dear a friend that it is horrible to see things as they are just now." Almost immediately Kautsky started trying to devise plans to get Bernstein out of England, suggesting that perhaps he could be made an editor of the *Neue Zeit*, which would at least allow him to live in Zurich. He even asked Adler if it would be possible for Ede to find sufficient work in Vienna and commented, "Ede in Vienna and me in Berlin, of all things that would be [an] upside-down world." However, as Bernstein continued to pursue his revision of Marxism, Kautsky's reaction began to harden. By late May 1898, he was warning Bernstein that his writings were aiding the enemies of social democracy. In August, he wrote to Adler of Ede's "unbelievable theoretical retrogression," but still he felt that a great deal of toleration was necessary. The following month found Bebel entering the fray, noting that Bernstein clearly misunderstood his isolation in the German party. By late September, Kautsky was still expressing his reluctance to attack Bernstein in print, because although "it may begin objectively and friendly, a polemic always ends with a quarrel." Finally on 24 September 1898, Bebel expressed his satisfaction that Kautsky had at last come to realize that Bernstein was beyond salvation and that a break between the two former inseparables was about to come.[65]

Having decided that Ede was no longer a Marxist, Kautsky pursued a three-pronged course vis-à-vis revisionism and Bernstein personally. First, in his letters to his friend, he became increasingly sharp in his criticism and more and more strongly urged Bernstein to show the courage of his convictions by ending his affiliation with the *Neue Zeit* and leaving the party. Second, in his public critique of Bernstein, Kautsky tried to moderate the growing severity of attacks by people like Luxemburg and Plekhanov by writing conciliatory articles. And third, in personal terms he wrestled with his attachment to Bernstein, the contradictory advice from Bebel and Adler, and his growing distress with Bernstein's failure to admit and live up to the isolation of revisionism within the party. Karl honestly sought to avoid the bitter split he dreaded but thought inevitable. To Bernstein, he wrote: "You declare false the value theory, the dialectic, materialism, the class struggle, the proletarian character of our movement . . . what of Marxism is left there?" He insisted that Bernstein was capitulating the bourgeois critics by trying to find a compromise between liberalism and Marxism. He warned that their cooperation could not continue because "as long as I edit [the *Neue Zeit*], it will be an organ of Marxism, not an eclectic organ *à la Soz[ialistische] Monatshefte* or *Revue socialiste*."[66]

Adler's advice was to avoid forcing Bernstein further to the right by moderating criticism of him still more. Adler felt that the tactical differences were not significant, but he did recognize that Kautsky "must tear his soul away from Ede, . . . the Kautsky-Bernstein double star no longer exists." Adler also warned against expelling Bernstein from the party because he might be more dangerous outside than in. But Bebel took a strikingly different position in the dispute. Besides arguing that Bernstein's tactics were fundamentally different from those of social democracy, Bebel also tied tactics and principles to one another, calling the revisionist controversy the "to be or not to be" of the party. Bebel argued that Adler had misjudged Kautsky's position, that Karl had tried for a year to "save" Ede. By late 1898, Kautsky had given up hope that Bernstein would leave the party and the *Neue Zeit* voluntarily. Although terribly saddened by Ede's position, he knew that nothing could prevent a nasty break.[67]

Bernstein, following Kautsky's suggestion, collected his observations into a book, and in March 1899 this most comprehensive statement of revisionism was published. It was entitled *The Presuppositions of Socialism and the Tasks of Social Democracy*, but its English translations are usually called *Evolutionary Socialism*. In order to set a moderate tone for the party discussion that was sure to follow publication, Kautsky and Bernstein both encouraged Adler to be the first to respond to the book. Adler reluctantly accepted the challenge, but cautioned Kautsky about his own "philistine scorn of theory," saying that he approached the book with "the preconceived desire to find it possible that Ede and the very, very many who are with him do not stand outside the scope of the party." This caution did not prevent Kautsky from writing Adler letters on two successive days denouncing Bernstein's book in no uncertain terms. "What [Bernstein] writes about the materialist conception of history is shallow platitude," Karl claimed; "about the dialectic, simply absurd; about value theory, baseless." Although the editors of the *Vorwärts* were pressing him to attack Bernstein, he declined to do so until he heard from Adler. But he also reported that he would give Dietz an ultimatum: "Either B[ernstein] goes or I go." Apparently Karl carried out this threat at a 16 March meeting attended by Dietz, Singer, Bebel, and Kautsky. All but the first agreed that Bernstein's close association with the *Neue Zeit* would have to end. When Dietz balked at dropping Bernstein unless he left of his own free will, Kautsky reported to Adler, "I replied that then I would go." In a later letter to Adler, Bebel supported Kautsky's account of the meeting.[68]

As far as Kautsky's role in the revisionist controversy was concerned, 16 March 1899 was an important day: He received the reassuring news that, having·read Bernstein's book, Adler was more upset with Bernstein than with Kautsky. Adler was bothered by Bernstein's arrogance, by his assumption that he was the "only cool head" in the party. But Adler was even more disturbed by the degree of cooperation with the bourgeoisie called for by Bernstein. Although he finally wrote to Bernstein urging that he end his permanent association with the *Neue Zeit*, the Austrian socialist leader also cautioned Kautsky against siding with the "literati and fanatics," like Plekhanov and Parvus. Adler still insisted that Bernstein's "foolishness" had not gone so far as to place him outside the party. On this day Kautsky's first lengthy public criticism of Bernstein appeared in the *Vorwärts*.[69]

On the following day Karl expressed his relief upon learning about Adler's negative response to *Evolutionary Socialism* and noted that he was receiving many other negative responses as well. He explained his relief to Adler in this way: "After the aplomb with which Ede came forward in Stuttgart, one had to think he was overladen with factual material, and now he has nothing other than a few hastily gathered, meaningless numbers from the *Handbook of Political Science*. That is a scandal for anyone who has the British Museum at his disposal." As for his own critique, the second installment of which appeared on 17 March, Kautsky contended that "it was as mild as possible," but he promised a sharper attack in the *Neue Zeit*.[70]

Shortly after Kautsky's first critique of Bernstein appeared in the *Vorwärts*, Bebel began to goad the party theoretician on to a sharper attack. Having given Kautsky more than two years to overcome his reluctance to criticize his friend, Bebel had decided that the time had come to strike hard against a dangerous deviation. This was the first of many times Bebel was to encourage Kautsky to adopt a more vigorous line of criticism. The party leader wrote to Karl: "I want to advise you to pounce sharply on Ede in working out your [new] articles; just no vagueness. Your articles for the *Vorwärts*, as I heard from many sides, did not make the impression they should have." Bernstein found Bebel's position curious because the dogmatism of his theory contrasted with his clearheaded practical leadership. But Bebel's view, in direct contrast to Adler's, was that just because Bernstein attracted a following, especially among the leading figures in the party, revisionism had to be pursued to the point of a break. While Kautsky, concerned about Bernstein's well-being after he left the *Neue Zeit*, discussed with Adler plans to set Bernstein up as the head of an English workers' secretariat to provide the continental press with regular information on the English movement, Bebel continued to marvel at how little Bernstein seemed to understand the precariousness of his position in the German movement. Bebel strongly advised Bernstein to admit the irreconcilability of his dispute with Kautsky and to leave the *Neue Zeit* voluntarily.[71]

Finally, the first phase of the revisionism crisis came to a close in late 1899. In preparation for the impending Hanover congress, Kautsky wrote his rebuttal to Bernstein's book and sent the proofs to Bebel for review. Bebel's immediate response was strongly positive. He felt that at last Bernstein would have to realize that further cooperation with Kautsky was impossible, and also that Bernstein, "if he possesses a morsel of self-awareness, will see how he goes astray." But a few days later Bebel sent Kautsky a sharply worded letter criticizing the last part of the second chapter of Karl's book. Bebel was very distressed that Kautsky had suggested that perhaps the party program should be changed in certain places, feeling that this was a concession to Bernstein that *"powerfully weakened"* Kautsky's critique. Bebel at first admitted that these changes might be necessary later, but that the time was not right for suggesting them; two days later he decided that no program changes were justified. When Kautsky accepted Bebel's criticisms and made all the recommended alterations, Bebel once again expressed his pleasure with the book. Bebel also praised Kautsky's *Neue Zeit* article aimed at setting the stage for a renunciation of Bernstein's views at Hanover in October. Of course that congress soundly rejected revisionism, and in May 1900, Bernstein announced his withdrawal from the journal to readers of the *Neue Zeit*. A few months earlier the formal break between the two friends had been marked when Kautsky stopped signing his letters to Bernstein with the nickname "Baron," used only with close party comrades and friends, and began to sign himself "K.K." or "K. Kautsky." This split lasted for some years.[72]

Relations between Kautsky and Bernstein deteriorated even further after 1900, despite Adler's efforts to preserve peace. For a time the prevalent emotion on Kautsky's part was sadness at the loss of a dear friend. From the Paris congress of the Second International, in September 1900, he wrote to Luise: "I also saw Ede. Victor [Adler] once again had the need for a great reconciliation scene. We touched hands and asked, *wie geht's,* and separated again. And that is all." But the persistence of the revisionist forces soon converted Kautsky's sadness into anger. He could not understand why Bernstein insisted on remaining in the party and felt that by so doing Ede was simply poisoning the SPD in order to destroy it. Kautsky's view was that the revisionists "do not form the right wing of our party, but a new party which is too cowardly or too weak or too unclear to detach itself from us, and which therefore bores into us." In the summer of 1901, Kautsky cut short a cold-water cure he was taking at the Sulz spa in Austria because he felt the need to return to Berlin to defend the *Neue Zeit* from the assaults of "Bernstein and his people." He had gone to Sulz to recover from the nervous stress brought on by overwork and the revisionist controversy.[73]

Despite Kautsky's wish to end the debate, revisionism persisted, and Bebel's frequent urgings to strike against the revisionists and their reformist allies forced a continuation of the polemic. Late in 1901, Bebel urged Kautsky to criticize those in the party who favored protective tariffs, which the party had traditionally opposed, and shortly before the 1903 Dresden party congress, Bebel once again exhorted Kautsky to be more severe with the revisionists. The loss of Bernstein's friendship, coupled with the constant aggravation of the polemic against the revisionists, sometimes made Kautsky long for Austria. He frequently expressed a feeling of alienation from even his closest German contacts like Bebel. He claimed that Adler was the person to whom he felt closest, but added that despite all the difficulties he would not leave Germany. "For my intellectual and political development," he wrote to Adler, "Germany is . . . more advantageous than Austria, and I dare not exchange this for anything."[74]

Between 1900 and 1904, Kautsky formulated a view of revisionism that explained the emergence of the doctrine as a result of European-wide developments in the politics of modern, capitalist society. Although he based his evaluation largely on the German situation, he also applied his analysis to other countries, especially France. The extent to which the revisionist debate and the continued political isolation of the SPD radicalized Kautsky's thought was clearly revealed in the tone of his work after 1900. Basically, he saw revisionism, the faction of French socialism led by Jaurès, and the emergence of a new progressive party in England with the decline of the Liberals as examples of the "renaissance of bourgeois radicalism." He argued that these groups formed a "historically necessary manifestation" that could achieve certain things that the socialists could not.[75]

> But they cannot replace social democracy. They much more presuppose a strong social democracy . . . which stiffens their backbone and moves them forward. The new party must remain theoretically fruitless because it wants to reconcile contradictions, [and] is therefore incapable of a unified position and must behave eclectically, must live on loans from socialism and liberalism, and finally, because of these contradictions, the new party can only lead an ephemeral existence. . . . Bernstein's historical role is this: that in social democracy he first gave expression to this need and with that loudly spoke the silent heartfelt desire of an entire section of the people.[76]

Kautsky faulted Bernstein for failing to fulfill his historical role in Germany, for not breaking away from the SPD to form a left-bourgeois oppositional party.

To support his thesis in the case of Germany, Kautsky marshaled a wide variety of arguments, taking off in almost all cases from claims made by revisionists. For instance, to counter the revisionists' contention that class conflict was declining because the workers were gaining concessions from the system, he argued that this position failed to take into account collateral advances of the power of the capitalists. Thus, while it was true that the number of workers' consumer cooperatives was increasing, the concentration of capital was increasing at a faster rate; trade unions were growing, but employers associations were expanding more rapidly; and while legislation that protected workers was increasing, state support for capitalism, as in growing military expenditures, was increasing even more. Kautsky concluded from this that the lines were being more clearly drawn between bourgeois and social democratic forces. While the upper ranks of the bourgeoisie tied themselves more and more closely to the government, the lower ranks were cut adrift. Instead of the famous reactionary mass, socialists were faced with a "reactionary confusion."

Into this confusion moved the revived petit bourgeois radicalism that Kautsky associated with revisionism, and that he had earlier associated with the south German, peasant-oriented faction of the SPD. At the same time he argued that the increasing strength of the German workers forced the upper bourgeoisie, mainly the large industrialists and financiers, to become increasingly conservative and to rely more and more on the brutal tactics of the Junkers. His most convincing evidence of this tendency was the failure of the German liberals to cooperate with the SPD in opposition to the Junker and agrarian demands for higher tariffs and the increasing support of liberals for military expansion.[77]

Kautsky also used more strictly political arguments to substantiate his theory. He argued that the revisionist dream of a great coalition of the left was a chimera because where social democracy was strong, liberalism was weak. Both drew their support, in large part, from the same sources and therefore could not both be strong together. As evidence of this Kautsky cited the dismal failure of the coalition concept as applied to the Prussian Landtag elections. He argued that although the election of SPD representatives was good, the decline in the number of Radical representatives matched the socialist increases, leaving the balance the same. For Kautsky this also proved that "German liberalism, given the opportunity, prefers the conservatives to the Social Democrats, . . . [and this] can henceforth be considered an irrefutable rule which is only confirmed by the rare exception." Thus the SPD must not rely on the liberal bourgeoisie; liberalism would continue to decline as socialism advanced.[78]

However, Kautsky did not conclude from this political analysis that the SPD could grow into power in Germany simply by winning votes and mandates. He insisted that the established forces would not allow that, and furthermore that the modern parliamentary system was a sham. In very radical terms he denied that infrequent elections among a widely scattered, poorly informed electorate yielded anything but a parliament that was a tool of domination by the ruling classes. He called for close party control of SPD representatives who had to be responsible to the majority, that is, the entire party, not the minority, that is, the separate constituencies. With this demand, Kautsky reached a high-water mark in his radicalization in the wake of the revisionist challenge. He was responding to what he thought was a dangerous erosion of the ideal of proletarian independence which the revisionist concept of coalition represented. He was also responding to the fact that a large percentage of SPD Reichstag and Landtag members favored revisionism. Unfortunately for his own views, Kautsky once again was unable to translate his theoretical criticisms into organizational reforms. The character of the party remained unchanged.[79]

While he recognized the difficulties of fighting revisionism in the German party, Kautsky was content with theoretical condemnations by various party congresses, especially the 1903 Dresden meeting which passed an unqualified rejection of Bernstein's theory. But since Kautsky also saw revisionism as part of a European-wide phenomenon, he felt the need to deal with the matter in the Second International. At the 1904 Amsterdam congress of that body, the SPD's Dresden resolution against revisionism was presented by Jules Guesde in the form of an international resolution. By passing this the Amsterdam congress would achieve two things. First, it would condemn any sort of regular socialist support for bourgeois governments. Jaurès and his followers, although they had adhered to the letter of the Paris resolution against entry into a bourgeois government, had been supporting Waldeck-Rousseau's cabinet since the Dreyfus affair. Guesde, Kautsky, and others saw this as a violation of the spirit of the Paris resolution and a reformist subterfuge. Second, if a strongly united International congress were to come down on Guesde's side against Jaurès, the former's position would be greatly strengthened in France, and the unified French socialist party everyone sought would emerge with a more radical orientation than that favored by Jaurès.[80]

Emile Vandervelde, the leader of Belgian socialism, and Victor Adler argued in favor of a counterresolution at Amsterdam that would have kept the question of relations between socialists and the bourgeoisie where Kautsky's Paris resolution had left it, namely a rejection of participation but not necessarily of informal cooperation. Jaurès argued in favor of this position, saying that the Guesde resolution would simply impose the political impotence of the German party onto the whole of international socialism. The commission appointed to draft the resolution approved Guesde's version, and the congress as a whole passed it also, twenty-seven to three with ten abstentions. Yet despite this apparent victory, Kautsky was dissatisfied with the results, and he was especially upset by Adler's support for the more moderate resolution. After the congress he patched up the differences with his Austrian friend, explaining that a chance to isolate and eventually eliminate Jaurès and his reformist followers had been missed at Amsterdam. Karl was angered that Adler and Vandervelde had spoiled the necessary spirit of unanimity, thus leaving the door open to Jaurès. He did not consider Adler himself a "secret revisionist," as Bebel had contended at Amsterdam, and in fact claimed that with respect to Austria, Adler's tactics were perfectly acceptable. But he did think that Adler was too easy on the deviations of others and not sufficiently sensitive to the dangers of revisionism or reformism.[81]

In a sense, the three years before the outbreak of the Russian revolution of 1905 represent an hiatus in Kautsky's career. In 1902, he published a book, *The Social Revolution,* in which he forcefully reiterated his orthodox line, and the success of the book encouraged him to believe that the way was being won, although he still had few illusions about the number of committed Marxists in the party. The year 1903 brought two major victories—the Reichstag elections, which gave the party more than a quarter of the popular vote and sent eighty-one socialists to the new house, and the Dresden congress which seemed to defeat the revisionists. But despite these achievements Kautsky was not entirely happy with things in the movement. For some time he had complained of a sort of "nervous degeneration" among the current group of German socialists. The iron men of the past, said Kautsky, men like Marx, Engels, even Lassalle and Liebknecht (who had died in 1900), were gone, and young and old alike stagnated. He argued that this resulted from "the rise of petty work, . . . because they see no great problems before them."[82]

Nonetheless, he still had great hope for the future. Even before the 1903 elections, Kautsky had perceived that "a great nervousness goes through the Reich." He anticipated that the stagnancy would soon come to an end since the government was being increasingly squeezed between an intractable agrarian-bourgeois ruling group and a rapidly growing, united socialist movement. He insisted that this situation could not last long.

> If [the government forces] imitate Gladstone and Waldeck-Rousseau, [if] they buy the leaders of the proletariat through some kind of cooperation, then we will have the same split which exists in France.
>
> But that is not likely. Neither the kaiser nor the Junkers and great industrialists are so clever as to follow this policy, which is most dangerous for us, which [Chancellor] Bülow would certainly do. Rather the opposite is to be expected. . . . we will catch a strong wind from above which [will] weld the party together and force the leaders of opportunism either to renounce opportunism or to join one of the less dangerous parties, . . . where they actually belong and to which they will be pulled when the comfort of social democracy comes to an end, and it does not merely pass out mandates, but also demands sacrifices.[83]

Kautsky realized that many might think this overly optimistic, but added, "what does life hold if one is not optimistic, if one does not see in the immediate future what will perhaps first be attained by our grandchildren?" This optimism was to be sorely tested by events after 1905.

CHAPTER FIVE

Challenge from the Left, 1905–1914

The Russian Revolution of 1905

BLOODY SUNDAY — 22 January 1905 — marked the beginning of the Russian revolution of 1905. On that day troops of the tsar fired on a peaceful protest march led by one Father Gapon, a police agent who was supposed to channel the despair of Russia's workers away from the tsarist government. The deaths and injuries that resulted symbolized the gap that had begun to open between Nicholas II, the "Little Father," and his people. In the months that followed, Russia, already badly strained by a losing war effort against the Japanese and the rule of an inept, archaic absolutism, was torn by rebellion. Urban workers and rural peasants, liberals and discontented intellectuals, but most importantly the navy and army, combined to protest land hunger, defeat, starvation, and the backwardness of the Russian state and society. In the end not much came of this revolution. By late 1906, the unrest had petered out as the sheer mass and inertia of governmental machinery wore down the protesters. A franchise law heavily weighted in favor of the landed and wealthy elected a parliament, the Duma, which had little power, and a few particularly offensive ministers were replaced by less incompetent men. But a promised constitution was never realized, and even the far-from-radical Duma was eventually dissolved. Fearing that any concession would spell the end of the glorious thousand-year rule of the Romanovs, Tsar Nicholas reneged on his promises and retired to safety behind the barriers of bureaucracy and loyal Cossack troops.[1]

International socialists were also rocked by the events of 1905. Since Nicholas I had aided in the suppression of the revolutionaries of 1848, progressive Europe had viewed Russia as a stronghold of the archconservative old order. If Russia could be so shaken, even nearly overturned by revolution, were not the hopes for socialist victory in the West much brightened? Furthermore, the Russian workers had shown the awesome potential of an old weapon, the mass strike. St. Petersburg, Moscow, and other major Russian cities had been paralyzed by a general walkout of factory and transportation workers. As early as 1893, discussion of the mass or general strike had been on the agenda of the Second International, and many times between then and 1905 such strikes in Belgium, Holland, and elsewhere had attracted the attention of socialists everywhere. But never before 1905 had the full potential of the mass strike been so graphically suggested. All of Europe's socialist parties, but especially the SPD, were gripped by a renewed and vigorous interest in the mass strike. For the SPD the debate over this weapon ended with a drastic change in the relationship between the party and the trade unions. As could be expected, Kautsky played a central role in the mass-strike debate.[2]

Like most non-Russian socialists, Kautsky had paid some attention to the land of the tsars before 1905, but he had not devoted a great deal of time to it. His view of Russia was that typically held by progressive Europeans in the late nineteenth century: It was an industrially backward, curiously foreign, and generally brutal country. Kautsky shared the anti-Russian prejudices of most German socialists, as evidenced by his singling out a Russian invasion as one possible justification for the formation of a broad coalition of the left in Germany. He also felt that Russia's backwardness would mean that the revolution in that country would not be a proletarian one, as it would in industrially advanced countries, but the traditional bourgeois revolution of an earlier period in western Europe. He argued that the revolution in Russia would find the proletariat leading the revolutionary intelligentsia, petite bourgeoisie, and peasantry to force their country into the modern era. He even suggested that a revolutionary element within the Russian officers corps would play an important part on the side of the revolutionaries, something he thought impossible in western Europe.[3]

Many of Kautsky's earliest works, including *Karl Marx's Economic Doctrines*, *Thomas More*, and *Class Struggles in France*, were translated into Russian within a year of their appearance in German. Through such works and personal contacts, Kautsky exercised a good deal of influence over the development of Russian Marxism. He also had closer personal ties with the Russian movement than did most leading figures in the SPD. During the Zurich years, Bernstein had introduced Karl to many Russian emigrés, most notably Pavel Axelrod, Vera Zasulich, and Georgi Plekhanov, three of the founders of Russian

Marxism. With Plekhanov and Axelrod, Kautsky established warm personal relations. Of all the figures in international socialism before World War I, few had more in common than Plekhanov and Kautsky. Both came from comfortable middle-class families; both had flirted with anarchism in their youth; and both ardently rejected organizational and administrative work in order to devote themselves to theory. Plekhanov held Kautsky in the highest esteem, and Kautsky frequently expressed his admiration for Plekhanov's intellectual abilities. Plekhanov and Axelrod, both of whom frequently contributed to the *Neue Zeit* and the rest of the German socialist press, were two of Kautsky's major sources of personal information on Russia and its Marxian movement.[4]

But Kautsky also had a third important source of information on Russian affairs in the brilliant Rosa Luxemburg. This remarkable young woman, born in 1871 of assimilated Jewish parents, came from the region of Poland dominated by Russia. Following her arrival on the German scene in the nineties, she became very close to the Kautsky family, especially Luise and the boys. Her relationship with Karl was at first that of respectful, but independent, student to acknowledged master; later one of equals; and finally one of icy and at times, at least on Luxemburg's side, vicious opposition. She was a harsh person who judged people in strict moralistic terms. An aggressive, effective polemicist, she had little compassion for human weakness or ignorance. She tended to overlook the possibility of honest disagreement, which she usually interpreted as personal attack or perfidy. Although Kautsky had great respect for her gifts, he also regretted her intolerance. In 1902, he observed that she was "an extraordinarily qualified woman, . . . but tact and a feeling of camaraderie are completely strange to her." The course of this interesting relationship will be followed more closely below.[5]

Kautsky's response to the 1905 revolution per se was characterized by unqualified support for the revolutionaries, cautions against overreliance on apparent liberal support, and sharp disagreement with the analysis of the revolution presented by the party leadership in the *Vorwärts*. In his first article on the revolution, he hailed the actions of the proletarian revolutionaries, but warned that even the cooperation of Russian liberals, like the leading figures of the *zemstvo* movement, would not win the revolution support from other European nations. He argued that because the workers had been the key to the first phase of the revolution, they had to expect that the European bourgeoisie, and eventually the Russian liberals also, would side with the tsarist government. Kautsky urged the French workers (this article appeared in a French socialist journal as well as in the *Neue Zeit*) to pressure their government not to aid the tsarist forces.[6]

The question of the role to be played by the Russian peasantry in the activities of 1905 provided material for the first of two major criticisms of the *Vorwärts* by Kautsky. The official party daily gave a great deal of coverage to events in Russia, most of it favorable to all factions of the revolutionaries. The *Vorwärts*, and other SPD journals as well, collected funds to support revolutionary activities and generally gave moral support to people they clearly perceived as enemies of the hated and feared tsarist state. Kautsky was in complete sympathy with these efforts. However, when the *Vorwärts* tried to predict what role the peasants would play in Russia, he dissented vigorously. This created a curious situation in which the man who for so long argued so ardently against the notion of a revolutionary potential among Germany's peasantry now argued just as strongly in favor of such a potential among the Russian peasantry. But this affair also reveals how flexible and subtle Kautsky could be in his analysis of events in different countries, and it further reveals his sensitivity, within the context of his materialist conception of history, to the variable course of development.[7]

Relying heavily on a liberal contributor from Moscow, a *Vorwärts* article predicted that the Russian ruling clique would foment peasant rebellion against the revolutionary intelligentsia in order to split the latter from its liberal allies, thereby weakening the forces of revolution. Kautsky faulted this analysis on three points. First, he argued that the assumption that the peasants would automatically turn against the student portion of the revolutionary intelligentsia, as had happened during the early 1870s in the "going to the people" phase of Russian populism, was false. During the earlier period the students had had few connections with the lower classes, either peasants or workers, but by 1905 that had changed. The students had established contacts with the workers, who in turn remained in touch with their home villages, thus serving as liaison between peasants and students. In the earlier period the students had been perceived as part of a privileged elite; now the peasantry saw them as part of the growing opposition to tsardom. Second, to contend that the peasants would oppose the revolutionary intelligentsia and not the liberals and the tsar was an absurd assumption in light of the major demand of the peasants—land. Who owned the land, the workers or the liberals and the tsar? Who would the peasants rise up against, the workers or the liberals and the tsar? Kautsky agreed that the liberals had something to fear from an uprising by the peasantry, but it was loss of their land, not a split within the revolutionary movement. Finally, Kautsky argued that the *Vorwärts* entirely missed the point of the activities in Russia if it failed to perceive that the very basis of the revolution was the need to liberate the country from its premodern forms, to distribute land to the peasantry and to establish progressive governmental institutions. In this way, Russia's politics and society would be brought into line with its emerging capitalist economics.[8]

In other words, Kautsky was arguing that the avant-garde of workers, reinforced by a rebellious peasantry, would force the revolution to its necessary historical conclusion—a capitalist, liberal Russia. In a later article, which was also the introduction to a new Russian edition of his *Das Erfurter Programm,* Kautsky expanded on this theme to predict that the temporary liberation of the peasantry that followed the acquisition of land, a concession necessary to win peasant support, would gradually be eroded as capitalism grew. Naturally his major point was that the growth of capitalism in the future depended upon the workers and peasants pushing the liberals into realizing in the present the system that would eventually give rise to the socialist revolution.[9]

Although this analysis is apparently the standard Marxist view of the course of modern history, three points of importance need to be made. First, Kautsky was in fact arguing against the application of the rigid Marxian view of the peasants as hopelessly reactionary, a view which the *Vorwärts* was accepting. While he thought a reactionary peasantry was characteristic of capitalist society, such as Germany, he did not think this was true in premodern societies, such as quasi-feudal Russia. Second, with the German model foremost in his mind, he feared that without the necessary push from the peasantry under the leadership of the proletariat, Russia's bourgeoisie would fail, as had Germany's, to eradicate all vestiges of the old order. And third, his view of the necessity of a worker-peasant coalition in 1905 corresponded very closely to the program adopted by Lenin and the Bolsheviks by 1917. Kautsky's analysis of the 1905 unrest in Russia was to provide the framework for his views of 1917.

As far as the Russian socialist movement was concerned, Kautsky publicly expressed confidence that its internal splits would not destroy its ability to take advantage of the revolutionary situation, although privately he was more pessimistic. He saw three kinds of divisions within the Russian movement: national, personal, and principled. The first included Great Russians against Caucasians; Poles and Latvians against Lithuanians; the Jewish *Bund* against them all; and the various combinations of conflicts implied by these divisions. That the groups were separate at all, said Kautsky, was largely a reflection of the inadequacies of the Russian state and the secrecy imposed by illegality. One such national conflict captured Kautsky's special attention, namely the antagonism between the Polish Socialist Party (PPS) and the Russian Marxian groups. The former argued that Polish independence was a more immediate, pressing problem than was political revolution in the entire Russian empire. Over twenty-five years earlier Kautsky and Engels had disagreed on this issue. Kautsky had argued that the political goals of socialism should overrule the desire for Polish liberation, while Engels had contended that Poland, and incidently also Ireland, had to be independent before they could have significant socialist movements. In 1905, Kautsky and Luxemburg, to say nothing of Plekhanov and Axelrod, were inclined to agree with Kautsky's earlier view.[10]

When in February 1905, Kazimierz Kelles-Krauz (1872–1905), a Polish socialist and occasional contributor to the *Neue Zeit*, submitted an article calling for a separate Polish movement to break away from the larger Russian issues and seek Polish independence, Kautsky rejected the article in no uncertain terms.

I am little edified by the politics put forward by you in your article. You wrote the unbelievable sentence that Poland certainly is ripe for democracy, *but perhaps not Russia*. This statement is the worst betrayal of the Russian revolution which one can think of and simultaneously reveals the most short-sighted parochialism. The PPS seems still not to know that the history of all nations living in the Russian empire will be decided in Petersburg, not Warsaw, that the destruction of tsarism is the precondition of the independence of Poland, that today it is a question of combining all the forces of revolution against the tsar. You think [you will] be able to win Polish democracy before the Russian is won, therefore you separate the Polish revolution from the Russian, and you make a struggle of the Poles against Russians out of the struggle of the Polish and Russian proletariat against the tsar.
    I cannot cooperate in that.[11]

After the national divisions, Kautsky discussed what he saw as essentially a personal division, that between the Mensheviks and the Bolsheviks, though he did not use those terms. He argued that in fact, as far as matters of principle were concerned, the Russian social democrats were more united than the German, since there were no revisionists in the Russian movement. On tactics and program, he wrote, revealing his ignorance of the true situation, the two groups did not differ at all, but on "the best form of party organization" they could not agree. And he argued that even this difference had drifted into the background as the dispute got more bitterly personal with time. He felt that a common enemy and the overwhelming need for unity would eventually overcome what was really a petty dispute. Privately Kautsky expressed respect for Plekhanov, Axelrod, and the rest of the *Iskra* Mensheviks, but argued that both they and Lenin's Bolsheviks had become too involved in the petty quarrels that so often plagued emigrés. The biggest problem, he said, was that the leaders had lost touch not only with Russia, but with activity of any sort. Instead of organizing, both sides criticized; instead of struggling, they speculated; instead of mixing theory and practice, they were pure theoreticians. Kautsky wished a plague on both their houses and hoped for the emergence of new leadership within Russia.[12]

The third division among Russian socialists was to Kautsky the most significant. On the one side were all those groups previously discussed, Poles and Russians, Mensheviks and Bolsheviks, and the *Bund*, — that is, the social democrats — and on the other side were those who called themselves revolutionary socialists, that is, terrorists. Kautsky discussed the historical origins of the peasant-based revolutionary socialists at great length and called for firm opposition to them, totally rejecting any suggestion of unity between the two groups: The future lay with organization and propaganda, not terror and assassination. He went on to argue, very optimistically, that these many splits were blown out of proportion by the small size and clandestine nature of the Russian movement. He saw the slowness of growth as a cause rather than a consequence of disunity and predicted that success would reduce the importance of the differences. Kautsky concluded his review of Russian socialism by claiming that not it but its opponents were in chaos, a chaos that would increase with the continued upsurge of peasant activity. Other observers of the Russian socialist scene at this time were less confident that events would favor unity and victory.[13]

The Mass-Strike Issue

The questions of division within the Russian movement and the role of the peasantry in Russian revolutionary activities took on much greater importance after the fact, that is, in 1917. The major impact of the Russian revolution of 1905 on Kautsky and the SPD was the fuel it added to the political debate over the mass or general strike. Other socialist parties had employed the tactic before 1905, and in fact, in the wake of the SPD's smashing victory in the 1903 election, Rudolf Hilferding, like Kautsky an Austrian-born intellectual who had attached himself to the German movement, suggested that the Germans consider the mass strike as a possible means of breaking out of the dead end of the country's pseudoparliamentary system. But prior to 1905, the German party leadership, backed by the trade-union leadership, had always managed to keep discussion of the mass strike at an absolute minimum. Even the mildly pro-mass-strike resolution at the 1904 Amsterdam congress of the Second International touched off no major polemics in the SPD. However, 1905 changed all this radically.[14]

What made the mass-strike debate particularly critical in Germany in 1905 was not just the Russian model, but also a major resurgence of economic strike activity by German workers. In that year more than half a million workers took part in work stoppages, either strikes or lockouts, more than in any previous five-year period. This new and extremely high level of activity had various effects on different parts of the socialist, working-class movement. The trade-union leadership, concerned with paying for strikes and conserving their jobs and their unions, tended to get increasingly cautious about calling their workers out. Since the turn of the century, powerful, wealthy, and highly conscious associations of industrialists and entrepreneurs had emerged in Germany, and they had begun to retaliate against the unions with lockouts and contributions to member firms experiencing strikes. The five-month-long lockout in the Crimmitschau-Zwickau textile industry during the winter of 1903–1904 had ended with an awesome display of power by the employers' associations and defeat for the unions. On the other hand, the strikes themselves and the increasing cost of living in 1904–1905 roused the rank and file of the trade unions to greater militancy. As one historian put it: "The same socio-economic situation which made the union leaders conservative had the opposite effect on the rank and file. The rising cost of living, the intense and widely shared experience of strike and lockout, and the unprecedented aggressiveness of the employers generated in the workers a new militancy and a receptiveness to radical political ideas."[15]

While these contradictory impulses were running through the trade-union movement, the SPD was experiencing internal difficulties. Traditional party superiority over the trade unions, which had in fact been weakening since the 1890s, was being seriously challenged. By 1905, the Free Trade Unions had surpassed the party in size, wealth, and probably also in organizational strength. As with nearly all trade-union movements, the German one was primarily concerned with specifically economic issues like wages, hours, and benefits and was cautious about spending its strength in political battles. When this inclination was coupled with the increased strength of the employers, the trade-union leaders, many of whom were also prominent party figures, began to insist that the party should no longer look upon the unions as automatic organizational allies in political struggles. Recognizing the importance of the trade-union membership, the party leaders, who were themselves becoming increasingly conservative, tended to side with the trade unionists and stayed away from any suggestion that the party adopt the mass-strike tactic for political ends.[16]

The leadership was not the party, however, and the more radical faction within the SPD looked at the mass strike with much different eyes than did the party bureaucracy. The people of this faction were almost all intellectuals, that is, they lived by their pens, and none had institutional responsibilities either to national or local party organizations or to trade unions. Some had close ties with party newspapers, like the *Leipziger Volkszeitung,* but none could be called part of the party bureaucracy. In large part this lack of responsibility, while allowing greater freedom, also meant that these intellectuals were not in regular contact with those in whose name they spoke—the workers. Kautsky, Luxemburg, Parvus, Hilferding, and the others all lacked the institutional framework that so often tempers abstraction. The radical faction of the party was also dissatisfied with the continued growth of votes and membership as ends in themselves and was anxious to see the party break out of what it felt would be the ultimately fruitless scramble for meaningless political power. Led by Luxemburg and Karl Liebknecht (Wilhelm's son), this radical faction strove to vitalize the party by taking advantage of the unrest in Germany and the mass-strike tactics so impressively used by the Russian workers. They hoped to use mass action to force the Prussian state to democratize and to combat German imperialism; they also sought to expand the party's influence among youth and the military forces. All this clearly contradicted the wishes of the party and trade-union leadership, and the resulting conflict continued through the war years, ending only with the split in German socialism during World War I.[17]

Paradoxically, though Kautsky started out in opposition to the party leadership, especially the editorial staff of the *Vorwärts,* in the mass-strike dispute, between 1905 and 1910 he emerged as the major architect of the theory that has variously been called centrism, fatalism, or integration ideology. In fact, beginning in late 1905 and persisting through mid-1910, Kautsky was more or less out of favor with the party leadership, who objected to what they considered his overly radical posture. Yet during this time, because an articulate left wing had emerged in 1905, he devoted himself to finding the "true" course between revisionism-reformism on the right and radicalism on the left. He was able to do this only by expanding to the fullest his rationalistic and optimistic analysis of the tensions in German society. Thus he remained out of favor with the party leadership because he insisted upon pointing out that the rigid Prussian-Junker state in Germany would not follow the wise course of compromising with the workers, but would ultimately force a resolution of societal tensions by revolution. On the other hand, he resisted what he thought were the putschist tendencies of the emerging left, reinforcing his long-standing view of the party as "revolutionary, but not revolution-making." The logic of Kautsky's analysis is hard to fault, but his rather naive faith that all would come out right in the end reflects his lack of sensitivity to the implications of the antirevolutionary organizational structure of the SPD. Furthermore, his strong humanitarianism made it difficult for him to call for revolutionary action, and therefore human destruction, unless he was certain of victory. Since revolutionary conditions are by their nature unpredictable and confusing, he never called for uncompromising revolutionary action in Germany.[18]

Several times before 1905 Kautsky had at least touched on the topic of the mass strike or general strike. Unlike many others in the party who dismissed it out of hand as nonsense, as had Wilhelm Liebknecht, Kautsky always considered the general strike a potentially useful weapon in the arsenal of social democracy, even if a dangerous and unpredictable one. A general strike in Belgium, which won minor concessions in easing the country's restrictive franchise law, brought the Second International to add discussion of this tactic to its agenda in 1893. For a general-strike commission at that congress, Kautsky drafted a resolution renouncing the worldwide general strike as totally impractical, but leaving open the possibility of using the general strike on a limited scale, under certain conditions. These conditions were, typically, left unspecified. Though the Zurich congress did not have time to consider the resolution, Kautsky's proposal received the approval of the commission. After the congress, he reinforced his views in letters to Engels and Adler. To the latter he wrote, "I am of the view that the strike has a great future and in the coming battle will play a great role." He argued that even if at present the general strike did not seem very likely, the party should not categorically renounce it. Rather, the general strike could serve both as a threat and a useful organizational aim. He also cautioned, however, that if the general strike ever were to be used, the party leadership would have to exercise close control in timing and execution, in order to ensure that it did not get out of hand. He most definitely did not perceive the general strike as a spontaneous action. If it came at all, it would be the result of disciplined action and centralized control, not a primal overflow of pent-up frustration.[19]

In the spring of 1902 a spontaneous general strike broke out in Belgium once again. The socialists took advantage of the situation to demand further alterations in the franchise law. When the national parliament responded to intimidation in the streets by refusing to change the law, the Belgian party was forced to face defeat or push the issue to civil war: It chose the former. Franz Mehring and Rosa Luxemburg published articles in the *Neue Zeit* that criticized the Belgian leaders for calling off the strike. Victor Adler, who had been trying for some time to head off a faction in his own party that favored the general strike, chastised both Kautsky and Bebel for not attacking the position taken by Luxemburg and Mehring. Kautsky disagreed with Adler, observing, "You are shocked by Rosa and Franz, I by the Belgian leaders." He added that "this is the first time (and I hope the last time)" that he and Adler had ever so clearly disagreed.[20]

Kautsky's grievance with the Belgians was not that they had called off the general strike, because, he said, that depended on local conditions and was endlessly debatable. Rather his complaint was that the leaders of the Belgian party had simultaneously pursued "two diametrically opposed courses." On the one hand, they had demogogically roused the masses to take to the streets demanding a general male franchise, while on the other hand they had secretly negotiated with the government for ministerial posts. Not only was this duplicitous, it showed a reckless disregard for the dangers of the general strike. In their almost grotesque eagerness to enter the government, Kautsky claimed, the Belgian socialists took their weapon too lightly; in their stupidity they toyed with "blood and lives. . . . Vandervelde and his people had no notion of the difficulties of the situation, of the seriousness of the struggle." Kautsky also noted that Singer and Bebel both agreed with this analysis.[21]

Adler's reply suggested that Kautsky, Singer, and Bebel were so upset because they thought of the Belgian leaders as revisionists. But Kautsky denied this, observing that the Belgians could not be revisionists since they had nothing to revise; they had always been eclectic and unsophisticated in theoretical matters. If prejudice of this sort were to be introduced into the discussion, said Kautsky, then what about Adler's irrational response to Luxemburg? Kautsky felt that his Austrian friend had reacted subjectively to the language of Luxemburg's article, rather than objectively to its content. According to him,

Adler failed, as had the Belgians, to realize that in Belgium patience and constant pressure would soon win the day for the socialists. "But strange to say," he added, "our *Realpolitiker* and statesmen are more impatient than our revolutionaries. They cannot wait until they become ministers, and this urgency for a ministry alone explains all the proceedings that simultaneously cheat with the liberals and incite the masses with bloated phrases."[22]

Before 1905 Kautsky's major concern with respect to the SPD was still the challenge from the right. For this reason, though he was hesitant to claim the general strike as a universally applicable, ultimate weapon of the working class, he was also reluctant to renounce it as useless. In defending Luxemburg's arguments in favor of the general strike, he generalized from the specific question at hand to broader issues. He asked Adler what options remained for a party which renounced force but "parliamentary cretinism and statesmanlike cunning." The renunciation of force was, according to Kautsky, central to the conflict between "the two methods which today struggle for dominance" in the SPD: Should the party develop as an independent power capable of forcing its desires on bourgeois society? Or should its program ask only for those things which are reconcilable with the bourgeois world? Kautsky obviously favored the first position. But lest he be suspected of an overemphasis on violence, he clarified his view of force: "My inclination is to understand force [*Gewalt*] as another means of power [*Machtmittel*], . . . organization is also a means of power. Every investigation of force must be an investigation of the means of power of the proletariat. Its fists are only one of its means of power and not the decisive one. Its most important means of power is its absolute necessity economically." He recognized the inherent dangers of, and threat to human life implied by, the general strike; he objected strenuously to using this weapon frivolously. But the "infathomable future" that lay ahead demanded that the party preserve the greatest possible tactical flexibility. Just as he had earlier refused to reject ministerialism in principle, so here he refused to reject the principle of the general strike. On such questions he was far from dogmatic and unrealistic, his major concern being preparation for the unknown.[23]

Few issues in the history of German social democracy before World War I more clearly illuminated the paradoxes and contradictions of the movement than did the great mass-strike debate of 1905-1906. Preoccupation with the issue began in earnest in May 1905, when, at their national congress in Cologne, the trade unions denounced not only the mass strike, but also any discussion of it. In June the radical, intellectual wing of the party launched its major response to the trade unions with the publication of *General Strike and Social Democracy,* by the Dutch socialist Henriette Roland-Holst, with an introduction by Kautsky. For the next year and a half, and then for long after that, through numerous party congresses and tons of printed matter, all factions of the party and trade unions debated the pros and cons of the mass strike and of talking about the mass strike. They hashed over the nature of the party and of party-trade-union relations and a vast multitude of other questions. In the course of this debate the centrifugal forces at work in the SPD were revealed as never before. To the extent that the mass-strike debate brought about changes in the internal relationships of the working-class movement in the Second Reich, it was even more important than the controversy over revisionism.[24]

This is a particularly difficult issue to deal with for many reasons. First, never before was a party debate so completely one of tone, of emphasis, rather than of substance, and never before were the arguments so obviously off the point. Second, Kautsky's position in this debate was even more severely rationalistic and finely drawn than his previous polemical postures. Third, the traditional anarchistic associations of the mass strike and the persistence of revisionists within the party meant that both sides could hurl irrelevant epithets at their opposition, thus blurring important distinctions and encouraging incorrect generalizations. Fourth, close analysis of the mass-strike debate reveals that what at the time appeared to be clear divisions between left and right, radical and moderate, were in fact overlapping and often contradictory alignments that render such labeling suspect. Finally, the issue of the mass strike was one that simply would not die, regardless of party and trade-union resolutions. Though both leadership groups made clear their hostility to the mass strike, though both organizations avoided any association with the mass strike, spontaneous mass action persisted through late 1905 and early 1906 and was to recur with discomforting frequency right up to 1914. The way in which the SPD responded to these persistent upheavals was a portent of reactions to the alarming events of 1914, 1917, and 1918.

During the course of the mass-strike debate, which for Kautsky consisted largely of an extended exchange between the editorial staffs of the *Vorwärts* and the *Neue Zeit*, he became more strongly associated with the party's radical faction than ever before. In large part this was the result of circumstances, namely the fact that the editorial board of the *Vorwärts* was dominated then by men whom Kautsky counted among the revisionists, above all Kurt Eisner and Richard Fischer. In July 1905, Kautsky called the *Vorwärts* staff "an inveterate evil." The hostility was mutual, and it tended to feed the mass-strike debate quite independently of the substantive content of the debate. Kautsky's radical posture was further exaggerated by the nature of the coalition he opposed, especially because the *Vorwärts* editorial board sided openly and aggressively with the trade-union leaders. Like the revisionists, the trade-union leadership had long considered Kautsky the kingpin of the distrusted orthodox Marxists. The intensity of the attack by both groups, as well as the intensity of Kautsky's counterattack, reflected these perceptions. Finally, Kautsky seemed to move to the left at this time because he was so closely allied with Rosa Luxemburg, whom more conservative party and trade-union leaders considered fanatical. Though the Kautsky-Luxemburg coalition was based on shared enemies more than on shared theory, an informal mutual defense pact was in effect between the two intellectuals during the mass-strike debate. Kautsky took it upon himself to defend his friend from trade-unionist attacks while she was in Russian Poland fighting for the revolution in its own territory. Kautsky's efforts earned him even more severe attacks from the right.[25]

Roland-Holst's *General Strike and Social Democracy* was a relatively cautious discussion of the history and potentials of the mass strike. It was not a revolutionary call for bloody action in the streets. But the editorial board of the *Vorwärts* chose to disregard the content of the book and to concentrate instead on the possible implications of a widespread mass-strike discussion. In taking this step the editors, like their allies the trade unionists, had to distort the tone of Roland-Holst's argument. At the same time they also condemned Kautsky for associating himself with the mass strike. Wrongly implying that Roland-Holst had assigned "unconditional and extraordinary significance" to the mass strike, the *Vorwärts* board argued that by so doing futile hopes would be aroused and attention and energy would be diverted from the more pressing, mundane, but also safer tasks of political and economic organization and struggle. The editors specifically rejected Kautsky's call, made in the foreword to the book, for further discussion and study of the mass strike as preparation for the future.[26]

The editors of the *Vorwärts* did not, however, categorically reject the mass strike as a potential weapon in the political efforts of the working class. Though careful to avoid using the expression *mass strike,* adopting instead one of the several code words that emerged during the debate, *Arbeitsverweigerung* (literally, "refusal to work"), the editorial board recognized such action as a possibility and only came down strongly against discussing it. For them the mass strike was something done, perhaps, but not something that was talked about. They emphasized that the SPD was revolutionary not because it condoned illegality and the use of force, but because its major aim was the achievement of socialism by the "revolutionization of heads," by the "conquest of the *Geist*" of the ever growing proletariat.[27]

Rebutting the *Vorwärts* attack was not difficult for Kautsky, since he had only to point out that the editorial board had misread Roland-Holst. Far from overemphasizing the mass strike, said Kautsky, both he and his Dutch comrade simply saw it as a complement to parliamentary activities, perhaps even as a logical continuation of the more reformist activities of socialists. Kautsky opened his response with a presentation of his own analysis of the limits and nature of the mass strike that was anything but radical. Even his sharpest condemnation of the *Vorwärts* editorial board, for siding with the trade unions in calling for a ban on discussion of the mass strike, was made because without discussion of the issue, opportunities for fruitful use of the mass strike might be missed or the mass strike might be used when it should not be. The failure of the *Vorwärts* to take the lead in a thorough discussion of the mass strike, he contended, meant that those presently responsible for the policies of the official party journal were unfit for their jobs.[28]

Kautsky's position was a curious combination of a genuinely leftist recognition of the sterility of purely parliamentary action and of a caution based on the conviction that the future belonged to socialism and on recognition of the strength of the military-bureaucratic machine that dominated Germany. Thus he argued that the growing interest in the mass strike among workers was not just the result of the Russian model, but also of a "growing disdain for parliamentarism." He saw the latter as a reaction to the failure of the SPD to bring about any changes in the wake of its smashing victory in the 1903 election, which the *Vorwärts* had loudly proclaimed as the advent of the peaceful conquest of political power by the party. When in fact nothing happened, Kautsky argued, the workers began to look elsewhere for the political strength necessary to begin the conversion to socialism. According to him, two things made it likely that this trend would continue. One was the steady decline in SPD fortunes in runoff elections, an indication of the party's increasing isolation; the other was the extent to which the Reichstag declined as a center of political activity as the SPD *Fraktion* grew. Kautsky concluded that as long as these tendencies persisted, interest among social democrats would increasingly be focused on extraparliamentary means of influencing the politics of the Reich.[29]

This portion of Kautsky's analysis was very radical in implication, and had he limited himself to this, his identification with the radical faction of the party could be accepted without qualification. But if attention is turned to his treatment of the specifics of the mass strike, the ambiguity of his position emerges. For he was extremely hesitant to suggest that the mass strike was a reasonable tactical consideration for the SPD. While he rejected the suggestion of some trade unionists that the mass strike *was* revolution, feeling that Belgium, Sweden, Holland, and Italy had shown otherwise, he did feel that in Germany "a successful mass strike is only conceivable in a revolutionary situation." To use the mass strike to support demands for franchise changes in a single city, like Hamburg, was foolish. He even cautioned against automatic response with the mass strike to governmental moves against the existing franchise, arguing that such moves might be intended as provocation. Kautsky's rational analysis of the potentials of the mass strike and his respect for the military and police power of the German state led him to conclude that, despite the growing popular attraction of extraparliamentary activity, the party would have to exercise great caution when contemplating the use of such a potent and dangerous weapon. In other words, he was urging discussion of the mass strike precisely because he was not eager to see it used.[30]

Such analytical niceties played little role in the heated debate that raged from July 1905 until after the 1906 Mannheim party congress. Kautsky claimed that because the *Vorwärts* editors did not want to talk about the mass strike, they must be intent upon compromise and cooperation with the government. The *Vorwärts* editorial board denied this accusation and countered with one of their own, implying that since Kautsky wanted to talk about the mass strike he was at least inclined toward anarchism. The validity of this charge was, of course, vigorously denied by the *Neue Zeit* editor, who had himself struggled against anarchists for years. The trade unions also entered the fray with attacks on Kautsky. Because he wanted to talk about the mass strike and because he claimed that the trade unions formed an elite vested interest opposed to the rising unrest among the rank and file, the trade unionists labeled Kautsky a *Nurpolitiker*, that is, one who was only interested in the political aspects of the workers' struggle and not in the cause of economic improvement. This charge contained only a grain of truth, because Kautsky had always staunchly supported the trade unions as schools for socialists. But he had also always argued that in the party-trade-union relationship, the party had to be superior.[31]

Two party congresses, in Jena, 1905, and in Mannheim, 1906, dealt with the mass-strike issue. Together they revealed in the clearest possible terms the paradoxes of the prewar German social democratic movement. At Jena, Bebel gave one of the longest speeches in the history of the party by way of introducing his mass-strike resolution.

For three-and-a-half hours, he demonstrated his political skills, his mastery of the party idiom, and the brilliant leadership that allowed him to simultaneously praise and criticize all factions of the party. Kautsky's 1893 Zurich resolution on the mass strike was praised as a model of clarity, but his emphasis on the sterility of the 1903 electoral victory was criticized as cryptoanarchist. The trade unions were praised for their great achievements in organizing and improving the lot of the workers, but their rejection of discussion of the mass strike was condemned as an attempt to ignore unpleasant realities *(Vogelstrausspolitik)*. He outlined the isolation and heroism of the party in stirring terms and on the whole emphasized the analysis of the radicals rather than the revisionists. His resolution referred to gaining and protecting general franchise rights and to the duty of the trade unionists to support social democracy, but it did not contain the words *mass strike*. In an obvious concession to the trade-union leadership, Bebel used another of the code words, *Massenarbeitseinstellung* ("mass work stoppage"); but even this was unsuccessfully opposed by the trade-union head, Karl Legien. The resolution was not a call for action, but it did imply party control of the mass strike, acceptance of the mass strike as a reasonable tactic, and party superiority over the trade unions.[32]

The speeches given for and against Bebel's resolution revealed what strange bedfellows this ambiguous issue created. Eduard Bernstein, the father of revisionism, and arch-radical Rosa Luxemburg, both spoke in favor of the resolution. Karl Legien, though condemning Kautsky's apparently radical stance on the question, was insightful enough to give powerful support to the latter's notion that the mass strike in Germany demanded a revolutionary situation. Luxemburg's brief but powerful speech was perhaps the most interesting of the congress. In highly emotional terms she hailed the appearance of spontaneous protest by the workers as the salvation of the party. Social democracy, she said, had only to follow the lead of its followers to break out of the stagnant quagmire into which it had fallen. Though many other speakers, among them Bebel and the prominent reformist, Eduard David, were shocked by Luxemburg's language and emotion, they accepted her as an ally on this issue. The final vote was predictably overwhelmingly in favor, 287 to 14, and of those opposed, most were trade unionists. Kautsky did not attend the Jena congress, but in his postcongress review, he hailed this vote as a victory for the party and implicitly for himself also. In the face of the opposition of the trade-union leaders, the very deep differences between Luxemburg's pro-mass-strike posture and that of Kautsky did not come out.[33]

Between the 1905 and the 1906 party congresses conditions within the German working-class movement changed drastically. Beginning in November 1905, and lasting through early 1906, spontaneous upheavals occurred in several German cities, especially in Saxony. These activities were largely undertaken by workers and were aimed at stopping the trend toward narrower franchise requirements on the provincial level. Faced with massive political strikes they could not afford to support, trade-union and party leaders signed a secret agreement in February 1906. Under the terms of the agreement, the party accepted fiscal responsibility for political strikes and agreed that the trade unions would be responsible in cases of economic strikes only. The party central committee also agreed to work against mass strikes in most instances. In one fell swoop, despite the Jena resolution and despite the decades-long tradition of party superiority over the trade unions, the backbone of any organized mass action by the SPD was broken in the vise of the vested interests of the trade unions. The party leadership's willingness to accede to the trade-union demands reflected the central committee's own aversion to mass action in the streets. After February 1906, for all practical purposes, the SPD was no longer in a position to lead an organized mass strike because its treasury, though comfortable for the needs of the party, was by no means sufficient to bear the costs of a strike by the much larger trade-union membership.[34]

For the most part this agreement did not change the mundane aspects of the working-class movement. The trade unions continued to be closely allied with the SPD in terms of membership, voting, political sympathies, and general outlook. Trade unionists remained as prominent figures in the party, and the party still relied heavily on the trade unions as educational and propaganda outlets. But if the SPD ever had the potential to lead organized mass action, this potential was greatly reduced by the agreement, which did not remain secret for long, but was leaked by the trade-union press soon after the meeting. Furthermore, those forces within the party who opposed the more radical tactics of mass action were greatly bolstered by the agreement; it became part of the growing impulse toward conservatism, along with the increased size, bureaucratization, and electoral success. Perhaps above all, the significance of the anti-mass-strike agreement lay in its timing. Early 1906 was a period of widespread enthusiasm for extraparliamentary action; it was also a period in which the ruling class seemed to be taking up the offensive against the working class with renewed vigor. If the revolutionary social democrats responded to these stimuli by surrendering one of their most potent weapons, what prospects did the future hold? Did this not mean the victory of the revisionists, the practical abandonment of the revolution that alone could bring socialism?

Bebel presented the mass-strike resolution once again at Mannheim, but this time his tone was much different. Besides attempting to achieve the rather remarkable feat of reconciling his Jena resolution and the February 1906 agreement, he now had to realign the majority of the party that followed him by limiting the mass strike to purely defensive purposes, that is, protecting old rights taken away in new attempts at repression. He now contended that most party members agreed that "the mass strike is not feasible without the cooperation of the trade unions," but still tried to maintain that the party had not, therefore, abandoned that tactic. He also revealed his own extremely cautious view in reporting that he had favored including in the present resolution a clause that would have required the calling of an extraordinary congress to ratify any decision of the central committee in favor of a mass strike. The rest of the leadership thought this process impractical, and it was not included in the resolution. Not surprisingly, the central committee and the trade unionists, headed by Legien, were allies at Mannheim. An amendment sponsored jointly by Legien and Bebel added to the main resolution a clause asserting that the Cologne trade-union resolution condemning the mass strike did not contradict the Jena party resolution. Despite the apparent absurdity of this clause, it passed by a vote of 323 to 62.[35]

Luxemburg, Kautsky, and others identified with the radical faction opposed the Bebel-Legien amendment, but once again in their speeches these supposed allies revealed how far apart they really were. Kautsky proposed an amendment which was a strong verbal reassertion of the ultimate supremacy of the party over the trade unions and of the need for the trade unions to act in accordance with the principles of social democracy, that is, to subordinate themselves to the party. It did not call for organizational or procedural changes to strengthen the hand of the party, and in fact would not have altered the substance of Bebel's resolution at all. In his speech on the mass strike, Kautsky powerfully reasserted his demand for party superiority over the trade unions. Yet when Luxemburg spoke in support of Kautsky's amendment, she once again emphasized the role and potential of spontaneity. As at Jena, Kautsky and Luxemburg were allies primarily because they had the same enemies. When the radicals were outmaneuvered by the leadership, which coopted the mildest part of Kautsky's amendment, a weak call for party-trade-union cooperation, both the *Neue Zeit* editor and his more radical friend voted with the majority to pass Bebel's resolution, 386 to 5.[36] Therefore, by the end of the Mannheim congress, the Cologne trade-union resolution condemning even discussion of the mass strike, the Jena party resolution reaffirming the mass strike as a potent weapon of the workers, and Bebel's resolution ratifying the secret agreement of February 1906 had been reconciled by democratic vote. Apparently Kautsky and other theoreticians who should have known better were not troubled by this muddle.

Theoretical Development

In the course of his discussion of the mass strike, Kautsky gave explicit form to many fundamental conceptions that formerly had only been implicit in his writings. Among the things so developed were three particularly important matters: the relative importance of political determinants, the relationship between spontaneity and objective conditions, and the nature and function of the socialist, working-class party. The first item had long been a central concern of Marxists and was important because of the apparent emphasis on the primacy of economics in Marx's own work. The second item, the relationship between subjective and objective factors, was for the most part not a major concern of most Marxists until after 1905, largely because of their concentration on organizing the workers and their rejection of the romantic and anarchistic notions of spontaneous upheaval. The final item, the nature of the party, would later become the most important single distinction between Lenin's communism and the older forms of social democracy. By clarifying his position on these matters, Kautsky gave much more precise form to his interpretation of Marxism.

Prior to the outbreak of the Russian revolution of 1905, in the wake of the Belgian general-strike discussion, Kautsky offered this analysis of revolutionary prospects among European countries: "Today, at least, an entire rank of states stands nearer the revolution than does Germany, despite the rapidity of its economic development and the growth of its social democracy. Today the German government is still the most powerful in the world." The German state had the strongest, best-disciplined army and bureaucracy, and it ruled a sober, peace-loving population with no revolutionary tradition. By contrast, Germany's neighbor to the east, though its proletariat was not fully developed, was in bad shape, economically and militarily. And Kautsky contended that everything was relative, even the revolutionary power of a class. Thus while Russia's proletariat was not far advanced, its government was weak, and therefore revolution was more likely in this backward, agrarian state than in the advanced industrial giants to the west. He did not argue that revolution was more likely in Russia because it had somehow to catch up with the West, but solely because its government was weak. He gave primary consideration to political determinants and specifically suggested that revolution would probably not come to Germany immediately because of the strength of its government.[37]

Not all of his opponents on the mass-strike issue in 1905–1906 accepted Kautsky's apparent radicalism. At least one right-wing party member, Friedrich Stampfer, an Austrian-born coeditor of the *Vorwärts*, upbraided Kautsky for excessive caution about using the mass strike to win franchise reform in Hamburg. He claimed that if the will were present in the masses, then the party must act with them. In fact, on this point Stampfer, Bernstein, and others of the party's right wing were closer to Luxemburg than to Kautsky. Kautsky pointed out that not will alone, but also something he called "actual conditions" determined historical development. In effect he was arguing against spontaneous mass action if it were dangerous according to rational analysis. During the debate with the *Vorwärts*, he had made the same point more elaborately. Here he quoted from a *Vorwärts* article that contended that the study of the material conditions of a revolutionary situation was "child's play, . . . but the stirring up of enthusiasm is the hardest part of political education, the decision for action perhaps the great tragic problem of world history." Though Kautsky admitted that part of his difference with the *Vorwärts* on this question was merely based on differences in perspective, he also added the following confession:

> Now for us Marxists, the "stirring up of enthusiasm" was never a problem the solution of which much occupied us. We believed that sufficient enthusiasm flowed from the class struggle, in which we take part, and from the scientific investigation of the conditions and tasks of the struggle, which brought us an abundance of the most inspiring new insights, the most magnificent view of the future, the most impressive aims, that we thought a special source of enthusiasm was no longer needed. And the spread of this enthusiasm and its concentration on action through concentrating on the class struggle and through the spread of scientific enlightenment seemed to us not "the great tragic problem of history," but a very hopeful, comforting task.[38]

This passage is worthy of closer analysis since one of the most frequent criticisms of Kautsky by his contemporaries and later scholars was that his theoretical positions, if they did not determine, at least reinforced the "revolutionary passivism" of the prewar SPD. As has already been discussed, quietism was implicit in the deterministic aspects of Marx's work, and the positivistic influences of the late nineteenth century tended to strengthen the inclination to rely on the inexorable march of history to bring about the socialist society. But Kautsky's position was not quietistic; he urged constant, vigorous participation in various endeavors, was particularly forceful in his demands for political activity, and argued that theoretical work was an integral part of socialist practice. As the above quotation shows, he felt that theory generated motivation to such an extent that promotion of action demanded no special attention; he most certainly was not calling for a do-nothing posture. Though the effect of Kautsky's position may have been to limit the potential of the SPD as a party of aggressive action, that was not his goal. In fact, his conviction that participation in the class struggle was radicalizing led him to make some startling suggestions about how the party could overcome the stagnation that he felt had prevailed since the turn of the century.

Twice during the mass-strike debate Kautsky suggested reforms to help turn the party from inaction to a more vigorous response to the unrest of the period, and in so doing he revealed much about his conception of the nature and function of the party. In a letter of August 1905 to Adler, with whom Kautsky was most unguarded, he gave fullest vent to his critique of the party, focusing attention on the makeup and personalities of the men on the central committee. Unlike the Austrian party, which was comprised of representatives of "the three great branches of the class struggle, parliamentarism, trade unions, [and the] press," Kautsky wrote, the German party was "a mere election mechanism," that is, the leaders were drawn exclusively from the party's Reichstag representatives. Kautsky thought the central committee "a collegium of old men who have become so absorbed in bureaucracy and parliamentarism that they curse every increase of their work load." Among the central committee members, only Bebel was a "fiery spirit," and even he was aging and beginning to tire easily. However, given the developments that were to come shortly, Kautsky's recommendations for changing this state of affairs seem incredible. He suggested adding "fresh blood" to the central committee in the form of "2–3 trade unionists and 1 press man." Though he knew that many radicals felt that adding trade unionists to the central committee would be a conservatizing influence, he did not share their fears because "the party masses remain as they are [that is, radicalized], conditions take care of that, and that reacts on" the central committee. In a later *Neue Zeit* article that dealt with the same question, Kautsky specifically argued that including the trade unionists on the central committee would not conservatize that body because the radicalizing influences of the political aspect of the class struggle would overcome the conservatizing influences of the economic aspect.[39]

Thus by the end of the mass-strike debate of 1905–1906, Kautsky had developed his mature view of the nature of German society, the role of the party, prospects for the future, and the relationship between politics and economics. It was this view that served as the basis for the emergence in 1910 of the "centrism" now most closely identified with Kautsky. He gave great prominence to political determinants in all these matters, seeing the political factor of the nature of the German state as overruling the expected effects of Germany's status as a major industrial society and arguing that the political aspect of the class struggle was primary to the economic. At the same time, he argued that it was another political quality of the Wilhelmine Reich— the sterility of the Reichstag—that ensured the continued interest of the workers in nonparliamentary activities. This line of argument implied two things that are of major importance in evaluating Kautsky's Marxism. First, if the workers turned to nonparliamentary actions because the state was not responsive, then it followed that in states with responsive governmental forms the workers would rely on parliamentary means to achieve their political ends. And this was precisely what he had suggested in 1898 when he pointed out the fallacies of Bernstein's political analysis as applied to Germany. Second, the ambiguity of his position was apparent in the implicit irreconcilability of the workers to a nonrepresentative government coupled with an objective evaluation that ruled out extraparliamentary forms of action except in revolutionary situations. After 1906 Kautsky remained radical insofar as he was hostile to the established state in Germany, but he was also moderate in his rejection of voluntaristic acts on the part of socialists to create or promote revolutionary situations. His view of the party was that it was revolutionary in its opposition to the state and its aims for the future, but not "revolution-making" because aggressive action not in accordance with objective conditions (that is, the strength of the German state) would only end in disaster. He was content to rely on further development of the inherent contradictions of German society to bring about a revolutionary situation and on the traditional tactics of the SPD to prepare the workers for taking advantage of the coming revolution.[40]

Private Life

Such was not the stuff of a vigorous revolutionary movement or of a fanatical revolutionary theoretician. But the SPD was not the former and Karl Kautsky most certainly was not the latter. He was not, except in the literal sense, a bohemian; rather he led the orderly, comfortable life of a successful intellectual. Though his incredible productivity is proof of his dedication and enormous capacity for work, he was occupied not with the frenetic labor of anticipating immediate revolution but with the long and difficult process of analyzing contemporary society and educating the workers in their historic responsibilities. Once when Adler, who was constantly in fiscal straits, hinted that he was sometimes criticized by party comrades because of his concern about earning a decent living, Kautsky stoutly defended his friend's right to basic comforts: "We may not carry on in conformity with anarchistic-nihilistic methods of propaganda which contend that the revolution comes very soon and which of necessity crumbles if the revolution does not come at the expected time. Our agitation must be calculated on a long duration, we must prepare ourselves so that we are able to conduct our struggle for decades; but for that it is necessary that the pioneers have an ordered domestic existence."[41]

Kautsky himself led such an existence. His days were largely devoted to work and his evenings to visiting, usually at home, and light reading. From nine in the morning to one in the afternoon he devoted himself to concentrated writing. After lunch and a nap (he was quite fond of sleeping), he would usually take long walks, often with his sons, during which he apparently worked out his thoughts on the multitude of issues that concerned him. The tradition begun by Engels of Sunday afternoon gatherings was continued in the Kautsky household. The Bebels, Rudolf Hilferding, Gustav Eckstein (two Austrians and close collaborators on the *Neue Zeit*) and, until her split from Kautsky in 1910, Rosa Luxemburg, were the most frequent guests. In addition to these regulars, the affairs were almost always swollen by foreign visitors; Russians were most numerous, but Austrian, French, Dutch, Belgian, and English socialists attended as well. The family's material needs were comfortably satisfied by Karl's income from the *Neue Zeit* and the royalties from his ever increasing literary production. Though he continually complained that he wanted more free time for scholarly work, as late as 1913 the responsibilities of maintaining his family prevented him from giving up his journal. Since the turn of the century Kautsky's burden of the *Neue Zeit* had been considerably lightened by the addition of Heinrich Cunow, as editorial secretary, and Emmanuel Wurm and Gustav Eckstein, who served as coeditors. But Kautsky still took upon himself a good deal of the work and discovered that having co-workers often required that he mediate in differences of opinion.[42]

The social life of the Kautskys was limited almost exclusively to contacts with socialists and family. More than in any other European

Karl Kautsky, 1881

Louise and Karl Kautsky, 1902

From left to right: Felix, Benedikt, and Karl, Jr., 1905

country, the political isolation of German socialists was carried over into social matters as well. While like all other people, socialists were either friendly or aloof from their neighbors, depending on personal inclinations, to a very great extent close contacts were limited by reason of societal prejudice to other socialists. This fact served to reinforce powerfully the sense of camaraderie and inner direction that came to characterize the SPD during the Wilhelmine years. The party provided a wide range of social and cultural events, such as singing and bicycling clubs, and eventually formed for its members a "state within the state" that protected the socialist workers and intellectuals from the hostilities of an enemy society. Party congresses were the focal point of much of this social aspect of SPD life, serving as an annual renewal of the bonds that held the party together. Though the congresses lasted only a few days, many socialists took advantage of the occasion to stretch out the period of pleasant contacts with good friends. Thus in 1893, Karl wrote to Luise (in English): "I am afraid I won't return home before Monday. August [Bebel] goes with me and wants to stay on Sunday somewhere on the Rhine to be merry." Furthermore, Kautsky's personal inclination to calm reflection on, and discussion of, the intricacies of the movement led him to value highly his evening visits from comrades. On one occasion, while Luise was in Vienna visiting her family, Karl reported that Bebel, Cunow, Hilferding, Eckstein, and he had spent an evening in discussion, adding in German, "es war sehr gemütlich," and then in English, "a quiet chat, just the thing I like."[43]

Luise Kautsky was, by the early years of the century, Karl's closest and most regular critic and co-worker. According to accounts of their sons, Luise read, and sometimes transcribed, every letter, article, brochure, and book that Kautsky wrote. At particularly critical times, as during the revisionism controversy and when the split with Luxemburg was coming to a head, Kautsky relied heavily on her counsel. But she was also a socialist author and translator in her own right, and frequently urged on by Rosa Luxemburg, with whom she remained on intimate terms even after her husband and her friend had split, she contributed to German, Polish, and English journals. Clara Zetkin, for years editor of a Berlin socialist journal concerned with women's issues, was also a close friend of the Kautsky family. Zetkin, Luise, and Luxemburg met regularly to discuss party and personal matters. One particularly thorny source of disagreement between Luxemburg and Kautsky was what she called his oppression of Luise. For his part, Kautsky felt that Luxemburg was meddling in personal affairs that were none of her business. Doubtless Luxemburg, who was herself a very independent person, especially in intellectual matters, was at least partially correct in seeing Kautsky's dominance over Luise as stifling, but interfering in the husband-wife relationship served no good end. By late 1918, Luise felt compelled by Luxemburg's increasingly radical position to break off personal contact, while apparently retaining the warmest personal regard for "Red Rosa."[44]

Regular vacations were a religiously kept ritual for the major figures in German socialism, and Kautsky frequently took trips with one or another of his sons. On these excursions they saw much of southern Europe, from Lisbon to Italy, but occasionally had some trouble getting away from Germans. From Maderno, Italy, Kautsky reported to Luise that their hotel was too expensive and too crowded and also that "the society is too much Berlin. I see here more Berlin people than I see in Berlin in one year." And his sons frequently wore him out on these vacations; while on this same trip with Karl, Jr., Kautsky told Luise, "I am rather tired, have made [sic] with Charley a walking tour for about two hours." The expense of such travel was sometimes too much for Kautsky. In 1910 while on vacation in Baden-Baden with his eldest son, Felix, Kautsky spent 250 marks during the first week and had to beg Luise for another 200 marks, pleading, "after a week I cry money! money!" On her vacation trips Luise usually spent time in Austria, but Karl more often went to Switzerland, at least once in the company of Rosa Luxemburg on a working vacation at Lake Geneva.[45]

Of all of Kautsky's friendships within the German party, none was more important or closer than his relationship with Bebel. With a few significant exceptions, Bebel and Kautsky stood together on most issues, and Kautsky's theory frequently reinforced Bebel's party positions. Two aspects of this relationship were of great importance to Kautsky. For one thing, he usually took his lead from Bebel in day-to-day political matters. Late in 1914, after the SPD had failed to fulfill its own legacy of opposition to war, Kautsky tried to assuage his guilt for having failed to convince the party to oppose the war by reference to Bebel's absence. "The feeling depresses me not a little," Kautsky wrote to Adler, "that I must now engage in practical politics without being able to follow a leader." First he had gladly followed Engels' lead, and after 1895, Bebel's. But with the latter's death in 1913, said Kautsky, "I have lost more than a friend, I lost my strongest support in practical politics." Without Bebel, Kautsky felt uncertain, and he regretted his own confusion at the outbreak of the war. Besides offering him guidance in politics, Bebel also frequently used Kautsky's writings to bludgeon party opponents. As a result much of Kautsky's reputation as dogmatic and intolerant derived from evaluation of strong positions he had taken at Bebel's urging. This was true during the assault on revisionism; it happened again in 1910 when Bebel urged strong language against the south Germans; in 1912 Bebel egged Kautsky on in his defense of the expulsion from the party of the extreme reformist, Gerhard Hildebrand; and for the last time, in July 1913, Bebel complained that Kautsky's attack on Franz Mehring was "not sharp enough" and specifically suggested that words like "my friend" be striken from the article. Bebel guided and used Kautsky in part because the two men shared similar views, but also because Bebel thought Kautsky overly optimistic, tactically inept, but still a useful polemicist.[46]

At least until 1910, the reputation for radicalism that developed during the mass-strike debate of 1905–1906 stuck with Kautsky. Shortly before the Reichstag election of 1907, he developed an explanation for the apparent contradiction of the materialist conception of history which the continued Junker domination of industrial Germany implied. Calling on the historical circumstance of the simultaneous emergence of working-class and bourgeois movements in Germany in 1848, Kautsky argued that the bourgeoisie failed in its historical role in Germany because it feared the workers. Furthermore, he contended that unlike the English model, where agrarian interests declined as capitalism grew, in Prussia the agrarian nobles oversaw the conversion of their own lands to capitalist production for the world market. In this way the Junkers maintained their military and government positions and at the same time preserved themselves economically, although with increasing difficulty and only with increasing state support. But the dominance of the Prussian agrarian nobility during the rise of Germany's industrial sector led to the Junkerization of the bourgeoisie, not only its commercial and industrial elements, but also its intellectual life. Thus, according to Kautsky, while in countries where the bourgeoisie had taken over the government, the typically bourgeois tactic of buying off, splitting up, and otherwise corrupting the proletariat was employed, in Germany the typically Junker tactic of brutal persecution was employed. "Nothing is more suitable," said Kautsky, "to the greater strengthening of the class consciousness of the proletariat, to arousing its revolutionary energy, to welding it together into a single strong body, than this last method." He contended that both the internal and external policies of the so-called new course were aimed at strengthening the hold of the Junkers and their bourgeois allies, while keeping the workers down. If there were any great politicians left in the German government, they would realize that the dominance of the ruling classes would be more secure the more the workers were won over. To achieve this end, he concluded, the government would have to win the support of the Center party, thus gaining the support of the Catholic workers. Instead the government launched an offensive against the Catholics and the Social Democrats.[47]

The offensive reached a climax with the Reichstag election of 1907. The increasing diplomatic isolation of Germany after the tragicomic Moroccan affair of 1905 and the Algeciras conference that followed made uneasy even those in the government who supported their irresponsible kaiser in his quixotic search for Germany's "place in the sun." Many Reichstag members were disturbed by Morocco and its aftermath, and when native revolts in the German-held territory in southwest Africa revealed the ineptitude of the colonial administration, opposition within the Reichstag, especially by the Center, threatened Chancellor von Bülow's position. In a move based on a perceptive analysis of the chauvinistic sympathies of much of the German electorate, and under pressure from the Center party, Bülow dissolved the Reichstag a year early and called on the people to support their government against the meddling of the people's representatives. Though similar calls from government heads who consider foreign policy their sacred preserve had been made before, and continue to be made even in republican nations, few such calls were as successful as Bülow's. In a highly orchestrated campaign, the governmental bloc, now joined by the formerly oppositional Progressives, launched an effective assault on the SPD, though it was less successful in its attack on public enemy number two, the Catholics, who actually gained five seats.[48]

Even though the SPD managed to gain more than 200,000 votes over its 1903 total, it lost thirty-eight seats, down to forty-three from eighty-one. In thirty-five of these lost districts, the vote against the socialists by the Progressives in runoffs was critical, but other factors were also important. For instance, various government-sponsored groups worked to turn out a considerably larger number of voters in 1907 than had voted in 1903; 84.3 percent of the eligible voters, over 11.2 million, voted in 1907, as opposed to 75.8 percent, less than 9.5 million, in 1903. Inasmuch as the SPD's gain was less than 12 percent of the increase in votes (200,000 of 1.7 million), the party's problem clearly lay with the voters who turned out because of the nationalistic agitation of the progovernment forces. Because the SPD had traditionally claimed that it was at least as interested in winning votes as it was in winning mandates, the election was probably not the disaster the loss of seats made it seem. On the other hand, the reformist and revisionist forces in the party were certainly more concerned with mandates than votes, and virtually all the party leadership saw the 1907 election as a severe blow to future prospects. If nothing else, the alliances against the SPD revealed its isolation and parliamentary vulnerability.[49]

Unlike most of the party, Kautsky was not tremendously upset by the 1907 election, and given his view of the tasks and nature of the party, his position is not surprising. Though he readily admitted that the socialists had underrated the potential of the colonial-nationalist issue, he emphasized that other things had also changed between 1903 and 1907. Two years of good harvests had made many peasants less inclined to oppose the government; the increasing cost of living was being blamed by the nonproletarian classes on the success of the trade unions, and the voters took out their frustration on the ally of the unions, the SPD. Furthermore, the radical ferment of 1905–1906 and even the SPD's victory in 1903 had roused fear of the socialists. But Kautsky denied that parliamentary work was an end in itself; rather it was only one tactic in the class struggle. He claimed that while the SPD may have lost "a few hundred thousand" votes from the nonproletarian classes that had supported it in 1903, it had made an absolute gain of 200,000 votes. Putting these two figures together, he made the rather dubious claim of a gain for the SPD of some "half a million new voters in the proletariat." Thus he was able to conclude that the future was with the socialists. Not only was the party's vote continuing to grow among the workers, but the newly forged Bülow bloc would have to rely on colonial policy successes to maintain control. And pursuing such policies would only increase the size of budgets and the military, and therefore taxes; intensify the isolation of Germany and the mistrust of foreign governments; and eventually bring foreign entanglements that could lead to war. He concluded that when this happened, the SPD, as the only party of peace in the Reich, would gain from the general aversion to war. Kautsky was arguing here that "worse is better," that greater international tension, higher taxes, and larger military budgets were good for the SPD. Never before had his optimism run quite so rampant.[50]

Historical and Political Writings

From early 1907 through early 1909, Kautsky was less concerned with party affairs and more occupied with his own historical research than he had been for years. His last major historical study had appeared in 1895, as part of the International Library series. This work, *The Precursors of Recent Socialism,* was later reissued as a two-volume study of the origin of communist movements associated with the Reformation. It was part of a strong Marxian tradition of investigating the socioeconomic aspects of religious movements and more specifically of rewriting the history of the German peasant wars of the early sixteenth century. Engels wrote on the peasant wars, as did August Bebel, Wilhelm Blos, and Ernst Belfort-Bax, the latter two at least sometimes self-professed adherents of Marxism. Kautsky's contribution to this literature was well received by Engels, who claimed to have learned a great deal from it. He had in fact done much more thorough research for his study than Engels had done for his, and this despite the younger man's acute sense of insufficiency about not having access to resources like those of the British Museum. Tussy Marx was so impressed with Kautsky's work that she heaped effusive praise on it. She found reading it a "rare delight," because of his "profound knowledge" and a writing style that was "so full of verve, of living palpitating interest, that one reads it like one of Stevenson's stories of adventure." Not even Kautsky himself thought that highly of his book.[51]

While Kautsky's first contribution to the International Library series has not stood the test of time very well, it was an interesting attempt to achieve a number of things. First of all, as with his study of Thomas More, he hoped to establish a respectable historical pedigree for socialism by revealing precursors in the past. In this case they were the communal religious sects of the late middle ages and early modern years, like the Hussites, Taborites, and Hutterites. Though he was careful to distinguish between this communism of consumption and the modern communism of production, Kautsky managed to claim continuity of the good aspects from the former to the latter. He was even more successful at tying things like the destruction of the family to the communism of consumption while disclaiming any association along these lines with modern productive communism.

Two weaknesses frequently associated with Marxian historians were not part of Kautsky's work. First, he did not simply project the present onto the past. He recognized that the vanguard of the revolutionary movement in Germany in the early sixteenth century was the peasantry and not some imagined proletariat or preproletariat. Second, he directly addressed himself to the problem of why the Reformation had for so long seemed a purely religious matter, after he had demonstrated what he saw as its socioeconomic roots. He claimed that the more widespread, the more sweeping a social movement becomes, "the greater becomes the necessity for establishing a rational connection between its separate claims." The more the larger movement was emphasized, the more "lofty general principles" seem to be motive forces. He was not able to eliminate religious motives completely, but he did attempt to explain away their uncomfortable persistence.[52]

One of the objections most frequently raised by contemporary critics of the study was that his contention that early Christians were primitive communists was not true. In his *Foundations of Christianity,* which first appeared in 1908, he set out to investigate the nature and origin of the faith of his culture, though it was not, of course, his faith. In so doing he reentered one of the great radical traditions of nineteenth-century German thought and in fact was reinvestigating a topic intimately associated with the origins of Marxism. But unlike the Young Hegelians and the young Marx, Kautsky was already certain that he had the tool necessary for a proper analysis of the pertinent information, namely, the materialist conception of history. Disclaiming any expertise in church or religious history, he concentrated on reviewing secondary materials and on subjecting available evidence to rational tests of internal consistency and compatibility. This work was not new scholarship; it did not present new evidence. Nonetheless, *Foundations* was the best history that Kautsky wrote—it had a bold confidence, a rational constancy, and an openness that make it readable still today.[53]

Foundations was also history with a purpose, which Kautsky made clear in his introduction: "To bring the proletariat to social insight, to self-consciousness and political maturity" by revealing that history is determined by the socioeconomic substructure of society and not by the repressive facade of the dominant bourgeois, Christian ideology. He did this by arguing for the class nature of early Christianity, largely the doctrine of the urban poor, and by setting the rise of the faith against the backdrop of the dissolution of the Roman Empire. He recognized early Christianity as a progressive force which assisted in the transition from ancient (slave) production to feudal production. But once again he denied that the ideology was anything but "religious garb" that helped the ignorant masses cope with "social forces they did not understand and which appeared to them as sinister." This analysis was obviously intended to reinforce the Marxian notion that because "scientific socialism" provided the means by which the proletariat could overcome its ignorance, the days of religion were past.[54]

In his introduction to *Foundations,* Kautsky contended that the materialist conception of history "guards us against the danger of measuring the past with the yardstick of the present," and to make this point even more plainly, he argued in the text that the difference in status and function of the ancient and modern proletariats made impossible much fruitful comparison of the two groups. But despite such denials, so much of his argument was based on parallels with modern history that his book was weakened by the very tendencies he rejected; on too many occasions he explained the period of the rise of Christianity by reference to the French revolutions of 1789, 1848, and 1871. An even more fundamental problem, one which Kautsky shares with most materialist historians, was that the arguments, for all their neatness and consistency, were based on assumptions that were not sufficiently investigated or demonstrated as true. Very convincing points were made about the relationship between the class nature of early Christian sects and the theological differences among the sects, but he failed to offer convincing evidence that the class analysis could be substantiated. For instance, once he had asserted that the Sadducees were nobles, the Pharisees bourgeois merchants, and the Essenes the "mass of the people," he gave satisfying nontheological explanations for the hatred that divided the sects and for the differing attitudes on the question of free will. However, because he did not investigate the validity of his assumptions, though it reads easily with its modern tone, *Foundations* is today little more than an intriguing period piece and a monument to Kautsky's doctrinal commitment.[55]

The relative calm of 1907-1908 was abruptly shattered in February 1909, when the central committee of the SPD refused to give its approval to a second edition of Kautsky's *The Road to Power,* which had been issued by the party's publishing house in January. The party leaders thought the work too radical. This book has frequently been described as the highest development of Kautsky's verbal radicalism, with the implication that he was radical in speech, but not in action. As a close look at the mass-strike debate has revealed, Kautsky was only apparently radical in 1905-1906 as well, since he rejected the use of the mass strike while urging discussion of it. But all this is hindsight, and in order to understand the reception afforded *The Road to Power,* the situation within the SPD in early 1909 must be understood. The years after 1906 were marked by a powerful resurgence of the right wing, a resurgence greatly stimulated by the loss of mandates in the 1907 elections. Despite being frozen out of effective parliamentary power by the Bülow bloc, the reformists and revisionists, often backed by the trade unions, tried to move the party further from its old radicalism in order to create a situation in which the socialists might gain acceptance into the dominant system. One particularly strong aspect of the right-wing revival was the increasing boldness of the south German SPD Landtag delegations in their support for provincial budgets. The national party had long had a tradition of opposing any budget that included funds for military expenditures or funds that would otherwise result in a direct or obvious strengthening of the hated state.

Though in fact this principle had often been challenged, especially in south Germany, the violators had never before been quite so bold as they became after 1906.[56]

Against this backdrop Kautsky wrote his book. Actually it was an expansion of an earlier series of *Neue Zeit* articles in which he had attacked the south Germans for supporting the budgets. In the course of this earlier exchange, two major themes had emerged: (1) the place of theory in the working-class movement; and (2) the effect of the so-called positive work of the socialists, that is, the pursuit of votes, election of candidates, and support for laws to protect and improve the lot of the workers. The opinions expressed by Kautsky were not new, but they were more clearly and forcefully articulated in *The Road to Power* than they had been previously. Furthermore, he could reach a considerably larger, more variegated audience in a small book distributed by the official party publishing house than he could in the *Neue Zeit*. When the central committee saw the first edition of 5,000 copies sell out in a few weeks' time, it felt compelled to oppose reissue because of the work's exaggerated radicalism. For the first time, Kautsky felt the pressure of trying to oppose the entrenched bureaucrats who made up the central committee.[57]

Why did the central committee find Kautsky's work offensive? Largely because it felt that the author had committed a tactical error by talking about the party's traditional but vague tie to revolution in the distant future. In *The Road to Power,* Kautsky had not demanded immediate action or a change of tactics, but had only reasserted the notion that the ruling powers in Germany would not allow the endless growth of the SPD and the trade unions, would not allow Germany to grow peacefully into socialism. Bebel articulated the central committee's objection in a letter to Adler: "With regard to the content of the brochure, I am of the opinion that one can think everything and also speak out in circles of trusted people, but to say it publicly is stupidity." He went on to point to the danger of feeding the opposition with extremism and claimed that "Kautsky has no feeling for such tactical questions, he gazes on the ends as if hypnotized, in all else he has no interest and no understanding." The times were hard for the politicians in the party. The loss of mandates in 1907 and the strength of the Bülow bloc created conditions that seemed ripe for renewed repression, which the party and trade-union bureaucracy feared more than anything.[58]

On the other hand, there was an additional possible source for the hostility of the central committee, namely Kautsky's powerful assertion that without theory, both as a consciousness-raising tool and as a source of direction, the mundane work of the movement would lead nowhere. This struck deeply into the heart of the growing socialist bureaucracy and attacked the basic rationale for its existence. By making this claim, Kautsky was once more inveighing against the "movement-is-everything" mentality that had emerged during the revisionism debates. His attack had three aspects. First, he scorned the party's emphasis on the "practical," which, he said, "signifies the insipid and insignificant." In order to have any coherent meaning, the practical activities of socialists had to be guided by long-term considerations, that is, by theory. Second, he claimed that the "positive work" of the party and the trade unions, far from being a reflection of the possibility of growing into socialism, was in fact a major source of continued antagonism between the bourgeois parties and the workers' party and also was the most important means of raising proletarian consciousness. And finally, he asserted that "however much the proletarian organizations grow, they will never in normal, nonrevolutionary times include the whole of the working class . . . but only an elite." This point applied not only to the trade unions, but also to the party itself. For while as much as three-fourths of the total population by its class nature could be considered a potential socialist bloc, the SPD received only about one-third of the votes cast, and less than one-fourth of all the eligible votes. The remainder of the population was "only revolutionary as a *possibility*, not a *reality*." And converting the possibility into a reality was the function of socialist propaganda, according to Kautsky.[59]

This entire analysis, though Kautsky claimed otherwise, clearly diminished the significance of the political and economic organizations vis-à-vis the activities of the intellectuals in the party. That this view offended the party bureaucracy was not surprising, and Kautsky certainly thought this was the source of the central committee's opposition to the second edition of *The Road to Power*. He complained to one friend that the party leaders, even Bebel, were knuckling under out of fear: "The situation today is that the most powerful social democratic party in the world has the most servile central committee in the world." To Adler, he emphasized the internal party struggle by this reference to the central committee: "The louts want to let the intellectual feel their power, to show him that he is merely their coolie and has to submit when they command." When the central committee refused to permit a second edition, Kautsky immediately launched an attack on its right to do that. He appealed to the party's control commission; he prepared for a legal and party battle; and he went to Austria for a few days, in part to consult Adler, in part to apply pressure on the central committee by suggesting that he might leave Germany altogether. He was, in fact, prepared to stay in Austria for up to six months, and in cooperation with Adler, who disapproved of the contents of *The Road to Power*, but objected even more to the central committee's effort to repress it, made plans to have the brochure reprinted in Vienna. In the end, mainly because of Clara Zetkin's determined support for her close friend, the control commission disagreed with the central committee's decision, and the latter gave in. Bebel called Kautsky back from Vienna, and the work was reprinted with very minor alterations. It rapidly sold out second and third editions of 5,000 copies each and eventually became one of Kautsky's best selling pieces.[60]

Centrism

Butting heads with the central committee did nothing to improve Kautsky's opinion of the party during the years of stagnation after 1905. He specifically identified one of the major problems within German socialism as the growth of a bureaucracy. "Incompetence and pettiness," he wrote to Adler, had cost the German party its leading role in the international movement. Kautsky had once thought the major problem was one of personnel, one that would be helped by a change in the composition of the central committee. But by 1909, he had come to realize that "the causes lie deeper." He then saw "an overgrowth of bureaucracy . . . that stifled every initiative from below." While he was not accusing the leadership of cowardice, only of over-conscientiousness, neither was he willing to urge agitation for mass action. Kautsky's conviction was that only spontaneous action could be sustained, and no amount of agitation could yield the long-term commitment necessary for revolution. On the other hand, he was convinced that the leaders of the party had to be prepared to take advantage of mass action if it were to come at the right time. However, first the trade unions and then the party had come to be led by people who were absorbed in "the administrative dealings of the enormous apparatus." Kautsky was at this time close to despair about the prospects of the German party, and once again he toyed with the idea of returning to Austria, only to be restrained again by material need and the lack of a trusted successor.[61]

Unfortunately, identifying the problems of the party and doing something about them were two different tasks. Though Kautsky was very good at the former, he was incapable of undertaking the latter. Through much of 1909 and into 1910, he dealt with the reformist-revisionist forces on a theoretical level, in the *Neue Zeit* and occasionally in the *Vorwärts*, but he never even attempted internal party reforms that might have helped the party break out of its stagnation. In large part this was because he simply was not a man of action, neither a politician nor an agitator. Furthermore, his entire world view, his conviction of the inevitable decay of capitalism, and his unquenchable optimism made him fall back increasingly on the traditional tactics of the party. Thus even when his own analysis boded ill for the future of socialism in Germany, he could do little but insist that the continued growth of the movement, in membership, votes, "positive work," in all ways, had to increase the tensions of German society until something broke. Once again, his logic was not so much at fault as was his failure to perceive that even when the crisis came his party would not be prepared to do anything but drift with the tide and protect itself. When the traumatic events of 1914 and 1918 occurred, he found that the party in which he had placed his trust was sorely wanting. At least part of the responsibility for this situation must be borne by Kautsky himself, because he failed to act on his own astute diagnosis of the illnesses of the SPD.

Strangely enough, the more Kautsky's concern about internal party developments increased, the more he insisted on the validity of traditional party tactics. By 1910 this tendency, along with two changes in the larger political scene of Germany, combined to bring him to articulate the theoretical position he called "centrism." In mid-1909, the Bülow bloc collapsed when the chancellor found it impossible to win conservative support for his finance reform bill that would have shifted much of the burden of state finances to direct property taxes. The end of the bloc seemed to open up the possibility of having the SPD help channel Reich politics in a more progressive direction by cooperating with the left-liberal parties against the conservative-Junker clique. This change naturally encouraged the right wing of the party to strengthen its demands for a more active parliamentary policy. But at about the same time there was also a resurgence of popular mass action protesting the restrictive franchise of Prussia and a growing popular protest over the kaiser's irresponsible conduct of Reich foreign policy. These developments encouraged the small but highly vocal left wing of the SPD to demand that the party take the lead in the protest movements. Kautsky's response to these contradictory pressures was to draw a narrow line between right and left and then to show the party how to walk that line.[62]

The first move came from the left, specifically from Rosa Luxemburg. Early in February 1910, the new chancellor, Bethmann Hollweg, who like all the chancellors before him was also head of the Prussian government, proposed a franchise reform bill for Germany's largest state that would have changed nothing essential. When popular protests against the proposal broke out, Luxemburg wrote an article in which she suggested that the party take this opportunity to use street demonstrations and the mass strike to win real reform. After the *Vorwärts* refused to print her article, Luxemburg sent it to Kautsky. The *Neue Zeit* editor at first accepted the article, then later rejected it, arguing that given the unrest at the time, to print the piece would have been inflammatory and dangerous. By rejecting Luxemburg's article, and by doing it in a manner which suggested outside influence (since Kautsky had changed his mind, Luxemburg felt that he had been pressured by the central committee) and perhaps fear of prosecution, Kautsky brought on the final break between himself and his radical friend. Though their relationship had been badly strained during the previous few years, the two had managed to remain civil until early 1910. Now Luxemburg, who felt she had been grievously wronged, unleashed her nasty pen and bitter tongue to get even with Kautsky for his influence and calm. She did not, however, break with Luise, and was not above using the wife against the husband, turning a doctrinal quarrel into a vicious personal assault. The more reasonable and plodding Kautsky was in the debate, the more irrational and frenzied was Luxemburg's response. She knew that she was fighting against an opponent supported by the massive inertia of the party leadership, and her only recourse was to ever sharper attack.[63]

For his part, Kautsky committed a serious tactical blunder, not so much by rejecting Luxemburg's article, as by taking up the polemic once the article appeared elsewhere. Of course had he not responded to Luxemburg's arguments, he would then have been even more open to charges of censorship and repression, but probably the acrimony and personal discomfort associated with such a situation would have been less than what followed from the actual debate. Furthermore, the debate itself was utterly fruitless and finally had to be abandoned altogether after becoming very awkward. Given the position of the party and trade-union leadership, which moved rightward after 1905, there was never much chance that the party would take an active role in the franchise-reform agitation. But even more, Kautsky had nothing new to say on the mass-strike issue, having said it all in 1906–1907. Once again he objected to calls for such action because the situation in the Reich at the time was not revolutionary. Once again he called for careful attention to the real situation in Germany rather than irrelevant analogies with other countries or emotional appeals that contradicted rational analysis. In the course of this debate Kautsky applied an old label, *Ermattungsstrategie,* or "strategy of attrition," to the long-term, traditional policies he espoused for the party. Social democracy would win, he said, not by employing the shock tactics of major upheaval, but by wearing down, by outlasting the opposition. An integral part of this tactic, however, was the continued pursuit of aggressive political positions by the party. Perhaps the only things gained by this involved exchange were public clarification of Kautsky's attitude toward the mass strike and the climax of the split with Luxemburg.[64]

In mid-July, the polemic with Luxemburg was interrupted when the SPD representatives in the Baden Landtag announced that they no longer felt themselves bound by the party's tradition of opposition to budget support and then voted for the state budget. Though by that time Kautsky had begun to see that the debate over the mass strike would lead nowhere, Bebel's swift and severe response to the Baden budget vote certainly encouraged a turn of the theoretical guns from the left to the right. Apparently this act by the south Germans finally broke Bebel's tolerance, because he immediately called upon Kautsky to "let the mess with Rosa go; now we have other things to do than quarrel about an unlaid egg." He urged Kautsky to attack "sharply" against the Badenese, forcing "either acknowledgment of and submission to party decisions or withdrawal from the party." Kautsky was happy to "let the mess with Rosa go," but because the matter had become so personal, he felt the need to explain his position to Luise. He argued that everyone had grown bored with Luxemburg's arguments and that the entire party felt that "she utters the wrong word in the wrong place." He further felt justified in dropping the mass-strike debate because Luxemburg had violated party courtesy by transforming theoretical disputes into personal hostility. Comrades, said Kautsky, did not do such things. For instance, Bebel, Marx, and Engels had often had differences with Wilhelm Liebknecht, "but they considered it stupid and improper to unbraid him publicly on that account, as Rosa [has] me." Although Luxemburg tried to prolong the polemic, sending a long article to Kautsky through one of her hangers-on, Hans Diefenbach, he rejected it, explaining, "Every polemic must end sometime."[65]

The conjunction of the budget vote and the mass-strike debate offered Kautsky a unique opportunity to give explicit form to the centrism that had begun to emerge after 1905. He did this in his most cleverly titled article, "Between Baden and Luxemburg," which appeared in the *Neue Zeit* number of 5 August 1910. Actually this article was part of the mass-strike debate, since the first eleven pages were devoted to a refutation of Luxemburg and the last five pages to an analysis of the prospects for mass strikes in Germany. On the latter,

Kautsky contended that mass strikes were more likely in countries without political rights for the workers, but more potent in countries with highly developed capitalist economies, and that in Germany a mass strike could not succeed unless it were a truly spontaneous phenomenon. Therefore, he concluded, the task of the party in Germany was to avoid the potential disaster of a premature or fabricated mass strike, but to be prepared to recognize and lead to victory a genuine mass strike. However, the greater significance of this article lay in its last two paragraphs. How was the party to fulfill the difficult task ahead of it?

> It will march to victory between Baden and Luxemburg.
> If we look at a map of the grand duchies of Baden and Luxemburg, we find that between them lies Trier, the city out of which Karl Marx came. If you go left from there, over the border, you come to Luxemburg. If you go sharply to the right, across the Rhine, you arrive at Baden. Today the situation on the map is a symbol of the situation in German social democracy.[66]

As Kautsky pointed out in this article, the number of party members arguing in favor of moving toward Baden was much greater than those arguing that the party should go toward Luxemburg; he therefore felt the threat from the right to be the greater and spent most of his time during the almost exactly four years before the war attacking the right. But in so doing he was being rational without being right, for in the entire debate with Rosa Luxemburg he had failed to address himself even once to the spirit, rather than the content of her argument. Luxemburg's point, though it was not specifically articulated, was that a party that only sat and waited would not be able to act when the time came. Kautsky's rebuttal was directed at the specifics of Luxemburg's position, and his conclusions made a good deal of sense. The German government did have the strength necessary to crush anything short of a truly massive popular movement, and the number of people who had taken to the streets in the spring of 1910 was probably not sufficient to carry the day. Kautsky himself had privately expressed serious doubts about the fitness of his party to lead the masses should they ever rise up. But rather than suggest reforms, rather than support tests and probes of mass action that might have sparked the party out of its lethargy, he only girded himself for a two-front war, against both right and left. The centrism that developed as a result of this posture made sense as an analysis of the prospects for socialism in Germany only if major emotional factors were ignored. Unfortunately, the decisive factors at the hour of crisis, in August of 1914, were to be emotional, not rational.

Emotions and overwork took their toll on Kautsky in 1910. Shortly after the Copenhagen congress of the Second International, he went to Baden-Baden for several weeks of rest and treatment at two sanatoria and did not return to Berlin until late November. Bebel was convinced that Karl's nervous breakdown was largely the result of the "struggle of souls" with Luxemburg and the "foolishly large amount of literary work" of the previous few years. Kautsky recognized these factors as causes, but also hinted at the impact of the more intimate aspects of the conflict with Luxemburg when he wrote to Luise that he was recovering slowly because "the course of neurasthenia as well as the course of true love never runs smooth." He revealed his problems with Luise and his odd ailments, humor, and English in another letter to his wife: "Its dreadfully cold and I feel icicles in the brain. I have found again the 1½ pounds of flesh I had lost last week [he had been down to 133 pounds]. And that in spite of my having paid my first weekly bill. They have charged me 9.50 [marks] per day. I am making progress and get daily more strength, was able today to make a nice walk. . . . Some warm underclothing, which I asked for a week ago, would do me good."[67] This was the second time, the first being after the dispute with Bernstein, that Kautsky had had to retire for peace and quiet after a particularly bitter confrontation with a former comrade. Perhaps because he did not engage in the public venting of his emotional distress over such polemics, because he did not turn theoretical attacks into personal attacks, Kautsky suffered seriously from such encounters.

Even if holding off the left caused Kautsky the greater anguish, he definitely perceived battling the right to be the more serious task. On at least two occasions before the outbreak of the First World War, he felt compelled to take up arms against the leftists again, once in late 1911 to rehash the question of mass action and once in mid-1914 to rehash the question of the mass strike, but mostly he concentrated on preventing the rightists from winning over the entire party. Bebel was partly responsible for this approach, but Kautsky's conviction that consciousness-raising and avoiding the pitfalls of compromise were the major tasks of socialist intellectuals was even more important. Delicately balancing between right and left was always a difficult job, but it was especially hard when his positions seemed to favor the right wing of the party. Thus in the months surrounding the election of 1912, in which the party broke with its decades-old tradition of not entering into electoral alliances, Kautsky seemed to be siding with the reformists by favoring such action. But of course he had always argued against the "one reactionary mass" slogan and in favor of using disputes among the opposition to the advantage of the socialists. As early as the Prussian Landtag elections of 1893, he had urged the party to form such alliances. As long as doctrinal purity was preserved, as Kautsky was convinced it had been, he thought such cooperation with the enemy entirely acceptable. While the smashing success of the party in the 1912 election—it more than recouped the losses of 1907, winning 110 seats and becoming the largest party in the Reichstag—reinforced Kautsky's conviction about the validity of the old tactics, another topic had begun to cause serious breaches in the solid ranks of the SPD. This was the question of imperialism, and it involved several fundamental issues facing an oppositional party in the Wilhelmine Reich—nationalism, militarism, and eventually war.[68]

Imperialism

Imperialism was one of the most complicated issues confronting socialists in the years before 1914; it was also an increasingly important matter as western Europe passed through successive crises in an atmosphere heavy with the threat of war. From the Boer and Spanish-American wars of the late nineties, through the Russo-Japanese war of 1904–1905, to the Moroccan crises of 1905–1906 and 1911, socialists, and many others in Europe, felt more and more that a major war would inevitably follow from imperialist conflicts. In general, international socialism was no more united in its view of the nature of imperialism than are present-day historians. But after 1902, with the publication of John A. Hobson's seminal work, *Imperialism*, socialists came increasingly to identify imperialism with capitalism. This tendency reached a climax for Marxists in 1917 in Lenin's *Imperialism, the Highest Stage of Capitalism*, but for German socialists before the war, the key work was Rudolf Hilferding's *Finance Capital* (1910). Kautsky's views of the nature and function of imperialism were strongly influenced by this tendency, and especially by Hilferding's study. He did not accept the identification of imperialism and capitalism, however, and he tended to emphasize its political aspects more strongly than its economic aspects.[69]

In his earliest work on the colonial expansion of western European nations, Kautsky had associated such activity with commercial-capitalist interests and with land-hungry, agrarian-oriented aristocrats. In 1898, and as late as 1909, in the midst of a resurgence of expansionism, he still expressed this opinion. But at the same time he began to see imperialism as a modern phenomenon, as intimately related to mature capitalism, rather than to the early phase of primitive capital accumulation. More importantly, he began to concentrate not on the nature and origins of imperialism, but on its effects. Kautsky was particularly concerned with three things. First, the imperial policies were popular, and the aggressive assault by the government on the SPD as unpatriotic, which reached its prewar peak in the 1907 election, forced Kautsky to deal with the political ramifications of imperialism. Second, the growing strength of the right wing within the SPD and international socialism and its demand for a socialist colonial policy brought Kautsky to reiterate his humanitarian and doctrinal objections to all colonialism. And third, the obvious relationship between constant imperialist rivalries and the seemingly endless armaments race led all socialists, including Kautsky, to discuss the imperialism-militarism-war question.[70]

Kautsky saw both nationalism, in the form of hostility to other countries, and imperialism as primarily bourgeois capitalist phenomena which were used by the German government to strengthen itself vis-à-vis worker opposition, to undermine the solidarity of the working class, and to draw the middle classes into an alliance with conservative Junkers. When in 1905, Bülow contended that the SPD was unpatriotic because it criticized the government's conduct in the first Moroccan crisis, Kautsky argued that just as all classes had distinct internal policies, so they had distinct foreign policies as well. While the "possessing classes" thought of the "Fatherland [as] the embodiment of their own riches, of their own power," and gave automatic support to governmental policies, the socialists did not. The workers were not antinational, because they, too, were concerned with the prosperity and security of their country. But when nationalism meant hatred of and conflict with other countries, as it had to under competitive capitalism, the workers rejected it. Though capitalistic nationalists could accept the slogan My Country Right or Wrong, a social democrat had "to have enough intelligence and courage to be able to recognize when the special interests of a nation, even his own, stand in the way of the struggle for the emancipation of the proletariat, and to act accordingly."[71]

Given his career-long rejection of the "one reactionary mass" concept, Kautsky's persistent claim that some among the bourgeois classes also opposed war is not surprising. Before he had been markedly influenced by Hilferding's book, Kautsky argued that socialists might cooperate with bourgeois and petit bourgeois pacifists against the government's imperialistic, warlike policies. And even after 1910, he still insisted that there were bourgeois groups opposed to war, though now he argued that the rest of their politics worked against their pacifistic desires. The tactic of cooperation proved to be singularly unsuccessful, however, inasmuch as even their opposition to war could not overcome the hostility of German bourgeois pacifists to the SPD. On the international level, Kautsky advised each socialist party to fight militarism and imperialism at home, arguing that attacking the policies of another country simply played into the hands of the militarists on both sides. He was particularly insistent on this point at the 1910 Copenhagen congress of the Second International, when the English socialist H. M. Hyndman asserted that as long as the German socialists could not prevent Germany from making war, which Kautsky readily admitted was impossible, the English socialists had to support increased armaments. Kautsky was convinced that this sort of fuzzy thinking vitiated the fundamental precepts of the International.[72]

In addition to these political objections, Kautsky opposed imperialism because it was exploitative, brutalizing, and racist. The humanistic values implicit in his position formed the basis for his strenuous rejection of anything resembling a socialist colonial policy, which he thought a contradiction in terms. On this he was fully supported by Bebel, who also found the idea of socialists administering colonies an absurd one. Following publication of Kautsky's pamphlet, *Socialism and Colonial Policy* (1907), Bebel gave high praise to the author's firm stand against socialist colonialism. But his praise was primarily for the political implications of the pamphlet, and Kautsky's position far transcended politics. He was not simply taking a stand against those within the SPD, mainly revisionists like Bernstein and opportunists like Ludwig Quessel, who argued for a socialist colonial policy. Kautsky's position revealed the limits to which he was prepared to extend the determinist implications of his Marxism, but even more it revealed the very basic humanist commitment that underpinned this Marxism.[73]

The major proponents of a socialist colonial policy used three kinds of arguments to support their demands. One was a very pragmatic and sensible suggestion that, since all colonial administrations were less than perfect, the socialists in national parliaments should work to improve conditions in the colonies. Second, carrying to an extreme the determinist implications of the dominant quasi-Marxist mode of thought, these people argued that before the colonies could become socialist, they would have to pass through the capitalist phase of economic development. This was, of course, simply the for-export version of the early deviation from Marxism that argued that the cause of socialism could best be served by promoting the development of capitalism. Third, the proponents of a socialist colonial policy argued that the interests of the native populations of colonies could best be served by bringing them civilization in the form of the new technological advancements provided by capitalism. The major figures with whom Kautsky debated this matter were the Dutch socialist Henri van Kol, at the 1907 Stuttgart congress of the Second International, and Emile Vandervelde, the leader of the Belgian party, who presented his position in a 1909 *Neue Zeit* article. At Stuttgart, van Kol presented the majority report of the colonial commission and Kautsky spoke in favor of the minority report which much more strongly rejected the colonial concept. The minority report was accepted overwhelmingly, and Kautsky's speech was soundly cheered.[74]

The most frequent objection Kautsky had to a socialist colonial policy was that all colonies were exploitative, and exploitation was exploitation whether "proclaimed openly in the name of profits or hypocritically in the name of Christ or even in the name of Karl Marx." When the imperialist frenzy of the time brought the Italian invasion of Tripoli, which many Italian socialists supported, Kautsky gave fullest vent to his disgust: "All of colonial politics rests on the conception, and is impossible without it, that the inhabitants of the noncapitalist lands are not human like we are, do not have human rights, but are inferior beings like mere animals. Humane colonial policy distinguishes itself from the ordinary only in that it demands that the human animals should be well treated, as animal protection leagues demand the same for horses and dogs." In response to Vandervelde, Kautsky claimed that far from being the advance of civilization, colonial expansion was based on the most shameless disregard for the human and property rights of the native population, and only the cultural egocentrism of the western nations made it seem otherwise. The only sort of reforms socialists should promote were those which either granted immediate freedom to the native population or were directed at increasing the power of the natives to resist foreign dominations. "Ethical speeches about culture and civilization," said Kautsky, only supported "colonial tyranny." Rarely did pre-1914 socialists hear the humanist doctrines of their cause more forcefully argued.[75]

As imperialist crises continued, a contradiction developed in Kautsky's thought. For one thing, under the influence of Hilferding's book, his attitude toward the relationship between capitalism and militaristic imperialism hardened. By 1912, he specifically rejected his turn-of-the-century position which held that the real militarists in German society were not industrial capitalists but the traditional landed aristocracy that dominated the army; he now accepted without significant qualification the doctrine that mature capitalism necessarily implied imperialism which necessarily implied militarism. But at the same time, as the threat of war increased, his aversion to, and horror of, war increased also. Whereas in 1904 he had been able to accept war as a regrettable, but nonetheless inevitable, result of modern society, by late 1910 and early 1911, the very real threat of impending war caused him to seek means of avoiding the disaster he knew it held, especially for the workers. Whereas earlier he had scoffed at the efforts of bourgeois pacifists to restrict armaments without ending capitalism, now he argued that "the armaments race is based on economic causes, but not on economic necessity. Its discontinuance is not in the least an economic impossibility." In 1912, he urged political opposition to armaments because he no longer thought of "the armaments race and the threatening war as something inevitable, for which the ruling parties are as guiltless as bourgeois society itself." The moral convictions that had brought him to socialism in the first place resurfaced after 1911. He rejected war as an inevitable result of the capitalist system he had struggled against for so long and assigned blame to the supporters of the system he was now convinced would bring the war he dreaded. In a direct confrontation between his logical analysis and his moral commitments, his humanistic aversion to a disastrous war won out.[76]

Here at last Kautsky's theory became fatalistic, because he also recognized that the party of the proletariat would not be able to prevent war. He had long accepted war as an extension of politics, and he argued that if socialists could not influence the politics that led to war, if the party could not bring reason to bear in times of peace, then the possibility of stopping war once it broke out was slim indeed. In 1905 he had rejected as impossible the stopping of a war by means of a mass strike. He argued that after war had begun the best that socialists could hope for was that a minority elite of the organized workers would respond to a call for such a strike. "The idea of a military strike," he concluded, "is therefore well meant, most noble and heroic, but an heroic folly." He was also convinced that a major European war would bring revolution, and he developed political tactics for socialists at the outbreak of a war which would be popular at the outset, but would eventually create the mass disaffection necessary for revolution. If war came, Kautsky said, then the socialists had to take the unpopular position of opposing it. This would cost the party politically in the first phase of the war, but as the conflict dragged on, more and more people would gravitate toward the socialist position. When the war finally brought the collapse of capitalist society, the socialists would have the popular backing that would allow them to lead the revolution. A principled but unpopular stance at the beginning of war would yield fruit at the end; thus Kautsky tied the inevitable revolution to the end of the war, not its beginning, as did many leftists in the international movement.[77]

This conviction, and the pragmatic demands of the immediate situation, molded Kautsky's response to the assassination of Archduke Franz Ferdinand and the mounting threat of war that followed. By late July 1914, Kautsky reported to Adler with regret that in Germany there were no manifestations of popular mass action against the war, but he still hoped that the conflict could be localized in the Balkan region as it had in 1912. But he was also well aware of the growing nationalistic sentiments within the SPD and wrote to Adler that if general war did break out, "we must be happy if we succeed in upholding party unity."[78]

On 3 August, Kautsky was invited to attend the conference of the SPD *Fraktion* at which a decision was to be made on whether to vote for or against or to abstain when the government's request for special war credits was laid before the Reichstag on the following day. Though Kautsky was not a member of the *Fraktion*, his status as party theoretician and the respect even his party opponents had for his views earned him the right, or the burden perhaps, of attendance. The situation had changed rapidly in the previous few days. On 31 July, the party central committee had discussed whether to abstain or reject; by 2 August it was deciding between rejecting and approving. On 1 August, the right-wing members of the *Fraktion*, including Eduard David, Robert Schmidt, and Eduard Bernstein among others, had met separately and decided to vote for the credits, regardless of the official decision.[79]

On 1 August, Kautsky and his closest ally on the central committee and in the *Fraktion*, Hugo Haase, had drafted a statement for the parliamentary group that was based on the assumption that it would refuse to vote for war credits. But once he discovered that even his urging to abstain would not be accepted by the *Fraktion*, Kautsky changed his tack, hoping to salvage as much fidelity to principle as possible. When appointed to a five-member committee to draft the party's official declaration, after a seventy-eight to fourteen vote had decided for credit approval, he joined with Gustav Hoch in urging that a sharp attack on the ruling classes and a clause demanding that the government renounce beforehand any annexations of territory or violations of neutrality be included in the declaration. In the final document this last effort to save face was stricken after the foreign office intervened. Kautsky had lost, and his party accepted the *Burgfrieden* ("civic truce") and made the war its own. In late November

1914, when another war credits vote came up, Kautsky once again urged that the rejected clause be included in the SPD vote statement. But after four months of war he knew that his worst fears had been realized, that the party had succumbed to the confusion and fears of the war situation. This time he knew his demand was a hopeless one, and he admitted to Adler, "I will make it merely in order to salve my conscience."[80] The SPD that Kautsky thought he had served died on 4 August 1914. The causes of death were perhaps natural, but Kautsky must share some of the blame for failing to prescribe preventive measures during the decades after 1890.

CHAPTER SIX

The Great War and
Two Revolutions,
1914–1924

IN RETROSPECT, Karl Kautsky lost the basis for his historical importance on 4 August 1914. The capitulation of most major socialist
parties to the nationalistic passions of the war, the apparent collapse of
the internationalist commitments of socialists, and, in 1917, the split of
the SPD, all were developments that contradicted Kautsky's preconceptions and convictions. With the Bolshevik seizure of power in late
1917, the focal point of world socialism began to shift from western
Europe to Russia and the nonwestern world. By mid-1919, Kautsky
was a man whom time had passed by. In 1924 he returned to Vienna to
live out the last years of his life as an isolated and all but forgotten
former doyen of Marxian socialism. The war and the rise of the
Bolsheviks changed the main thrust of Marxism in such a way that
Kautsky became a peripheral figure, at first viciously attacked and
subjected to ridicule and scorn, but finally merely rejected.

Kautsky's fall from prominence symbolized the resolution, at least
for a time, of the ambiguities of Marxism as the theory of revolutionary
movements. Kautsky represented the more deterministic, less violent,
more humanistic implications of Marx's writings. Lenin represented
the more voluntaristic, more violent, less humanistic implications of
those same writings. The savage brutality of war and the hostility of
both internal and external opponents drove first Russian and then a
large proportion of international Marxism further and further from
Kautsky's milder interpretations. But it was historical circumstance
that determined the shift, not the inherent qualities of Marxism,
whether of Lenin's or of Kautsky's brand. Despite the claims of the
ideologues, Kautsky's interpretation of Marxism was not incorrect, it
was just on the losing side. Unfortunately for his historical and per-

sonal reputation, historians, like sports fans, are attracted by, and compelled to deal with, winners.

Opposition to the War and the Party

Once formal declarations of war had been made, Kautsky's major concern was to preserve as much theoretical integrity as possible in the face of the overwhelming national enthusiasm for war. This enthusiasm was widespread, affecting not only the great majority of the SPD *Fraktion*, but also the mass of the working-class population. Kautsky had long felt that if the socialists could not significantly influence the politics that led to war, they certainly could not hope to stop it once it had broken out. For this reason he contended that once conflict erupted, the major practical question was not war or peace, but victory or defeat. However, as will be shown below, he was very suspicious of the motives of the German government. He placed very narrow limits on the extent to which socialists could cooperate with the ruling classes in the pursuit of victory. After the war credits vote of 4 August, his major efforts were directed at keeping the party from splitting over the war issue, and providing theoretical clarity in the muddle of the first weeks of war.

Kautsky contended that though the socialist workers' movement was internationalist, each separate movement had a perfectly legitimate and necessary interest in defending national integrity. He made a distinction between the national state (*Nationalstaat*) and the nationalistic state *(Nationalitätenstaat),* the former being characterized by shared language and interests, the latter being primarily an aggressive, negative concept based on recognition of common enemies. The workers, said Kautsky, had always and would always recognize the validity of national states, but their internationalism made them reject nationalistic states, which were associated with the economic and political predominance of the bourgeoisie. This argument was an expansion of a position Kautsky had put forth in a much different context in 1907. During the first two-and-a-half years of the war, Kautsky used this position primarily against the right-wing members of the SPD who completely capitulated to war fever. But as the war dragged on, the leftist opposition within the German party became more vociferous in its insistence that national defense contradicted Marx's contention that the workers had no country. Kautsky pointed out to the left that even in the *Communist Manifesto,* Marx explicitly recognized that the workers did have national interests, but that they were qualitatively different from those of the bourgeoisie in that workers' nationalism was not defined in opposition to the interests of other nations.[1]

For most of the war Kautsky felt that preserving the unity of the party was of the utmost importance. His notion of how the socialists would fare during and after the war was predicated on the assumption that the party would remain united and pursue the tactic of moral opposition. Furthermore, like most other political observers at the time, in August and September 1914, Kautsky assumed that the war would be a short one, perhaps only three months, but certainly not more than six months to a year long. He was convinced that the massive demands made by modern warfare on human and natural resources, industrial and financial systems, and military machines could not be sustained for very long. Thus, though he was acutely aware of the divisive impact of the war on the SPD, as long as he assumed the war would be short, he restrained his own criticism for the sake of preserving the unity that would be vital after the war ended.

As the war continued, Kautsky came increasingly to realize that the requirement of party unity was difficult to reconcile with the friction created by the enthusiastic support given the war effort by the party's right wing. Even in late November 1914, when the war was approaching its fourth month, he began to suggest that the duration of the war would make it extremely difficult for critics of the party's official policy to remain silent. At this time he was still inclined, in private, to see the Luxemburg-Liebknecht left as the major threat to party unity. He was clearly uncomfortable about being lumped together with the extreme left by right-wing critics and felt that Luxemburg's major aim was to create her own party since she could not dominate the SPD. As he wrote to Adler on 28 November: "If she [Luxemburg] cannot direct the large party, she wants to have a small one." But even at this early date Kautsky felt that the extremism of the right wing—David, Südekum, Heine, and the trade unionists especially—was a major factor in Luxemburg's appeal. By its enthusiastic support for the government the party had opposed for so long, the right wing encouraged the workers to turn to the left, so that they were drawing closer to Luxemburg's position with each day of the war. By February 1915, Kautsky's position had clearly shifted; he now felt that the greatest threat to party unity came not from the *Rosauriern,* the followers of Rosa Luxemburg, but from the right. At that time he only very reluctantly, out of a continuing commitment to unity and because of the pressures of wartime censorship, refrained from an outright condemnation of the party leadership, especially the *Fraktion*. From early 1915 until mid-1917, he concentrated almost exclusively on countering the party's right wing. His centrist position was most clearly revealed in his defense of the Second International against attacks from both the right and the left.[2]

Kautsky's distinction between the national state and the nationalistic state allowed him to contend that the workers of the major European nations had the right to national self-defense while also arguing that the war did not spell the end of the Second International. In addition, because he had never deluded himself, as had some proponents of the International, that this world organization of socialist parties had any but moral force at its command, Kautsky did not see socialist support for defensive war as a betrayal of internationalism and the destruction of the International. On this more than any other issue, the typical criticism of Kautsky as unrealistic is nonsense. He knew very well that socialists alone could not stop war, that massive popular protests would not occur once war had started, that the best the socialists of the world could hope for was to maintain moral superiority by not supporting aggressive, acquisitive war. Thus, unlike the right-wing socialists who abandoned internationalism in the same proportion as they accepted chauvinism, and unlike the left socialists who denounced the Second International to the extent that their unrealistic hopes were dashed by socialist support for the war, Kautsky doggedly insisted that the International had not been destroyed by the war. Rather he contended that the true nature and limits of the effectiveness of the International had been revealed by the response to the war.[3]

Through early 1915, then, Kautsky's position on the war and the SPD's response to it may be summarized as follows: Though clearly not enthusiastic about it, Kautsky argued that socialists had to support the war to the extent that it was a war of national self-defense, because the very real interests of the workers were at stake; though suspicious of the government's justifications for the war and of the enthusiasm of many socialists for the war, he moderated his criticisms out of considerations of party unity; and finally, assuming that the war would not last long, and that therefore party tensions would not reach intolerable levels, he looked forward to the impending peace and the advantages the socialists would reap from the war brought on by bourgeois imperialism.

These positions were all consistent with ones Kautsky had espoused long before the war, and each makes some sense in and of itself, but more than ever before, the shortcomings of his reliance on rational analysis were to be revealed by the more than four years of war. While he dealt with the war and the issues it raised in a calculating, sensible fashion, the revolutionary frustration and disgust of the left and the chauvinism of the right both increased quite independently of objective factors. But equally important to Kautsky's position during the first months of the war was his assumption that the conflict would not last long. Had the war been a short one, his restraint for the sake of unity might well have been justified by later events. But because the war dragged on for over four years, the internal conflicts of the party were exacerbated to the point of a split. Against the backdrop of this development, Kautsky's early caution could not win much support. Victor Adler was a more astute judge of human nature than was his close friend. In late March 1915, Adler wrote to Kautsky: "You think all men are like you, that [they] make decisions on reason. Quite the contrary. They act as they must and are able, and then they look for the theoretical foundation."[4] The enthusiasms of the extremes increasingly meant Kautsky's isolation.

Although entirely willing to hold off on intraparty criticism during the first few months of the war, Kautsky rejected the concept of *Burgfrieden* from the very beginning. He could not accept its implicit assumption that the German government was faultless with regard to the origins of the war, nor did he feel that his own concept of the validity of national self-defense demanded unquestioning support for the political and military actions of the German government and armed forces. He made a distinction between the "decision" of 4 August, that is, the war credits vote, which he felt was justified by the demands of national self-defense, and the "policy" of 4 August, that is, the *Burgfrieden* and the growing chauvinistic, imperialistic pronouncements of the socialists who supported the war. He rejected the "policy" of 4 August because it went beyond the reasonable requirements of national self-defense, demanding that socialists support imperialism, territorial aggrandizement, and the most extreme forms of national hatreds. He therefore regularly and fervently argued against the *Umlerner,* those who held that the party had to change its theories to correspond to the supposed new realities represented by the war.[5]

Rightists in the party were the major targets of Kautsky's polemics throughout the war years. Although he also objected to the leftist position of defeatism or turning the war into revolution, he was compelled by circumstance to concentrate his attack on the supporters of the war. There were three major reasons for this. First, in number and prestige those within the SPD who supported the war far outstripped those who opposed it, although the latter group did increase slowly and steadily. Second, wartime censorship had a dual effect on Kautsky's polemics. On the one hand, because the right-wing socialists argued in favor of the war, the censors allowed much more of their material to be printed than was so for the critics of the war. The same principle applied to Kautsky's responses, that is, in his criticism he could more easily discuss the concepts presented by the rightists than he could those presented by the leftists. On the other hand, the very fact that censorship existed at all meant that the German press could not discuss a large variety of topics, and thus, just as in the earlier antisocialist law period, the closest thing to freedom of expression was the immunity afforded Reichstag members. Since the rightists dominated the *Fraktion*, their voices were most frequently heard, a fact which probably tended to make the capitulation of German socialists to chauvinism seem even more widespread than it was, at least to foreigners and those who had only the press to rely on for information. Third, because of his conviction that the International had to play an important role in the peace that followed the war, Kautsky was determined to combat the tendency on the right to attack enemy socialists with ever increasing violence. He was critical of German socialists who denounced the French or the English as inveterate evils, but he also rejected the efforts of French or English writers to blame the war solely on the Germans.[6]

Differences of opinion about the war created within German socialism extensive realignments of left-right affiliations that at least for the war years often had little to do with prewar sympathies. The two most outstanding examples, as far as Kautsky was concerned, involved Eduard Bernstein and Heinrich Cunow. Following their split in 1899, Bernstein and Kautsky had not been in close or frequent contact, and though articles by Bernstein appeared occasionally in the pages of the *Neue Zeit*, the two men remained on very distant terms. During the first days of the war, it seemed unlikely that this situation would change. Bernstein was one of the right-wing *Fraktion* members who had decided on 2 August to vote for war credits regardless of the decision made by the *Fraktion* as a whole. But within weeks of the outbreak of the war, Bernstein moved toward Kautsky's position, and close personal contacts between the two men resumed. Bernstein became one of the major contributors to the *Neue Zeit*, and he and Kautsky worked together closely in an effort to combat the rising chauvinism of the party majority. They issued joint statements, argued in favor of one another's positions, and, with Hugo Haase and Georg Ledebour, formed the core of the old-timers who left the party in April 1917 to found the Independent German Social Democratic Party (Unabhängige sozialdemokratische Partei Deutschlands — USPD). After over fifteen years of separation, the reestablishment of the Kautsky-Bernstein relationship was greatly satisfying to both men.[7]

In stark contrast to the revival of his friendship with Bernstein was the change in Kautsky's relationship with Heinrich Cunow. Long a close co-worker with Kautsky on the *Neue Zeit*, an editor of the *Vorwärts* since 1905, and generally considered a member of Kautsky's Marxist center, Cunow followed a course opposite to that of Bernstein. When the first vote to support war credits was cast by the SPD *Fraktion*, he denounced it. But in a matter of weeks, he became not only a partisan of the German war effort, but also one of the leading figures of the *Umlerner*. As had happened so often in the past, Kautsky found himself opposed by an old friend and, furthermore, subjected to vitriolic personal attacks. Although some of the *Umlerner* struck Kautsky as simply ludicrous, largely because they had never understood Marxism very well to begin with, he thought Cunow's position more formidable in theoretical terms. Nonetheless, he insisted that Marxism was neither a hastily conceived nor a narrowly limited theory and held that though some minor rethinking might be necessary as a result of the war, nothing like the wholesale changes Cunow thought necessary was justified. He was particularly harsh in his attack on Cunow's efforts to redefine the role of the state to make it an agent of socialization on a large scale. Kautsky further pointed out that the harsh condemnation being leveled by Cunow against the "old" orthodoxy could equally be applied to Cunow's earlier work. As usual he refrained from bitter personal polemics, but he clearly felt keenly the loss of yet another former comrade. When in August 1917 the party leadership stripped Kautsky of the *Neue Zeit* editorship, it was given to Cunow.[8]

The apparent endlessness of the war not only affected Kautsky's evaluation of proper tactics, it also placed him in an increasingly difficult position vis-à-vis the split that developed as a result of the war. Never was the label "centrism" more appropriate for Kautsky's position than during the war years. While convinced of the need to preserve party unity and opposed to the defeatism and the anti–Second International posture of the extreme left wing of the German party, the ever more extreme capitulation of the right wing to imperialism, chauvinism, and acquisitive war aims forced Kautsky to define his own position almost exclusively in terms of opposition to the party majority. Furthermore, as the war proceeded he became much more aware that the deck was stacked in favor of the majority and that in conjunction with governmental censorship, the restrictions on the propaganda of the minority (or "opposition" as it was called) were very stringent. Like many of those further to the left, Kautsky came to realize that the highly centralized, well-disciplined, and united party he himself had helped to create could very effectively suppress dissent simply by calling upon party discipline, the need to preserve unity, and party tradition. Under the conditions that prevailed during the war, when party congresses were considered impossible, leadership shifted almost exclusively to the *Fraktion*, where the tradition of unanimity effectively stifled public dissent. Not until the early spring of 1916 did collective opposition, as opposed to individual deviation, appear within the *Fraktion*, when Hugo Haase led the opposition representatives in the formation of the *Arbeitsgemeinschaft* ("working group").[9]

This first manifestation of organized parliamentary opposition placed Kautsky in a difficult position. His sympathies were definitely with the oppositional group. Even before the war he had long objected to the influence that seemed to flow to the Reichstag *Fraktion* regardless of considerations of theory or ability. Kautsky also had objected in the past to the fact that the SPD representatives tended to be more responsive to their electoral constituents than to the party, and in wartime this meant, to Kautsky at least, that these men deviated even more than ever from orthodoxy. But convinced that unity was vital, Kautsky had decidedly mixed feelings about the succession of the Reichstag oppositional group. Nonetheless, he had laid the basis for a personal split with the party majority in a series of *Neue Zeit* articles that ran from late October through early December 1915. In the introduction to the pamphlet version of this series, he explained that he had been driven to the conclusions expressed in this work by the suppression of dissent by the party majority. Not only was the minority virtually excluded from the party press, but it was silenced even in the Reichstag, where it might have hoped to be heard. Formerly, on issues of major importance, when presenting the party's positions to the Reichstag, the *Fraktion* had chosen a second speaker from the minority. But since the war had revealed the deep split within the party, the majority now denied even this traditional platform to the minority. Kautsky therefore justified what amounted to a theoretical foundation for a party split by reference to the majority's unwillingness to tolerate dissent.[10]

Kautsky began his arguments by referring to the constant and inevitable conflict between personal conviction, that which moves people to take stands on issues, and the means by which this conviction can be converted into effective action, namely, cooperation with large numbers of like-minded individuals. Now because no two individuals are exactly alike, he argued, cooperation for action always involves a measure of compromise with personal conviction. Fortunately, in a mass, working-class party the individual members come from generally similar environments and therefore have less individual variation, a stronger sense of common purpose, and less need for repressive discipline. However, such a party, while seeking a maximum of inclusiveness, that is, in trying to increase its size, does so at the expense of spontaneous enthusiasm, that is, by bringing about the need for greater individual submission to the collective will.[11]

According to Kautsky, reconciliation of the conflict between size and enthusiasm in order to attain an optimum level of both values could only be achieved by the "fullest freedom of expression of opinion within the party organizations." Not only were differences of opinion inevitable, they were also essential if the party was to avoid ossification. He argued further that party members had not only the right to dissent, but also the duty to listen to the dissent of others. Here he arrived at the nub of his argument: Under the extraordinary conditions of war, the right to dissent was suppressed and the duty to listen was ignored. Though the SPD previously had always insisted on discipline once congressional and parliamentary decisions were reached, now the majority used its superior position to prevent even a modicum of discussion; in so doing the majority violated party custom. Kautsky further challenged the right of the majority to act against the minority for violating party discipline since the majority itself had already declared that the extraordinary conditions of war justified contradiction of party decisions against budget support. He concluded this portion of his arguments with an enticement, a warning, and a challenge. The enticement was that the public forum, if the minority were allowed access to it, might have a moderating influence on the views of the opposition. The warning was that suppression bred extremism. The implied challenge was to the majority to test its ideas against those of the minority out in the open.[12]

At first blush these arguments, coming from the man so often called the "party pope" and condemned for dogmatism, might seem absurd and opportunistic. But certain things are worth recalling at this point. First of all, Kautsky's arguments rested on the assumption that freedoms and access formerly accorded to minority opinion within the SPD had been eliminated by the war. In a rebuttal to Kautsky, Otto Braun argued that in the *Neue Zeit* alone the previous twenty-one numbers had carried forty-six articles by oppostionists and only fourteen by supporters of the majority, but this contention was obviously feeble given the restrictions of censorship. Second, Kautsky's journal had always, from its very first issue, carried articles by authors whose opinions differed from his own, and this tradition extended into the war years. Certainly Kautsky frequently took advantage of his position as editor to ensure that he had the upper hand in polemics, but he always gave opponents space to say their piece. Third, strictly speaking, Kautsky was not arguing in favor of schism, but warning the majority not to force a split. And fourth, though the arguments he presented bear a striking resemblance to liberal-bourgeois arguments in favor of individualism, he consistently developed his position within the context of the party, defined as the collective of the working class. He explicitly recognized a need for discipline and even argued that it was the majoritarian Reichstag representatives who followed individual conviction by enthusiastically supporting the war. He was convinced that were the entire party free to express an opinion, the majority of its members would favor the position of the minority of the *Fraktion*.[13]

But even more important to evaluating the opinions Kautsky expressed in this pamphlet is the realization that for the first time since he entered the socialist movement over forty years earlier, he found himself fundamentally and apparently irreconcilably opposed to virtually all of the leadership of his party. Furthermore, because of the nature of the issues involved, he could no longer accept the premise, as he had on most occasions when he found himself at odds with this or that faction, that simply misinformation or mistaken judgment was involved. Now he was forced to face the fact that his position would not carry the party because his access to the public forum was severely limited and because the differences were probably too great to be reconciled anyway. Thus though undoubtedly he really did feel his position was more representative of the majority of the party, he was also quite aware that the extraordinary conditions imposed by war had trapped everyone. To this extent this pamphlet was in fact laying the theoretical groundwork for the party split everyone felt was coming. However, until late 1916 at least, Kautsky continued to hope that unity could be preserved, and even in April 1917, he only reluctantly participated in the split. To the bitter end he continued to hope that he could outwait the chauvinistic party leadership and, with the end of the war, aid in the restoration of reason to his party.[14]

Nationalism and Democracy

Increasing insistence on the need for freedom of expression within the context of the party was only one aspect of Kautsky's thought that underwent a major change of emphasis as a result of the war. Two other major issues, nationalism and democracy, were also significantly affected. A closer look at how his position was altered is justified for two reasons. First, in a different context, Kautsky had already written quite extensively on democracy and nationalism, but the war introduced complications that forced him to clarify certain ambiguities. While there is little doubt that he had always assumed that socialism could only be attained by means of a majoritarian movement, the revisionism debate had found him arguing that in Germany at least, the proletarian movement took precedence over any imagined democratic movement postulated by Bernstein and his followers. Though the revisionist crisis had established this distinction clearly enough, the importance of the democracy issue during the war and its aftermath finally brought Kautsky to a more explicit presentation of his views. The same is generally true for nationalism, a matter on which Kautsky, like Marx, had always been ambiguous. The second reason for looking more closely at Kautsky's stance on democracy and nationalism during the war is the significance of these positions for his evaluation of Bolshevism and the Russian Revolution. Coupled with his attitude toward revolutionary violence, as developed during the mass-strike debates of 1902 to 1906, his views of democracy and nationalism formed the basis for his judgment of Lenin and the Bolsheviks. In addition to creating the conditions that made the Russian Revolution of 1917, the First World War and its impact on German socialism also gave shape to the premises from which Kautsky would criticize that revolution.

"Social democracy is an international and a democratic party. . . . But what is the struggle for democracy other than the struggle for the self-determination of people, and how is international democracy possible other than that self-determination be demanded not only for the people to which one belongs, but for all people in the same degree?"[15] With these words Kautsky opened a pamphlet entitled *The Liberation of Nations*, which was written in mid-June 1917. He came to these conclusions not as a result of debates with left-socialist revolutionaries, not in order to defend petit bourgeois democracy and nationalism against the violent, determined, "new democracy" of the soviets, but because during almost four years of war, he saw his party and his adopted country develop war aims that disregarded the rights of other nations, that presumed that the might of the victor proved national superiority and justified conquest and domination. Through most of the war he was far less concerned with the increasing extremism of the left socialists than he was with the chauvinism and arrogance that came to characterize the right, and he refined his views of democracy and nationalism in response to the latter. Only after having developed his critique of the right did he use the same arguments against what he considered the equally perverted and dangerous arrogance of the left.

The two issues, democracy and nationalism, were inextricably linked in Kautsky's response to the increasing chauvinism of his party. As early as August 1914, he insisted that any acceptable peace had to recognize "above all the independence of people, i.e., democracy." During the war he repeatedly emphasized that national independence "is an essential part of democracy, which is a necessary basis for the struggle of the proletariat." In a pamphlet written in early 1915, to combat both the leftists who rejected the concept of national bound-aries and the rightists who argued that democracy was consistent with the expansion of Germany into non-German areas, Kautsky distin-guished between national and nationalistic states. He then went on to observe that democracy "means not merely the domination of state power by the populace, but also the equality of rights of the individual vis-à-vis state power. This equality of rights is also prejudiced in na-tionalistic states." But he was careful to distinguish between democracy as an end and democracy as a means. This distinction was for Kautsky the major difference between bourgeois and social democracy.

> Social democracy has taken over from bourgeois democracy the striving for the national state. Certainly we are not bourgeois democrats, but we differ from them not in that democracy is for us something insignificant or entirely superfluous. As the lowest class in the state, the proletariat can gain its rights in no other way than through democracy. Only we do not share the illusion of bourgeois democracy that the proletariat would already have its rights if it attained democracy. This forms the basis from which it struggles for its rights. The proletarian struggle for emancipation does not stop with democracy, it only assumes another form.[16]

Kautsky also found it necessary to combat the tendency of the right and the left to see imperialism as a necessary consequence of economic development and to equate imperialism with capitalism. The right concluded from this view that because socialists recognized that the development of capitalist society would inevitably lead to socialism, they had to support imperialism. Kautsky had, of course, taken on similar arguments before. The leftists argued that since imperialism *was* capitalism, the only alternative to imperialist war was the im-mediate establishment of socialism. Kautsky countered the first posi-tion by contending that imperialism was a political, not an economic, consequence of capitalism and, furthermore, that socialists have not always supported the advance of capitalism without qualification. He pointed out that some of these same rightists had earlier been the most vociferous in demanding higher wages for workers, when all would agree that low wages were to the advantage of capitalism. He also argued vigorously that economics were only deterministic "in the last instance," that shifts in political power of the various classes "under certain circumstances can fundamentally alter the entire system of production." Therefore, he concluded, despite the economics of capitalism, socialists could oppose imperialism on political grounds. On the other hand, Kautsky argued that the leftists' demand that imperialism be ended immediately by the establishment of socialism sounded very radical, but only served to drive into the imperialist camp those who recognized the continuing obstacles to the immediate attainment of socialism.[17]

Of course Kautsky's arguments did not heal the wounds caused by the war. He continued to reiterate his assertion that democracy and nationalism were fundamental means in the fight for proletarian emancipation, always against the background of growing support among the socialist leadership for expansionist war aims. When German socialists began to accept lebensraum arguments and to urge the formation of a *Mitteleuropa* under German domination, Kautsky countered by arguing that "democracy does not merely mean freedom and self-determination for one class or one people, but for all. . . . One is no democrat if one demands freedoms for oneself and participates in the assault of others." He also tied national independence and proletarian internationalism together by claiming that just as high wages and short hours at home were threatened by low wages and long hours in neighboring countries, so domestic freedom was endangered if neighbors were oppressed. When more specific issues of expansion by Germany came up, such as the conquest of Poland or Belgium and the fate of Serbia, Kautsky addressed himself to these topics also. In all three of these cases he concluded that only national independence or autonomy made sense, given modern developments.[18]

National independence was not a simple, universally applicable principle for Kautsky. He recognized that given certain historical traditions of multinational political organization, specifically Russia and Austria, national autonomy within a federative framework provided the necessary guarantees of freedom from oppression. He also argued that the historical tendency toward national independence was only one aspect of the dialectical development of modern society. A contrary tendency was represented by the increasing economic interdependence of all countries with the advance of technology and specialization. Because he recognized these contradictory tendencies, Kautsky did not flatly claim that each nationality should have its own state. Furthermore, in response to the increasing clamor for a German-dominated *Mitteleuropa,* he postulated a United States of Europe, an association of sovereign national republics cooperating economically for the good of all. He even suggested that this was a possible future stage of capitalist development, a peaceful division of world markets quite in contrast to the imperialist war raging through Europe at the time. Kautsky's treatment of the question of nationality, while it did not begin to deal with all the complexities of the problem, especially the emotional, almost irrational aspects, was not simpleminded.[19]

One significant change in Kautsky's political thought appeared very early in the war. In his most radical phase, during and immediately following the revisionist crisis, Kautsky had harshly condemned bourgeois parliamentary government as a fraud because of the expense, the time between elections, and the ignorance of the voters. By early 1915, however, the tendency of the right wing to disregard the duly elected representatives of non-German peoples and call on some semimystical notions of destiny to justify expansion, caused Kautsky to change his attitude. Recognizing that parliamentarism was flawed and easy to criticize, that at times more "primitive democratic" means, like direct legislation or the mass strike, might be necessary to break deadlocks under parliamentarism, he contended that these means could not permanently replace parliamentarism; it was an imperfect necessity. This not only represented a significant change in his attitude toward the existing political institutions of much of Europe, it also served as a basis for Kautsky's response to the Russian soviets and the German *Räte* that appeared in 1918. Having decided that parliamentary government, despite its weaknesses, was the only viable long-term form that democracy could take in complex modern societies, he was to regard the Russian-inspired forms as at best temporary institutions.[20]

The Party Split

By early 1917, Kautsky was forced by party developments to recognize that a split had to come. First of all, the war continued, and in fact the announcement by Germany in January 1917 of the resumption of unrestricted submarine warfare guaranteed that the war would be prolonged. This move ended any possibility of a peace based on the military stalemate that had characterized 1916. As long as the war continued, the basic cause of the split within the SPD persisted. Moreover, the majority socialists continued their assault on the minority, denying the opposition access to the press, refusing it a forum in the Reichstag, and even expelling it from local party organizations. In mid-October 1916, the party central committee joined forces with the military high command to censor the party's official daily, the Berlin

Vorwärts. Kautsky had warned earlier that continued persecution by the majority would only further radicalize the opposition, and his prophecy proved true. The final factor which forced a split was the increasing opposition to the war among the working class and the increased vociferousness of the radical opposition within the SPD. Both of these tendencies were greatly stimulated by the Russian Revolution of 1917.[21]

A formal split was slow in developing, even though Liebknecht's vote against the second war credits bill on 2 December 1914 was a tocsin of things to come. In April 1915, Franz Mehring and Rosa Luxemburg founded the radical oppositional journal *Internationale,* and in early May, Kautsky, Bernstein, and other prominent theoreticians joined Rudolf Breitscheid in the more moderate oppositional journal *Sozialistische Auslandspolitik Korrespondenz* (later renamed *Der Sozialist*). These two journals constituted the first organized opposition within the German party. In mid-June a thousand low-level functionaries and other leftists issued a manifesto calling for a radical change in the party's policy toward the war, and on 19 June, Haase, Bernstein, and Kautsky issued their own more moderate, but also more influential critique of the majority policy, "The Demand of the Hour." Less than a year later, on 24 March 1916, Haase led the oppositional members of the Reichstag delegation in the formation of their own *Fraktion,* the *sozialdemokratische Arbeitsgemeinschaft*. Despite his own hesitation about splitting, Kautsky played a major role in the process that led to the formation of the USPD. At a 7 January 1917 meeting of the opposition, his manifesto on a peace without victors or vanquished, calling for an international, democratic peace with self-determination for proletarian-based governments, received the unanimous approval of the 157 delegates attending. On 9 February, the leadership of the *Arbeitsgemeinschaft,* which had stopped just short of calling for a split at the January meeting, denounced the disciplinary tactics of the SPD and called for independent political action. In a few days the local organizations of Berlin, Leipzig, Braunschweig, Bremen, Halle, and elsewhere proclaimed their solidarity with the Haase group.[22]

Kautsky responded to this sharpening conflict with a series of four articles in the *Neue Zeit* dealing with the impending split. He emphasized the majority's responsibility in forcing the split through its policy of supporting the war and adopting as its own the chauvinistic, expansionistic war aims of the government. He developed further his insistence upon democracy for the proletariat by rejecting the majority's call for cooperation with the National Liberals within the framework of the imperial regime, arguing that both the National

Liberals and the regime of the kaiser were antidemocratic. Only through democracy could the workers rule, he claimed, and therefore the majority's position entailed the abandonment of the principle of proletarian political power. Referring to the failure of the bourgeois revolution of 1848, Kautsky claimed that only its economic strength allowed the bourgeoisie to be the dominant, though not the ruling class. By contrast, the proletariat could only become the dominant class, that is, establish the socialist order, by first becoming the ruling class, that is, by seizing political power. Kautsky's reluctance to support calls for a new party derived from his conviction that the potential of the workers to establish and use a democratic state form would be greatly hampered if they had two parties instead of one. He warned that like war, a split was much easier declared than ended, and though he felt the war to be the major source of division in the ranks of the proletariat, he knew it was not the only source. His fear that a split in social democracy would emasculate both the movement and the new, democratic state he expected at war's end was to prove very well founded. He was convinced that by implicitly abandoning democracy and by constant persecution of the minority, the majority socialists were dangerously imperiling the prospects for successful proletarian revolution.[23]

The sharpening conflict within the German workers' movement in late 1916 and early 1917 also led Kautsky to elaborate on his differences with the extreme left. The more disgust with the war grew, the more strident the leftists became in their assault on the war and on the governments and socialist parties that supported the war; the more strident the leftists became, the more sweeping and simplistic their arguments became. Kautsky increasingly found himself in the center, with the chauvinistic majority attacking him from one side and a putschist-inclined extreme left attacking him from the other. Although circumstances threw him together with the extreme left, he adamantly rejected its simpleminded notions about the war. He drew a parallel between those who saw the war as everywhere and in all aspects imperialistic and those who accepted the notion of "one reactionary mass." Though there was often a theoretical need to speak of only two classes, the reality of political and economic life clearly revealed intermediary, undifferentiated classes. Similarly, though the war was theoretically imperialistic, in fact there were varieties of imperialism and various degrees of imperialism in the several capitalist states. Kautsky contended that the world was extremely complex, and that simply labeling all nations as indistinguishably imperialistic and guilty in the war could do little to explain or justify proletarian action.[24]

Kautsky argued against monolithic capitalism and specifically against the notion that imperialism was capitalism. Political, demographic, and other variations differentiated the imperialism of the capitalist states. Thus American imperialism in the Philippines was qualitatively different from Belgian imperialism in the Congo; though imperialism was generally tied to protective tariffs, colonies, and a strong military, imperialistic England had low tariffs, imperialistic Germany lacked exploitable colonies, and imperialistic America had neither a strong army nor a strong navy. Kautsky concluded from this analysis that though economic factors lay at the base of imperialistic expansion, imperialism was not an economic necessity, but only an activity that sprang from the striving for profits of certain segments within a capitalist society. Imperialism was therefore a question of power politics, and the proletariat had to deal with it accordingly. Kautsky rejected as obfuscatory nonsense the arguments of radicals like Karl Radek, who held that since Belgium had colonies, the proletariat that was fighting to defend Belgian independence was serving the interests of the imperialistic bourgeoisie. Kautsky asked if Belgium would have been spared the war if it had not had any colonies. When Radek claimed to have discovered imperialism in Switzerland in the form of foreign investments, Kautsky countered by asking if, because of their investments in Russia, German financiers favored a Russian victory, or if French capital worked for a Turkish victory because of French investments in Turkey. The increasingly extreme rhetoric of the left was too simpleminded for Kautsky. He felt that such gross generalizations and distortions would only mislead and eventually undermine the proletarian opposition in Germany. Proper Marxists had to find a balance between the extremism of both the left and the right.[25]

Unfortunately for Kautsky and the unity of the German proletariat, the war and, after early March 1917, the Russian Revolution did not provide an environment conducive to balancing between extremes. From 6 to 9 April 1917, 143 delegates of the socialist opposition met in Gotha to give more concrete form to their movement. The group that gathered together on this occasion was highly eclectic, from the extreme leftists such as Luxemburg's Spartacists and the International Group to the moderates such as Kautsky and Haase. All factions agreed on only two things—opposition to the war and the need to prevent bureaucratic domination from subverting the new party as it had the old. Even the issue of forming an entirely separate party did not carry unanimously. Kautsky and Bernstein were on the losing side of a seventy-two to forty-four vote in favor of a complete split, including a new name. In his opening address Haase emphasized primarily the errors of the SPD vis-à-vis the war. Wilhelm Dittman followed with organizational proposals for a decentralized, locally autonomous party, and he was seconded by Fritz Rueck of the International Group, who added a demand for a highly action-oriented party. Georg Ledebour was the principal speaker on the tasks of the party. He placed strong emphasis on representative democracy, including short-er terms of office and female franchise, but criticized the left's blanket rejection of national self-defense (*Verteidigungsnihilismus*) as well as the majority's total support for the war.[26] Common enemies did not breed harmony in the new party, and lack of unity on goals and means would soon be a significant factor in the failure of the USPD.

For Kautsky this founding congress was significant in two contradic-tory ways. First, the increasing hostility of the Luxemburg-Liebknecht left to Kautsky and his centrist followers was fully revealed to the congress by Fritz Heckert. Speaking on the tasks of the party, Heckert spent much of his time assailing Kautsky, who, according to Heckert, was no better than Ebert and Scheidemann. Heckert's basic argument was that "if you are not with us you are against us." He denounced Kautsky for imagining that imperialism could ever be peaceful and for hoping that the war could be ended in any way but by revolution. Haase rose in defense of his friend and mentor, and Kautsky gave a spirited self-defense as well. In the end Heckert's attack carried little weight, for the second way in which this congress proved significant for Kautsky was that his manifesto declaring the goals of the new party was accepted with only one dissenting vote. The manifesto blamed the split on the majority socialists and denounced their national-social aims and means, including their acceptance of the monarchy and implicit rejec-tion of republican governmental forms. It included a call for political amnesty, democratization of the franchise, traditional press, speech, and assembly freedoms, and a socialist peace based on self-determination, limited armaments, and international arbitration.[27]

One episode in the USPD founding congress exposed a striking difference between the leftists and the moderates of the party and also foreshadowed its future dissolution. In his attack on Kautsky, Heckert mocked the call for a peace without annexations on the basis of self-determination. Haase interrupted, asking: "Do you want annexa-tions?" Heckert retorted: "Marx was for annexation where it was in the interests of historical progress."[28] This was symbolic of the "hards" against the "softs" in the USPD, of the radical-moderate split that was to characterize Marxism after World War I, and of the Bolshevik–social democratic debate that was to occupy so much of Kautsky's time in the last two decades of his life. The arrogance and revolutionary passion of the leftists gave them confidence to presume to know the future. They refused to get caught up in the old means-end dilemma; they did so simply by rejecting the notion that means were causally related to ends, by justifying all actions only in terms of announced aims. This position was abhorrent to the more moderate opposition like Haase, Ledebour, and Kautsky, all of whom lacked not the conviction, but the single-mindedness and ruthlessness of the extreme left. The humanist consciousness of the older, social democratic mentalities of the USPD could not accept the extremism of the younger radicals.

In his postcongress summary of Gotha, Kautsky expanded on the calls for local autonomy that had been made during the gathering, arguing that limiting the size of the bureaucracy and electing good people would not be enough to prevent the USPD from falling victim to the same illness that had undermined the old party. He urged regular, active, democratic participation by the rank-and-file membership as the best check against an overly powerful leadership. This sort of grass-roots participation was especially important in controlling the party press and administering the party treasury, particularly since exclusive control of the treasury made the leaders virtually independent of the party membership. Kautsky also revealed why he chose to join the new party rather than stay with the old. While recognizing that party unity was important, he noted that the mass of the workers was becoming increasingly alienated from the SPD leadership, especially given the radicalizing influence of the Russian Revolution. He concluded that "still far more important than the unity of the party is the trust of the working mass in it."[29]

From the creation of the new party to the outbreak of the German revolution in November 1918, Kautsky was mainly preoccupied with efforts to bring the war to an end. During the summer of 1917, he kept himself available to go to Stockholm and participate in what was ultimately an abortive effort to reactivate the Second International and have it bring pressure on the warring states to stop the slaughter. Hugo Haase, head of the USPD Stockholm delegation, was to send word to Kautsky if it seemed that he could help in the revival. However, given that the Bolsheviks played a key role in the Stockholm negotiations, Kautsky's presence would probably have proven a liability. After the negotiations failed, Axelrod scornfully reported in a letter to Kautsky that the Bolsheviks valued the extremism of a Radek more than "you, really more than Marx and Engels." Kautsky remained in Berlin during the Stockholm meetings, writing considerable propaganda encouraging the Stockholm effort. He felt that a reasonable and swift peace was critical to the survival of revolutionary Russia, quite accurately perceiving peace to be the most important demand of the anti-tsarist forces. He was also convinced that the sooner the war ended, the easier it would be to reunite the divided German social democratic movement. Although the German government gave its approval to the SPD delegation to Stockholm, the cabinet and military leadership also used the publicity generated by the gathering in their persecution of the USPD. As late as August 1917, the government was apparently considering the possibility of prosecuting both Kautsky and Bernstein for treason on the basis of articles that had appeared in the foreign press regarding the two men's views of the war. The proceedings were dropped, however, because Kautsky and Bernstein could not have been proved to be the authors of the articles, which in any case contained no new material useful to the Allied powers or likely to strengthen their will to fight.[30]

The efforts of the SPD to combat the new party and suppress the opposition continued with renewed vigor after the split. Almost immediately after Gotha, Clara Zetkin was removed as editor of the *Gleichheit,* and in the fall of 1917, Kautsky lost the *Neue Zeit.* Though he had edited the journal for almost thirty-five years, and was in fact internationally identified with it, once the decision had been made by the SPD leadership, Kautsky was given no notice and was not allowed to publish any parting message to his readership. Naturally he was extremely bitter about the shabby treatment he received, but since the journal legally belonged to the SPD, he could not dispute its right to remove him from the editorship. He felt that the central committee had taken this action merely to deprive him of a platform from which to address German socialists. He predicted that the journal's readership, which had already fallen drastically during the war, would decline further after his departure, since most of the *Neue Zeit* subscribers were Independents. Certain that the war made founding a new journal impossible, he felt he would be forced to rely on pamphlets to conduct his polemics, and he knew this would make his work difficult. "Therefore it is certainly possible," he wrote to Adler, "that I am put in cold storage for the duration of the war."[31]

Kautsky was not put in cold storage for the duration, but the journals to which he had access were either far less influential than the *Neue Zeit,* like the *Sozialistische Auslandspolitik,* or had leftist inclinations that did not fit comfortably with Kautsky's position, like the *Leipziger Volkszeitung.* Not until the founding of the USPD's *Freiheit,* shortly after the German revolution, did Kautsky once again have regular access to a journal with fairly widespread circulation, at least in Berlin, and with which he was in close agreement. After mid-1919, however, his ties with the *Freiheit* weakened considerably as the journal moved to the extreme left, and he began to publish more and more in Austrian journals like *Der Kampf* and the *Arbeiter-Zeitung,* both of which were Viennese social democratic organs. During late 1917 and 1918, he did write several short works, including an attack on the *Umlerner* entitled *War Marxism,* and his major critique of the Bolshevik takeover in Russia, *The Dictatorship of the Proletariat.* He also wrote *Social Democratic Notes on the Transitional Economy,* in which he discussed the impending conversion to peacetime production and the implied conversion from capitalism to socialism. But *War Marxism* and *Dictatorship* were first published in Vienna, and *Social Democratic Notes,* though written in March 1918, was barred by the censors until after the revolution. Thus, though he remained active, at least until November 1918, the loss of the *Neue Zeit* severely restricted his influence on German socialists.[32]

The Russian Revolution

Losing his regular forum for discussion of significant developments in theory and world events hit Kautsky hard in late 1917, because it coincided with the Bolsheviks' victory in Russia and their rising influence in the world socialist movement. These developments were important to Kautsky for a number of reasons, some immediate and practical, some more theoretical. For instance, shortly after the German revolution, he worked in the foreign office and attended meetings of the cabinet at which the question of reestablishing diplomatic relations with the Russians was discussed. Because he had come to distrust the Bolsheviks and opposed their influence on the German leftists, he joined with Haase in counseling caution in dealing with the Soviet government. In addition to their distrust of the Bolsheviks, Kautsky and others obviously feared Allied reprisals if German socialists made encouraging overtures to the Russians. Finally, Kautsky, at least, did not think the Bolsheviks would remain in power long enough to justify the effort of recognizing their government; over a decade later he was still predicting the imminent collapse of the Soviet state. Another practical concern raised by Lenin's victory in Russia was the role of soviets or workers' councils in the revolution of the proletariat. This and other matters would occupy much of Kautsky's attention in late 1918 and 1919 when they became important in Germany.[33]

In the long run the most important impact on Kautsky of the Bolshevik Revolution came in the realm of theory, where he was forced by the Russian experience to clarify and make explicit his views on revolution, the coming of socialism, and the role of democracy in both processes. His attitude toward the Bolsheviks was conditioned by his initial response to the March revolution in Russia, by his personal contacts with many prominent Mensheviks, by his experience with the SPD majority's repression of the antiwar minority in the party, and by the effect of the Bolsheviks on the German and international movements. Many years before 1917, he had argued that because of its decaying government and growing working-class movement, revolution was more likely in Russia than in the major nations of western Europe. In January 1916, he repeated this prediction, adding that revolution was then even more likely in Russia because of the terrible conditions brought on by the war. "Today Russia is no longer merely the land of despotism against which Marx and Engels formerly demanded a war," Kautsky wrote, "but a land of revolution." As usual he was not willing to make specific predictions about the form and timing of the coming revolution, but he was certain that it would cause "a powerful echo in western Europe."[34]

The March 1917 revolution in Russia made a major impression on most of the world, and different people saw in it different things. The Allies, and most of the early leaders in the new Russia, were convinced that the revolution would allow the country to begin to pursue the war with renewed vigor and success. Woodrow Wilson contended that the end of tsarism allowed the United States to enter the war on the side that was now truly the side of democracy against autocracy. In Germany the major impression of the March revolution was that Russia would now leave the war, a move which the military and prowar forces contemplated with joy since it would allow Germany to concentrate all its might on the western front. Kautsky's view was that the revolution was certainly a victory for the Russian peace party, but the conclusions he drew about this victory were much different than those of the militarists. He argued that with Russian despotism gone, the SPD backers of the war would have to change their tune, since it was now clearly despotic Germany and Austria against the democracies. Furthermore, he was convinced that in order to assure the continued victory of the peace party in Russia, the German government had to offer generous peace terms. But here Kautsky was wrong. In fact the persistence of the war—the feeble and tragic efforts of the provisional government to continue the Russian war effort—was the single most important reason for the meteoric rise in the fortunes of the only Russian party willing to accept peace regardless of the cost, the Bolsheviks.[35]

When the revolution was less than a month old, Kautsky defined it as bourgeois and democratic—bourgeois in that it destroyed the remnants of feudalism in Russia, setting the stage for modernization and the growth of capitalism, and democratic in that it opened the channels to political power to all classes. He firmly rejected an observation by the SPD's *Vorwärts* that Russia had only replaced the domination of absolutism with the domination of the bourgeoisie. This position confused state form with the rule of a class. What had really happened was that the form of the Russian state had changed in such a way as to allow the proletariat to develop freely and openly into a majoritarian movement that could then oversee the conversion of Russia from a capitalist to a socialist society as economic conditions ripened. Kautsky's position clearly presupposed a long period of development, both political and economic, before Russia could become proletarian and then socialist. It also included an implicit distinction between a political and a later social revolution. The political revolution would give the proletariat access to political power and would be a short-term, definite event; the social revolution would emerge from the economic conditions that make the proletariat a majority and socialism a necessity, and it would be a long-term, indefinite event.[36]

As if to anticipate his conflict with the Bolsheviks, Kautsky outlined the tasks confronting the revolutionary, largely proletarian regime in Russia.

> There are two things that the proletariat urgently needs: democracy and socialism. Democracy, that is, far-reaching freedoms and political rights for the masses of the people, which alters the arrangement of state and community administration to mere tools of the mass of the people. And then socialism, that is, nationalized [*staatliche*], communal or cooperative production for the needs of society. The proletariat needs both to the same degree. Social production without democracy could become the most oppressive fetter. Democracy without socialism would leave in existence the economic dependence of the proletariat.[37]

Although he recognized that the proletariat shared the demand for democracy with other classes, he argued that the proletariat was most eager for democracy and best able to use it. Socialism was the demand of the proletariat alone, but only democracy could be achieved immediately by seizing political power: Socialism depended on the development of capitalism. Kautsky also suggested that despite Russia's backwardness, heavy industry and mines might be nationalized, the land of the royal family, religious orders, and large landowners seized, and reforms such as minimum wages, maximum hours, worker-protection laws, and other measures legislated. Though he admitted that most of these things were not socialistic, he contended that their quantity, coupled with the shock of the fall of the old order, would create a qualitative change in the tone and mood of Russian society.

Kautsky closed his evaluation of the prospects of the Russian revolution by arguing that despite the small urban population in Russia and despite the very small size of the organized, conscious workers' movement, democratic forms were still very much to the advantage of the proletariat. In fact, he argued that because the countryside was so backward, because the peasants were so ignorant and amorphous, the conscious, organized proletariat would all the better be able to sway the politics of the country. Furthermore, he concluded that *at the moment* democracy was even more important than the economic improvement of the proletariat because in order to rule, the workers had not only to be numerous and have the necessary material conditions, but they had also to develop the ability of self-rule. This could only come from mass participation, not from secret committees. The great imponderable of the revolution was, however, the peasantry. On it rested the fate of the new order, because it comprised the army, and if the army supported the counterrevolution, the workers would be crushed. But if the workers had free access to political activity, Kautsky was convinced the peasants could be won over.[38]

Although his specific analysis of the Russian situation in the spring of 1917 was based on a number of misconceptions — for instance, the new government was not democratic, except by proclamation, and was furthermore very slow to organize elections for a democratic assembly, though admittedly it was also confronted with enormous complications — what is important in Kautsky's critique is what it revealed about his conception of the nature of the revolution in Russia and other nondemocratic countries. He had moved a step closer to making explicit his earlier implicit distinction between political and social revolution. Marxists had long argued that proletarian socialist society could only emerge from the womb of bourgeois capitalist society, just as bourgeois capitalist society had grown out of aristocratic feudal society. This view presupposed that the economic substructure of society would undergo gradual but regular changes — intensified internal contradictions in Marxian terms — that would eventually create a situation in which the political-social-ideological superstructure would be obsolete vis-à-vis the economic substructure. At some unspecifiable point this contradiction would lead to revolution that would bring the substructure and the superstructure into closer relationship. Marx and most of his followers made the best historical case for this process by pointing to the example of the French Revolution of 1789, but by analogy the process could also be applied to the coming transition from capitalism to socialism.

Two aspects of this view of historical development are important as far as Kautsky's theory of revolution was concerned. First, the revolution that resulted from the inherent contradictions of any system would be a political revolution because it would force the superstructure of society—the juridical and political forms, the distribution of political power, the dominant ideology that reflected the distribution of political power—to catch up with the economic substructure. To this extent, Marxism presupposed that the realm of conscious activity was politics, not economics: What revolution does is change the superstructure, not the substructure. Kautsky's analysis of Russia after March 1917 reflected this view. His assumption was that Russia's economic substructure had become sufficiently capitalist to create tensions between it and the essentially precapitalist superstructure that could only be resolved by a revolution that would bring the dominant economic class, the bourgeoisie, to political and social dominance. This conflict had, of course, been greatly accelerated by the ineptness and collapse of the tsarist superstructure during the war. However, a second aspect of the Marxian view of revolution also played an important role in Kautsky's analysis. Obviously all countries did not develop internal contradictions at the same rate. Most Marxists recognized that the French Revolution was only another example of what had happened over a century earlier in England, and half a century later, incompletely, in Germany. In Russia, however, the same revolution was delayed so long by historical circumstances that for the first time in history a bourgeois revolution had occurred in a country with a conscious and organized working class. This fact encouraged Kautsky to believe that aggressive and vigorous action on the part of the workers, in conjunction with the peasantry, could force the Russian bourgeoisie to complete swiftly the transition to capitalist society. This in turn would accelerate the process of internal contradiction within the new order that could only end in socialism.

Because of his firm conviction that history could only serve the cause of the proletariat, Kautsky was certain that even in apparently backward Russia the proletariat would soon become a majority and that it would do so as the country became more capitalist. Therefore, as the economic substructure more and more created socialism through concentration and collectivization, the growing proletarian majority would increasingly assume political power, if the political superstructure were democratic. In this way, Kautsky argued, the violence that had characterized all previous reconciliations of contradiction between substructure and superstructure could be minimized. He could make these claims and still adhere to Marxism because he concentrated his attention on politics, the realm in which conscious activity determined developments. Like Marx and Engels, he argued not only that bourgeois capitalist society created its own gravediggers in the proletariat, but also that by means of a favorite bourgeois political form, the democratic republic, the workers would assume power. Once they had attained this power, the workers could then use it to ease further the process of reconciling the contradictions that developed in the maturing society. For Kautsky, Russia was a special case in modern history only to the extent that the dominance of bourgeois capitalist society would be of shorter duration there than in more advanced countries.

Phrased in such general terms, Kautsky's view of the Russian Revolution does not seem much different from that of the Bolsheviks. They, too, emphasized the political nature of the Revolution; they, too, emphasized the need for the proletariat to push the Revolution to completion; they, too, claimed that for the moment all that could be done in Russia was to abolish the old order and make way for bourgeois capitalism; they, too, argued that in Russia the course of history would be shortened, or "telescoped," as it was often called at the time. But in fact the Bolshevik seizure of power and Kautsky's response to it gave rise to the longest, most complicated, and ultimately most hopeless of the many ideological disputes Kautsky engaged in. This conflict represented the split between social democratic Marxism and communist Marxism, between the "hards" and the "softs" of the world socialist movement. It was a very involved dispute, with Kautsky on one side and Lenin, Trotsky, Radek, and later Bukharin as the major figures on the other. That Lenin in 1918, Trotsky in 1920, and Radek in 1921, would all take time from their busy days in revolution and civil war to write works attacking Karl Kautsky's theories attests the Russians' respect for his influence among European socialists and his position as leading theorist of the Second International. Prior to 1914 all these Russians had accepted Kautsky as the master of theoretical Marxism and were therefore driven to renounce their aged teacher as apostate. They now revealed their own obsession with theoretical justification, and perhaps also their lack of understanding of developments in western socialist movements, when they continued their attacks long after Kautsky had ceased to exert a major influence on the world movement. For his part, Kautsky continued to criticize the Soviet system, and to predict its imminent collapse, to the very end of his life.[39]

The two works that began the debate identified all the important differences between the two positions. The great mass of writings that followed embellished and expanded the basic positions, but rarely added anything new of general importance. Kautsky's response to the Bolshevik takeover appeared in book form as *The Dictatorship of the Proletariat* in the late summer of 1918. This was based on a series of articles that had appeared in the *Leipziger Volkszeitung* and the *Sozialistische Auslandspolitik* in early 1918. With various title changes and minor alterations in content, *Dictatorship* was published in at least five different editions in 1918 and 1919. Lenin's response to Kautsky was *The Proletarian Revolution and the Renegade Kautsky*. It was written in the late fall of 1918, and first appeared in the West shortly after the German revolution in November. Actually this was the third major work since the beginning of the war in which Lenin argued that Kautsky was no longer a Marxist. Lenin had criticized Kautsky's theory of imperialism in *Imperialism, the Highest Stage of Capitalism* in 1917, and Kautsky's view of the state in *The State and Revolution* in early 1918. In addition, in numerous articles between 1914 and 1918, Lenin had severely criticized Kautsky's stand on the war (without ever being quite clear on what that stand was) and his view of the fate of the Second International. The *Renegade* was, however, the harshest and most thorough attack on Kautsky ever made by anyone.[40]

Kautsky criticized the Bolsheviks on three main counts. First, he asserted that socialism's goals were not the socialization of the means of production and the political domination of the proletariat. These were the means to the real end which was "the abolition of every kind of exploitation and oppression." For this reason, he argued, any regime, whether it called itself a dictatorship of the proletariat or whatever, could not be truly socialist if it were based on oppression; only democratic forms could yield true socialism. Second, Kautsky contended that Russia was bourgeois or petit bourgeois country with an especially prominent peasantry. Therefore, any effort to rule Russia against or even without the support of the peasantry would be futile and short-lived. And third, he saw the efforts of the Bolsheviks to rule Russia as an example of the dangers of letting revolutionary will outstrip the limits of objective conditions. According to Kautsky, will was a necessary, but far from sufficient, element in the course of human history. His critique of Bolshevik rule was neither ill-considered nor unsympathetic; he freely recognized the difficulties confronting the new regime and was little inclined to assign personal blame or to pass moral judgment. But he was convinced that the Bolsheviks could not long hold power and that while they did, the cause of the proletariat would not be well served. Less than ten days after the Bolshevik seizure, Kautsky wrote to his close Menshevik friend, Pavel Axelrod: "In the present crisis I am very critical of the Bolsheviks and fear they will founder and pave the way for the counterrevolution."[41]

The notion that even the process of socialization was only a means to a higher end was not exactly new with Kautsky. Beginning with Marx himself, the assumption that socialism would serve human liberation was a now explicit, now implicit, assumption in the speech and writings of most people who adhered to the movement. These people had assumed all along that postcapitalist society would liberate humanity from the oppressive burdens of labor and class rule. But not until socialists actually assumed power somewhere did it become clear that the transition period from capitalism to socialism would necessarily involve oppression. Given their own definition of the state as a tool of class rule, the Marxists recognized that once the workers controlled the state it would be used to control the opponents of the proletariat. Kautsky did not argue that no repression would be necessary, but he did argue that the more oppression and violence a workers' government had to employ, the less historically justified such a regime would be, and the less likely long-term survival would be.

As the title suggests, one of Kautsky's major concerns in his first analysis of the Bolshevik state was with the concept and reality of the dictatorship of the proletariat. Like Lenin, Kautsky accepted the phrase as descriptive of the transition period between capitalism and socialism, but unlike Lenin, Kautsky emphasized that the dictatorship of the proletariat was a "political *condition,* not a *form of government.*" In part Kautsky substantiated his position by picking quotes from Marx and Engels; in part he argued by analogy, for instance, if the Commune of 1871 were a dictatorship of the proletariat, then such a condition could not rule out general suffrage since that is what the Commune had. But the major thrust of his argument was more telling. Dictatorship implies government by one person or one party, but certainly not one class, since classes can only rule, not govern. Governing implies an organization and cohesion that classes do not have, thus at best only a political party can govern. But party and class are not coterminous entities—a class can split up into various parties, as had the workers in Russia and Germany. Under such conditions, Kautsky argued (with an eye to the split in German socialism), the dictatorship of the proletariat in fact becomes the dictatorship of one faction of the proletariat over the others, as well as over the nonproletarian classes.

Therefore, since Marx clearly had in mind the rule of the entire class of conscious workers during the transition period, Kautsky concluded that the dictatorship of the proletariat could only refer to the general condition in which the workers used their superior consciousness and organization in democratic forms to mold society in their own image. He was particularly insistent that while the soviets had an important future as agencies through which the workers could advance the economic aspects of the transition period, they were inadequate as the basis for a new form of government because they were too exclusive.[42]

Although he approved of the idea of a proletarian-peasant coalition in Russia to force the revolution to completion, Kautsky adamantly insisted that given the economic conditions, given the overwhelming numerical preponderance of the peasantry and their unshakable desire for private property, even proletarian-peasant cooperation could only yield a bourgeois revolution. With this in mind, he made a specific distinction between social revolution, a "protracted" and "profound transformation of the entire social structure brought about by the establishment of a new method of production," and the political revolution, which precedes and precipitates the social revolution, and is "a sudden act, which is rapidly concluded." He objected to the opportunistic approval by the soviets of peasant land seizures, arguing that such seizures were usually carried out by those peasants who already had good-sized holdings. He saw only two possible courses for the revolution under the leadership of the Bolsheviks. Either it would become increasingly dominated by the peasantry, thus turning from a progressive bourgeois revolution into a regressive, petit bourgeois revolution, or, in order to feed the depressed urban population, the Soviet government would more and more have to rely on violent expropriation of the products of the peasantry. In the latter case, the Soviet government would be breeding civil war, further chaos, and ultimately totally oppressive rule. Neither of the two alternatives corresponded to Kautsky's vision of the victory of the revolution. He felt the workers should have given moral and physical support to the peasantry in its struggle against the old order, but also worked with the poorest elements among the peasantry to encourage cooperative farming, thereby advancing socialist consciousness among them. Given Russian conditions the workers had to recognize the importance of the peasants, but the proletariat could neither opportunistically adopt private property slogans as its own nor force the peasants through violence to give up the yield of their privately held land. The maintenance of production for the market was a temporary but necessary concession to the nature of Russian economics.[43]

Kautsky concluded that the errors of the Bolsheviks proved they had tried to make a workers' revolution by relying on sheer will in opposition to objective conditions that militated against such a revolution. His position was not the simpleminded one of those like the Russian "economists" who argued that since socialism was the inevitable result of historical development the workers had to do nothing to bring it about; Kautsky frequently disputed this interpretation in its various forms. He argued that "the will to socialism is the first condition for its accomplishment," and that "ripeness for socialism is not a condition which lends itself to statistical calculation . . . it is wrong . . . to put the material prerequisites of socialism too much in the foreground." But he also contended that to a great extent the necessary will was dependent upon the development of industry. In his earlier debate with party comrades about the 1905 revolution, Kautsky had argued that the necessary enthusiasm for revolutionary activity would follow naturally from comprehension of the course of historical development. Now he argued that an artificially generated enthusiasm for proletarian revolution would be futile in the face of the objective conditions of Russia. He was certain that not even the "strongest will" could make the revolution in Russia anything but a bourgeois revolution.[44]

By the time Lenin wrote his critique of *The Dictatorship,* he and most of his followers had abandoned their earlier view that the Russian Revolution was bourgeois in form and content. Now that political power had been seized in the name of the proletariat, it should be held in the name of the proletariat by any means necessary. Thus Lenin assumed that the Revolution was not essentially bourgeois; Kautsky assumed that it was. This difference of fundamental view meant that some of Lenin's sharpest and most frequent criticisms missed the mark because they presupposed an agreement that did not exist. For instance, Lenin repeatedly argued that Kautsky's insistence on legality and democracy, his rejection of violence, and his defense of the constituent assembly over the soviets, constituted "objective" support of the bourgeoisie. But since Kautsky assumed that the entire Revolution was bourgeois, Lenin's quite valid observation did not undermine the essence of Kautsky's position. On the other hand, Lenin did score heavily on some points, as when he ridiculed Kautsky's assumption that the months from March to October were the democratic period in the Revolution. However, Lenin's view of this period was often equally distorted because he identified it as the period of Menshevik rule, which it certainly was not.[45]

Another significant contrast between the two men was the very different personalities revealed by the form and content of their arguments. Lenin's work was characterized by an iron conviction of his own correctness, by a strong propensity to mockery and ridicule, and by vicious ad hominem attacks. Although he frequently referred to bygone days when Kautsky had been a Marxist (generally 1909 and before), Lenin also used phrases like "civilized belly-crawling and boot-licking before the capitalists" to charge that Kautsky crossed the line from unconscious to conscious service to the cause of the bourgeoisie. Kautsky's critique of the Bolsheviks and their regime was almost entirely devoid of personal attacks of any sort. Lenin's conviction allowed him to accept and justify internecine struggle among socialist factions, civil war in Russia, and further destruction and disruption of Russia's productive capacity, all in the name of a greater good. Kautsky lacked this fanatical conviction and retained an acute awareness of the tendency for such extreme measures to develop a self-energizing need for survival.[46]

Lenin closed his criticism with what he thought was a telling and final observation:

The above lines were written on November 9, 1918. That same night news was received from Germany announcing the beginning of a victorious revolution, first in Kiel and other northern towns and ports, where the power has passed into the hands of Soviets of Workers' and Soldiers' Deputies, then in Berlin, where, too, power has passed into the hands of a Soviet.

The conclusion which still remained to be written to my pamphlet on Kautsky and on the proletarian revolution is now superfluous.[47]

This judgment was to prove rash and ill-informed, but the outbreak of revolution in Germany did offer Kautsky further opportunity to examine the nature of revolution, this time in an advanced industrial society that still lacked the forms of government Marxists usually associated with the economic dominance of the bourgeoisie. His evaluation of Germany was amazingly consistent with the general principles outlined in his writings on the Russian Revolution.

Revolution in Germany

Kautsky's debate with the Bolsheviks was rapidly, if only temporarily, pushed into the background by the growing revolutionary sentiments in Germany. Dissatisfaction with severe rationing of foodstuffs and the growing burden of labor and self-sacrifice created tensions among the workers that increasingly took the form of strikes and protest marches. On a few occasions before 1917, protests with political motives had occurred, as in the summer of 1916 when the drafting and prosecution of Karl Liebknecht had roused the workers to demonstration. But only after the Russian revolution of March 1917 did workers' protests regularly include political demands, as well as objections to the shortages and hardships of war. In the spring of 1917 the first of the workers' councils (*Arbeiterräte*), modeled on the Russian soviets, appeared in Leipzig. The political demands of such groups, with rare exceptions, were liberal republican and moderate socialist, not the extremist demands for total revolution favored by the Spartacists in Germany and the Bolsheviks in Russia. In Germany in 1918–1919, local and national organizations of the workers' councils were consistently dominated by the more moderate workers who sought only a democratic republic which would allow the proletariat to identify fully with its state and country. Even at the height of revolutionary activity, the extreme left never came close to having enough support to get the councils to declare themselves masters of Germany. To this extent, the German revolution of 1918 always remained more moderate than the Russian activities of the previous year. By the same token, the achievement of radical revolution in Germany would have required even more aggressive and brutal force than that employed by the Bolsheviks in Russia. Neither the SPD nor the majority of the USPD was willing to accept the violence and threat of civil war implicit in demands for radical revolution.[48]

Besides lacking a large radical faction among the working class, Germany in 1918 differed from Russia in 1917 in another decisive way—the fate of the nation in the war. The utter collapse of the economy, the incompetence of the tsarist regime, massive desertion by the war-weary peasant-soldiers were all clear in Russia by late 1915 and throughout 1916. Most Russians did not want to fight on by early 1917, and the society could not support the material and human demands of war any longer. When revolution came in March, the attitude of the army was decisive—enormous numbers of soldiers and sailors deserted, and most of those who remained refused to fight to save the tsar. Russia collapsed, crushed by the war. In Germany the picture was quite different. Despite the incredible demands made on the combatants and the civilian population, despite the duration and rapaciousness of the war, Germany was still able to launch a major offensive in the spring of 1918. Even when the initial successes turned to defeat, the military leadership refused to admit it, and the political leaders of Germany remained subordinate to the high command of the army.

The Kiel sailors' mutiny that marked the beginning of the revolution in Germany was not an expression of radical defeatism, but a demand by the sailors that their lives not be wasted in a lost cause. The lack of a pervasive sense among the populace as a whole that the war was being lost was of great importance for the revolution. Certainly this meant that when defeat did come, it was a great shock. But equally the majority of the population of Germany, including the majority of the workers, had not been conditioned by the war experience to accept radical, decisive change. Losing the war did not create the anarchy necessary for the seizure of power by a small, determined group of extremists.

None of this prevented a great many German socialists—from the left wing of the SPD through the USPD moderates like Kautsky and Haase to the extreme left of the Spartacists and the revolutionary shop stewards—from assuming that the events of early November 1918 heralded the arrival of the socialist revolution. This hodgepodge of forces disagreed vehemently on how to proceed with the establishment of socialism. Disagreement occurred over the instruments of revolution—the constituent assembly or workers' and soldiers' councils. The pace of the transformation was debated—gradually over years or very rapidly. Proper techniques were also disputed—violence or persuasion, socialization with compensation or expropriation by force. But in this debate only the extreme left abandoned the traditional commitment of the German movement to the concept of democracy: adult suffrage in a republic. Thus most socialists, increasingly aware that they were not a majority, gradually gave up demands for swift socialization and accepted as inevitable, given the situation, what was for them an incomplete revolution.

Because the German revolution came at the end of the war, just as Kautsky had predicted as early as 1907, the SPD-USPD coalition that assumed power in early November 1918 was confronted with staggering internal and external problems. For one thing, the revolution failed to eliminate or even seriously weaken many of the prerevolutionary bastions of power—most notably the military, the state bureaucracy, the courts, and the large industrialists—and thus the socialists who took office were restricted to moderate and cautious activities. The split of German social democracy before the revolution greatly weakened the ability of socialists to take advantage of the turmoil of November. They failed to achieve some of the fundamental reforms that were possible within the narrow limits of the peculiar situation of Germany. Because the SPD had capitulated to chauvinism during the war and virtually abandoned its traditional opposition to the imperial regime, Ebert, Scheidemann, Noske, and other leading figures of the party were not willing to press their momentary advantage. The confusion and sense of incompleteness, and ultimately the failure of Weimar Germany, derived primarily from the fact that the only class that was enthusiastic about the revolution, the proletariat, was divided on most fundamental questions raised by the abdication of the kaiser and the loss of the war.

Kautsky had, of course, feared that just such a situation would arise if revolution came at a time when the proletariat was politically split. Therefore at least until the end of December 1918, when the agreement between the SPD and the military began to yield its bloody fruit, Kautsky counseled in favor of reunification of the USPD with the SPD. He felt that reunification was possible because the major cause of the schism, the war, was gone, and that reunification was necessary if the revolutionary moment were not to be lost. In fact, though he accepted the necessity of revolutionary violence to end the old order and begin the new one, he recognized that long and excessive violence would add to the difficulties of the transition by breeding a civil war that would end any chance of the reunification of the socialist movement. In a broadsheet distributed in Berlin during the hectic early days of revolutionary unrest, Kautsky called for restraint and an absolute minimum of violence. With the Russian experience clearly in mind, he wrote that "violence always leads to civil war." Unfortunately the extreme left of the USPD was not willing to accept the incomplete revolution of November, and the SPD leadership was willing to use its alliance with the military to suppress the leftists. For a time in early 1919, the civil war Kautsky feared raged in the streets of Berlin.[49]

In assuming that the basis for the socialist revolution had been won in November, Kautsky badly miscalculated conditions in Germany. Even though his fear that continued violence would breed civil war was a sound one, he falsely assumed that no further forceful measures had to be taken to secure the democratic, worker-dominated forms he thought necessary for the transition from capitalism to socialism. The survival of the military and much of the old bureaucracy with their prestige only slightly tarnished necessarily undermined the potential for the creation of a new state free of atavistic remnants of the prerevolutionary order. Their survival ensured that a large and extremely important part of the machinery of the new state would be in the hands of people who regretted the passing of the old Reich. In practical terms, Kautsky's opposition to any but an absolute minimum of violence was as dangerous for the revolution he desired as was the blatantly counterrevolutionary, violent suppression of the leftists by the

SPD government. He was disgusted by the government-backed violence, but his false conviction that the day had been won in November brought him to see the actions of the left as irresponsible putschism rather than as efforts to complete the revolution.

According to Kautsky, leftist pressures to force the revolution to more radical extremes were a major factor contributing to the difficulties of the German revolution. He was particularly harsh in his condemnation of the Spartacists because he felt that their putschist tendencies, especially in January 1919, were responsible for the counterrevolutionary actions of the SPD, though he was also appalled by the eagerness with which Noske used the *Freikorps* to suppress the workers. By late 1918, Kautsky had developed a critique of the Bolshevik regime in Russia that condemned Lenin and his followers for fratricide, that is, for killing fellow socialists and oppositional workers. In January 1919, Kautsky passed the same judgment on the SPD, but he placed a good deal of responsibility for the situation on the shoulders of the Spartacists for inciting the workers to violence. He flatly rejected the Spartacists' argument that just as the eighteenth-century French and the 1917 Russian revolutions passed from moderate to increasingly radical phases, so the German revolution had to do the same thing. To suspend democracy, destroy production, and risk a new war because of some supposed "natural law" of revolutions struck Kautsky as absurd. He argued that the German revolution was different primarily because it was the work of only one class, the proletariat. Though he recognized that there were differences within the class, represented by the SPD and the USPD, these differences were only ones of timing and methods, not the class differences of the earlier revolutions. The greatest danger in Germany was that the extreme left, by misreading the nature of the revolution, would force the right into counterrevolution. By calling for rapid, extensive socialization of industry, the Spartacists were undermining one of the basic requirements of the revolution—orderly transition. By rejecting a democratic parliament in favor of action in the streets, the Spartacists were pursuing a course fraught with dangers and putting the fate of the revolution in the hands of the previously unorganized and unenlightened masses. This was the degradation, not the advancement of the revolution.[50]

Violence was the first, but by no means the only, aspect of the leftists' position to which Kautsky objected. He was also distressed by their rejection of a democratically elected constituent assembly as the ultimate source of political power in the new German state. The Spartacists, once again following the lead of the Russians, looked to the newly created workers' and soldiers' councils as a revolutionary alternative to the national assembly, which they felt was an essentially bourgeois governmental form. Kautsky himself had on occasion observed that elected representative bodies were hardly the best agents for the achievement of the socialist society. But the constant growth of the socialist movement in the years before the First World War had encouraged him to believe that someday the workers could vote in socialism if only they had access to political control of the state. The repressive tactics of the SPD during the war had caused him to emphasize more than ever the need for constant grass-roots activity by the masses in order to overcome what he saw as the tyrannical tendencies of an overly powerful leadership. So strong was his faith in the masses that he was convinced during and after the war that only a truly democratic system would allow for the development of the free, socialist society he sought. The increasing disaffection of the populace with the imperial government during the last months of the war encouraged Kautsky even further in his belief that the day would come when socialism would be backed by a majority of the population. The relatively easy overthrow of the old regime and the obvious popularity of the new order among the workers convinced him that the old repressive form of parliament could be transformed into an instrument for domination by the socialist-conscious working class.

Kautsky was willing to accept the councils as revolutionary, and therefore temporary, bodies, but in politics he thought their utility strictly limited to the period of transition from the old Reich to the new republic. He did foresee an important economic function for the workers' councils, as local administrators of a gradual socialization plan necessary for the implementation of socialism. But he objected to the councils as permanent political bodies. First, by their very nature the councils disenfranchised enormous numbers of people, not just entrepreneurs and landowners, but professionals, white-collar workers, peasants, artisans, servants, and even housewives. If the republic were to be secured, these people had to accept it as the legitimate government; limiting political power to the workers would not only contradict the democratic principles of the socialist tradition, but also create a large and potentially very dangerous opposition to the new order. Therefore, to solidify the gains of November, a constituent assembly was a necessity. Second, he argued that limiting political participation to the workers and their soldier allies would only accentuate the differences within the already badly divided proletariat. In a national assembly, however, the predominant interests would be those of class rather than faction, and the solidarity of the workers would be reinforced. This would facilitate the task of giving the new state the proper socialist direction. Finally, Kautsky claimed that since immediate, total socialization was impossible, during the period when Germany had a mixed economy the mixture had to be reflected in its political bodies, that is, in a democratically elected assembly.[51]

This issue, the workers' and soldiers' councils versus the constituent assembly, finally brought Kautsky's break with the USPD in mid-1919. During the earlier months of the revolution, his strong support for a national assembly was broadly accepted by the USPD, albeit with the reservation that the elections be delayed to allow time to educate the electorate about the revolution. But from late December 1918, and through most of 1919, the majority of the party was radicalized and turned toward the councils. This was in large part a reaction to the repressive measures taken by the SPD leaders, with whom the cause of the national assembly was closely identified. But after the January elections, when the SPD and USPD together did not win a majority, many oppositional socialists turned to the councils as the only means of preserving and furthering the revolution. By the second congress of the USPD, in March 1919, sentiment for the councils was clearly on the rise; by the third congress, November 1919, the party accepted the concept of the dictatorship of the councils. By this time Kautsky had broken with his new party without returning to the old.[52]

Through much of 1919, Kautsky's usually awesome optimism was seriously challenged by his increasingly despairing view of the fate of socialists in Germany. In May he rejected a unity invitation from the SPD faction of the *Räte*, claiming that under present conditions such a step would seem to be capitulation to Noske. In May he also rejected any possibility of unity with the communists who had split with the USPD in January. At this time he introduced a pet proposal that he was to hold to throughout the year. This was the idea that unity between the left wing of the SPD and the right wing of the USPD, based on a reconstruction of the prewar Marxist center, was the only feasible step, given current conditions. The right wing of the SPD, the party majority, was too eager to suppress the workers; the left wing of the USPD was no different from the violent putschists of the Spartacist movement. Therefore, Kautsky concluded that those caught in the middle were the only candidates for unity. But the increasing radicalization of the left and the continued suppression of the workers by the SPD government brought Kautsky to the brink of despair by mid-October. In an article that was part of a series on the question of socialist unity, Kautsky wrote: "Never was the unity of the social democratic organizations of Germany more necessary than now; never was it less possible." He saw no way out of the dilemma of a three-way split in socialism, of governmental socialists butchering and imprisoning oppositional socialists, of the lack of a strong socialist international to bring pressure for reunification. Probably during no other period of his life did Kautsky come so close to losing hope.[53]

The debate within the USPD over the councils had many aspects — the Russian model, the spontaneous nature of the councils, seizing power versus building socialism, dictatorship and democracy as form or condition, and many others. But in fact the central issue was a vague but extremely important one of tone or mood. Kautsky represented a school of socialist thought that was highly rationalistic and analytical, with a decided inclination to order. This school placed a good deal of emphasis on the deterministic aspects of Marx's writings. An orderly man in his private life and intellectual activities, Kautsky was convinced that sufficient consciousness and leadership could yield an orderly revolution. But revolutions are not orderly, and they often demand flexible, highly innovative thought and action. Frustrated in their hopes that the workers themselves would push forward to the fuller revolution socialism needed, the left of the USPD turned to the councils, which, of course, had already rejected the concept of "all power to the soviets." The left eventually looked to a Bolshevik-style revolutionary party to save their dreams.

At the Berlin congress of the USPD, in the spring of 1919, Kautsky presented the case for the moderates, and Clara Zetkin captured the revolutionary mood of the left. At this meeting he reiterated his opposition to the soviets in his report on the recent Bern conference, which had attempted to revive the Second International. He argued that he was not opposed to the concept of the dictatorship of the proletariat, but claimed that dictatorship was not a form of government. It was a general condition in which the will of the proletariat would stamp itself on the nation through a united and concerted effort of the workers and their political party within democratic, representative forms. Zetkin responded by arguing that the central choice was not between democracy and dictatorship, but between "empty, bourgeois, formal, political democracy" and "vigorous, combative, proletarian, socialist democracy." Zetkin's speech was far less a detailed analysis of conditions and options in Germany than an emotional plea to the party not to lose the noble vision of the socialist society in the morass of principles and hard realities. Zetkin spoke for the frustrated and singleminded in the party. She spoke for those who saw in the Russian Revolution proof that an active, sufficiently determined, ruthless party could win the day. The disappointed hopes of the early weeks of the German revolution and the new state drove many within the USPD to accept the Russian model, abandon the majoritarian ideals of the social democratic movement, and look to the new forms of council and disciplined revolutionary party for salvation.[54]

Of course both sides erred in their evaluation of conditions in Germany. Despite the proof offered by the January 1919 constituent assembly elections that the socialist cause was not a majoritarian movement, Kautsky clung to the belief that it would become the majority without extreme measures. He continued to believe until his death that the freedom to propagandize and the continued maturation of capitalism had to bring socialism, eventually. He held to this opinion in the face of all evidence to the contrary. On the other hand, the leftists simply did not reckon with the German facts and the requirements of the revolution. The Bolsheviks, notwithstanding their own claims, had not made the Russian Revolution, because revolutions are not made, they happen. The Bolsheviks were prepared, when no one else in Russia was, to seize power and use it ruthlessly to shape the nation in their own image. In Germany only the figureheads of power had fallen—the army and bureaucracy survived the lost war and the abdication of the kaiser—and all the socialist determination in the world could not have overcome the odds. Perhaps a united working class headed by a united socialist party could have achieved more. But as it was, a badly split proletariat and its even more factionalized political parties could only accept defeat or an incomplete revolution. At least the second alternative had the advantage of less bloodshed.

Conceivably something more vigorous could have been done, even within the apparently narrow limits of action open to the German socialists. For instance, in his speech to the USPD congress of March 1919, Kautsky pointed out that the officer corps had not been purged of the men still loyal to the old Reich. He called for a revamping of the military hierarchy to ensure that it became "completely democratic and social democratic," identifying one of the major weaknesses of Weimar Germany, namely, that its last line of defense was a military that always remained only marginally loyal. Kautsky called the failure to purge the officer ranks one of the basic mistakes of the SPD government. And yet his own parliamentary inclination really offered no solution to this dilemma. The USPD had not done well in the January elections, winning only 22 seats, hardly 5 percent of the total. The party's ability to bring about military reform by parliamentary means was therefore extremely limited. Even if Kautsky's advice had been followed, and the two socialist parties had come together in the new republic, the combined socialist representation in the constituent assembly was only 185 seats, less than 44 percent. As the SPD had earlier formed an alliance with the military, Kautsky's call for a purge yielded nothing. On the other hand, had the USPD been able to influence the workers' and soldiers' councils, it is possible they could have been used to apply pressure from without to achieve reforms that would have made Weimar Germany more stable and stronger. But Kautsky's narrow view of the councils prohibited him from seeing the possibilities of these new bodies.[55]

The revolution of 1918 catapulted Kautsky into the political arena to an extent he had never known before. As an elder statesman of German socialism—he was sixty-four when the revolution broke out—he was looked to by the USPD leadership and accepted by the SPD leadership as an expert in several fields. His long record of commentary on economic matters won him the post of chairman of the socialization commission which was appointed nine days after the deposition of the kaiser. He also became an outside advisor (*Beigeordneter*) in the foreign office, charged with supervising the publication of official papers pertaining to the question of responsibility for the origins of the war. Largely because of his official position, he became a citizen of the new German state in 1919. As socialist contact in the foreign office, he attended several meetings of the Council of the People's Representatives, or the cabinet, which headed the government from early November 1918 until the constituent assembly elected Ebert president on 11 February 1919. But Kautsky's tenure as a government official was extremely brief. As a member of the USPD, he followed Emil Barth, Wilhelm Dittmann, and Hugo Haase, when on 28 and 29 December 1918 they left the government to protest the bloody suppression of a sailors' revolt of 23 and 24 December. Thus he held his positions for less than two months, though he continued to edit the war documents through the spring of 1919, and in January reported to representatives of the government and the *Zentralrat,* the central committee of the national congress of the workers' councils, on the conclusions of the socialization commission.[56]

By decree of the Council of People's Representatives, the socialization commission was constituted on 18 November 1918. The *Freiheit* announced the original commission as consisting of five socialists—Kautsky, Emil Lederer, Rudolf Hilferding, Heinrich Cunow, and Otto Hue—and four bourgeois economists and businessmen, including Walter Rathenau. Rathenau, a major architect of the German domestic war effort, was not particularly popular with the antiwar socialists; the hostility of the Independents on the commission forced him to resign soon after being appointed. Eventually three other men were appointed, including the then little-known Austrian economist Joseph

Schumpeter. When the first meeting was held on 5 December, Kautsky was chosen as chairman. After almost a month of meetings, as a whole and in parts, and despite a lack of cooperation from, and covert and overt sabotage by, the official economic ministry, Kautsky submitted the commission report to the government on 10 January 1919. The conclusions of the commission were very moderate, recommending no fixed program of socialization but one that adapted itself to the varying development of the different industries. The plan also specifically rejected the notion that socialization meant nationalization (that is, control by the state), and its one definite recommendation was the socialization of coal mines, with compensation and autonomous committees of entrepreneurs and workers to run them; everything else would have to wait. In fact, of course, even this had to wait. In the January elections, a socialist majority failed to materialize and as a result so did even modest socialization.[57]

Kautsky's view of how socialism would come out of capitalism was based on three preconceptions: the process would be gradual; it had to occur in a condition of plenty; and the state was not an appropriate agency for the socialization of production. Each of these preconceptions was revealed in Kautsky's writings on socialization, and he repeatedly insisted that the transition had to be orderly, because disorder would interrupt the process of production, thereby creating shortages, unemployment, and other hardships. His notion of the world of socialism was a world of plenty, not want; for this reason he rejected the idea that the transition from capitalism to socialism must necessarily include a period of lowered production. To ensure that socialization did not totally disrupt production, Kautsky argued, the owners of property taken over in the conversion had to be compensated. This was necessary because socialization would be gradual, and the capitalists who retained their property at the beginning had to be confident that they would not someday suddenly lose everything without compensation, otherwise they would simply stop producing immediately. Kautsky recognized that the capitalists could be forced to produce, but he argued that this not only would subvert democracy, it would also result in lower levels of production and inferior products. He felt that if the unexpropriated capitalists were certain of eventual compensation, they would continue to produce in an orderly fashion.[58]

In addition to the requirements of order and increased productivity, Kautsky felt that the pace and specifics of socialization had to correspond to the level of technical development in each particular area of production. He argued that socialist production was to be based on the achievements of capitalist production, that socialism was in this sense a direct outgrowth of highly developed capitalism. He defined six criteria for determining the appropriateness of socialization: corporations before individual holdings; large enterprises before small; cartels before those companies in free competition; concerns which produced only for the domestic market before those which produced for export; firms with regular markets before those without; and finally, companies with relatively simple production techniques and few products before those with complicated techniques and a large variety of products. He also insisted that in the conversion from capitalism to socialism, the technicians, experts, and intellectuals who provided the technical know-how of large-scale production had to be won over to the new order. Just as he did in the political aspects of the revolution, he sought as much order and as little violence as possible in its economic aspects.[59]

Perhaps the most interesting of Kautsky's ideas on socialization were the close relationship between democratic political forms and socialism he saw as vital to the survival of the new society and the mechanisms of economic administration he postulated. On the first matter he argued that because "constant political movement, constant economic and political struggle is the essence of democracy," socialism, particularly during the period of transition from capitalism, had to be tied to democracy. His point was that only under democratic forms would it be possible to work out class conflicts exclusively on a political level, without any disruption to production. If the workers had political control of the state, they could use it to settle their disputes with the remaining bourgeois forces and to adjust differences within the proletariat itself. Maximum hours, minimum wages, worker-protection laws, and other matters of importance to the workers would be dealt with on a political level, without resort to strikes and other forms of economic disruption. In fact, he proposed that in a socialist republic, no strikes would be allowed. He felt that calm and order could be achieved and maintained not by the oppressive tactics of a police regime, but by the workers' domination of political power.[60]

Nationalization in the form of state socialism or state capitalism was not what Kautsky meant by socialization. Though he postulated an important role for the state in the process of socialization—as a central clearing house, as the source of general economic plans, as the agent of compensation, and as the capital source for concentration in agriculture—he did not assign to the state a permanent role as administrator or even supervisor of socialized holdings. His notion was that economic control in the socialist society would be shared by collegia made up of equal numbers of representatives from the state, the workers, and consumers. The workers' councils would be the means by which the proletariat influenced the process of production. In every industry not immediately socialized, entrepreneurs, workers, and consumers would share equally in management. He also foresaw the creation of peasant cooperatives to manage the large holdings created by the state's buying up of small holdings. Housing cooperatives, consumer cooperatives, and other forms of local organization would provide a high degree of decentralized, direct popular control of the economic aspects of everyday life. Far from being dominant in economics, the state would only be a facilitating factor in the conversion and an equal partner with workers and consumers in major industry.[61]

Kautsky's proposals for implementing these plans were far les imaginative than the plans themselves. The socialization commission had only advisory powers, and the leaders of the new German state were not about to act on the commission's modest recommendations until after the constituent assembly elections. When those returned a nonsocialist majority, the plan became a dead letter. At the second congress of the workers' and soldiers' councils, April 1919, his plan for socialization was read by Luise, Kautsky himself being ill at the time. This plan reiterated many of his earlier arguments, but called on the councils to pressure the new government into dealing with socialization. To this end he urged the congress to press for reunification of the two socialist parties. United, the proletariat could exert greater influence for a more thorough purging of elements of the old order and for more vigorous pursuit of socialism. But the congress could not respond to his pleas because the two parties were at the time moving even further apart. Moreover, his opinion carried much less weight in the spring of 1919 than it had earlier; his advice no longer was a significant factor. Finally, Kautsky probably would not have supported the councils if they had gone beyond moral pressure and into the streets to give their demands more substance. He was not present at the congress, but he probably would have favored the resolution calling for the socialization issue to be turned over to the *Zentralrat*. The resolution was carried over cries from the leftists of "trash!" and "academic nonsense [*Kathedersozialisten*]." Once again his ideas were not translated into action.[62]

Work in the foreign office commanded more of Kautsky's time and created more headaches for him than did his work with the socialization commission. Not the least of his problems was his own lack of experience in public affairs in general and with the protocol and processes of the foreign office in particular. He was acutely aware of his own weaknesses in this regard. Another serious obstacle was the strong personal conflict between Kautsky and the foreign minister, Wilhelm Solf, a career diplomat-politician appointed in the waning days of the old Reich. Solf, like most imperial holdovers, was offended by the presence of a socialist in his department; he distrusted Kautsky's motives, training, and abilities. He even tried to get Kautsky out of the country by arguing that he was needed to establish contacts with French and British socialists in Bern. Since Kautsky's primary function as an outside advisor in the foreign office was to arrange for the publication of documents that would fix responsibility for the war on the old order, Solf's attitude was not surprising. Kautsky soon found that he could not do his job properly because Solf was limiting his access to critical documents. His threat to resign unless Solf left the foreign office added to the growing demand that the foreign minister be replaced. In early December 1918, Solf was implicated by innuendo in an abortive conservative coup attempt; a few days later Kautsky accused the news bureau of the foreign office of spying on the Spartacists, and on the same day Solf and Haase exchanged harsh words over Solf's accusation that the USPD had received financing for their revolutionary activities from the Russians. Finally, on 12 December the *Freiheit* announced Solf's impending departure; on the eighteenth his resignation was announced and the cabinet began looking for a successor; and on 21 December, Count Ulrich Brockdorff-Rantzau was named to the post.[63]

Although Kautsky got along much better with Rantzau than he had with Solf, the work at the foreign office was complicated by a number of other factors. For instance, leftist critics charged Kautsky with incompetence and whitewashing when rumors circulated that important foreign-office documents had been burned. Kautsky denied that any such burnings took place while he was working on the project. Some critics argued that he should have published the documents as they came to light, rather than waiting until the entire collection was ready. Kautsky defended his methods on the grounds that defenders of the old Reich could not then claim that the documents were taken out of context. Bourgeois and conservative journals claimed that publishing the documents would make it harder to gain a fair peace. Kautsky argued that the documents would prove that the deposed kaiser and his clique had been responsible for the war, not the German people, and that this should ensure a better peace. Other right-wing critics, like the *Deutsche Tageszeitung*, complained that sensitive state documents were in the hands of a foreigner because Kautsky was a Czech. The *Freiheit* defended Kautsky against the charge, arguing that he was not a

Czech, but a "Prague-German." This article closed by suggesting that Germany would gain a great deal "if a man like Karl Kautsky" were to replace Solf in the foreign office. Kautsky certainly never entertained such grandiose designs for public office, and fortunately conditions did not permit his being appointed to such a post.[64]

Two literary works resulted from Kautsky's efforts in the foreign office. After a long delay, during which the government published a white paper on the war-guilt question, a four-volume publication entitled *The German Documents on the Outbreak of War, 1914* was issued. Kautsky had finished his work by late March, but for a variety of reasons — most of them associated with trying to get a better deal from the Allies — the collection was not published until October. At that time, Max Montgelas and Walter Schücking were identified as primary editors, and Kautsky as compiler. This collection has long since been superseded by more complete collections of documents, but when it was published, the left was shocked to discover how correct it had been in condemning Germany for the war, while the right argued that the documents proved that the kaiser and his clique had not caused the war. The intention of the government in sponsoring the project had been to forestall a harsh peace by blaming the war on the old Reich, not the German people. Obviously this end was not realized.[65]

The second work to come out of Kautsky's foreign office experience was his analysis of the documents he had edited, *How the World War Began (Wie die Weltkrieg entstand)*, which is usually given a much more descriptive title when translated into English, *The Guilt of Wilhelm Hohenzollern*. This, too, has been superseded by more recent studies, but at the time of its publication the topic was of immediate concern to many people, and Kautsky's book received wide notice. The study began with a brief review of imperialist conflicts and German diplomatic isolation and then turned to the events between the assassination of Archduke Franz Ferdinand and the war declarations of early August. While Kautsky assigned first responsibility to Austrian incompetence and folly, he clearly presented Kaiser Wilhelm as committed to and eager for war at least as early as 4 July and probably by 30 June. The bulk of the book purported to show that the political, diplomatic, and military elites of imperial Germany conspired with the Austrian leadership to dupe both peoples into a senseless war. In Germany, Kautsky argued, the people were purposely lied to; they went into war enthusiastically because they did not understand the true motives of the kaiser. The point of this study, according to Kautsky's own introduction, was to demonstrate that German statesmen, not the German people, were responsible for the war.[66]

Naturally Kautsky's arguments did not go unchallenged. From moderate conservatives like Hans Delbrück, prominent historian and editor of the influential *Preussische Jahrbücher,* to reactionary chauvinists like Theodor Schiemann, historian, friend of the ex-kaiser, and editor of the conservative *Kreuzzeitung,* critics took on Kautsky's preconceptions, his use of documents, and his interpretation of facts. Delbrück's criticism was the most measured and professional. He objected primarily to Kautsky's tendency to impute nefarious motives to the Germans and Austrians while taking the French and the English at their word. The more right-wing critics, like Schiemann, simply denounced Kautsky as a traitor and a liar. Other right-wingers, like Friedrich Freksa, a Munich literary figure, emphasized Kautsky's non-native status, repeatedly referring to him as a Czech. Eventually the furor over Kautsky's book died down, though, of course, the argument over war guilt still rages. But the response to his study did demonstrate that in the early years of the shaky Weimar Republic, Kautsky was still prominent enough to attract the attention of scholars and politicians.[67]

Kautsky's historical work was not directly connected with his socialist activities, and his active participation in socialist affairs dropped off drastically during the spring of 1919 as the USPD moved further to the left. As this leftward movement accelerated, Kautsky came under increasing fire from the Bolsheviks and the German left for deserting the cause of revolution. But as these attacks increased, Kautsky became even more adamant in defense of his distinction between political and social revolution. In a July 1919 letter to his youngest son, Benedikt, he offered the clearest exposition of his fully developed view:

> I completely agree with you on this, in that I hold the English way of socialization to be the most fruitful future course. Many now see this as capitulation to Bernstein. But whoever thinks so has forgotten (or never knew) what my opposition to Bernstein was.
>
> [Bernstein] held that Marx's prognosis of economic development was false, that the proletariat would not grow, and therefore that socialism was only attainable with the aid of the socially sensitive part of the bourgeoisie. He saw this portion growing as the class struggle was channeled into milder forms, and above all considered revolution unnecessary or dangerous. I have actively fought that, and in this I was right in the end.
>
> These people have never been able to distinguish between social and political revolution. This [latter] can only be a sudden act, and it was indispensible in eastern Europe. The military monarchy was not to be overthrown otherwise. But now that has

happened. The task is now above all only the social revolution—except in Asia and the colonies. This revolution is only feasible gradually [and] therefore often not externally recognizable as a revolution. It is impossible to say exactly when and where capitalism began, and so it is also impossible to say: now capitalism has ended, now socialism begins.

That the *social* revolution will only be a gradual process is a view which I have always taken, as for example in the Erfurt program. . . . I have not changed sides in this.[68]

Such a view was perhaps implicit in the Erfurt program, but Kautsky did not make this explicit distinction until the pressure of two revolutions forced him to do so. By that time many people who had learned at least part of their Marxism from Kautsky were dedicated to forcing the pace of both political and social revolution. Other former party comrades had abandoned their dreams of social revolution altogether and were satisfied with, or even found too precipitate, a political revolution that left the workers in a minority. Kautsky's position was no longer popular, and he found himself without a party.

From mid-1919 to 1924, when he and Luise left Germany to return almost permanently to Vienna, Kautsky was little involved in party affairs. A long visit, full of complications, to the Menshevik-dominated government of independent Georgia kept him out of Germany from August 1920 to May 1921. This trip was originally intended as a fact-finding visit by a delegation of old Second Internationalists, but he fell ill during the trip, and was forced to stop in Rome. The Mensheviks who headed this short-lived government considered him a mentor, and he was treated to a long visit once he did arrive. He was in Georgia from late September until early in January. Kautsky enjoyed this experience, and wrote an account called *Georgia: A Social Democratic Republic,* which was little more than an attack on the Bolsheviks and a rather rose-colored look at the Georgian situation. Before Kautsky returned to Germany from Georgia, the Red Army had invaded and conquered it. Upon his return, Kautsky found the USPD a shambles, with most of the membership having gone over to the newly formed communist movement following the Halle congress of October 1920. The remainder of the party was still far from united, and it gradually disintegrated completely.[69]

After the dissolution of the USPD, Kautsky drifted back toward the SPD without ever again playing a significant role in its affairs. He contributed very little to the official party press, fewer than a score articles in the *Vorwärts* after 1919. His contributions to the Austrian and other foreign socialist presses increased after 1920, and he spent a good deal of time writing books and articles criticizing Bolshevik Russia. The great war destroyed the party that had been his since 1880; as a result, he lost the journal he had edited for nearly thirty-five years. The victory of the Bolsheviks in Russia and the incomplete revolution in Germany created a situation in which his reasoned and relatively cautious brand of Marxism no longer appealed to a working class hardened by war and revolution. In 1924 he returned to Vienna, retiring forever from active political life.

CHAPTER SEVEN

Return to Vienna,
1924–1938

DURING THE LAST FOURTEEN YEARS of his life, Kautsky's active involvement in a socialist, working-class party virtually ceased. By 1924 and his return to the Austrian capital, he was seventy years old. He had devoted nearly all of the previous forty-five years of his life to the most intimate daily contact with the German movement, albeit as an intellectual and not a politician, organizer, or party functionary. But from 1924 on, his concern shifted from German party affairs to highly abstract theorizing, on the one hand, and to criticism of Bolshevik Russia, on the other. In conjunction with the latter, Kautsky devoted a great deal of time to urging the Russian emigré opponents of Bolshevism to abandon their incessant infighting and prepare for the inevitable collapse of the communist order in their homeland. So convinced was he that the communist state in Russia was a historical contradiction that he repeatedly predicted its imminent demise. The indomitable optimism that led him to this conclusion also caused him to maintain the increasingly absurd conviction that the German, Italian, and Austrian fascist movements were only fleeting aberrations. But when he died in October 1938, the world he had hoped to live to see, the world of socialism and human justice, was never further from being realized.

Critique of the Bolsheviks

Kautsky's critique of Bolshevik Russia developed along three main lines in the years after 1919. First, he persisted in his argument that because objective conditions had not been ripe for a socialist revolution in Russia in 1917, the Bolshevik regime simply could not survive. Soviet Russia lacked a firm industrial base; therefore, the exigencies of modern production would force Lenin to make his peace with the capitalist countries in order to acquire the necessary capital investment and technological improvements. In 1921, he wrote to the Menshevik Irakli Tseretelli that "the complete capitulation of Lenin before the capitalism of western Europe is inevitable." He also contended that for the same reason—the lack of the necessary preconditions for the development of a modern industrial society—the Soviet government would be forced, eventually, to pander to the peasantry or fall. However, he also emphasized that all efforts to secure Russia's economic base had to end in failure because either the massive peasant majority would be pushed to rebellion by the ruthless exploitation necessary to develop industry solely from internal sources, or both the workers and the peasants would rebel against the foreign domination implied by the capital investments that were necessary. One way or another, Kautsky was convinced that the new Soviet state and society were historical abominations that could not long survive.[1]

Historical parallel provided Kautsky his second line of anti-Bolshevik critique. Referring to the examples of France during the generation from 1799 to 1830, central Europe for the ten years after 1848–1849, and France from 1871 to 1877, he argued that every period of revolution was followed by a period of counterrevolution. In Russia, the Bolsheviks, once the most radical and ruthless of all the revolutionary parties, had been forced by circumstances to take over "the function of the counterrevolution"; the "white tsarism" of the old order had been replaced by the "red tsarism" of the new. Although he was realistic enough to admit that the "counterrevolutionary" government of the Bolsheviks was both more efficient and more vicious than the tsars' governments had been, in 1923 he very optimistically maintained that modern history had shown that each counterrevolutionary period was shorter than its predecessor and that therefore the reign of the Bolsheviks would not be as long as the counterrevolutionary period following the Paris Commune. That he firmly believed this last notion is doubtful; he made the prediction in a letter intended to help unite the badly split Georgian Menshevik emigré clique. But there is little doubt that he did see the oppressive Bolshevik state as a manifestation of an inevitable counterrevolution; during the 1930s he argued that Bolshevism and Nazism were both counterrevolutionary movements.[2]

Finally, Kautsky emphasized that Bolshevik Russia would collapse from the sheer weight of its internal contradictions; he rejected any notion of mounting an invasion or even promoting internal unrest by putschist activities, at least until the inevitable collapse was at hand. His repeated advice to his Menshevik emigré friends was to settle their own disputes and to cooperate with all the forces of opposition, especially the peasantry, in order to ensure the ultimate victory of democratic forces. The state that succeeded Bolshevik rule would have to be a peasant republic, according to Kautsky, but the united social democratic forces of Russia could exercise influence in this new state to ensure fair treatment for the workers and to prepare the transition from peasant capitalism to socialism. In 1929, he went so far as to argue to Theodore Dan that after the collapse of their state, even the Bolsheviks would have to be included in the social democratic coalition.[3]

Knowing full well that this last suggestion would not win favor with the Mensheviks, Kautsky pressed hard on the issue of sectarianism. First he insisted that despite the errors of the communist leadership, there were "highly valuable elements to be found among the communist workers," and in a Russia numerically dominated by the peasantry, the social democrats would need all the worker support they could muster. Kautsky also lectured Dan on practical politics, arguing that "compromises are necessary in practical politics." Echoing his earlier distinction, he contended that theoretical or propagandistic compromises were not acceptable, but compromises in practice, in the shaping of laws or practical programs, had to be made. Just as in the years before the First World War he had condemned both the Bolsheviks and Mensheviks for their petty theoretical and personal disputes, so now Kautsky argued that Russian sectarianism would have to be put aside to save Russia. Twice he referred to the fatal, uncompromising attitude of the German extremists, Rosa Luxemburg and Karl Liebknecht, to make his point about the self-destructive potential of narrow sectarianism. He had no illusions about the willingness of the communists to relinquish their domination in Russia, but he argued that in order to take fullest advantage of the inevitable collapse of the Soviet system, the social democrats would have to be prepared to cooperate with the chastened, but still useful communist forces. "A politician must be able to forget," he wrote, especially to forget past theoretical and tactical differences that no longer have practical significance.[4]

The International Socialist Movement

In rather stark contrast to his advice to the Menshevik exiles, Kautsky took an increasingly hard line on the relationship between the Bolsheviks and the international socialist movement. From the last days of the war, he had worked diligently to get the defunct Second

232 · KARL KAUTSKY

International revived. Early in 1919, representatives from most of the European parties of the old International met in Bern to discuss the prospects of reorganizing an international association. Kautsky was a delegate for the USPD, and Germany was also represented by SPD delegates. At the USPD congress in March 1919, Kautsky delivered a report on the Bern conference in which he claimed that the old International was not entirely dead. He pointed out that only the United States, Serbia, Belgium, Switzerland, and Italy were not represented. But he failed to point out that the only socialist party then in power, the Bolsheviks, had boycotted Bern, and he failed to discuss the significance of the absence of the Swiss and the Italians. He also reported that personally he was reserving judgment on the Bolsheviks until more information was available. But in fact, at Bern he had sided with forces which were extremely hostile to the Bolsheviks, although his own speech on Russia was not entirely hostile to Lenin's government. He had urged the Bern conference to recognize the monumental problems facing the new Russian regime even as he supported the implicitly anti-Bolshevik resolution. As on so many other occasions, he failed to take into account the emotional implications of his rational analysis. A strong statement on the desirability of democracy, which was little else than an implied attack on the Bolsheviks, was much less likely to discourage further Allied intervention in Russia, as Kautsky claimed it would, than it was to strengthen the anti-Bolshevik forces. Whatever the merits of democracy over dictatorship, he was being either foolish or disingenuous in failing to perceive the potential impact of such a statement.[5]

Actually Kautsky was willing to accept the Bolsheviks into some reconstituted Second International long after the Bolsheviks had made it very clear that they were not willing to share in any such activities with Kautsky and those whom Lenin labeled "social patriots" and "social chauvinists" because they were not willing to make a clean break with prewar socialism. Despite constant and vituperative personal attacks by the communists, Kautsky was still arguing as late as 1920 that all the Russians had to do to be accepted into a revived International was to stop insisting on splits in national working-class movements and to end their forceful repression of "socialist brother parties." He contended that even parties advocating soviet-style democracy could be tolerated, despite the fact that he had by that time broken with the USPD over its accepting the soviet concept. But by 1920 he had ceased to pull much weight in German socialist circles. Furthermore, the tide of revolutionary excitement had been on the side of the Bolsheviks since late 1917; they, not Kautsky, had the power and prestige to decide who would be tolerated in a new International and who would not. Kautsky's increasing isolation was made even more obvious by the success of the Third International and the final disappearance of the rump of the Second.[6]

Eventually, a noncommunist, socialist international was organized after the First World War, but Kautsky had very little to do with it. Two meetings, in Bern in December 1920, and in Vienna in February 1921, resulted in the formation of the Internationale Arbeitsgemeinschaft sozialistischer Parteien. In 1923, the first congress of the new international, the Labour and Socialist International (L.S.I.), which grew out of the Arbeitsgemeinschaft conferences, met in Hamburg. Successive congresses were held in Marseilles (1925), Brussels (1928), and Vienna (1931), with a final conference in Paris in 1933. This International was derisively referred to as the "two-and-a-half" by its opponents, a reference to its rejection of the old Second and also its distance from the new Third. The major parties of the L.S.I. were the Independent Labour Party of Great Britain, the SPD, the Social Democratic Workers' Party of German-Austria, and the French Socialist Party. The USPD had been active in the organization of the Arbeitsgemeinschaft, but the party's vote to affiliate with the Third International at the Halle congress in October 1920 soon reduced the USPD to insignificance. One of the conditions of affiliation was the adoption of the name "communist," and the secession of some 300,000 members to the German Communist Party left the USPD in shambles. It finally dissolved into obscurity. Nonetheless, the L.S.I. had as members parties which at various times ruled alone or in coalition in England, Austria, Germany, and Sweden. It also included the exiled Mensheviks, Georgians, Ukrainians, and other Russian parties. Among the leading figures of the L.S.I. were Friedrich Adler, Emile Vandervelde, Otto Bauer, and Leon Blum.[7]

The L.S.I. was organized because the member parties felt that the Third International was narrowly focused and attempted to impose on the world movement tactics based on the peculiar conditions of Russia. But the L.S.I. and many of its member parties were not unreservedly hostile to the Soviet Union, and on occasion Kautsky's anti-Bolshevism put him at odds with L.S.I. policies. He was on his Georgian trip when the new international was being organized and was an official delegate at only one congress, in Vienna, 1931. But his lack of active participation in L.S.I. affairs and his occasional divergence on policy matters did not prevent his being honored by the new international and its member parties as a major figure of the socialist movement. Friedrich Adler, who was general secretary of the L.S.I., often called upon Kautsky to

Rosa Luxemburg and Karl Kautsky, Jr., 1907

From left to right: Eduard Bernstein, Pavel Axelrod, Karl Kautsky, 1922

Karl Kautsky's last public speaking appearance, Vienna, 1932

attend and speak at commemorative celebrations sponsored by the L.S.I., including the sixtieth anniversary of the founding of the First International in 1924 and the fiftieth anniversary of the Wyden congress of the German party in 1930.[8]

The L.S.I. congresses resembled the fraternal pageants of the Second International. The Vienna congress was preceded by the second Arbeitsportsolympiade, a working-class Olympics; on the eve of the congress, 24 July, a concert sponsored by the L.S.I. was held in the Rathausplatz; on the twenty-fifth, the delegates gathered in assembly to honor the athletes who had just finished their competition; and on the twenty-seventh, another concert was held at the Vienna Burggarten. Speakers at the formal sessions dealt with the decline of capitalism, the threat of fascism, and, in particularly heated fashion, with the appropriate response of socialists to these issues. Although he was an official Austrian delegate at this congress and met extensively with other delegates in private, Kautsky did not speak on any of the topics addressed. His most public activity in connection with the congress was a speech in honor of Victor Adler given before the busts of dead Austrian party comrades.[9]

The Materialist Conception of History

As part of the festivities associated with the 1931 congress of the L.S.I., the Austrian socialist Fritz Brügel wrote a brief history of the various worker-socialist internationals. After reviewing the major personalities of the Second International—Adler, Bebel, Wilhelm Liebknecht, Luxemburg, Jaurès, Guesde, Turati, Plekhanov, Vandervelde, and others—Brügel referred to Engels and to "Karl Kautsky, who must be named at the head of all others, who further developed the teachings of Karl Marx, and has produced the scientific basis on which the edifice of modern socialism is raised."[10]

In addition to the general impact of Kautsky's life-long devotion to the continuation of Marx's work, Brügel was also alluding to Kautsky's magnum opus, *The Materialist Conception of History*, which had been published in 1927. Kautsky himself referred to this eighteen-hundred-page, two-volume study as "the quintessence of my life's work." Pavel Axelrod called it "a worthy advancement [*Fortsetzung*] of the theoretical work of Marx-Engels." Peter Garwy, another Russian exile active in the L.S.I., praised the work also, saying that it would put to rest the "primitive, vulgar materialism of Lenin, Bukharin, etc." History has, however, passed a much different judgment on *The Materialist Conception*. It is now little read and certainly did nothing to counter the prestige of the theories associated with the victors in the Russian Revolution. No Kautskyian school of Marxism exists today. Marxism-Leninism is the common starting point for almost all the multitude of doctrinal disputations that still today generate a great deal of heat and very little light.[11]

Kautsky's intention in *The Materialist Conception of History* was to provide "a systematic and exhaustive" presentation of historical materialism, which he argued was not a mere "empirical theory, . . . but one into which a great world view has been incorporated, with which it stands and fails." This world view was that of the natural sciences. It accepted the absolute reality of the world external to the "I" and the validity of the notion of cause and effect. It held that the basic principle of the history of all living things was that changes in organisms and their organization followed only from changes in the environment, and humans are, like all animals, products of the workings of natural forces. Kautsky emphasized Darwin as one of the major figures in the establishment of this world view, but laid greater stress on the importance of Engels, particularly his *Origins of the Family* and *Anti-Dühring.* This treatment of historical materialism was clearly a product of Kautsky's early fascination with the sweeping biological theories and positivism of the last half of the nineteenth century. As if to prove this connection, he included as part of his magnum opus articles on the natural origins of social instincts in humans and animals which he had written over forty years earlier. *The Materialist Conception* was an effort to make explicit what Lenin once referred to as "the *inseparable* connection between the instinctive materialism of the natural scientists and *philosophical materialism* as a trend known long ago and hundreds of times affirmed by Marx and Engels."[12]

One of the most persistent criticisms of Kautsky's theory has concerned his emphasis on the affinities of Darwinian, evolutionary natural science and Marx's historical materialism. A contemporary Marxist critic, the German Karl Korsch, called Kautsky a bourgeois cryptorevisionist who substituted evolution for the dialectic and thus eliminated the subjective, active component of Marx's theory to focus exclusively on "objective, historical evolution [*Werden*] in nature and society." More recent critics have repeated and expanded on Korsch's line of argument, until the standard view of Kautsky as a positivistic Marxist has been firmly established. The connection in Kautsky's mind between the natural sciences as they developed in the late nineteenth century and Marxism is irrefutable, but the idea that he viewed human society as simply a subdivision of larger natural history and subject to the same developmental laws is false. In *The Materialist Conception of*

History, he specifically and repeatedly denied that the laws of nature and the laws of society are interchangable.[13]

"The materialist conception of history rests on the one hand on the recognition of the uniformity of events in nature and society, on the other hand it demonstrates the particular of societal development in the generality of world development." "The materialist conception of history means nothing other than the application of [the methods of natural science] to society—naturally with consideration to its peculiarity." According to Kautsky, two things made human societal history distinctly different from natural history: the mode of development and the role of human intellect and will. While natural history is characterized by an evolutionary mode of development, human history is not—for humans, development is dialectical; it occurs as a result of "the conflict of opposites." He specifically contended that his dialectic had more in common with Hegel's than with Engels', because Hegel's dialectic was an exclusively human phenomenon while Engels argued that dialectical development was characteristic of all of nature. When his Russian friend, Theodore Dan, objected to the apparent reduction of the dialectic to insignificance in *The Materialist Conception,* Kautsky responded that it was precisely in the realm of *"human society"* that he saw the dialectic as operative.[14]

Dialectical development in human society was for Kautsky the product of the interaction of human intellect and the environment in which humans live. Marxists differed from Kantian and Hegelian idealists said Kautsky, because "for us it is never the idea alone, but the reciprocal action between thinking humans and their environment which produces the dialectical process." On the one hand, the human intellect yielded will, moral commitment, the subjective, active component of social development; but on the other hand, and of even greater importance for Kautsky, human intellect was the source of technological change. Virtually the entire second volume of *The Materialist Conception of History* was devoted to a discussion of the impact on human development of the unique ability of humans to manipulate the environment through technology. From the harnessing of fire to the division of labor and the emergence of classes to the formation of states to the rise of modern capitalism, Kautsky emphasized human action as a vital part of the material change that yielded development. By simultaneously insisting on the natural origins of social instincts and the similarities of natural and social development, while at the same time stressing the subjective role of humans in the process of history, he blended the ambiguous legacy of the Marxian notions of will and determinism into a coherent, if not entirely persuasive, world view.[15]

One obvious weakness of Kautsky's presentation of the materialist conception of history is its very comprehensiveness. Enlightened observers must preserve a measure of skepticism about any system that purports to present the history of the world and humanity as part of an all-encompassing schema. Particularly historians who have delved into the intricacies of the past and politicians who try to cope with the complexities of the present must balk at sweeping linear explanations. As Kautsky himself once observed, the world is too complicated to be reduced to gross generalizations, and in fact, he was aware of this as an inherent problem of Marxism. At the opening of *The Materialist Conception*, he attempted to clear up one particularly difficult matter by refuting the notion that Marxism was the same thing as economic determinism. "Certainly we see the 'moving force' of history in economics," he wrote. "However it does not drive psychology, but history." He claimed that for Marxists, not economic interests, but economic development was the moving force of history. Furthermore, he argued that the "general law of social development" and the notion of the necessity of social revolution, both of which Marx discovered, were applicable only to the period after the arrival of industrial capitalism. According to Kautsky, Marxists do not seek to explain the humanly universal, but the historically specific. However, his own effort to provide a comprehensive world view belied this conviction.[16]

Finally, Kautsky laid claim to something that he had often said did not exist, namely objective truth that was not determined by class. Forgetting his own frequent statements on the relativity and class nature of all political, historical, and intellectual activities, he asserted that as "pure scientific teaching," the materialist conception of history was not bound to the proletariat, though in its practical application it was, presumably because the interests of the proletariat were being served by history. In stark contradiction of his own half-century of struggle for theoretical clarity among German socialists, Kautsky denied that acceptance of the materialist conception of history should be a precondition for membership in social democratic parties. These parties, he wrote in the foreword of *The Materialist Conception*, "must stand openly with all who want to fight the struggle for the freedom of the proletariat, the struggle against all oppression and exploitation, however this desire may be theoretically based, whether materialist or Kantian or Christian or whatever." Unlike the communists, the lesson Kautsky learned from the disasters of world war and the Russian Revolution was not the need for greater discipline and theoretical unity, but the need for a more broadly based, amorphous coalition to counter the rising tide of oppression.[17]

240 · KARL KAUTSKY

Nazism

At no time were the strengths and weaknesses of Kautsky's strongly rationalistic Marxism more obvious than when he attempted to analyze the fascist movements of the interwar years. Of course the fascist phenomenon was difficult for all Marxists to interpret. The qualities and composition of these new mass movements defied the categories of Marxist explanation. For the most part Kautsky's discussion of fascism in general and nazism in particular was not markedly different from that of many other Marxists. He saw the new movements as part of the inevitable despair that follows the apparent failure of revolutions to achieve their ends. This was the same counterrevolutionary argument he had used in 1923 to explain the Bolsheviks. Fascism was a manifestation of antiprogressive, antidemocratic mature capitalism which won popular support from the insecure, unconscious, petit bourgeois and peasant masses. The appeal of dictatorship and militarism was successful, he said, because of a bad peace and the growing world economic crisis. He contended that a good deal of responsibility for the failure of Weimar Germany had to be born by "the democratic victor states" for their harsh, unjust treatment of the conquered German people.[18]

All this was both obvious and formalistic, but also not much to the point. The fact of the matter was that Kautsky could not come to grips with fascism because his own rationalism prevented him from understanding the desperation and fear that seized so many people in the aftermath of war and revolution or the threat of revolution. He tended to see the violence and extremism of fascism and communism as an overreliance on will or as pandering to the ignorant and primitive among the masses. As his own brand of reasoned Marxism rapidly lost ground to the more vigorous and militant movements of the right and left, he insisted increasingly on the need for less passion and more calculation. Trying to explain the problems of European social democracy to an American friend in 1935, he wrote; "The position of these people [the extremists] is more favorable than ours. [This is] because we demand from the workers that they learn and think, while they flatter their ignorance and appeal to the most primitive instincts. That got Lenin his successes, then Stalin, Mussolini as well as Hitler."[19]

Sympathizers with Kautsky's general theoretical positions tried to convince him that the times demanded more excitement from Marxism than he was offering. Gregory Bienstock, a young Russian exile, argued that right thinking and proper analysis were not enough. "Who in all the world has thought more correctly than we Marxists?" Bienstock asked Kautsky. In an impassioned plea for a Marxism that offered more adventure and daring, and would therefore be more attractive, Bienstock suggested that "we have promoted all too much science and too little mythology." Bienstock recognized the tenor of his times and sought to adjust Kautsky's Marxism to it.[20]

Kautsky's response to Bienstock reflected the older man's rationalism and the strength of his conviction. While the first quality may have prevented an effective response to the crisis of the interwar years, when coupled with the second, it yielded a powerful, hopeful message. Kautsky asked Bienstock two penetrating questions: "But how would discussion be possible between science and mythology?" and "What is 'our time'? The last year or the last hundred years?" Obviously, "the sober do not fit into the society of the drunken," but the temporary success of the drunken does not justify the abandonment of reason. "My time will come again," he concluded, "of that I am firmly convinced." Later he restated the same sentiments in more stirring terms:

> The victory of Hitlerism for the moment does not in the slightest provide occasion for us to become ruthless in our methods, as we are now frequently urged to become, if by becoming ruthless is meant to become bloodthirsty and unscrupulous. . . . The brown barbarians may arrest us, may throw us into concentration camps, may shoot us "in flight," but they shall not succeed in making us prisoners of their depravity. Under all circumstances we shall remain the champions of democracy and humanity. We reject as senseless and cruel and ruinous to both our cause and our nation the suggestion that we strive to arrive at humanity by the methods of brutality.
>
> The circumstances that made Hitlerism are temporary. The German working class, however, remains basically the same as it was before the world war and will again do its duty when circumstances change and make possible the overthrow of the Hitler regime.[21]

This was in 1934, after little more than a year of Nazi rule in Germany, long before the Anschluss was to drive home the brutality of the Hitler regime to the Kautsky family. But even as things went from bad to worse, Kautsky did not lose his hope that history would prove him right.

Withdrawal from Public Life

Public comment on contemporary political events was a decidedly secondary occupation for Karl Kautsky after 1924. The return to Vienna in that year marked his retirement from active politics, but hardly from literary labors. Increasing age and nagging ill health did little to reduce the extent of his writing. In the last fourteen years of his life, he wrote and had published over four thousand pages of theoretical and historical study, including a collection of his correspondence with Engels comprising more than four hundred pages. But this productivity did not mean that he appealed to a large audience. Probably the best testimony to his fall from prominence was the fact that he could get the Engels correspondence published only after the Czech socialist party promised to buy 500 copies. On occasion even the very sympathetic Austrian socialist press rejected his articles as politically irrelevant in the troubled 1930s. Attacks on the Bolsheviks found ready outlets and translators, but his major theoretical and historical works from this period have remained untranslated to this day.[22]

Kautsky was not entirely forgotten, however, as the curious reaction to his two-volume study of war revealed. Originally planned as a four-part project, only the first and third volumes saw the light of day. The second volume was completed, but the manuscript was lost following the Nazi takeover in Germany in 1933. The first volume, *War and Democracy* (1932), discussed the politics of war in theory and practice from the Reformation to 1848. The second volume to appear, *Socialists and War* (1937), concentrated on socialist attitudes toward war. This work retraced historical ground of the first volume in part one, covered the period from the Crimean War to the Russo-Turkish War in part two and the imperialist period in part three, and closed with a detailed look at socialists and the First World War. These volumes are notable primarily for the strong antiwar sentiments which prevail throughout, and for Kautsky's striking willingness to understand without excusing the dilemma of the German socialists who had to take a stand on war credits in early August 1914.[23]

Many postwar, noncommunist European socialists felt that these two volumes by Kautsky merited his nomination for a Nobel peace prize. At the prompting of the Menshevik exile Paul Olberg, fifteen Swedish social democratic parliamentarians, led by Richard Lindstroem and Harald Akerberg, submitted Kautsky's name to the peace prize committee of the Norwegian parliament on 22 January 1938. In the weeks that followed, a considerable number of European socialists, mostly parliamentarians and intellectuals, petitioned the prize committee in Kautsky's favor. A particularly strong French contingent of 154 parliamentary representatives, including Leon Blum, urged that Kautsky be awarded the prize. On 26 January 1938, the official organ of the French socialist party (SFIO), *Le Populaire,* asked its readers to send telegrams of support for Kautsky's nomination. *Le Populaire* and another French socialist newspaper, *Le Peuple,* both referred to Kautsky as the "doyen de la doctrine marxiste" in expressing their support. An impressive list of Czech, Hungarian, Bulgarian, Yugoslavian, Dutch, Danish, and Austrian socialists, and a few nonsocialists, also promoted Kautsky's candidacy. One past and one future president of Austria, Karl Seitz and Karl Renner, emphasized the universality of Kautsky's antiwar appeal in their letter to the Nobel prize committee. In the end, Kautsky's work was too partisan and his contribution to world peace too limited; the 1938 prize went to the Nansen International Office for Refugees.[24]

While Kautsky's study of war won the praise of noncommunist socialists, it was sharply attacked by the followers of Leon Trotsky. This extreme reaction and the obsessive concern of communists with Kautsky remain something of a mystery. In 1937, when Kautsky was eighty-three and had little influence in the world socialist movement, when fascism and Stalinism were making a shambles of the revolution Trotsky and his followers sought, when Trotsky himself was in exile, isolated, and harassed, the first number of a new journal of Trotsky's Fourth International, *Der einzige Weg,* still found time to attack Kautsky. Only two books were reviewed in this number, *The Case of Leon Trotsky* and *Socialists and War.* The review of the Kautsky book was little more than a mocking, vituperative slap at "the old master of renegadery," at the "social patriot Kautsky," at "the hoary renegade."[25] Of course, Kautsky scraped bare a lot of old wounds in his discussion of the First World War, but even that does not fully explain the reaction of Trotsky's followers. Once again it seems that the sense of betrayal felt by so many who had learned their Marxism from Kautsky compelled this almost ludicrous attack. By giving space and time to such polemics in 1937, the Fourth International revealed its isolation and irrelevance.

Not all of Kautsky's opponents were as obscure and powerless as the followers of the Fourth International. Kautsky was not a major figure in the enormous group attacked by the Nazis as enemies of the Third Reich, but he and his family were jeopardized by the increasing fascist sympathies in Austria during the thirties and by the threat of a German invasion, largely because of Kautsky's politics. Yet like so many others in a similar predicament, family and emotional ties, the problems of leaving home and work, and the persistant belief that "it can't happen here," kept the Kautskys in Austria until after the Anschluss had begun. On 13 March, two days after Nazi troops began their invasion, Karl and Luise left Austria under the auspices of the Czech embassy. A native-born Bohemian, Kautsky was granted protection as a prominent Czech national. After brief stops in Pressburg and Prague, the

Kautskys flew to Amsterdam, where they settled in late March. Karl had begun his memoirs in late 1936, and he continued to work on this project after leaving Austria. On 17 October 1938, advanced cancer of the pancreas, complicated by old age, the disruption of exile again, and years of heavy toil for the cause he dearly loved, brought death to Karl Kautsky. He was one day past his eighty-fourth birthday when he died.[26]

Other members of the Kautsky family fared even less well after the Anschluss. Only Felix, the eldest son, managed to escape Nazi imprisonment and make his way to Los Angeles. Benedikt ("Bendel"), the youngest and most politically active of the boys, was imprisoned in May 1938. He spent the entire war in various concentration camps, including Buchenwald, where he was in 1945. Karl, Jr., who was a doctor specializing in obstetrics and gynecology, was imprisoned for several months while the Nazis tried to fabricate evidence of a Jewish doctors' conspiracy to exploit Aryan women through abortion. When this failed to yield anything, he was released, and he joined his wife and daughters making their way from Austria to Sweden and eventually to New York. It was dangerous to be a Kautsky in Austria in 1938.[27]

Luise Kautsky survived her husband by six years. Although friends had arranged for her to leave the continent for England or even the United States, Luise remained in Amsterdam in order to keep in touch with her youngest son, Bendel, while he was imprisoned. For nearly six years, including four in which Holland was occupied by the Germans, Luise lived in Amsterdam. But shortly after her eightieth birthday, in August 1944, she was arrested on a technical violation of identity-card regulations. She was sent to Auschwitz, and for most of the next three months worked in the camp hospital. Bendel was in a different part of the same camp, but they did not meet, though they did manage to communicate by smuggled letters. In early December, the incredible rigors of camp life killed Luise. She died a relatively peaceful death in the midst of great horror and brutality.[28]

Conclusion

The hurried flight from Vienna and the tragic fate of much of the Kautsky family after 1938 constituted a dramatic end to the paradoxical life of Karl Kautsky. Personally a peaceful, almost passive man, he was for years an outspoken proponent of vigorous antiestablishment activities. And though he had long served what the ruling classes called the "unpatriotic" and "dangerous" Social Democrats, it was only after fifteen years of retirement that his earlier political activities bore dangerous fruit. With the exception of his brief encounter with the counterrevolutionary troops in January 1919, he experienced no physical persecution or serious threat of persecution until the Nazi invasion of Austria in 1938. A native-born Bohemian Austrian, he was the leading theoretician of German socialism for almost three decades, only to be saved in his twilight years from German aggression by his Czech citizenship. Finally, even though he did more to popularize and standardize Marxism—to create an orthodoxy—than did any other individual, save possibly Friedrich Engels, no major movement anywhere in the world calls itself Kautskyist. The honor and tribute that came after 1919 were based on very general qualities of his work, his anti-Bolshevism, his humanism, and his optimism, rather than on any specific theoretical, political, or organizational contributions he had made to Marxism.

For a number of reasons, the standard criticisms of Kautsky made by both communist and noncommunist critics seem to make a good deal of sense. The communists generally have seen him as deficient in his ability to translate theory into practice. They argue that he was unwilling to accept the logical conclusion of his analysis of modern, capitalist society, and unwilling to insist on vigorous, assertive action by the proletariat to take advantage of the critical point in history, the chaos of World War I, in order to make revolution. Lenin and his successors have pointed to Kautsky's theoretical failures—his refusal to identify capitalism with imperialism; to his personal failures—his "petit bourgeois" aversion to violence that prevented him from pressing for vigorous action in the streets to advance the proletarian cause; and to his tactical failures—above all his rejection of the soviet concept and his insistence on more traditional representative democracy. Communist critics have blended this broad-ranging collection of complaints into a general view that emphasizes two points: Because Kautsky was an armchair revolutionary, because he did not participate directly in the day-to-day struggle, he failed to appreciate the practical demands of the proletarian movement; and because he abandoned, or never fully understood, the dialectical conception of history, he failed to perceive the qualitative gap between the old order and the new.

Noncommunist critics have emphasized different things, although at times the two schools come together. One of the most persistent noncommunist criticisms has been that Kautsky, because he stressed evolutionary development, was fatalistic in his view of the future. This argument concludes that in fact Kautsky was a sort of secret revisionist who really thought the new order would come as a result of gradual, quantitative change, rather than dramatic, short-term revolutionary change. Other noncommunist critics fault him for his revolutionary rhetoric and for his failure to realize how accurate the revisionist analysis was, finding the source of these errors in his obsession with theory and his lack of contact with grass-roots politics and the trade-union movement. Thus, the communist and noncommunist critics agree that Kautsky was too theoretical and ꞓnat ꞓe clung to a conception of social development that was evolutionary rather than revolutionary and dialectical.

Of course, both lines of criticism have a certain validity. Kautsky's family background, his youthful experiences, the influence of the intellectual currents of the time, did yield a personality more inclined to reflection than action. The mildly alienated atmosphere of the theatrical milieu and the Czech minority status of the Kautsky family were sufficient to make him receptive to the romantic and noble socialism of George Sand. The serious, but somewhat undisciplined intellectualism of the Kautsky home reinforced his interest in theoretical abstraction, and an intrinsic and pragmatic aversion to public politics further oriented him toward theory rather than practice.

While the difficulties of being a socialist and a member of a respectable bourgeois family associating with workers in Austria during the 1870s should not be overlooked, Kautsky's commitment to the movement clearly did not derive from a powerful personal sense of alienation or from personal contact with the hardships of the laboring classes. As a youth he was attracted to socialism because it offered him the chance to satisfy romantic desires to serve the underprivileged and because it provided him a channel for his mildly rebellious reaction to the comfort and complacency of his family. A penchant for the natural sciences also caused him to be powerfully attracted by the strongly scientific overtones of much of socialist theory.

Kautsky also inherited from his family an inclination for work, a diligence, and a serious devotion to occupation that help account for his incredible productivity. His commitment to socialism was neither casual nor frivolous; being a socialist meant working as a socialist, full time. He was not pressed by his family to establish a respectable career, nor were his parents eager to push him out on his own. But the middle-class values of industry and respectability did effect Kautsky's approach to life, if not the content of his theory and politics. Except for two or three years of hardship during the early 1880s, he provided comfortably for himself and his family solely by his own hard work and the support given him and many other intellectuals by the SPD. During his long years of association with working-class socialism, he enjoyed the comforts of a modestly successful, middle-class intellectual. Once again, the sometimes personally offensive pariah status associated with being a socialist in Wilhelmine Germany should not be overlooked. A generous measure of personal integrity and commitment was required of any middle-class intellectual who chose to associate publicly with the workers' party. But Kautsky did not suffer the poverty and persecution often associated with revolutionaries.

Finally, Kautsky was not a political activist. He was not a party organizer or candidate; he was not a frequent or particularly impressive speaker; he did not participate in trade-unionist activities. He was an intellectual, an editor, and an author. On occasion he worked effectively at party conventions to rally support for his own and party leadership positions, as at the 1891 Erfurt party-program congress and the 1895 Breslau congress at which the party's peasant program was debated. But for the most part he took his lead in political matters from others, including Andreas Scheu, Friedrich Engels, Eduard Bernstein, August Bebel, and Victor Adler. He declined to take active part in politics in part because he realized he lacked the skills of a good politician. But even more importantly, he was convinced that practice would largely take care of itself, while theory required closer attention. Of all of Kautsky's assumptions, this last one was the source of his greatest weakness. He consistently failed to see his theoretical positions translated into effective action because of it, and he consistently failed to perceive that practice tended to be self-perpetuating quite independently of theory.

For almost all of his long career in the German working-class movement, Karl Kautsky was a prominent figure, but he never was a really powerful figure. Largely because he had so little interest in day-to-day political matters, and because he took his lead in politics from others, he was not a major shaper of policy. Certainly he was in frequent and close contact with party leaders, especially Bebel, Singer, Haase, Dietz, Zetkin, Auer, and others, but there is no evidence that these people were swayed by his specific political opinions. Bebel was doubtful of Kautsky's political acumen from the beginning of their close association in the 1880s; Engels had been equally suspicious even before then. The party leadership up to the First World War did not call on Kautsky to contribute to ongoing political debates except in the most general terms. And after the war, he was not a significant force in either the SPD or the USPD.

All of this is not to say, of course, that Kautsky was without influence. At Erfurt in 1891 and again at Breslau in 1895, he was able to stand up against even Bebel and carry the day on important issues. However, most of the time he was simply not part of the effective leadership of the party. He did not participate regularly in the inner workings of the SPD Reichstag *Fraktion;* he did not sit on either the executive committee or the control commission of the party; he did not plot election strategies; he did not determine editorial policies of the party's daily press. In a party dominated by a massive bureaucracy, Kautsky was not a bureaucrat.

What influence Kautsky did have usually came from his usefulness to SPD policy makers, especially August Bebel. Bebel used him to give intellectual legitimacy to policies derived from the necessities of intraparty and larger German exigencies. But the relationship between Kautsky's theory and Bebel's practice was neither crude nor exploitative; Kautsky was rarely, if ever, manipulated by Bebel. Rather the two men usually cooperated out of shared interests and conviction, but they worked on different levels. Bebel needed the theoretical respectability Kautsky could give; Kautsky gained a forum from which to expound his views. Until Bebel's death in 1913, Kautsky was assured of continued influence in the party hierarchy. Afterward, he found himself increasingly isolated, both because of the changes taking place within the SPD and because he no longer had a special relationship with the party leaders.

At least as far as Kautsky's particular case is concerned, this relationship reveals something important about the role of theory in the German party. The theory of the SPD was far less important as an objective analysis of the inevitable course of human history than as a rationalization of the socioeconomic and political realities of the Wilhelmine state. Kautsky's orthodoxy repeatedly prevailed over Bernstein's revisionism and Luxemburg's radicalism because Bernstein failed to perceive the sense of isolation and exclusiveness prevalent among party members and Luxemburg overrated the willingness of the workers to act aggressively.

Kautsky captured in theory many of the ambiguities of the Second Reich. He may have insisted on an exclusively working-class party because Marx's theory demanded it, but the SPD was receptive to this concept because most of its members felt themselves to be isolated in, and excluded from, the rest of society. Similarly, Kautsky's position prevailed on the so-called peasant question because his theory rationalized the workers' hostility toward, and suspicions of, what they saw as a conservative and backward peasantry. At the same time, by avoiding the vituperative extremism of the radical left, he managed to keep in touch with the majority of party members that recognized the power of the opposition and was willing to bide its time, reinforced by Kautsky's assertion that history was with the socialists so long as they were alert to opportunities but not reckless and overanxious.

If Kautsky's influence within the German party derived from his association with the political leadership of the SPD, his influence within the Second International and the world socialist movement was largely dependent upon his association with the SPD and on the more important role played by theory on the international level. Thus, on the one hand, he spoke with considerable authority in the International because he was assumed to be a spokesman for the largest party in that organization. Some critics of the prominence of the Germans in the Second International, like Jean Jaurès, were acute enough to realize that through Kautsky's theory the peculiar conditions of the Wilhelmine state were being imposed on the entire world movement. On the other hand, the Second International was not an active political organization in the same way that most of its member parties were at home. Therefore, its concerns tended to be less pragmatic and more theoretical. At the congresses of the International, Kautsky was in his element, and he frequently took full advantage of the situation.

Theory was Kautsky's realm, and his fame and historical significance are dependent upon his theoretical contributions. But he was primarily a popularizer of Marxism, not an innovator. He wrote several histories that helped Marxism gain a measure of intellectual stature, but he did not significantly advance the scope or subtlety of historical materialism. He wrote several party programs that helped establish the general outline of Marxian working-class parties before Lenin, but there is no hallmark to identify these programs as uniquely Kautskyian. Not until after the German revolution and the Bolshevik victory in Russia did he clarify the ambiguities of his own theory sufficiently to justify the label "Kautskyism" when he introduced the distinction between the social revolution and the political revolution. But by that time he had lost the party support that would have allowed him to press for changes in organization and tactics in accordance with the newly clarified theory; he had lost the chance to see the formation of a Kautskyian party.

To the extent that critics have dealt with Kautsky's failure to translate theory into practice and with his inability to see the logic of the practice he could not influence, they have been substantially correct in their evaluations. But efforts to find the roots of his practical failures in his theory fall short of the mark. He was never cryptorevisionist because he always insisted that the class struggle between the proletariat and bourgeoisie could not be overcome by passive reconciliation of conflicting interests and because he always insisted on an exclusively working-class party, at least until the rise of fascism. He was not a fatalist; he was always convinced of the necessity and significance of human action as a determinant in history, although his willingness to push for vigorous action was restrained by his abhorrence of violence. And finally, Kautsky specifically rejected a natural-scientific, evolutionary mode of development for human social history as early as 1885, held to this position consistently throughout his years as an important figure in the SPD, and reaffirmed it in his 1927 work, *The Materialist Conception of History.*

Much of Kautsky's theory can be viewed as an effort to interpret and balance the thorniest of the ambiguities of Marx's writings, the voluntaristic implications within an apparently deterministic historical analysis. Very early in his career as a Marxist, he rejected as absurd the interpretation of Marxism that held that the specific course of history was determined only by developments in the economic substructure, and that, therefore, the communist society would come regardless of human actions. Much later in his life, he denounced Russian and German communists for presuming that by mere acts of will they could force the pace of history and achieve communism before objective conditions were ripe for it. He sought diligently for a middle ground between the deterministic Scylla and the voluntaristic Charybdis.

In 1899, during the most vigorous debate over revisionism, Kautsky took issue with Bernstein's assertion that Marxism in its Kautskyian guise included a collapse theory, that is, the notion that "a business crisis will usher in the social revolution, or that the proletariat can only conquer political power during a business crisis." Kautsky staunchly denied that he or Marx or Engels ever made such a fatalistic suggestion. While not rejecting the notion of recurrent crisis in capitalistic economics, he argued that to tie the occurence of the transition from capitalism to socialism to the collapse of the former was one-sided, because "the class struggle remains unmentioned in this description." In other words, he was asserting that despite the historical necessity of recurrent capitalist crisis, a critical part of the process of social revolution was the voluntaristic element implied by the class struggle. The transition from capitalism to socialism would not be automatic, the proletariat had to engage in the class struggle to win power.[29]

Many years later, Kautsky had occasion to address himself to precisely the same question again. During the great depression of the 1930s, many communists and socialists argued that this event marked the collapse of capitalism and the rise of socialism, but Kautsky disagreed.

> But let us assume that capitalism is about to break down. Will it not mean the same thing as the victory of socialism? Unfortunately not. . . .

We must, therefore, guard against interpreting the materialist conception of history in an automatically mechanistic way, as if social development went by itself, being impelled by necessity. Human beings make history, and the course of history is propelled by necessity only to the extent that human beings living under the same conditions and prompted by the same impulses will of necessity react in the same manner.

Marx expected the victory of socialism to come not from the collapse of capitalism; . . . Marx expected it to come as a result of the growing power and maturity of the proletariat.[30]

His contention at this time, as it had been for decades, was that the new social order would not come mechanically as a product of inevitable development, but only in conjunction with conscious, collective action on the part of the proletariat.

Kautsky was to a great extent also trying to find a balance in the voluntarist-determinist dichotomy when in 1917-1919, he turned his attention to the notion of the dictatorship of the proletariat. He agreed with Lenin and the communists that this dictatorship was the transition period from capitalism to socialism, but he disagreed entirely about its nature. He argued that the dictatorship of the proletariat was a general condition that characterized postrevolutionary society, not a specific form of government. Just as under capitalism the bourgeoisie exercised its dictatorship in various forms—republic, constitutional monarchy, military monarchy, and others—so after the revolution, the proletariat would dominate despite the specific form of government adopted. Furthermore, since even in Germany in 1918 capitalism had not developed sufficiently to eliminate all nonproletarians, Kautsky contended that, in the interests of stability, nonproletarians must continue to have a voice, even within the dictatorship of the proletariat. He was willing to await further development, and even to accelerate this development by speeding up the socialization of certain critical industries. Thus while emphasizing in deterministic terms the fact that Germany, and even more so Russia, was not yet completely ripe for socialism, he argued in favor of certain voluntaristic acts to promote socialism. In addition to limited socialization, he urged that military and bureaucratic strongholds of the old order be neutralized. Although this position obviously fell far short of the more extensive demands of the extreme left, it was not the fatalistic acceptance of an incomplete revolution.

Similar efforts to balance voluntarism and determinism are apparent in the explicit distinction between social and political revolution which Kautsky first made in 1918–1919. He quite simply argued that since politics was the realm in which conscious human action could shape history, political revolution could be made. He held that political revolution was not so completely dependent upon the historical development of specific objective conditions as to narrowly limit the effective range of conscious activity. He tended, as did many other Marxists, to see the more or less despotic governments of central Europe as historical accidents anyway, so that a political revolution in which the proletariat won access to the channels to power by the establishment of a representative form of government was for him entirely consistent with the determined course of history. Social revolution, on the other hand, dealt with areas that could not so readily be altered by conscious human action, and therefore social revolution would have to await the slower course of the inevitable development of the economic substructure of society. Here Kautsky clearly gave considerable weight to determinism, while not entirely ruling out the influence of voluntarism. But of course, he offered the analysis of social revolution versus political revolution only after the fact. This distinction was only implicit in his pre-1917 work.

The impact of Kautsky's efforts to strike a balance between voluntarism and determinism can be seen in a number of other theoretical positions he took. For instance, because he limited his conception of voluntary action largely to the realm of politics, he stressed the need to raise the consciousness of the workers and the necessity of a mass party. But because he contended that social revolution could not be made, he did not see the need for a highly disciplined, elitist core of revolutionaries to force the revolution to its extreme conclusion in a short period of time. Furthermore, because he was convinced that in the long run historical development would ensure the victory of the proletariat which had access to political power, he was quite willing to tolerate mixed governments of bourgeois and worker representatives. At any rate, he held that to push politics too far beyond socioeconomic developments would only invite bloodshed and, ultimately, failure. For these reasons, he emphasized democracy over discipline, both in party organization and state political form.

No issue more clearly reveals Kautsky's ambiguity on political issues than the matter of democracy and representative government. In his more radical periods, as during the high point of the revisionism debates, he denounced bourgeois parliaments as trickery. As his position during the Millerand affair showed, Kautsky was also opposed to any long-term commitment by socialists to the concept of coalition government. By the same token, he was generally opposed to making the SPD a truly democratic mass party in that he strenuously opposed expanding the party's appeal beyond the industrial working class. But at the same time, he repeatedly urged the German socialists to engage in political activities that would allow them to take advantage of differences among the nonproletarian portions of the population. For instance, he strongly urged that the SPD use election compromises to try to break the conservative stranglehold on the Prussian Landtag, and he consistently rejected the "one reactionary mass" concept, arguing that socialists had to take advantage of the oppositional elements within the bourgeoisie. In fact, the core of his dispute with Bernstein was not whether nonproletarian opposition should be cooperated with, but whether such forces should be allowed into the SPD. Kautsky was willing to enter into the spirit of parliamentary government, of give-and-take on issues, of campaign coalitions, as long as his party remained staunchly proletarian and as long as it was not irreconcilably compromised by governmental participation.

When the German revolution came, this ambiguity on political questions was forced to a reconciliation. Kautsky advanced three major arguments favoring a democratic, republican government rather than a proletarian, soviet government. First, he rejected the violence and economic dislocation that would have been necessary for the total seizure of power by the proletariat. Second, he developed his distinction between a determined social revolution and a voluntaristic political revolution, arguing that the aim of the latter was to win the proletariat access to political power. And third, he relied on what he saw as the inevitable victory of a majoritarian proletariat to justify accepting less than a complete proletarian revolution. Even though immediate victory was not possible, ultimately history would serve the cause of the proletariat.

These positions point up the outstanding characteristics of Karl Kautsky. His aversion to violence and widespread disruption was based on strongly humanist feelings that rejected the disregard for human life that is a necessary part of an extensive revolution. He came to see "that every bloody struggle . . . in the long run demoralizes its participants, and far from increasing, actually reduces their capacity for constructive effort in the field of production as well as in political life."[31] This is hardly the conviction of a dogmatic revolutionary, and it contributed to Kautsky's failure to see his ideals realized in his own lifetime. However, it is also a hard sentiment to reject without adopting an attitude of superhuman superiority.

Distinguishing between social and political revolution was part of Kautsky's apparent need to explain and understand all things in theoretical terms, and coupled with his antipathy to violence and his conviction of future victory, it was an effort to rationalize his moral commitment. Kautsky's exchange with Bienstock in 1934, and the amazement of other correspondents with Kautsky's unfaltering optimism during the 1930s, were examples of the strength of his conviction. He clung to his belief in the future, arguing that like Marx in 1848, most Marxists had correctly forseen "the direction in which events were moving, but . . . misjudged the rate at which they were moving." Many years earlier Kautsky had asked Adler, "What does life hold if one is not optimistic, if one does not see in the immediate future what will perhaps first be attained by our grandchildren?" The disasters of the twenties and thirties, the rise of communism and Stalin, the conquest of Germany by Hitler's fanaticism, and the depression shook but could not conquer this optimism. Like many others in Europe at the time, he continued to see World War I as a major turning point in history, and also like many others, he began to look outside of a decadent Europe for hope. In 1935, he expressed a slightly desperate, but highly typical wish. "I do not trust much anymore to the labor movement in Europe, on the continent. The war and its consequences have demoralized the whole European society and the workmen are impaired by it. I think the labor movement of the world may yet rise upward out of the crisis when the Anglo-Saxons take the lead. . . . Socialism can't keep its ground anymore without the Americans."[32] Like so many other of the noble but less than realistic dreams of Karl Kautsky, this one, too, came to nothing.

NOTES
BIBLIOGRAPHY
INDEX

Abbreviations

Adler	Friedrich Adler, ed., *Victor Adler Briefwechsel mit August Bebel und Karl Kautsky* (Vienna, 1954).
Bebel	Karl Kautsky, Jr., ed., *August Bebels Briefwechsel mit Karl Kautsky* (Assen, 1971).
Bebel-Engels	Werner Blumenberg, ed., *August Bebels Briefwechsel mit Friedrich Engels* (The Hague, 1965).
Bernstein	Helmut Hirsch, ed., *Eduard Bernsteins Briefwechsel mit Friedrich Engels* (Assen, 1970).
Blumenberg	Werner Blumenburg, *Karl Kautskys literarisches Werk* (The Hague, 1960).
Engels	Benedikt Kautsky, ed., *Friedrich Engels' Briefwechsel mit Karl Kautsky* (Vienna, 1955).
E&E	Karl Kautsky, *Erinnerungen und Erörterungen* (The Hague, 1960).
IRSH	*International Review of Social History* (Amsterdam).
KA	Kautsky archive, International Institute for Social History, Amsterdam.
KFA	Kautsky family archive, International Institute for Social History, Amsterdam.
Lichtheim	George Lichtheim, *Marxism: An Historical and Critical Study* (New York, 1961).
Marx-Engels (1942)	Karl Marx and Friedrich Engels, *Selected Correspondence* (New York, 1942).
Marx-Engels (1960)	Karl Marx and Friedrich Engels, *Selected Correspondence* (Moscow, 1960).
NZ	*Die neue Zeit* (Stuttgart, 1883–1917).
Osterroth	Franz Osterroth, *Biographisches Lexikon des Sozialismus* (Hanover, 1960).
Protokoll	Sozialdemokratische Partei Deutschlands, *Protokoll über die Verhandlungen des Parteitages* (Berlin, 1891–1925).
Schorske	Carl E. Schorske, *German Social Democracy, 1905–1917: The Development of the Great Schism* (New York, 1955).

Notes

Chapter One: Introduction

1. The first translation into Chinese of a work by Kautsky was *Ma-k'o-ssu ching-chi hsueh-shuo* [Karl Marx' ökonomische Lehren] (Shanghai, 1911). James P. Harrison, *The Communists and Chinese Peasant Rebellions* (New York, 1969), p. 26, suggested that this may have been the first book-length Marxist work translated into Chinese. A Chinese translation of *Dictatorship of the Proletariat, Lun wu-ch'an chieh-chi chuan-cheng*, appeared in Taiwan in 1971. In the same year, Kautsky's *The Class Struggle* was reissued in the United States. The Soviet-bloc states have published many translations of Kautsky's works since World War II.

2. The most important work by Lenin in establishing the precedent for almost unqualified vilification of Kautsky by communists was *The Proletarian Revolution and the Renegade Kautsky*, written in 1918. Contemporary expansion and refinement of this position will be dealt with in the notes when appropriate. The noncommunist attack is best represented by James Joll, *The Second International* (New York, 1960), and John P. Nettl, *Rosa Luxemburg*, 2 vols. (London, 1966), and their criticisms will also be dealt with below. George Lichtheim, *Marxism: An Historical and Critical Study* (New York, 1961), and Hans-Josef Steinberg, *Sozialismus und deutsche Sozialdemokratie* (Hanover, 1967), are the only two authors of major works who have, in my opinion, done well by Kautsky. John H. Kautsky, "The Political Thoughts of Karl Kautsky" (Ph.D. diss., Harvard University, 1951), exaggerates certain aspects of Kautsky's work. He is a grandson of Kautsky, and, at least in 1951, a defender at the expense of reasonable perspective. See pp. i, 8, and 11 of his dissertation for examples of this distortion.

3. Lichtheim and Steinberg fall into this category.

4. Lenin, Nettl, and Joll are examples of this approach.

5. I give my sincere thanks to Artur Rachwald for providing me with an analysis of Waldenberg's book. Karl Renner, an Austrian socialist, self-professed student of Kautsky, but during World War I an opponent of his mentor, wrote a brief and laudatory biographical sketch, *Karl Kautsky* (Berlin, 1929). In 1954, Hermann Brill published an interesting but very limited review of some aspects of Kautsky's socialist career in "Karl Kautsky," *Zeitschrift für Politik* 3 (September 1954), 211–40.

6. "Sozialistische Kolonialpolitik," *NZ* 27:2 (1908–09), 39.

7. On many occasions Kautsky discussed the tendency of individual variation to decrease in statistical importance as the size of the population increased. For a

particularly thorough treatment, see "Klasseninteresse - Sonderinteresse - Gemeinin-teresse," *NZ* 21:1 (1902–03), 240–45, 261–74.

8. "Allerhand Revolutionäres," *NZ* 22:1 (1903–04), 655–56.

9. Kautsky to Engels (4 December 1880), Engels, p. 10.

10. A most interesting discussion of the ambiguous nature of Wilhelmine Germany may be found in Ralf Dahrendorf, *Society and Democracy in Germany* (Garden City, N.Y., 1967), pp. 31–52.

11. Andrew G. Whiteside, *The Socialism of Fools* (Berkeley, 1975), p. 51, quoted Kautsky on what Whiteside called "his fellow Jews." The quote is accurately cited, but the context is wrong, since Kautsky was referring to the Jews he first met upon entering the Austrian socialist movement in the mid-1870s. See Benedikt Kautsky, ed., *Luise Kautsky zum Gedenken* (New York, 1945), and Kautsky's own explanation in *E&E*, pp. 36–37.

Chapter Two: Prague and Vienna, 1854–1879

1. *E&E*, pp. 36–78, 148–49, 273. This is a memoir begun by Kautsky in 1936 and left uncompleted at his death in 1938. It covers only the years up to 1883, but constitutes the only major published source on Kautsky's early life.

2. *E&E*, pp. 35, 79–80, 102–05, 112; Kautsky to Adler (12 December 1904), Adler, pp. 441–42.

3. *E&E*, pp. 108–09, 170–72, 194.

4. Wilhelm Liebknecht to Kautsky (4 October 1876), in George Eckert, ed., *Wilhelm Liebknechts Briefwechsel mit deutschen Sozialdemokraten*, vol. 1, *1862–1878* (Assen, 1973), p. 708; Marx to Jenny Longuet (11 April 1881), Marx-Engels (1942), p. 389; Engels to Kautsky (27 August 1881), Engels, p. 39. See also Engels to Bebel (25 August 1881), Bebel-Engels, p. 114.

5. *E&E*, pp. 10–12, 96–97, 113–33, 137–39, 152.

6. Ibid., pp. 78, 141, 175–76, 180–81.

7. Ibid., pp. 181–83, 227, 235–37, 273–74, 397–98; Kautsky to Ernst Haeckel (28 October 1882), KFA 8.

8. Kautsky to Engels (10 February 1881), Engels, pp. 1 (Kautsky's introduction), 16; Engels to Bebel (22–[24] June 1885), Bebel-Engels, p. 228.

9. Engels to Bebel (24 July 1885), Marx-Engels (1942), p. 440.

10. Engels to Kautsky (1 February 1881), Engels, p. 13.

11. *E&E*, pp. 238–42, 249–51, 253–60 (summary of *Atlantic-Pacific Company*), 260–64, 266–68, 273–74; contract between Edmund Gerson and Karl Kautsky, "dramatic author," 14 November 1878, KFA 3.

12. *E&E*, pp. 66–70, 88, 104–07, 160–61.

13. Ibid., pp. 162, 340; Blumenberg, pp. 12–13; Engels, p. 1; Kautsky to Luise (11 February 1911), KFA 36.

14. For example, Walter Holzheuer, *Karl Kautskys Werk als Weltanschauung* (Munich, 1972), tries to tie Kautsky's early work very specifically to Buckle and Haeckel.

15. *E&E*, pp. 212–13. The two authors who most emphasized the importance of Darwin to the development of Kautsky's thought were Karl Korsch, "Die materialistische Geschichtsauffassung: Eine Auseinandersetzung mit Karl Kautsky," *Archiv für die Geschichte des Sozialismus und der Arbeiterbewegung* 14:2 (1929), 179–279, and, following Korsch's lead, Erich Matthias, "Kautsky und der Kautskyanismus," *Marxismusstudien*, 2nd ser. (1957), pp. 151–97.

16. *E&E*, pp. 155–61.

17. Ibid., pp. 88, 101.

18. Ibid., pp. 99, 186.

19. For Palacky and his influence on Czech nationalism, see Joseph F. Zacek, *Palacky: The Historian as Scholar and Nationalist* (The Hague, 1970); Hans Kohn, *Not By Arms Alone* (Cambridge, Mass., 1940), pp. 69–83; Arthur J. May, *The Hapsburg Monarchy, 1867–1914* (Cambridge, Mass., 1960), p. 24; and Jan Havranek, "The Development of Czech Nationalism," *Austrian History Yearbook* 3 (1967), 242–43.

20. Kautsky discussed the impact of the Commune on his own development in several places, most notably in *E&E*, pp. 178–86. Marx and Engels both claimed the Commune as a model for the future with few reservations; for Marx, see *The Civil War in France*, and for Engels, see the introduction he wrote for an 1891 edition of Marx's work. Though Lenin was more critical of the Commune, he too accepted it as both symbol and model of the workers' state. However, the Commune was not the product of agitation by members of the First International; the Communards were not exclusively workers; and even among the minority of socialists, followers of Marx were not numerous. It was widely held for years that the Commune had been socialist and even Marxist. See David McLellan, *Karl Marx* (New York, 1973), pp. 388–404.

21. *E&E*, pp. 187–89. In 1896, Kautsky recommended *M. Antoine* to Victor Adler for serialization in the Austrian party newspaper. Kautsky to Adler (2 June), Adler, p. 209.

22. *E&E*, pp. 186, 190; Kautsky to Luise (11 February 1911), KFA 36.

23. George Sand, *The Sin of M. Antoine* (Philadelphia, 1900), pp. 155, 167–68, 171.

24. *E&E*, pp. 190–93, 203–07.

25. Lassalle and the German workers' movement were covered in some detail by the liberal Viennese press; for example, see "Zur Arbeiterfrage," *Neue Freie Presse*, no. 91, 30 November 1864. Kautsky briefly discussed his own relationship with Christian deism at this time in *E&E*, pp. 210–12. See also Holzheuer, *Karl Kautskys Werk*, pp. 2–11, for a discussion of the replacement of a Christian, humanist world view by a "natural-scientific materialism as *Weltanschauung*."

26. Probably it would be better to use scientism instead of positivism here, but it would also be pedantic. Walter M. Simon, *European Positivism in the Nineteenth Century* (Ithaca, N.Y., 1963), suggested that such a substitution be made in all treatments of nineteenth-century intellectual history. However, positivism has come to be used very generally to refer to that vague but widespread European movement which held that the investigatory and analytical techniques of the natural sciences should be applied to all fields of human knowledge, and placed its faith in science rather than in ethics or religion for the salvation of mankind from the evils of itself and the outer world. As used here, "positivism" does not mean the school that identified with the doctrines of August Comte. This distinction is critical because of the importance of Darwin to the development of Kautsky's thought. Virtually all of the Positivists (in the Comtian sense) greeted Darwin's theory of natural selection with hostility, contending that it was "rationalistic but not experimental, ingenious but lacking sufficient evidence" (Simon, p. 25). This distinction between the rationalistic and the experimental is what separates most of the followers of Comte from the larger positivist movement in an epistemological sense; most Comtians were not in the mainstream of the Enlightenment tradition to the extent that they rejected rationalism. Marx, Engels, Kautsky, and virtually all Marxists were rationalists, and therefore they fall into this mainstream. For a discussion of epistemology in the nineteenth century, see Ernest Cassirer, *The Problem of Knowledge* (New Haven, 1950), especially pp. 118–216. See also Herbert Marcuse, *Reason and Revolution* (Boston, 1960), pp. 323–88.

By materialism I do not mean to imply strict philosophical materialism which rejects the reality of ideas, but rather that tendency which seeks to identify material determinants of ideas and actions, whether in economics or biochemistry or elsewhere. This too is a tendency present in the Enlightenment tradition. For a discussion of Marx and materialism, see Z. A. Jordan, *The Evolution of Dialectical Materialism* (New York, 1967), pp. 13–64. Jordan argues that Marx should be called a naturalist, rather than a materialist, a distinction that is important only if the terms naturalism and materialism are taken out of Marx's historical milieu and given strict philosophical interpretations.

27. *E&E*, pp. 212–13. The interrelations of materialists in Europe at mid-century could hardly be better demonstrated than by the fact that Buckle's German translator was none other than Arnold Ruge, one of the central figures of the Young Hegelian movement.

28. Ernst Haeckel, *The History of Creation*, 2 vols. (London, 1876), I, 170–74. For a very thorough discussion of Haeckel, see Daniel Gasman, *The Scientific Origins of National Socialism* (London, 1971).

29. Haeckel, *History*, I, 256, 281, 313, II, 307–10, 321. For Kautsky's explanation of the origins of less culturally developed races, see "Die Entstehung der ethischen Begriffe," *Vorwärts*, 30 December 1877.

30. Haeckel, *History*, I, 4, 169, 179, 203–26, 237, 350.

31. *E&E*, pp. 518–21; Adler to Dr. Johannes Volkelt (13 September 1882), Adler, pp. 4–6; Kautsky to Haeckel (28 October 1882), KFA 8; Gasman, *Scientific Origins*, p. 151; Hans-Günter Zmarlik, "Der Sozialdarwinismus in Deutschland als geschichtliches Problem," *Vierteljahrshefte für Zeitgeschichte* 11 (July 1963), 259 n.19. In a letter to Engels, Kautsky identified *Kosmos* as "a liberal German Darwinist technical journal," the editor of which had socialist sympathies. Kautsky to Engels (12 March 1884), Engels, p. 103.

32. Ludwig Büchner, *Force and Matter* (New York, 1891), pp. v–vii (1855 preface), 71, 75, 156, 222, 232–40, 242, 254, 289, 301–15, 367, 393. In this edition (it is reprinted from the fourth English edition, translated from the fifteenth German edition) Haeckel is cited or discussed on pp. 2, 67, 71, 132, 141–46, 153, 156, 161–64, 176, 238, 337, 350.

33. Ibid., pp. v, 57, 171, 189–90, 299, 343.

34. *E&E*, pp. 212–13.

35. *Force and Matter*, pp. 382–83.

36. "Entstehung," *Vorwärts*, 30 December 1877.

37. Büchner, *Force and Matter*, p. 388.

38. Henry Thomas Buckle, *History of Civilization in England*, 2 vols. (New York, 1939), I, 4, 5, 13. See also p. 163 for an incredible paean to progress.

39. Ibid., I, 29–30, 81–93, 106, II, 2–7. Büchner contended almost precisely the same thing and cited Buckle as a source. *Force and Matter*, pp. 370–71.

40. Buckle, *History*, I, 113, 162, 171, 209, 599, 600, 627, 688–89.

41. Many of Kautsky's articles appeared in several parts, as was customary in socialist journals. In 1875, he published a four-part article on "Darwin und der Sozialismus," in the *Gleichheit;* in 1876, a two-part article on "Der Sozialismus und der Kampf um das Dasein," in the *Volksstaat;* in 1877, a five-part article on "Der Kampf um's Dasein in der Menschenwelt," in the *Vorwärts;* in 1877–1878, a four-part article on "Die Entstehung der ethischen Begriffe" and a three-part article on "Das Bevölkerungsgesetz und die Bewaldung," in the *Vorwärts.* These comprise his major discussion of natural science and socialism. Much of his more reportorial work on Austrian affairs appeared in the "Correspondenzen" column of the *Vorwärts.* After the virtual elimination of the German socialist press following the passage of the antisocialist law in late 1878, most of Kautsky's articles for the remainder of the year and for all of 1879 appeared in the Austrian press, especially in *Der Sozialist.* The latter year was the only one in which the majority of his work appeared in that country.

42. "Der Sozialismus und der Kampf um das Dasein," *Volksstaat*, 28 and 30 April 1876.

This article was signed "von einem Serben," one of several pseudonyms Kautsky used at that time.

43. Ibid., 28 April.

44. Ibid., 30 April.

45. Ibid., 28 April.

46. *E&E*, pp. 325, 367, 375-77; "Geschichte und Sozialismus," *Vorwärts*, 8 March 1878. As an example of his familiarity with Marx, see "Der Kampf um's Dasein in der Menschenwelt," *Vorwärts*, 30 March, 1, 6, 8, and 11 April 1877, where Kautsky identified Marx and Darwin as the two men who had finally provided the means by which history based on "the naturalist laws of human development" could be written. Darwin provided a satisfying materialist world explanation, and Marx traced intellectual developments "to the history of production" (30 March 1877).

47. Engels to Bebel (15 October 1875), Marx-Engels, p. 365, and Bebel-Engels, pp. 40-41.

48. *E&E*, pp. 367-70, 373-74; "Entstehung," *Vorwärts*, 6 February 1878. The editorial note appended to the latter pointed out that Kautsky's contention of a low level of ethical and cultural development in China was probably wrong, referring the reader to a review of Herbert A. Giles's *Chinese Sketches* which had appeared in the *Vorwärts* of 1 February.

49. Engels, p. 4; Peter Gay, *The Dilemma of Democratic Socialism* (New York, 1952), p. 43. A more thorough discussion of *Anti-Dühring* and its impact on Kautsky will be taken up in the next chapter.

50. "Die Physiognomie der heutigen Gesellschaft," *Vorwärts*, 31 March 1878; "Sozial-Conservatives," *Vorwärts*, 14 April 1878; Engels, p. 7.

51. Herbert Steiner, *Die Arbeiterbewegung Oesterreichs, 1867-1889* (Vienna, 1964), pp. 73-78, 82, 121, 169; *Vorwärts*, 3 June 1877; Havranek, "Czech Nationalism," pp. 224-29.

52. Steiner, *Arbeiterbewegung*, p. 131.

53. Ibid., pp. 3, 7-9, 61-69, 82-101.

54. Ibid., pp. 132-35, 157-61, 171-83, and 197-208.

55. Ibid., pp. 13-15, 28-31, 37-39, 66, 104-11, 115-17, 119-20, 169, 244. For Kautsky's account of the early history of the Austrian socialist movement, see "Die Arbeiterbewegung in Oesterreich," *NZ*, 8 (1890), 49-56, 97-106, 154-63.

56. *E&E*, pp. 227-31, 307, 316. Kautsky's first contribution to the Austrian socialist press was an attack on the moderates, "Oberwinders Schwanengesang," *Gleichheit*, 29 May 1875.

57. *E&E*, pp. 285, 317, 334-38. For a discussion of the genesis and function of these observers at working-class gatherings, see Richard Reichard, *Crippled from Birth: German Social Democracy, 1844-1870* (Ames, Iowa, 1969), pp. 116-18.

58. "Correspondenzen," *Vorwärts*, 4 October 1876, 18 May and 3 June 1877.

59. "Die Parteien und die Wissenschaft," *Vorwärts*, 3 October 1877.

60. *E&E*, pp. 344-46, 359, 362, 413; "Correspondenzen," and "Aus Oesterreich," *Vorwärts*, 29 May and 7 June 1878. A few years after the fact, Kautsky also suggested that the moderation of Kaler-Reinthal's 1876 program changes and the reunion with the former Oberwinderians caused a backlash in the direction of anarchism. Steiner, *Arbeiterbewegung*, p. 128 (quoting Kautsky to Herman Schlueter, 30 December 1884, International Institute for Social History). For further discussion of Kautsky's attitude toward Most and the Austrian anarchists, see Adolf Braun, "Kautsky in Oesterreich," and Eduard Bernstein, "Kautskys erstes Wirken in der deutschen Sozialdemokratie," both in *Karl Kautsky: Der Denker und Kämpfer* (Vienna, 1924), pp. 61-63, 67-68; Vernon Lidtke, *The Outlawed Party: Social Democracy in Germany, 1878-1890* (Princeton, 1966), p. 111; Steiner, *Arbeiterbewegung*, pp. 155-59.

61. *E&E*, pp. 283-84. Braun, "Kautsky in Oesterreich," p. 62, suggested that Kautsky's

eventual failure to turn much of the Austrian party away from Most influenced him to move even closer to the Germans.

62. *E&E*, pp. 353, 412-13, 415-17, 419-20; Engels, p. 7; Steiner, *Arbeiterbewegung*, p. 17.

Chapter Three: The Peripatetic Decade, 1880-1890

1. *E&E*, pp. 420-21; Mary Lefebvre to Kautsky (18 April 1880), KFA 4; Engels, p. 122 n.5; Bebel, p. 87 n. 8; Eduard Bernstein, *My Years of Exile* (London, 1921), p. 107; August Bebel, *Aus meinen Leben*, 3 vols. (Stuttgart, 1910-14), III, 96.

2. *E&E*, pp. 448, 450. For an account of the German socialist exiles in Zurich, see the pertinent passages in Lidtke, *The Outlawed Party*, and in Bernstein, *My Years*.

3. *E&E*, pp. 431-33, 461-62, 491-92; Kautsky to Engels (10 February 1881), Engels, p. 16.

4. *E&E*, pp. 433-34, 440; Bebel, xxx (quoting Kautsky, *Die Volkswirtschaftslehre der Gegenwart* [Berlin, 1924], p. 10); Engels, p. 7; Bernstein, "Kautskys erstes Wirken," p. 70; Bernstein, *My Years* p. 108; Gay, *Dilemma*, p. 51.

5. *E&E*, pp. 462-70; Engels, p. 8; Bebel to Engels (26 December 1880), Engels to Bebel (20-[23] January 1886), Bebel-Engels, pp. 100, 250-51; Bernstein to Engels (6 February and 9 September 1881), Engels to Bernstein (12 March, 14 April, and 25 August 1881), Bernstein, pp. 18-19, 25, 33; Lidtke, *The Outlawed Party*, pp. 91-93; Gay, *Dilemma*, p. 47; Bebel, *Leben*, III, 168.

6. Kautsky to Engels (4 December 1880), Engels to Kautsky (1 February 1881), Engels, pp. 9-10, 12-13.

7. *E&E*, pp. 470-72, 475, 481-82, 484; Engels, pp. 17, 23.

8. Marx to Jenny Longuet (11 April 1881), Marx-Engels (1942), p. 389; Engels, pp. 88-89.

9. Engels to Bernstein (14 April 1881), Bernstein, p. 25; Engels to Bebel (25 August 1881), Bebel-Engels, p. 114.

10. Engels to Bebel (30 April 1883), Bebel-Engels, pp. 152-53.

11. *E&E*, pp. 429, 439, 474, 498-502, 505; Engels, pp. 8, 10-11; Lidtke, *The Outlawed Party*, pp. 169-70. Höchberg's party activities ended completely in 1883, and he died in 1885. Kautsky and Höchberg never met again after the former left Zurich in 1882, but they continued to correspond.

12. *E&E*, pp. 508-09; Kautsky to Engels (11 and 31 May, 6 September 1882), Engels, pp. 54, 58-59, 61; Steiner, *Arbeiterbewegung*, pp. 173-80, 208, 216, 221, 233. Among the many attacks on the anarchists Kautsky published in the Viennese socialist journal *Wahrheit*, see especially "Das Raubattentat an Merstallinger" and "Mit allen Mitteln," both 1 September 1882, reprinted in Ludwig Brügel, *Geschichte der österreichischen Sozialdemokratie*, 4 vols. (Vienna, 1922-23), III, 268-72.

13. Bernstein to Engels (13 July 1882), Engels to Bernstein (15 July 1882), Bernstein, pp. 116, 118; Kautsky to Engels (11 and 31 May, 6 September 1882), Engels, pp. 57-59.

14. *E&E*, pp. 514-17, 523-25, 528; Kautsky to Engels (11 October 1882), Engels, pp. 64, 68.

15. For the radical-moderate split of the antisocialist years, see Lidtke, *The Outlawed Party*, pp. 82-83, 89-90, 129-38, 152, 154, 158. For the ambiguous, petit bourgeois and democratic roots of German socialism, see Reichard, *Crippled from Birth*.

16. *E&E*, pp. 374-75; Kautsky to Engels (11 October and 11 November 1882), Engels to Kautsky (15 November 1882), Engels, pp. 64-66, 68. In the first year of the *Neue Zeit*, Kautsky wrote articles on "Die sozialen Triebe in der Tierwelt," "Der Kampf ums Dasein

in der Pflanzenwelt," "Die Traditionen der sozialen Tiere"; the second year opened with a three-part article on "Die sozialen Triebe in der Menschenwelt."

17. Kautsky to Engels (14 September and 3 October 1883, 15 April and 29 May 1884), Engels to Kautsky (18 September 1883), Engels, pp. 81–82, 85, 110–11, 118–19.

18. Kautsky to Engels (5 August and 3 October 1883), Engels, pp. 79–80, 82, 85–86, 88, 91; Kautsky to Bebel (30 October 1884), Bebel, pp. 19–21. Apparently Liebknecht vetoed this move to London.

19. Kautsky to Engels (29 May and 2 June 1884), Engels, pp. 117–18, 122; Kautsky to Dietz (30 May 1884), KFA 8. In his memoirs, Blos made only a brief passing reference to his participation on the *Neue Zeit.* See Wilhelm Blos, *Denkwurdigkeiten eines Sozialdemokraten,* 2 vols. (Munich, 1914–19), II, 69.

20. Kautsky to Engels (29 May and 23 June 1884), Engels, pp. 117–18, 125; Bebel to Engels (8 June 1884), Bebel-Engels, p. 184.

21. Bebel to Kautsky (13 September 1884), Bebel, pp. 18–19.

22. Kautsky to Bebel (8 November 1884), Bebel, p. 24; Engels, p. 165.

23. Engels to Kautsky (19 July 1884), Kautsky to Engels (26 June, 18 August, and 26 October 1884, 9 January 1885), Engels, pp. 129, 137–38, 140, 152–53, 161–62; Bernstein to Engels (16 July 1884), Bernstein, p. 284. Liebknecht played a very inconsistent role in all these developments; he seemed motivated by a need to try to maintain unity at all costs and by the personal interests of Geiser.

24. Engels to Kautsky (26 April 1884), Kautsky to Engels (29 April 1884), Engels, pp. 111–13; Kautsky to Bebel (3 October and 8 November 1884), Bebel, pp. 21, 25; Lidtke, *The Outlawed Party,* p. 130.

25. Kautsky to Bebel (3 October 1884, 14 February 1885), Bebel, pp. 20–21, 26–28.

26. Kautsky to Engels (22 October, 22 December 1884, 9 January 1885), Engels, pp. 152–53, 157–58, 160–62.

27. Kautsky to Engels (30 July and 9 August 1886), Engels to Kautsky (31 July 1886), Engels, pp. 165–67, 194–95, 198; Kautsky to Adler (15 March 1887), Adler, p. 28; Walter Emden and secretary to Kautsky (6 May 1887 through 30 April 1888), KFA 2.

28. Kautsky to Engels (9 January 1885), Engels, pp. 161–62; Kautsky to Bebel (14 February, 10 and 16 March, and 22 April 1885), Bebel, pp. 27–28, 35–39.

29. Kautsky to Bernstein (5 April 1885), Bernstein, pp. 434–35; Engels to Bebel (22–[24] June 1885), Bebel-Engels, p. 228; Lidtke, *The Outlawed Party,* pp. 193–204. *Vertrauensmann* is virtually untranslatable in the sense implied here; it was used by the socialists during the antisocialist law period to describe the person who served as a party contact for several other more or less clandestine socialists to keep them informed of party developments and help disseminate illegal literature. Obviously these people were highly respected and trusted in party circles.

30. Engels to Kautsky (23 May 1884, 1 April 1890), Kautsky to Engels (2 April 1890), Engels, pp. 115, 251–52; Kautsky to Bebel (15 December 1885, 25 October 1886), Bebel, pp. 46–47, 57; Bebel to Engels (5 July and 7 December 1885, 9 April 1890), Bebel-Engels, pp. 231, 245–46, 388.

31. Engels to Kautsky (17 October 1888), Engels, pp. 212–14, 222–24; Bebel to Engels (15 October 1888), Engels to Bebel (25 October 1888), Bebel-Engels, pp. 337, 340; Natalie Liebknecht to Engels (27 November 1888), in Wilhelm Liebknecht, *Briefwechsel mit Karl Marx und Friedrich Engels,* ed. Georg Eckart (The Hague, 1963), p. 320; Chushichi Tsuzuki, *The Life of Eleanor Marx* (Oxford, 1967), pp. 244–47. For Engels' somewhat muddled account of the Kautskys' split, see Engels to Laura Lafargue (13 October 1888), in Friedrich Engels, Paul and Laura Lafargue, *Correspondence,* trans. Yvonne Kapp, 3 vols. (Moscow, 1960), II, 157–58.

264 · NOTES TO PAGES 60-67

32. Kautsky to Bebel (14 and 22 September 1888), Bebel, pp. 68–69, 70–71; Engels to Kautsky (15 September 1889), Engels, pp. 247, 249 n.5; Tsuzuki, *Eleanor Marx*, pp. 257–63.

33. Engels to Kautsky (18 and 28 January, and 20 February 1889), Kautsky to Engels (5 and 26 February 1889), Engels, pp. 227–30, 232–60, 265; Kautsky to Adler (5 August 1891), Adler, p. 75.

34. Kautsky to Engels (13 May, 20, 27, and 28 June, and 10 July 1892), Engels to Kautsky (17 May, 25 June, and 5 July 1892, and 21 May 1895), Engels, pp. 339–57; Tsuzuki, *Eleanor Marx*, p. 247.

35. Engels, pp. 433–50; Bebel to Adler (17 November and 20 December 1890, 5 June 1892, and 18 September 1895), Adler, pp. 63–64, 66–67, 90, 187.

36. Kautsky to Engels (9 April and 22 August 1890), Engels, pp. 213, 251, 253–55, 258; Kautsky to Luise Ronsperger (drafts and letter, 29 December 1889), KFA 35.

37. Testimony by Kautsky to the importance of *Anti-Dühring* occurs in many places, see especially Engels, p. 4, and *E&E*, pp. 436–37 and 483–84. For the changes in Marxism made by Engels, see Erhard Lucas, "Marx' und Engels' Auseinandersetzung mit Darwin: Zur Differenz zwischen Marx und Engels," *IRSH* 9 (1964), 433–69; Dieter Groh, "Marx, Engels, und Darwin: Naturgesetzliche Entwicklung oder Revolution?" *Politische Vierteljahresschrift* 8 (1967), 544–59; Donald C. Hodges, "Engels' Contribution to Marxism," *The Socialist Register 1965* (New York, 1965), pp. 297–310; Alfred Schmidt, *The Concept of Nature in Marx* (London, 1971), pp. 51–61; Paul Walton and Andrew Gamble, *From Alienation to Surplus Value* (London, 1972), pp. 51–76; Lichtheim, pp. 234–58.

38. Friedrich Engels, *Anti-Dühring* (London, 1943), pp. 15, 31.

39. For the debate on Kautsky, see Korsch, "Geschichtsauffassung"; Matthias, *Kautsky;* and Steinberg, *Sozialismus*, pp. 51–53.

40. "Der Darwinismus und die Revolution," "Die urwüchsige Form des Kampfes um's Dasein," "Der Staatssozialismus," "Phäkenthum," *Sozialdemokrat*, 4 and 18 April 1880, 15 September and 8 December 1881, 6 July 1882; "Die sozialen Triebe in der Tierwelt," *NZ* 1 (1883), 20–27, 67–73; "Die sozialen Triebe in der Menschenwelt," *NZ* 2 (1884), 13–19, 49–59, 118–25; "Die Indianerfrage," *NZ* 3 (1885), 17–21, 63–73, and 107–16. In "Menschenwelt," p. 124, Kautsky wrote, "Just as with the social animals, so also with humans the social instincts have been mechanically bred, without the intervention of an idea."

41. "Das winzige Mauslein," "Verschwörung oder Revolution?" "Der Staatssozialismus," *Sozialdemokrat*, 30 January, 20 February, 6 March, 29 September, and 8 December 1881.

42. "Ein materialistischer Historiker," *NZ* 1 (1883), 538–39. This critique of materialist historians of the Enlightenment might well be applied to Kautsky's own work up to 1884.

43. Kautsky to Engels (29 December 1883, 14 February and 12 March 1884, 9 August 1886), Engels to Kautsky (5 February 1885, 11 August 1886), Engels, pp. 91–92, 97–98, 103, 197–99; Blumenberg, pp. 39–40. The straight presentation of Marx is also represented by the series of articles entitled " 'Das Elend der Philosophie' und 'Das Kapital,' " *NZ* 4 (1886), 7–19, 49–58, 117–29, 157–65.

44. *The Economic Doctrines of Karl Marx* (London, 1936). Since World War II this book has been reissued in the Soviet Union and many Soviet-bloc states. See Blumenberg, pp. 39–40.

45. "Die Aussichtslosigkeit der Sozialdemokratie," *NZ* 3 (1885), 179–88, 193–202; "Die Quintessenz des Sozialismus," *NZ* 3 (1885), 515–19; "Aus dem Nachlass von Rodbertus," *NZ* 4 (1886), 258–63; "Juristen-Sozialismus," *NZ* 5 (1887), 48–62. In "Aussichts.," Kautsky argued that Schäffle changed his mind about socialism as his personal de-

pendence on the state increased, thus implying both opportunism and cowardice. For Kautsky's denial of the importance of those being criticized, see Kautsky to Bebel (15 December 1885), Bebel, p. 46. For Engels' similar disavowals, see Engels to Laura Lafargue (2 November 1886), Engels, *Lafargue Correspondance*, p. 406.

46. Kautsky to Engels (29 May and 11 October 1884), Engels to Kautsky (26 June and 20 September 1884), Engels, pp. 118–19, 126–27, 144–45, 147; Kautsky to Bebel (8 November 1884, 15 December 1885), Bebel, pp. 25, 46; Engels to Bebel (20–[23] January 1886), Bebel-Engels, pp. 250–51. Vernon L. Lidtke, "German Social Democracy and German State Socialism, 1876–1884," *IRSH* 9 (1964), 202–25, gives the background for the anti-Rodbertus debate, concluding that at least among the Reichstag *Fraktion* the appeal of Rodbertus and his followers was significant.

47. Karl Kautsky, "Das 'Kapital' von Rodbertus," "Eine Replik," "Schlusswort," *NZ* 2 (1884), 337–50, 385–402, 494–505, and 3 (1885), 224–32; C. A. Schramm, "K. Kautsky und Rodbertus," "Antwort an Herrn K. Kautsky," *NZ* 2 (1884), 481–94, and 3 (1885), 218–23.

48. Review of Anon., *Die Aristokratie des Geistes als Lösung der Sozialen Frage, NZ* 3 (1885), 90–92. As early as 6 July 1882, in "Phäkenthum," *Sozialdemokrat,* Kautsky had argued that Darwin himself had suggested that humans were not inalterably bound to act in accordance with the same natural laws that governed the lives of animals. He eventually added to his general observation about the inapplicability of natural-scientific laws to social situations when he specifically denied that Marxism and Darwinism were related. "Sozialismus und Darwinismus," *Oesterreichischer Arbeiterkalender für das Jahr 1890,* pp. 49–54, cited in Steinberg, *Sozialismus,* p. 42, and Gasman, *Scientific Origins,* pp. 123–24. See also "Darwinismus und Marxismus," *NZ* 13 (1894–95), 709–16.

49. See chapter 2, "First Publications," for Kautsky's earlier views.

50. "Die chinesischen Eisenbahnen und das europäischer Proletariat," *NZ* 4 (1886), 537; "Kommunistische Kolonien," *NZ* 5 (1887), 30.

51. "Notizen," "Statistische Revue," *NZ* 1 (1883), 245–46, 388–89; "Die Erhaltung des Kleinbauernstandes," *NZ* 3 (1885), 321–29; "Die technische Entwicklung," *NZ* 5 (1887), 510–15; "Statistische Schönfärberei," *NZ* 6 (1888), 29–34; "Herrn Dr. Stiebling's Theorie der Wirkungen der Kapitalsverdictung," *NZ* 6 (1888), 164–69; "Die Verschwendung in der kapitalistischen Produktionsweise," *NZ* 7 (1889), 25–35 (the quote is from p. 26).

52. "Soll Deutschland Kolonien gründen?" *Staatswirtschaftliche Abhandlungen* 1 (1879–80), 394–400; Kautsky to Engels (11 May 1882), Engels, p. 56. See also "Kommunistische Kolonien,", *Sozialdemokrat,* 27 March and 3 April 1881, in which Kautsky flatly rejected colonization and emigration as parts of the socialists' program.

53. "Auswanderung und Kolonisation. I.," *NZ* 1 (1883), 365–70; "Tongking," review of R. E. Jung, *Deutsche Kolonien* (Leipzig, 1884), and "Das Recht auf Arbeit," *NZ* 2 (1884), 156–64, 237–39, 300; "Die deutsche Auswanderung," *NZ* 3 (1885), 253–57.

54. "Auswanderung II," *NZ* 1 (1883), 393–404; "Die sozialen Triebe in der Menschenwelt," *NZ* 2 (1884), 118–24; "Die Indianerfrage," *NZ* 3 (1885), 17–20; "Kamerun," *NZ* 6 (1888), 15–26.

55. "Auswanderung II," *NZ* 1 (1883), 404; "Tongking," *NZ* 2 (1884), 158, 163–64; "Indianerfrage," *NZ* 3 (1885), 116; "Kamerun," *NZ* 6 (1888), 27.

56. "Der Übergang von der kapitalistischen zur sozialistischen Produktionsweise," *Jahrbuch für Sozialwissenschaft und Sozialpolitik* 1:2 (1880), 59–60; Kautsky to Engels (18 August 1884), Engels to Kautsky (22 August 1884), Engels, pp. 140–42; Kautsky to Adler (15 March and 7 June 1887), Adler, pp. 29–33. Lenin's dictum was that on their own the workers are capable of developing only trade-union consciousness. See *What is to Be Done?* (Moscow, 1947), p. 42. In this work (first published in 1902), Lenin quoted at

266 · NOTES TO PAGES 75-82

length some "profoundly true and important utterances by Karl Kautsky" (p. 51) on the subject of the need for supervision in the development of the workers' socialist consciousness.

57. Kautsky to Engels (7 and 29 April 1884), Engels, pp. 106–07, 112–13. Steinberg, *Sozialismus*, pp. 48–49, correctly pointed out that much of Kautsky's early writing on the future state was typically utopian-socialistic—paying more for unpleasant than for pleasant work, using technology to eliminate repellent work, gradually equalizing wages, etc. See "Die Vertheilung des Volks-Einkommens im Zukunftsstaate," *Der Sozialist*, 27 and 31 October 1878; "Die Vertheilung des Arbeitsertrages im sozialisten Staate," *Jahrbuch für Sozialwissenschaft und Sozialpolitik* 2 (1881), 88–98. But even this speculation was tempered by a measure of realism. In "Übergang," pp. 59–68, he argued that the transitional institutions would have to be based on institutions that already existed, that were presently to the advantage of the workers, and that would strengthen socialist inclinations. Thus he rejected state monopolies, because they failed to meet requirements two and three, and producers' co-ops, because they failed to meet requirement three, but accepted trade unions as meeting all three requirements. See also "Die Abschaffung des Staates," *Sozialdemokrat*, 15 December 1881.

58. Kautsky to Engels (6 September 1882), Engels, p. 60; Kautsky to Bebel (15 December 1885, 17 August 1886), Kautsky to H. W. Fabian (2 January 1885), Bebel, pp. 47, 53–54, 364; "Übergang," *Jahrbuch*, 1:2 (1880), 63; "Der Staatssozialismus und die Sozialdemokratie," "Der Staatssozialismus," "Abschaffung," *Sozialdemokrat*, 6 March, 8 and 15 December 1881; "Historiker," *NZ* 1 (1883), 542; "Die chinesischen Eisenbahnen," *NZ* 4 (1886), 518; "Die moderne Nationalität," *NZ* 5 (1887), 403, 405; "Verschwendung," *NZ* 7 (1889), 29; "Bodenbesitzreform und Sozialismus," *NZ* 8 (1890), 397.

59. "Soll Deutschland," *Staats. Abhand.*, 1 (1879–80), 398; "Die Bourgeoisie und die Republik," "Abschaffung," *Sozialdemokrat*, 24 April and 15 December 1881; "Nationalität," *NZ* 5 (1887), 442.

60. "Die chinesischen Eisenbahnen," *NZ* 4 (1886), 516–17; "Die Arbeiterbewegung in Oesterreich," *NZ* 8 (1890), 100.

61. "Verschwörung," "Wahlen und Attentate," *Sozialdemokrat*, 20 February and 5 June 1881; "Die internationale Arbeitsgesetzgebung," *Jahrbuch für Sozialwissenschaft und Sozialpolitik* 2 (1881), 111–12.

62. "Bourgeoisie," "Freiheit," *Sozialdemokrat*, 24 April and 7 July 1881.

63. "Freiheit. Antwort an den Genossen A.B.C. [Robert Seidel]," "Klassenkampf und Sozialismus," *Sozialdemokrat*, 8 and 28 September 1881.

64. "Übergang," *Jahrbuch* 1:2 (1880), 61–63; "Darwinismus," *Sozialdemokrat*, 4 April 1880; "Arbeitsgesetzgebung," *Jahrbuch* 2 (1881), 112; "Die Sterblichkeit der Kostkinder," *NZ* 1 (1883), 191–96.

65. Engels, pp. 178–80; *E&E*, pp. 521–22; *Thomas More and His Utopia* (New York, 1959); *Die Klassengegensätze im Zeitalter der französischen Revolution* (Stuttgart, 1908); "Die Entstehung der biblischen Urgeschichte," *Kosmos*, 7 (1883), 201–14; "Zum Luther jubiläum," *NZ* 1 (1883), 489–96; "Die Entstehung des Christentums," *NZ* 1 (1883), 481–99, 529–45; "Die Bergarbeiter und der Bauernkrieg, vornähmlich in Thüringen," *NZ* 7 (1889), 289–97, 337–50, 410–17, 443–53, 507–15. Engels had high praise for these last articles. See Engels to Kautsky (15 September 1889), Engels, p. 247.

66. Kautsky to Engels (18 and late August 1887), Engels, pp. 208, 210; *More*, pp. 4, 12, 142, 146, 153, 159, 171, 186, 206–10.

67. Engels to Kautsky (20 February 1889), Kautsky to Engels (26 February 1889), Engels, pp. 232–36.

68. *Klassengegensätze*, pp. 3–5, 9, 10, 23, et passim.

Chapter Four: Challenge from the Right, 1890-1904

1. Julius Braunthal, *History of the International,* 2 vols. (New York, 1967), I, 233, 252; Lichtheim, p. 267. For Kautsky's role in the Hungarian party, the 1903 program of which he drafted, see Tibor Erenyi, "The Activities of the Social Democratic Party of Hungary During the First Decade of the Century," in *Studies on the History of the Hungarian Working-Class Movement, (1867-1966),* ed. Henrik Vass (Budapest, 1975), pp. 55-88.

2. Erich Matthias and Eberhard Pikart, *Die Reichstagfraktion der deutschen Sozialdemokratie 1898 bis 1918,* pt. 1 (Düsseldorf, 1966), xv-xxii; William H. Maehl, *German Militarism and Socialism* (Lincoln, Neb., 1968), pp. 75-78; Schorske, p. 7; Lidtke, *The Outlawed Party,* 299. For the SPD's place in the politics of Wilhelmine Germany, see Fritz Fischer, *World Power or Decline* (New York, 1974), pp. 5-6; Dieter Groh, *Negative Integration und revolutionärer Attentismus* (Frankfort, 1973), pp. 331-35, 577-682; Konrad H. Jarausch, *The Enigmatic Chancellor* (New Haven, 1973), pp. 47-49, 89-91, 106-08, 208-09, 439-40 n. 27; George D. Crothers, *The German Elections of 1907* (New York, 1941).

3. Kautsky to Engels (16 February, 6 April 1892), Engels, pp. 329, 336; Kautsky to Adler (15 October 1892), Kautsky to Emma Adler (22 March 1895), Adler, pp. 106, 194; Kautsky to Luise (13 September 1896), KFA 35; Kautsky to Max Zetterbaum (30 October 1893), KFA 8; Kautsky to Paul Ernst (20 December 1893), KFA, 8.

4. Kautsky to Engels (21 December 1890, 5 April 1891, 19 February 1892), Engels, pp. 267, 291, 329, 453; Adler to Kautsky (19 May 1887), Kautsky to Adler (13 December 1892), Adler, pp. 31, 114; Kautsky to Bernstein (2 February 1896), KA, C115.

5. Kautsky to Engels (3 July 1890), Engels, p. 257; Kautsky to Luise (7 May 1896), KFA 35.

6. Kautsky to Engels (18 February 1891, 23 January 1892), Engels, pp. 278, 325; Kautsky to Luise (24 August 1891), KFA 35. The first child was named Felix; the third son, Benedikt, was born in 1894.

7. Kautsky to Engels (25 November 1890, 5 April 1891, 19 May, 11 October 1893), Engels to Kautsky (7 April 1891, 3 November 1893), Engels, pp. 264, 291-92, 381, 388-91; Kautsky to Adler (13 October 1893), Adler, pp. 121-23; Kautsky to Luise (26 August 1893), KFA 35. Bruno Schoenlank (1859-1901) was the editor of the *Leipziger Volkszeitung* (1893-1901), a co-worker on the *Vorwärts* (1892), and an SPD Reichstag representative (1893-1901); Franz Mehring (1846-1919) was the most prolific of contributors to the *Neue Zeit* until his break with Kautsky in 1912-1913; Max Schippel (1859-1928) was at one time a young radical SPD journalist and later a rightist and a Reichstag representative (1890-1905). See Osterroth, pp. 219-20, 263-64, 267, 269-70.

8. Engels to Kautsky (4 December 1892), Kautsky to Engels (11 October 1893), Engels, pp. 373, 388-89; Kautsky to Adler (26 November 1890, 13 October 1893), Kautsky to Hugo Heller (28 December 1895), Adler, pp. 65, 121-22, 195; Kautsky to Bernstein (several letters from 4 May 1895 through 24 June 1896), KA, C107-38.

9. Engels to Kautsky (4 December 1892), Kautsky to Engels (19 December 1892), Engels, pp. 372-75; Kautsky to Bebel (end of November 1892), Bebel, pp. 80-81; Kautsky to Adler (13 October 1893), Adler, pp. 121-22; Kautsky to Bernstein (25 January 1896), KA, C114.

10. Kautsky to Luise (26 August 1893), KFA 35; Kautsky to Engels (1 and 25 November 1893), Engels, pp. 389-90, 395; Kautsky to Adler (15 October 1892, 13 October, 1 November 1893, 29 April 1894), Adler, pp. 107-08, 122-23, 125-26, 150.

11. Kautsky to Engels (19 December 1892), Engels, pp. 373-75; Kautsky to Luise (2 August 1895), KFA 35.

12. Kautsky to Luise (2 August 1895), KFA 35; Kautsky to Hugo Heller (10 January 1896), KFA 8; *Protokoll,* 1894, pp. 63-84.

13. Tussy Marx (22 and 28 August, 17 September 1895, 3, 10, 20, and 29 February 1896), KA, D XVI, 437–39, 447, 449–51; Kautsky to Bernstein (25 January, 24 and 29 February, 19 and 31 March 1896), KA, C114, 118–20, 123; Kautsky to Hugo Heller (28 December 1895, 23 March 1896), Adler to Kautsky (27 March 1896), Adler, pp. 198, 205–07.

14. Kautsky to Luise (12 March, 28, 29, and 30 April, 7 May 1896), KFA 35; Kautsky to Bernstein (19 March 1896), KA, C120; Tussy Marx to Kautsky (1 April, 20 May 1896), KA, D XVI, 452, 455; Kautsky to Adler (18 April 1896), Adler, pp. 203–04.

15. Kautsky to Adler (13 June, 15 October 1892, 25 October 1901, 4 April 1903), Adler, pp. 92–93, 107–09, 375, 415–16. For a precise summary of Kautsky's view of the function of socialist intellectuals, see "Akademiker und Proletarier," NZ 19:2 (1900–01), 89–91. For an earlier, more elaborate discussion, see "Die Intelligenz und die Sozialdemokratie," NZ 13:2 (1894–95), 10–16, 43–49, 74–80.

16. Kautsky to Engels (9 April 1890, 25 November 1893), Engels, pp. 254, 395; Kautsky to Adler (13 October 1893, 12 November 1896), Adler, pp. 121, 222; Kautsky to Luise (7 and 9 October 1895, 16 September 1902), KFA 35; Polizeipräsident, Abteilung I. (Berlin) to Kautsky (14 January 1919), KFA 5. The items to Luise cited here were written while Kautsky was at party congresses; he almost always wrote this correspondence to Luise in English. I have edited these letters and postcards for punctuation, but not for grammar or vocabulary. The communication from the head of the local police announced that a payment of 150 marks had to be made before the application for citizenship could be processed. Kautsky did once begin the process of becoming a citizen while he was in Stuttgart, but it came to nothing. See Kautsky to Hugo Heller (31 March 1897), Adler. p. 230.

17. Kautsky to Engels (25 November 1893), Engels, p. 395. In a letter to Engels of 19 May 1892 Kautsky reported that Dietz considered him an "incorrigible optimist." Engels, pp. 381–82.

18. Protokoll, 1887, p. 47; Protokoll, 1890, pp. 158–59, 181.

19. Kautsky to Engels (8 September 1890), Engels to Kautsky (18 September 1890, 7 January, 23 February 1891), Engels, pp. 260–61, 268, 281–83.

20. Kautsky to Bernstein (8 January 1891), KA, C81.

21. Kautsky to Engels (8 and 13 January 1891), Engels to Kautsky (15 January 1891), Engels, pp. 269–71.

22. Kautsky to Bernstein (29 January 1891), KA, C82.

23. Kautsky to Engels (9 and 18 February, [9 March] 1891), Engels to Kautsky (3 and 23 February 1891), Engels, pp. 272, 276, 278–83, 285–86. Kautsky's conciliatory article was "Unsere Programme," NZ 9:1 (1890–91), 680–90; see also the first few pages of "Der Entwurf des neuen Parteiprogramms," NZ 9:2 (1890–91), 723–25.

24. Kautsky to Engels (6 February 1891), Engels, pp. 273–75.

25. Kautsky to Engels (4 June, 26 September 1891), Engels, pp. 299, 306; Kautsky to Adler (5 August 1891), Adler, p. 96; "Entwurf," NZ 9:2 (1890–91), 726–27, 730, 749–54, 781, 789–91.

26. "Entwurf," NZ 9:2 (1890–91), 750, 753–55.

27. Kautsky to Luise (15 October 1891), KFA 35; Kautsky to Engels (30 October 1891), Engels, p. 316; Protokoll, 1891, p. 81.

28. Kautsky to Luise (18 October 1891), KFA 35; Protokoll, 1891, pp. 12, 81, 325–33, 358.

29. Kautsky to Bernstein (9 October 1891), KA, C85; Engels to Kautsky (28 September, 14 October, 3 December 1891), Kautsky to Engels (30 October 1891), Engels, pp. 307–10, 312–15, 317.

30. Kautsky to Engels (3 March, 6 April 1892), Engels to Kautsky (5 March 1892),

NOTES TO PAGES 100–06 • 269

Engels, pp. 331, 335; *The Class Struggle* (New York, 1971), p. 1. For some reason English translations of this book have usually taken their title from the fifth section, "The Class Struggle." This is inappropriate and unfortunate, because *The Erfurt Program* is much more than a discussion of the class struggle.

31. *Class Struggle,* pp. 9–87, 90, 122, 127–29, 132, 135–48, 158.

32. Ibid., 90–93, 159, 177, 186–88. The charge of cryptorevisionism was made by Matthias, "Kautsky," pp. 163–64, 168.

33. Tussy Marx to Kautsky (22 August 1895, 30 September, 7 October 1896), KA, D XVI, 437, 457–58; Kautsky to Luise (2 May 1896), KFA 35.

34. Tussy Marx to Kautsky (17 September, 27 December 1895, 19 and 30 April, 20 May 1896), KA, D XVI, 439, 445, 453–55; Engels, p. 453; Blumenberg, p. 69. Kautsky had become close friends with Tussy during his 1880s stay in London, and their correspondence concerning the *Nachlass* is marked by warm friendship and affection. The image of Tussy that comes out of these letters is one of a bright but frustrated woman. Her frequent and touching allusions to the Kautsky children, whom she never met, and her eagerness to have Karl and his family come to London reveal a lonely woman who regretted her own childlessness. Tussy's pseudo-husband, Edward Aveling, was a shady, two-timing schemer who often begged money from Kautsky and many others. Eventually Karl made a virtually direct accusation that Aveling murdered Tussy, who died under strange circumstances in the spring of 1898. See Tussy to Kautsky (20 February, 18 September 1895, 10, 20, and 29 February, 30 September, 7 October 1896, 5 April 1897, 1 January 1898), KA, D XVI, 435, 440, 449–51, 457–58, 464–65, 483; Edward Aveling to Kautsky (5 December 1887, 20 January, 14 February 1888), KFA 2; Kautsky to Adler (9 April 1898), Adler, pp. 244–45. For Tussy's melancholy life story, see Tsuzuki, *Eleanor Marx.*

35. Roger P. Morgan, *The German Social Democrats and the First International, 1864–1872* (Cambridge, 1965), pp. 19–20, and 29–30. Liebknecht's association with the Saxon People's Party earned him Engels' scorn. Engels once referred to the "primitive middle-peasants of lower Saxony," and argued that the "narrow-minded South German, republican, petty-bourgeois notions systematically drummed into the heads of the workers by Liebknecht are much harder to get rid of" than Lassallean notions. See Engels to Marx (20 July 1851), Engels to Kugelmann (10 July 1869), Marx-Engels (1960), pp. 66, 267.

36. "Die Bauern und der Sozialismus," *Sozialist,* 7, 10, 14, 17, 21, 24, 28 November 1878; "Die Agitation unter den Bauern," *Jahrbuch für Sozialwissenschaft und Sozialpolitik,* 1:2 (1880), 14–25; "Die soziale Frage auf dem Lande," *Staats. Abhand.* (1879–1880), pp. 449–60. Presumably Kautsky wrote the *Jahrbuch* article before leaving Austria. *E&E,* p. 423.

37. Kautsky to Engels (23 July 1881), Engels, p. 35; "Die Zins-Sklaverei des deutschen Bauernthums," "Die Sozialdemokratie und des Bauernthum," "Die revolutionäre Kraft des amerikanischen Kornes," *Sozialdemokrat,* 16 May, 10 and 24 October 1880; "Italiens oekonomische Verhältnisse," *NZ* 1 (1883), 47–48.

38. For a discussion of the Bund der Landwirte, see Hans-Jürgen Puhle, *Agrarische Interessenpolitik und preussischer Konservatismus* (Hanover, 1966), and Sarah R. Tirrell, *German Agrarian Politics After Bismarck's Fall* (New York, 1951).

39. *Protokoll,* 1894, pp. 141–42, 145–46, 148, 157–58.

40. Kautsky to Bernstein (14 November 1894), KA, C102; Kautsky to Engels (14 and 23 November 1894), Engels, pp. 413, 415.

41. Various letters from Kautsky and Ledebour in the *Vorwärts,* 20, 21, and 25 November, 19 December 1894; Kautsky to Hugo Heller (22 December 1894), Bebel, p. 371; Kautsky, "Das Erfurter Programm und die Landagitation," *NZ* 13:1 (1894–95),

278; Osterroth, pp. 183–84. See Bebel, pp. 87–90, for Kautsky's letters to the party central committee protesting Ledebour's assault and the efforts of the *Fraktion* to prevent Kautsky from defending himself in the *Vorwärts*.

42. Kautsky to Bernstein (14 November 1894), KA, C102; Kautsky to Luise (7 October 1895), KFA 35; Kautsky to Engels (14 November 1894, 30 July 1895), Engels, pp. 413, 443–44; Kautsky to Hugo Heller (6 August 1895), Bebel, p. xxiii; Singer to Adler (26 November 1894), Adler, p. 163.

43. "Das Erfurter Programm," *NZ* 13:1 (1894–95), 280; "Unser neuestes Programm," *NZ* 13:2 (1894–95), 612–20; "Die Konkurrenzfähigkeit des Kleinbetriebes in der Landwirtschaft," *NZ* 13:2 (1894–95), 485–86, 491.

44. "Unser neuestes Programm," *NZ* 13:2 (1894–95), 559–65, 586–94, 610–13, 621; "Noch einige Bemerkungen zum Agrarprogramm," *NZ* 13:2 (1894–95), 812; "Arbeiterschutz und Bauernschutz," *NZ* 14:1 (1895–96), 19–21. For a discussion of state socialism, see Kautsky, "Vollmar und der Staatssozialismus," *NZ* 10:2 (1891–92), 705–13, and "Der Parteitag und der Staatssozialismus," *NZ* 11:1 (1892–93), 210–21; and Lidtke, "German Social Democracy." For a more detailed discussion of democracy versus the dictatorship of the proletariat, see Kautsky, "Die direkte Gesetzgebung durch das Volk und der Klassenkampf," *NZ* 11:2 (1892–93), 516–27.

45. Kautsky to Luise (30 September 1895), KFA 35; "Unser neuestes Program," *NZ* 13:2 (1894–95), 558–59, 613, 616–19, 623; "Noch einige Bemerkungen," *NZ* 13:2 (1894–95), 812.

46. *Protokoll*, 1895, pp. 100–01, 104–05; Kautsky to Luise (9 October 1895), KFA 35. The entire debate covers pages 98–176 in the *Protokoll*.

47. *Protokoll*, 1895, pp. 109–10, 112–14, 117–19, 121, 124, 126–27. Clara Zetkin also gave a long speech in support of Kautsky's resolution, and she closed with a stirring call for the party to reject the agrarian program and thereby "hold firmly to the revolutionary character of our party" (p. 143). Zetkin's speech met with stormy, prolonged applause. The popularity of her position was reflected in the fact that at this congress she was elected to the party control commission for the first time.

48. *Protokoll*, 1895, pp. 176–77; Kautsky, "Der Breslauer Parteitag und die Agrarfrage," *NZ* 14:1 (1895–96), 108–13; Bebel to Adler (20 October 1895), Adler, pp. 193–95.

49. Kautsky, *Die Agrarfrage* (Stuttgart, 1899); David, *Socialismus und Landwirtschaft* (Berlin, 1903); Kautsky, "Sozialismus und Landwirtschaft," *NZ* 21:1 (1902–03), 677–88, 731–35, 745–58, 781–94, 804–19. Hans G. Lehmann, *Die Agrarfrage in der Theorie und Praxis der deutschen und internationalen Sozialdemokratie* (Tübingen, 1970), pp. 113–262, discusses the agrarian question in Germany. I disagree with Lehmann's conclusion that Kautsky was responsible for the failure of the SPD to come up with a good agrarian program. Lehmann overrates the influence of both Kautsky and theory. Heinrich Dade, *Die landwirtschaftliche Bevölkerung des deutschen Reichs um die Wende des 19. Jahrhunderts* (Berlin, 1903), pp. 56–57, discusses the 1882 and 1895 census figures. Hellmut Hesselbarth, "Der aufkommende Revisionismus in der Bauernfrage und Karl Kautsky," *Marxismus und deutsche Arbeiterbewegung* (Berlin, 1970), pp. 365–97, is an excellent discussion of Kautsky on the agrarian question. On the south German party, see Paul Frölich, "Die süddeutsch Fronde," in Rosa Luxemburg, *Gesammelte Werke* (Berlin, 1925), III, 399–407.

50. *Protokoll*, 1893, pp. 253–69; Kautsky to Engels (11 October 1893), Engels, p. 388; Kautsky to Adler (5 May 1894), Adler, pp. 152–54. Bernstein's position in 1893 was presented in "Die preussischen Landtagswahlen und die Sozialdemokratic," *NZ* 11:2 (1892–93), 772–78.

51. "Umsturzgesetz und Landtagswahlen in Preussen," *NZ* 15:2 (1896–97), 275–82;

"Die preussischen Landtagswahlen und die reaktionäre Masse," *NZ* 15:2 (1896–97), 580–90.

52. "Die preussischen Landtagswahlen," *NZ* 15:2 (1896–97), 586.

53. "Was ist ein Kompromiss? Nachlese zur Diskussion über die preussischen Landtagswahlen," *NZ* 16:2 (1897–98), 356–62; *Protokoll*, 1897, pp. 168, 217; Bebel to Adler (5 June 1897), Adler, pp. 231–32.

54. For the impact of the Dreyfus and Millerand affairs on international socialism, see Joll, *Second International,* pp. 83–99, and Braunthal, pp. 255–74.

55. "Jaurès' Taktik und die deutsche Sozialdemokratie," *Vorwärts,* 26 July 1899; "Jaurès und Millerand," *Vorwärts,* 1 August 1899; "Eine internationale Umfrage über sozialdemokratische Taktik," *Vorwärts,* 5 October 1899.

56. *Compte rendu sténographique non officiel du cinquième Congrès socialiste international tenu à Paris du 23 au 27 septembre 1900* (Paris, n.d.), pp. 99–170; "Die sozialistischen Kongresse und der sozialistische Minister," *NZ* 19:1 (1900–01), 36–44; "Bürgermeister und Minister," *NZ* 19:2 (1900–01), 794–96; Engels, p. 454.

57. Eduard Bernstein, "Probleme des Sozialismus," *NZ* 15:1 (1896–97), 164–71, 204–12, 303–11, 772–83; *NZ* 15:2 (1896–97), 100–07, 138–43; *NZ* 16:2 (1897–98), 225–32, 388–95.

58. Kautsky, "Die materialistische Geschichtsauffassung und der psychologische Antrieb," *NZ* 14:2 (1895–96), 652–59; Kautsky, "Was will und kann die materialistische Geschichtsauffassung leisten?" *NZ* 15:1 (1896–97), 213–18, 228–38, 260–71; Kautsky, "Utopistischer und materialistischer Marxismus," *NZ* 15:1 (1896–97), 716–27; Bax, "Synthetische contra Neumarxistische Geschichtsauffassung," *NZ* 15:1 (1896–97), 171–77; Bax, "Die Grenzen der materialistischen Geschichtsauffassung," *NZ* 15:1 (1896–97), 676–87.

59. The standard English treatment of Bernstein is Gay, *Dilemma.* This work dignified the intellectual content of revisionism beyond deserved limits. Gerhard A. Ritter, *Die Arbeiterbewegung im Wilhelminischen Reich, 1890–1900* (Berlin, 1963), called Bernstein's work *"Illusionismus,"* and claimed that the furor over revisionism had little to do with its theoretical content. Calling the latter a *"feuilletonistischen* popularization of the bourgeois critique of Marxism," Ritter argued that revisionism attracted so much attention simply because it was the first internal critique of Marxism. See Ritter, pp. 196–204, especially p. 197, n.129, where he suggested that Gay misinterpreted revisionism.

60. *Protokoll,* 1899, pp. 94–244; *Protokoll,* 1903, pp. 298–420.

61. *Protokoll,* 1898, pp. 126–30. The Kautsky-Bernstein debate was conducted in the *Neue Zeit,* the *Vorwärts,* the *Sozialistische Monatshefte* (Bernstein only), and in one book by each man, Bernstein's *Die Voraussetzungen des Sozialismus und die Aufgaben der Sozialdemokratie* (1899) and Kautsky's *Bernstein und das sozialdemokratische Programm: Eine Antikritik* (1899). For a particularly straightforward presentation of Kautsky's view of theory, see "Missverständnisse über Missverständnisse," *Vorwärts,* 29 May 1901.

62. Kautsky to Bernstein (30 August 1897), KA, C175 (cited in Holzheuer, *Karl Kautskys Werk,* pp. 68–69).

63. *Patriotismus und Sozialismus* (Leipzig, 1907), p. 10.

64. Kautsky to Luise (1 May 1896), KFA 35; Kautsky to Bernstein (30 August 1897, 13 and 26 February 1898), KA, C175, 180–81; Adler to Kautsky (9 November 1896), Adler, p. 219; *Protokoll,* 1898, pp. 122–25. For Plekhanov's active role in the revisionism dispute, see Samuel H. Baron, *Plekhanov: The Father of Russian Marxism* (Stanford, 1963), pp. 164–85; for Luxemburg's role, see Nettl, *Luxemburg,* I, 202–50. Kautsky later remarked that his first perception of Bernstein's antirevolutionary inclinations came late in 1897 from Bernstein's "Menge und das Verbrachen," *NZ* 16:1 (1897–98), 229–37. See

Kautsky to Adler (21 May 1899), Adler, p. 303. Actually Kautsky's first printed criticism of Bernstein was a brief article entitled "Taktik und Grundsätze," *Vorwärts*, 13 October 1898.

65. Kautsky to Luise (9 March 1898), Bebel to Kautsky (9 and 24 September 1898), Kautsky to Hugo Heller (22 September 1898), Bebel, pp. xxxii–xxxiii, 110–11; Tussy Marx to Kautsky (15 March 1898), KA, DXVI, 489; Kautsky to Bernstein (26–27 May 1898), KA, C191; Adler to Kautsky (4 April 1898), Kautsky to Adler (9 April, 4 August 1898), Bebel to Adler (29 September 1898), Adler, pp. 242–43, 245–46, 249, 252.

66. Kautsky to Bernstein (23 October 1898), KA, C209 (reprinted in Adler, pp. 272–73). Gay, *Dilemma*, pp. 79–80, found Kautsky's position at this time "strange if not sinister." I think Kautsky's actions were those of a man who felt he was losing a dear and trusted friend. His first concern was saving Bernstein from personal anguish and disgrace, and there is nothing sinister in that. *Sozialistische Monatshefte* was the major organ of revisionists and reformists in Germany; *Revue socialiste* played a similar role in France.

67. Adler to Bebel (1 November 1898), Bebel to Adler (4 November 1898), Kautsky to Adler (4 November, 23 December 1898), Adler, pp. 266–71, 281–82.

68. Kautsky to Adler (23 December 1898, 7, 8, 17 March 1899), Bernstein to Adler (3 March 1899), Adler to Kautsky (7 March 1899), Bebel to Adler (8 April 1899), Adler, pp. 281–82, 287, 291–95, 301, 307–08.

69. Adler to Kautsky (16 March 1899), Adler to Bernstein (17 March 1899), Adler, pp. 296–97, 299.

70. Kautsky to Adler (17 and 21 March 1899), Adler, pp. 301, 303; "Bernsteins Streitschrift: Die Zusammenbruchstheorie; Liberalismus und Sozialismus; Demokratie und Klassenkampf," *Vorwärts*, 16, 17, and 18 March 1899. Kautsky continued his critique with "Nochmals Bernsteins Streitschrift: Die neueste Lesart der Marxschen Zusammensbruchtheorie; Die demokratische-sozialistische Reformpartei; Unsere Taktik," *Vorwärts*, 8, 11, and 12 April 1899; "Prinzipieller Gegensatz oder Voreingenommenheit? Noch ein Wort zur Diskussion mit Bernstein," *Vorwärts*, 26 April 1899.

71. Bebel to Kautsky (22 March, 3 August 1899), Bebel to Bernstein (3 August 1899), Bebel, pp. 113, 115, 118; Bernstein to Adler (28 March 1899), Bebel to Adler (8 April 1899), Kautsky to Adler (10 April 1899), Adler, pp. 306–09, 312.

72. Bebel to Kautsky (3, 9, 11, 13, and 22 September 1899), Bebel, pp. 118–24; Kautsky to Bernstein (10 February 1900), KA, C242; *NZ* 18:2 (1899–1900), 160.

73. Kautsky to Adler (25 September 1900), Bebel, xxxvi; Bebel to Adler (8 July 1901), Kautsky to Adler (31 May, 5 and 6 June, 9 September 1901), Adler, pp. 352, 355, 357, 359, 366–67.

74. Bebel to Kautsky (25 October 1901, 9 September 1903), Bebel, pp. 143, 161–62; Kautsky to Adler (9 September, 15 November 1901, 18 October 1904), Adler, pp. 367, 377, 434. In the spring of 1903, Bebel also urged Kautsky to be more critical of David's book on the agrarian question. Kautsky to Adler (4 April 1903), Adler, p. 415.

75. Kautsky to Adler (5 June 1901, 18 October 1904), Adler, pp. 356–57, 432–33.

76. Kautsky to Adler (18 October 1904), Adler, pp. 432–33.

77. "Der Münchener Parteitag," *NZ* 20:2 (1901–02), 804–09; "Was nun?" *NZ* 21:2 (1902–03), 389–98; "Klasseninteresse-Sonderinteresse-Gemeininteresse," *NZ* 21:2 (1902–03), 240–45, 261–74; "Literarische Rundschau," review of Paul Kampffmeyer, *Wohin steuert die ökonomische und staatliche Entwicklung?*, *Vorwärts*, 5 May 1901; "Der Wahlkampf und die Aufgaben des kommenden Reichstages," *Vorwärts*, 30 May, 3 June 1903.

78. "Zum Parteitag," *NZ* 21:2 (1902–03), 729–39; "Die preussischen Landtagswahlen," *NZ* 22:1 (1903–04), 225–31; "Wahlkreis und Partei," *NZ* 22:2 (1903–04), 36–46.

79. "Allerhand Revolutionäres," *NZ* 22:1 (1903–04), 588–98, 620–27, 652–57, 685–95, 732–40.

80. Joll, *Second International,* pp. 100–06; Braunthal, *History,* pp. 276–84.

81. Kautsky to Adler (18 October 1904), Adler, pp. 431–35; *Sixième congrès socialiste international: Compte rendu analytique* (Brussels, 1904), pp. 130–208. Joll's account of the disagreement at Amsterdam includes the observation that Kautsky was "a fanatic who did not believe in compromise." (p. 102). This is an example of the typically extremist evaluations that historians have made of Kautsky. Like most such evaluations, this one is less than judicious. Apparently others in the German party also saw Adler as a "secret" revisionist, including Clara Zetkin. See Bebel to Kautsky (29 August 1903), Bebel, p. 157.

82. *The Socialist Revolution* (Chicago, 1905); Kautsky to Adler (21 November 1901, 28 January 1903), Adler, pp. 381–82, 412.

83. Kautsky to Adler (4 April 1903), Adler, pp. 416–17.

Chapter Five: Challenge from the Left, 1905–1914

1. For a complete account of these affairs, see Sidney Harcave, *First Blood: The Russian Revolution of 1905* (New York, 1964).

2. For an excellent brief discussion of the SPD and the Russian revolution of 1905, as well as the mass-strike debate, see Schorske, pp. 29–58. See also Richard W. Reichard, "The German Working Class and the Russian Revolution of 1905," *Journal of Central European Affairs* 13 (1953), 136–53.

3. Kautsky to Adler (15 October 1892, 5 June 1901), Adler, pp. 105, 354; Kautsky to Plekhanov (6 October 1904), KA, C525. References to Russia appear in numerous works by Kautsky before 1905, beginning as early as "Deutschland und Russland," *Der Sozialist,* 15 November 1877.

4. Kautsky's relationship with Axelrod has been masterfully dealt with by Abraham Ascher, "Axelrod and Kautsky," *Slavic Review* 26 (1967), 94–112. For Plekhanov, see Baron, *Plekhanov,* pp. 1–46, 124–25, 174–76, 225. For Kautsky's praise of Plekhanov, see Kautsky to Engels (15 February 1884, 7 December 1891), Engels, pp. 98, 319; Kautsky to Adler (26 January 1893), Adler, p. 118. Kautsky's *Class Struggle* apparently came out in Russian, in the *Review of the North,* almost immediately after publication in German, though Blumenburg did not refer to this translation. See Engels to Kautsky (15 September 1889), Engels, p. 247.

5. Kautsky to Dietz (probably 1902), Bebel, p. xlii. Luxemburg's life is dealt with impressively by J. P. Nettl in an outstanding biography. However, Nettl's treatment of Kautsky is not up to the high standard of the rest of his work, and his discussion of the Kautsky-Luxemburg relationship is one-sided. For a taste of Luxemburg's contacts with the Kautsky family, and for examples of her frequently charming and disarming personal style, see her *Letters to Karl and Luise Kautsky from 1896 to 1918* (New York, 1925).

6. "Die zivilisierte Welt und der Zar," *NZ* 23:1 (1904–05), 614–17.

7. Anon., "Die Politik der russischen Regierung," *Vorwärts,* 10 February 1905; Kautsky, "Die Bauern und die Revolution in Russland," *NZ* 23:1 (1904–05), 670–77.

8. "Die Bauern und die Revolution," *NZ* 23:1 (1904–05), 670–77.

9. "Die Agrarfrage in Russland," *NZ* 24:1 (1905–06), 412–23. Kautsky also forcefully argued this analysis in "Die Folgen des japanischen Sieges und die Sozialdemokratie," *NZ* 23:2 (1904–05), 406–08. In this article he agreed with Luxemburg's comparison of Gleb Struve, a leading Russian socialist-turned-liberal, with Jaurès. Kautsky's popularity in Russian socialist circles at this time is amply testified to by the fact that no less than five different editions of *Das Erfurter Programm* were published in Russia in 1905—two in Moscow, one each in Kiev, Odessa, and St. Petersburg, and another appeared in St.

Petersburg in 1906. For Kautsky's postmortem on the revolution, see "Triebkräfte und Aussichten der russischen Revolution," *NZ* 25:1 (1906–07), 284–90, 324–33, in which he reiterated his earlier analysis.

10. "Die Differenzen unter den russischen Sozialisten," *NZ* 23:2 (1904–05), 68–69; Kautsky to Engels (8 November 1881), Engels to Kautsky (7 February 1882), Engels, pp. 46–48, 50–53.

11. Kautsky to Michael Lusnia, one of several pseudonyms used by Kelles-Krauz, (4 February 1905), KFA 8. A year after this letter, Kautsky received a request from a Warsaw publisher to print a total of 42,500 copies of seven of his books. Apparently Kautsky's popularity ran high in Poland at this time. See Towarzystwo Wydawnietw Ludowych to Kautsky (28 March 1906), KFA 4. For Kautsky's views on Poland vis-à-vis Russia, see "Allerhand Revolutionäres," *NZ* 22:1 (1903–04), 620–27.

12. "Differenzen," *NZ* 23:2 (1904–05), 69–71; Kautsky to Adler (20 July 1905), Adler, pp. 464–66. For a more detailed discussion of Kautsky and the Menshevik-Bolshevik split, see Ascher, "Axelrod and Kautsky"; Dietrich Geyer, "Die russische Parteispaltung im Urteil der deutschen Sozialdemokratie, 1903–1905," *IRSH* 3 (1958), 195–219, 418–44; Peter Lösche, *Der Bolshewismus im Urteil der deutschen Sozialdemokratie, 1903–1920* (Berlin, 1967), pp. 27–34. Kautsky remained in the midst of this split for far longer than he liked, because he was one of the administrators of the famous Schmidt inheritance of the Russian party. See Lösche, pp. 60–66.

13. "Differenzen," *NZ* 23:2 (1904–05), 71–79.

14. Hilferding, "Zur Frage des Generalstreiks," *NZ* 22:1 (1903–04), 134–42. This volume also had five other articles on the general strike, including a five-part series by Kautsky, "Allerhand Revolutionäres," 588–98, 620–27, 652–57, 685–95, 732–40, but none of this had aroused major polemics. The 1904 resolution was presented by Henriette Roland-Holst, and it was only a very cautious expansion of the acceptable limits of the mass strike as a weapon of the working class. See Braunthal, *History*, pp. 285–304, for a discussion of the general strike and the Second International.

15. Schorske, pp. 29–32. For a contemporary discussion of the employers' associations, see Gerhard Kessler, *Die deutschen Arbeitgeberverbände* (Leipzig, 1907).

16. The literature on the tendency of both trade-union and party leadership to become more conservative is vast. A contemporary observer of the SPD wrote insightfully on the topic, Robert Michels, *Zur Soziologie des Parteiwesens in der modernen Demokratie* (Leipzig, 1910). Most studies of the German socialist movement have emphasized this tendency to a greater or lesser extent. See especially Schorske, pp. 8–16. Of course, Kautsky also discussed the tendency to independence and self-preservation among bureaucracies. See chap. 3 above, "Literary Work of the 1880s."

17. For Luxemburg, see Nettl, *Luxemburg*, I, 295–364. I am not suggesting, as does Schorske, that the radical-moderate split as it developed after 1905 was the prelude to and cause of the "great schism" that led to the formation of the German Communist Party. I agree with Dieter Groh's conclusion, in *Negative Integration*, pp. 121–25, 163–85, 482–502, that the war was the source of the schism. It is true that radical-moderate tensions reached new highs after 1905 and persisted until after the war, but a person's position during these years was not a good indication of his or her stand on the war. In a more immediate sense, the cause of the eventual split was a question of party discipline, with the majority forcing the minority to a split. Susanne Miller, *Burgfrieden und Klassenkampf* (Düsseldorf, 1974), pp. 155–56, makes this argument most persuasively.

One exception to the radicals' lack of institutional responsibilities was Clara Zetkin. She was a member of the party control commission after 1905, and she usually aligned herself with the radicals.

18. Centrism was Kautsky's own label for his post-1905 theory. *Fatalismus* was used by Steinberg, but has implications that are too negative to fit Kautsky's position. Matthias labeled Kautsky's theory *Integrationideologie*, but this expression is neither accurate nor useful, since neither the revisionists nor the radicals accepted Kautsky's positions. Groh's *revolutionärer Attentismus* is perhaps the best expression, but it is virtually untranslatable into acceptable English; "revolutionary attentiveness" is best. German writers concerned with Kautsky have long fished around for labels to put on his work. In addition to the four mentioned here, Darwino-Marxism is a favorite. A Frenchman has added another: Guy Desolre, "Henri de Man et le marxisme: Critique critique de la critique," *Revue européene des sciences sociales* 12:31 (1974), 37, called Kautsky's theory *"le fatalisme optimiste."*

19. Braunthal, *History,* p. 287; Kautsky to Engels (25 November 1893), Engels, p. 394; Kautsky to Adler (26 November 1893, 9 March 1894), Adler, pp. 129–30, 136–37; "Allerhand Revolutionäres," *NZ* 22:1 (1903–04), 685–95, 732–40.

20. Adler to Kautsky (17 May 1902), Kautsky to Adler (19 May 1902), Adler, pp. 395–96. The articles that upset Adler were Mehring, "Ein dunkler Maitag," and Luxemburg, "Das belgische Experiment," *NZ* 20:2 (1901–02), 97–101 and 105–10, respectively. Mehring had introduced the Belgian strike with "Belgien," *NZ* 20:2 (1901–02), 65–69. Vandervelde responded to Luxemburg and Mehring, though mistaking the latter's article for an editorial piece, in "Nochmals das belgische Experiment," *NZ* 20:2 (1901–02), 166–68, to which Kautsky attached a note defending Mehring's tone, and Luxemburg rebutted Vandervelde in "Und zum dritten Male das belgische Experiment," *NZ* 20:2 (1901–02), 203–10, 274–80. This exchange typifies the role of the *Neue Zeit* as a forum for international socialist debate.

21. Kautsky to Adler (19 May 1902), Adler, pp. 396–97.

22. Adler to Kautsky (21 May 1902), Kautsky to Adler (23 May 1902), Adler, pp. 399–402. In his biography of Luxemburg, Nettl accused Kautsky of plagiarizing the idea of impatience on the right and on the left from a 1910 Trotsky letter (I, 433–34). The 1902 quote I have given here clearly shows that Nettl's accusation is false. Kautsky had developed this notion long before 1910. This episode points out one of the few weaknesses of Nettl's otherwise excellent book. He tended to adopt as his own Luxemburg's view of Kautsky. This led him to deal harshly and unfairly with Kautsky, particularly in terms of personality. Dr. Karl Kautsky, Jr., has pointed out other errors in Nettl's treatment of Kautsky in a letter appended to the German edition of the Luxemburg biography (Berlin, 1967), pp. 830–34.

23. Kautsky to Adler (9 June 1902), Adler, pp. 404–05.

24. Henriette Roland-Holst, *Generalstreik und Sozialdemokratie* (1905; rpt. Dresden, 1906); Schorske, pp. 39–42. In theoretical terms the revisionism controversy was far more important than the mass-strike debate, but the latter more clearly revealed contradictions and had a real impact on relations between trade union and party. In part because it focuses on Kautsky, my discussion of the mass-strike conflict differs substantially from Schorske's, who identified Kautsky too glibly with the "radical" position. As will be seen below, Kautsky's position was radical and not-radical at the same time.

25. Kautsky to Adler (20 July 1905), Adler, p. 464; Kautsky, "Genossin Luxemburg über die Gewerkschaften," *Vorwärts,* 18 April 1906, and "Die Genossin Luxemburg und die Gewerkschaften," *Vorwärts,* 5 May 1906.

26. Anon., "Über politischen Streik," *Vorwärts,* 25 June 1905.

27. Ibid.

28. "Die Folgen des japanischen Sieges," *NZ* 23:2 (1904–05), 494–95.

29. Ibid., pp. 495–99. The party's success in runoff elections declined steadily from a

high of 63 percent (15 of 24) in 1884 to a low of 16 percent (14 of 90) in 1907. The 1912 election reversed this trend when the party won 38 percent (46 of 121). See Matthias and Pikart, *Reichstagfraktion,* p. xxiii.

30. "Folgen," *NZ* 23:2 (1904–05), 493–94. Gay's identification of Kautsky with the pro-mass-strike forces (*Dilemma,* p. 239) is incorrect.

31. Anon., "Unmögliche Diskussion," *Vorwärts,* 19 July 1905; "Ein Hausen Unrichtigkeiten," *Vorwärts,* 20 July 1905; "Debatten über Wenn und Aber," *Vorwärts,* 2, 5, 6, 8, 9, 10, 13 September 1905; Kautsky, "Die Fortsetzung einer unmögliche Diskussion," *Vorwärts,* 1 September 1905, and *NZ* 23:2 (1904–05), 681–92; "Noch einmal die unmögliche Diskussion," *Vorwärts,* 15 September 1905 (with critical footnotes by the *Vorwärts* editors), and *NZ* 23:2 (1904–05), 776–85; "Zu den Parteidebatten: Richtigstellung," *Vorwärts,* 16 September 1905; "Der mögliche Abschluss einer unmögliche Diskussion," *NZ* 23:2 (1904–05), 795–804. For Kautsky on the trade unions, see "Partei und Gewerkschaften," *NZ* 17:1 (1898–99), 420–23; "Die Neutralisierung der Gewerkschaften," *NZ* 18:2 (1899–1900), 388–94, 429–33, 457–66, 492–97; "Die Lehren des Bergarbeiterstreiks," *NZ* 23:1 (1904–05), 772–82; "Der Kongress von Köln," *NZ* 23:2 (1904–05), 309–16; "Partei und Gewerkschaft," *NZ* 24:2 (1905–06), 716–25, 749–54. The trade unionists' charges against Kautsky were repeated in this last article.

32. *Protokoll,* 1905, pp. 142–43, 285–313. Bebel's speech took the entire morning session.

33. Ibid., pp. 314–42.

34. Schorske, pp. 54–59.

35. *Protokoll,* 1906, pp. 131–32, 232–33, 239–40, 304–05.

36. Ibid., pp. 143, 256–62, 305–07.

37. "Allerhand Revolutionäres," *NZ* 22:1 (1903–04), 620–27, 652–57.

38. Friedrich Stampfer, "Wahlrechtsbewegung und Massenstreik," *NZ* 24:2 (1905–06), 755–58; Kautsky, "Der mögliche Abschluss," *NZ* 23:2 (1904–05), 796–97, and "Grundsätz oder Pläne?," *NZ* 24:2 (1905–06), 781–82. The *Vorwärts* quote is from "Debatten über Wenn und Aber. V.," 9 September 1905.

39. Kautsky to Adler (2 August 1905), Adler, pp. 466–67; "Zum Parteitag," *NZ* 23:2 (1904–05), 753–55.

40. For the reasons I have given in this paragraph, I do not agree with Dieter Groh's contention (*Negative Integration,* p. 191) that "the knowledge must have been bitter" for Kautsky that the masses were only converted by practice and not theory, and that if the German government were to adopt reformist tactics "à la Lloyd George or Waldeck-Rousseau" the revisionists would gain the upper hand (quoting from Kautsky to Rappaport [8 June 1911], KA, C571). My argument is that Kautsky would have been a reformist himself if the German government had been a responsive one. After the German revolution Kautsky said as much in a letter to his son Benedikt (31 July 1919), Bebel, pp. xxxix–xl.

41. Kautsky to Adler (5 September 1892), Adler, p. 97. For Adler's economic problems, see Julius Braunthal, *Victor und Friedrich Adler* (Vienna, 1965), pp. 32–33, 90–100.

42. Benedikt Kautsky, "Karl Kautsky: Persönliche Erinnerungen an meinen Vater," *Arbeiterkalender, 1954* (Vienna), pp. 104–05; Kautsky to Bebel (18 July 1913), Bebel, pp. 353–54. Apparently the more spirited Rosa Luxemburg found the Sunday afternoon gatherings somewhat disgusting, as she began to pull away from Kautsky; see Nettl, *Luxemburg,* I, 410.

43. Kautsky to Luise (28 October 1893, 13 February 1911), KFA, 35 and 36.

44. B. Kautsky, "Persönliche," p. 109; Kautsky to Luise (17 July 1910), KFA 36; Luxemburg, *Letters,* pp. 137–39, 154–55, 227–30. Luise Kautsky also wrote a memorial to

Luxemburg, *Rosa Luxemburg: Ein Gedankbuch* (Berlin, 1929). I have relied upon information provided to me in personal interviews with Dr. Karl Kautsky, Jr. Nettl's account of the Kautsky's relationship is often highly speculative and rarely substantiated. See *Luxemburg*, especially I, 410–12.

45. Kautsky to Luise (13, 17 March 1907, 19 April 1910), KFA 35 and 36; Luxemburg, *Letters*, pp. 137–38.

46. Bebel to Kautsky (14 July, 5 August 1910, 8, 9, 13 October 1912, 16 July 1913), Kautsky to Bebel (18 July 1913), Bebel to Luise (4 September 1910), Bebel, pp. 220–21, 226, 229–31, 313–14, 317–38, 351–53; Bebel to Adler (12 January 1912), Kautsky to Adler (28 November 1914), Adler, pp. 545, 605. Kautsky's comments on Hildebrand are in "Ein Ketzergericht," and his review of Hildebrand's book, *Sozialistische Auslandspolitik*, *NZ*, 31:1 (1912–13), 1–6, 36–38, respectively. For the critique of Mehring, see "Ein Vertrauensmann," *NZ* 31:2 (1912–13), 600–02. For the explanation of Dr. Karl Kautsky, Jr., as to why his father was sometimes called "the Grand Inquisitor" and the "party pope," see Bebel, p. xv.

47. "Die Situation des Reiches," *NZ* 25:1 (1906–07), 453–57, 459–60, 486–87, 497–98. See also "Ausländische und deutsche Parteitaktik," *NZ* 25:1 (1906–07), 724–31, 764–73, where Kautsky elaborated his notion that in the wake of the 1907 election, it was even clearer that the bourgeoisie and the workers could not cooperate in Germany.

48. Crothers, *German Elections*, pp. 129–48, 208–53. For the SPD and the election, see Schorske, pp. 59–66.

49. Crothers, *German Elections*, pp. 175–78; Matthias and Pikart, *Reichstagfraktion*, p. xv. Most of the calculations in this paragraph are my own.

50. "Der 25. Januar," *NZ* 25:1 (1906–07), 587–96.

51. Kautsky, *Vorläufer des neueren Sozialismus*, 2 vols. (Berlin, 1923), published in English, less the first 160 pages of volume one, as *Communism in Central Europe in the Time of the Reformation* (New York, 1959); Kautsky to Engels (5 March 1895), Engels to Kautsky (21 May 1895), Engels, pp. 422–23, 435; Tussy Marx to Kautsky (20 February 1895), KA, DXVI. Engels' study was reprinted in *The German Revolutions* (Chicago, 1967); in 1891 Blos edited a new edition of the classic by Wilhelm Zimmermann, *Geschichte des grossen Bauernkrieg*, which first appeared in three volumes in 1841–1843; Belfort-Bax's work was *The Peasant War in Germany* (London, 1899); and Bebel wrote *Der Deutsche Bauernkrieg* (Braunschweig, 1876).

52. Kautsky, *Communism in Central Europe*, pp. 12, 15, 127, 214–15, 220–21. Abraham Friesen, "The Marxist Interpretation of the Reformation" (Ph.D. diss., Stanford University, 1967) has dealt exhaustively with the works of Zimmermann, Engels, Kautsky, and others. Though Friesen is weak on Marxism, and often confuses objective evaluation with debatable epistemological-philosophical positions, his review of the historiography of the tradition is sound. For Kautsky's place in it, see pp. 65–69, 92–93, 230, 253–59, 324–26, 356–57, 384, 390–94, 397, 470–74, 486–87, 560–65, 576–79, and 634.

53. *Foundations of Christianity* (New York, 1953), pp. xi–xiii, originally published as *Der Ursprung des Christentums* (Stuttgart, 1908). This book was one of Kautsky's big money-makers, going through at least thirteen editions in German. For an example of the sort of criticism Kautsky was confronting, see A. K., "Der sogenannte urchristliche Kommunismus," *NZ* 26:2 (1907–08), 582–91.

54. *Foundations*, pp. xx, 25–59, 138, 146, 253.

55. Ibid., pp. xv, 47–48, 229–48, 250, 258, 264–65, 274, 278. Though this work is now rarely cited in scholarly works on Christianity, it does on occasion appear in the footnotes of studies that attempt to analyze societies in terms of socioeconomic substructures. For an example of this, see Bernard Magubane, "A Critical Look at Indices Used in the Study

of Social Change in Colonial Africa," *Current Anthropology* 12:4-5 (October–December 1971), 419-30. *Foundations* is cited on p. 426, where Magubane uses it to substantiate his observation that "social tendencies of a people, therefore, always arise from actual needs within the people, and not through mere imitation of foreign models."

56. Schorske, pp. 88-115. Nettl (*Luxemburg*, I, 408-09) made a particular point of Kautsky's verbal radicalism in *Der Weg zur Macht*. For an earlier discussion of budget nonsupport, see Kautsky, "Die Budgetbewilligung," *NZ* 26:2 (1907-08), 809-26.

57. The articles in the *Neue Zeit* began on 6 October 1908 with Kautsky's "Maurenbrecher und das Budget," *NZ*, 27:1 (1908-09), 44-50, and continued with Maurenbrecher, "Offener Brief an den Genossen Kautsky," pp. 148-53, ending with Kautsky, "Reform und Revolution: Eine Antwort," pp. 180-91, 220-32, 252-59. A great deal of correspondence concerning the second edition of *Der Weg* was reprinted in Ursula Ratz, ed., "Briefe zum Erscheinen von Karl Kautskys 'Weg zur Macht,' " *IRSH* 12:3 (1967), 432-77. See also Bebel, pp. 202-03, for another important letter from Zetkin to Kautsky. For evidence of the speed and breadth of the circulation of Kautsky's work, see Kautsky to Luise (28 February 1909), KFA 35.

58. *The Road to Power* (Chicago, 1909), pp. 11-12, 30, 54-55; Bebel to Adler (6 March 1909), Adler, p. 495.

59. *Road,* pp. 25, 27, 30, 45-46, 66, 70-72.

60. Kautsky to Hugo Haase (14, 19, and 25 February 1909), in Ratz, "Briefe," pp. 438, 440, 449; Kautsky to Adler (7 and 9 March 1909), Adler, pp. 496-98; Bebel to Kautsky (2 March 1909), Bebel, pp. 202-03; Kautsky to Luise (28 February 1909), KFA 35.

61. Kautsky to Adler (26 September 1909), Adler, pp. 501-02.

62. For conflicting discussions of the effects on the SPD of the break up of the Bülow bloc, see Schorske, pp. 146-96, and Groh, *Negative Integration,* pp. 121-185.

63. Nettl, *Luxemburg,* I, 416-34; Kautsky, "Eine neue Strategie," *NZ* 28:2 (1909-10), 335-36. Dr. Karl Kautsky, Jr., felt very strongly that Luxemburg had used her friendship with his mother to attack his father. See Bebel, pp. xlv and 192 (letter 139 n.1).

64. Kautsky's part in the debate consisted of the following articles in the *Neue Zeit* 28:2 (1909-10): "Was nun?" pp. 33-40, 68-80, "Eine neue Strategie," pp. 332-41, 364-74, 412-21, "Zwischen Baden und Luxemburg," pp. 652-67, and "Schlusswort," pp. 760-65. Luxemburg's first article, "Was weiter?" appeared in the *Dortmunder Arbeiterzeitung*, 15 March 1910; to the above issue of the *Neue Zeit* she contributed "Ermattung oder Kampf?" pp. 257-66, 291-305, "Die Theorie und Praxis," pp. 564-78, 626-42, and "Zur Richtigstellung," pp. 756-60.

65. Kautsky to Minna Kautsky (11 July 1910), Bebel to Kautsky (14 and 18 July, 5 August 1910), Bebel, pp. 220-22, 226; Kautsky to Luise (15 and 21 July, 3 August 1910), KFA 36.

66. "Zwischen Baden und Luxemburg," *NZ* 28:2 (1909-10), 665-67. Later Kautsky referred to himself, Eckstein, Cunow, Bebel, and Hilferding as the "Marxist center." Kautsky to Adler (26 June 1913), Adler, p. 573.

67. Bebel to Kautsky (5 August 1910), Bebel to Luise (4, 12, and 29 September 1910), Bebel, pp. 226, 229-31, 233-37; Kautsky to Luise (7 September-15 November 1910, numerous letters), KFA 36. On several occasions during the next two years, Bebel, who at over seventy had slowed down somewhat himself, cautioned Kautsky against overworking again. See Bebel to Kautsky (30 August 1911) and Bebel to Luise (16 March 1912), Bebel, pp. 269-70, 291.

68. For mass action, see "Die Aktion der Masse," *NZ* 30:1 (1911-12), 43-49, 77-84, 106-17. For the mass strike, see *Der politische Massenstreik* (Berlin, 1914). For the 1912 elections, see "Praktische Wahlagitation," *NZ* 29:2 (1910-11), 32-36; "Die Revanche der

Niedergerittenen," *NZ* 30:1 (1911–12), 545–49; "Die Wurzeln des Sieges," *NZ* 30:1 (1911–12), 577–81; "Der neue Liberalismus und der neue Mittelstand," *Vorwärts*, 25 February 1912; "Nochmals der neue Mittelstand," *Vorwärts*, 3 March 1912; "Unser Stichwahlabkommen," *Vorwärts*, 5, 6, and 7 March 1912. Kautsky's clearest, most straightforward discussion of the validity for Marxists of electoral alliances came in an article entitled "Der erste Mai und der Kampf gegen den Militarismus," *NZ* 30:2 (1911–12), 100–06.

69. John A. Hobson, *Imperialism* (London, 1940); Lenin, *Imperialism, the Highest Stage of Capitalism* (New York, 1933); Rudolf Hilferding, *Das Finanzkapital* (Frankfurt, 1968). Kautsky's praise for Hilferding's book is in "Finanzkapital und Krisen," *NZ* 29:1 (1910–11), 764–72, 797–804, 838–46, 874–83. For contrasting discussions of Kautsky on imperialism, see John H. Kautsky, "J. A. Schumpeter and Karl Kautsky: Parallel Theories of Imperialism," *Midwest Journal of Political Science* 5:2 (May 1961), 101–28; and Ursula Ratz, "Karl Kautsky und die Abrüstungskontroverse in der deutschen Sozialdemokratie," *IRSH* 11 (1966), 197–227. For Kautsky's rejection of the identity of imperialism and capitalism, see "Der Imperialismus," *NZ* 32:2 (1913–14), 908. Although not published until 11 September 1914, this article was written some weeks before the war in anticipation of the 1914 congress of the Second International that never met.

70. "Ältere und neuere Kolonialpolitik," *NZ* 16:1 (1897–98), 769–81, 801–16; "Sozialistische Kolonialpolitik," *NZ* 27:2 (1908–09), 35–36. Roger Chickering, *Imperial Germany and a World Without War* (Princeton, 1975), pp. 272–77, deals with Kautsky's attitude toward the threat of war in the few years before 1914. Chickering errs on three points. First, he misunderstands Kautsky's general attitude toward the SPD's relationship to German society: Kautsky did not encourage the SPD "to insulate itself as far as possible from capitalist society," as Chickering writes (p. 266). Second, Kautsky's views had not undergone a "dramatic change" by 1911, as Chickering claims (p. 273), because the SPD theorist had long argued that aggressive expansionism and its threat of war were not part of *industrial* capitalism (see, "Ältere und neuere Kolonialpolitik" cited above). And third, Chickering suggests that the different role assigned to finance capital by Kautsky, on the one hand, and the bourgeois pacifist Alfred Fried, on the other, was "of peripheral significance" (p. 276, n. 198). But like most Marxists, and unlike most bourgeois pacifists, Kautsky steadfastly argued that finance capital increasingly dominated commercial and industrial capital (see, for instance, *The Social Revolution*). The role of finance capital was, therefore, hardly peripheral to Kautsky's position. In placing more emphasis after 1910 on the need for the SPD to cooperate with bourgeois antiwar forces, Kautsky was reaffirming his long-held conviction that the nonsocialists in German society did not form "one reactionary mass" and giving further expression of his conviction that politics were often paramount.

71. "Patriotismus, Krieg und Sozialdemokratie," *NZ* 23:2 (1904–05), 346, 348; "Patriotismus und Sozialdemokratie," *Vorwärts*, 16 December 1905; "Kriegsursachen," *Vorwärts*, 18 February 1906; *Patriotismus und Sozialdemokratie* (Leipzig, 1907), pp. 11–13. This last was a reprint of articles which originally appeared in the *Leipziger Volkszeitung*, 4, 6, and 7 May 1907.

72. *Patriotismus*, pp. 9, 22–23; "Der Kongress von Kopenhagen," *NZ* 28:2 (1909–10), 775–76; "Weltpolitik, Weltkrieg und Sozialdemokratie" (written for the party central committee in mid-August, 1911), in *Dokumente und Materialen zur Geschichte der deutschen Arbeiterbewegung* (Berlin, 1967), pp. 356–61; "Der Baseler Kongress und die Kriegshetze in Oesterreich," *NZ* 31:1 (1912–13), 339–40.

73. Kautsky, *Sozialismus und Kolonialpolitik* (Berlin, 1907); Bebel to Kautsky (15 October 1907), Bebel, pp. 190–91.

74. Vandervelde, "Die belgischen Sozialisten und die Kongofrage," *NZ* 27:2 (1908–09), 732–39; *Internationaler Sozialisten-Kongress, Stuttgart, 1907* (Berlin, 1907), pp. 24–40, Kautsky, "Der Stuttgarter Kongress," *NZ* 27:2 (1908–09), 724–30.

75. "Methoden der Kolonialverwaltung," *NZ* 26:1 (1907–08), 616, 621; "Sozialistische Kolonialpolitik," *NZ* 27:2 (1908–09), 36–38; "Banditenpolitik," *NZ* 30:1 (1911–12), 2; *Internationaler Sozialisten-Kongress*, pp. 34–35. For further commentary on this topic, see "Ein Buch über Zentralafrika," *NZ* 31:2 (1912–13), 371–78; "Armee und Volk," *NZ* 32:1 (1913–14), 402–05.

76. "Patriotismus, Krieg und Sozialdemokratie," *NZ* 23:2 (1904–05), 365–66; "Der erste Mai," *NZ* 30:2 (1911–12), 106–07, 109; *Patriotismus*, p. 20. Ratz, "Abrüstung.," p. 220, identifies this change in Kautsky as the point at which "the Marxist criterion for judgment of war was no longer that of social democracy." This strikes me as an arbitrary, *ex post facto* evaluation of the nature of Marxism, i.e., after the Russian experience. Before the Russian model emerged, the possible developments of Marxism covered a much wider spectrum than they seem to now. Ratz also suggests that by arguing that disarmament could work, Kautsky was implicitly accepting the possibility of peaceful imperialism (p. 205). I think that Kautsky was simply responding to the immediate pressures of the time, namely the increasing threat of war, and that he still felt imperialism to be dangerous and something to be eliminated.

77. "Patriotismus," *NZ* 23:2 (1904–05), 369–70; *Patriotismus*, pp. 4–5; "Krieg und Frieden," *NZ* 29:2 (1910–11), 104; "Der erste Mai," *NZ* 30:2 (1911–12), 108–09,

78. Kautsky to Adler (25 July 1914), Adler, pp. 596–97.

79. Kautsky, *Sozialisten und Krieg* (Prague, 1937), pp. 436–80; Groh, *Negative Integration*, pp. 630, 640, 642–43, 675–84.

80. Kautsky to Adler (28 November 1914), Adler, p. 606; *Sozialisten und Krieg*, p. 460; Groh, *Negative Integration*, pp. 676, 692–93, 695–96, 698.

Chapter Six: The Great War and Two Revolutions, 1914–1924

1. "Die Sozialdemokratie im Kriege," *NZ* 33:1 (1914–15), 1–2; "Die Vorberietung des Friedens," *NZ* 32:2 (1913–14), 876–77; "Neue sozialdemokratische Auffassung vom Krieg," *NZ* 35:1 (1916–17), 321–24. Kautsky presented variations and expansions on the themes outlined here in numerous works during the war years. See especially "Die Internationalität und der Krieg," *NZ* 33:1 (1914–15), 225–50, and the introduction to the pamphlet from this article, published by Dietz in December 1914; *Nationalstaat, Imperialistischer Staat und Staatenbund* (Nürnberg, 1915); "Äussere und innere Politik," *NZ* 34:1 (1915–16), 20–25, 41–49; "Noch einige Bemerkungen über nationale Triebkräfte," *NZ* 34:1 (1915–16), 705–13.

2. "Der Krieg" and "Wirkungen des Krieges," *NZ* 32:2 (1913–14), 844, 947–48; "Internationalität," *NZ* 33:1 (1914–1915), 243; "Eine Richtigstellung," *NZ* 33:1 (1914–15), 634–36; Kautsky to Adler (28 November 1914, 11 February 1915), Adler, pp. 606–07, 611.

3. "Vorbereitung," *NZ* 32:2 (1913–14), 881–82; "Wirkungen," *NZ* 33:2 (1913–14), 981; "Die Internationale und der Burgfrieden," *NZ* 33:1 (1914–15), 18–19; "Internationalität," *NZ* 33:1 (1914–15), 225–26, 237–38, 248–49. Some of the evidence Kautsky used to substantiate his claim that the International was not dead was not very concrete. See "Aus der Partei: Danksagung," *Vorwärts*, 20 October 1914, where he argued that the many birthday greetings he had received from foreign socialists "prove that the supposedly dead International lives and gladly grasps every opportunity to announce its continuity."

4. Adler to Kautsky (20 March 1915), Adler, p. 617. So as not to be caught unprepared when the war ended, on 28 August 1914, Kautsky launched what he hoped would be a major discussion of the impending peace, see "Vorbereitung," *NZ* 32:2 (1913-14), 876-82.

5. "Internationale," *NZ* 33:1 (1914-15), 19; "Internationalität," *NZ* 33:1 (1914-15), 225, 246; *Internationalität*, pp. 2-5 (introduction); "Sozialdemokratische Anschauungen über den Krieg vor dem jetztigen Kriege," *NZ* 35:1 (1916-17), 300-01. Kautsky developed this critique most fully between April and July 1915, in two long polemics with Heinrich Cunow and Eduard David in *NZ* 33:2 (1914-15). For the Cunow debate, see "Zwei Schriften zum Umlernen," pp. 33-42, 71-81, 107-16, 138-46; "Nochmals unsere Illusionen," pp. 230-41, 264-75; "Zum Schluss der Diskussion," pp. 347-48. For the David debate, see "Eine Verteidigung der Zustimmung zu den Kriegskrediten," pp. 313-17; "Die Sozialdemokratie im Weltkrieg," 321-29; "Wohin geht die Reise?" pp. 394-402; "Ein objectiver Richter und gewissenhafter Historiker," pp. 453-63; "Ein Schlusswort," pp. 566-73. The two works that set Kautsky off against the *Umlerner* were Paul Lensch, *Die deutsche Sozialdemokratie und die Weltkrieg* (Berlin, 1915), and Heinrich Cunow, *Partei-Zusammenbruch? Ein offenes Wort zum inneren Parteistreit* (Berlin, 1915).

6. For Kautsky's efforts to combat the rise of national hatred among socialists, see "Eine Erörterung des Rechts auf Erörterung," *NZ* 33:1 (1914-15), 737-40; "Zwei Schriften," *NZ* 33:2 (1914-15), 34-38; "Ein objektiver Richter," *NZ* 33:2 (1914-15), 459, 461-63; "Imperialistischer Tendenzen in der Sozialdemokratie," *NZ* 34:1 (1915-16), 97-101; "Von Radek zu Bethmann," *NZ* 34:2 (1915-16), 473-80; "Wie englische Arbeiter deutsche Sozialdemokraten von einem internationalen Kongress ausschlossen," *NZ* 34:2 (1915-16), 618-20; "Die Wahrheit auf dem Marsch," *NZ* 35:1 (1916-17), 169-75.

7. For evidence of the Kautsky-Bernstein cooperation during the war, see "Das Gebot der Stunde: Aufruf Bernsteins, Kautskys und Haases," *Leipziger Volkszeitung*, 19 June 1915, reprinted in Eugen Prager, *Geschichte der U.S.P.D.* (Berlin, 1922), pp. 72-74; "Aus der Partei: Bernstein und Kautsky über ihren Aufruf," *Vorwärts*, 11 July 1915; "Ein Phantasie-Interview mit Kautsky und Bernstein," *Vorwärts*, 25 February 1916. After the war Kautsky and Bernstein remained on close personal terms and the years of split were largely forgotten. Kautsky had high praise for his old friend; see "Eduard Bernstein zu seinem fünfundsiebzigsten Geburtstag," *Die Gesellschaft* 2 (1925), 1-22. Here Kautsky identified 1912 as the turning point, when Bernstein reestablished a closer relationship with the *Neue Zeit*, but the war years brought closer personal relations.

8. Prager, *Geschichte*, pp. 30-31, 34; "Zwei Schriften," *NZ* 33:2 (1914-15), 76-80, 108-16; "Illusionen," *NZ* 33:2 (1914-15), 230-41, 264-75. In 1918, Kautsky wrote a longer refutation of the *Umlerner*, this time focusing on the work of Karl Renner. See *Kriegsmarxismus: Eine theoretische Grundlegung der Politik der 4. August* (Vienna, 1918).

9. Prager, *Geschichte*, pp. 93-96; Kautsky, *Mein Verhältnis zur Unabhängige Sozialdemokratischen Partie* (Berlin, 1922), pp. 3-8.

10. These articles were published as a pamphlet in early 1916 along with polemical responses by Otto Braun and Hans Marckwald, whose contributions had also first appeared in the *Neue Zeit*. This pamphlet, *Überzeugung und Partei*, was published by the left-wing Leipzig party publishing house. For Kautsky's introduction, see pp. 5-6.

11. *Überzeugung*, pp. 7-11.

12. Ibid., pp. 11-13, 17-20.

13. Ibid., pp. 31-32, 37, 41-42. Kautsky continued these arguments through the rest of 1916. See in *NZ* 34:2 (1915-16): "Die Spaltung der Fraktion," pp. 33-36; "Eine mahnende Erinnerung," pp. 65-71; "Zur Geschichte des Zentralorgans der Partei," pp.

321-31, 353-65. He also admitted in late 1916 that the original tactics he had espoused in response to the war had been based on several false assumptions. See "Mein Irrtum," *NZ* 35:1 (1916-17), 216-20.

14. A party conference was held in late September 1916, and though representation procedures greatly favored supporters of the *Fraktion* majority, and though very little was resolved, Kautsky was gratified that at least a split had been avoided. See "Die Parteikonferenze," *NZ* 35:1 (1916-17), 1-5. For an account of this conference, see Prager, *Geschichte,* pp. 108-14.

15. *Die Befreiung der Nationen* (Stuttgart, 1917), p. 5.

16. "Die Vorbereitung des Friedens," *NZ* 32:2 (1913-14), 876-77; "Die Sozialdemokratie im Kriege," *NZ* 33:1 (1914-15), 4; *Nationalstaat,* pp. 10-11, 14. The long quote is from p. 11.

17. *Nationalstaat,* pp. 17-21. Kautsky continued to combat the economic arguments of the right throughout the war. See "Äussere und innere Politik," *NZ* 34:1 (1915-16), 47-48.

18. "Äussere," *NZ* 34:1 (1915-16), 43. For Kautsky's discussion of the cases of particular nations, see "Das neue Polen," *NZ* 35:1 (1916-17), 153-56, 177-89, and *Serbien und Belgien in der Geschichte* (Stuttgart, 1917). In *Die Vereinigten Staaten Mitteleuropes* (Stuttgart, 1916), Kautsky used a review of Friedrich Naumann's *Mitteleuropa* as a basis from which to attack those socialists, like Karl Renner, who sympathized with Naumann's position.

19. *Nationalstaat,* pp. 70, 75-77; *Staaten,* pp. 43-45; "Noch einige Bemerkungen über nationale Triebkräfte," *NZ* 34:1 (1915-16), 710-11.

20. *Nationalstaat,* pp. 8-9. Of course soviets had appeared in Russia in 1905, but Kautsky did not then comment in any depth on their significance.

21. For evidence of the assault by the majority on the opposition, see Prager, *Geschichte,* pp. 39-40, 52-55, 87-91, 93-96, 102-04, 116-20, 129-31.

22. Prager, *Geschichte,* pp. 67-75, 93-96, 124-29, 133-36 (Kautsky's manifesto is reprinted on pp. 127-29); Robert F. Wheeler, "The Independent Social Democratic Party and the Internationals" (Ph.D. diss., University of Pittsburgh, 1970), pp. 14-16.

23. The articles, which ran in the issues of 23 February, 9, 16, and 23 March 1917, *NZ* 35:1 (1916-17), are: "Parteispaltung?" pp. 489-98; "Sozialdemokratie und nationalliberale Taktik," pp. 537-45; "Die Wendung zum Nationalsozialismus im Kriege," pp. 561-69; "Zwei Arbeiterparteien," pp. 585-91.

24. "Der imperialistische Krieg, *NZ* 35:1 (1916-17), 449-54, 475-87. This article appeared in the issues of 9 and 16 February 1917.

25. Ibid., pp. 478-80, 482, 484, 486-87. Kautsky made these same arguments again on 4 May in "Imperialismus und reaktionäre Masse," *NZ* 35:2 (1916-17), 102-15. Here he railed against those Marxists who saw theory not as a guide to lead them through the labyrinth of reality, but as a magic formula which allowed them to skip the labyrinth and get right to the ends. "Theoretical abstraction," he wrote, "is the way, the only way, to deeper understanding of reality, it is not its pure image" (p. 104).

26. Prager, *Geschichte,* pp. 143-51; USPD, *Protokoll über die Verhandlungen des Parteitages* (Berlin, 1917), pp. 12, 16-23, 38, 49-50, 52-53, 55-58. Many years later, participants in the Gotha congress of 1917 were still debating the true nature of this event. Early in 1930, Kautsky and Wilhelm Dittmann exchanged letters on this topic. Dittmann argued forcefully that the split had already occurred *before* the congress and that it was the result of expulsions of antiwar socialists by the SPD central committee. Kautsky had apparently sought Dittmann's opinion on the question of whether or not the formation of a new party was a foregone conclusion before the congress. Dittmann thought so, at least from

a 1930 perspective; Kautsky thought not. See Dittman to Kautsky (19 February 1930), KFA 2.

27. USPD, *Protokoll*, 1917, pp. 61–67, 73–74, 76, 79–82; Prager, *Geschichte*, pp. 147–51.

28. USPD, *Protokoll*, 1917, p. 66.

29. "Die Gothaer Konferenze," *NZ* 35:2 (1916–17), 50–53.

30. Kautsky to Axelrod (3 October 1917), Axelrod to Kautsky (10 October 1917), 16:5:88, Nicolaevsky Collection, Hoover Institution, Stanford, California; "Stockholm," *NZ* 35:2 (1916–17), 505–12; Prager, *Geschichte*, pp. 157–60; Wheeler, "Independent Social Democratic Party," pp. 47–64; Bundesarchiv, Coblenz, R43F/film 2714/Bd. 2447, Staatssekretär Reichsjustizamt an Reichskanzler (23 August 1917). I am indebted to Jim Robertson for providing me with this last item.

31. Prager, *Geschichte*, pp. 154–55; Kautsky to Adler (4 October 1917), Adler, pp. 640–42. Kautsky's prophecy of decline in the subscribers to the *Neue Zeit* was correct, but since the decline had started at the beginning of the war, it was not a particularly drastic event when, after Kautsky's departure, the subscription list went from about 4,800 to 3,000. The decline through the war years was typical of most of the party journals, while the *Neue Zeit* drop in late 1917 was unique. See *Protokoll*, 1914–17, p. 25, and *Protokoll*, 1919, p. 36. By late 1920, the *Neue Zeit* still had not recovered many of the lost subscribers, and by 1924 the journal had come to an end; see *Protokoll*, 1920, pp. 48–49.

32. *Kriegsmarxismus* (Vienna, 1918); *Volksherrschaft oder Gewaltherrschaft* (Berlin-Bern, 1918), also published in Berlin under the title *Demokratie oder Diktatur; Die Diktatur des Proletariats* (Vienna, 1918); *Sozialdemokratischen Bemerkungen zur Übergangswirtschaft* (Leipzig, 1918).

33. Charles B. Burdick and Ralph H. Lutz, eds., *The Political Institutions of the German Revolution, 1918–1919* (New York, 1966), pp. 70–72 (cabinet meeting of 18 November 1918); Kautsky, "Die Friedensbedingungen," *Freiheit*, 11 May 1919, no. 224; Kautsky to Theodore Dan (23 April 1919), KFA 8.

34. *Staaten*, pp. 54–55.

35. "Eispalast," *NZ* 35:2 (1916–17), 609–13.

36. "Die Aussichten der russischen Revolution," *NZ* 35:2 (1916–17), 9–11. This number of the *Neue Zeit* was dated 6 April 1917.

37. Ibid., pp. 11–12.

38. Ibid., pp. 12–20.

39. Lenin's major contribution to this debate will be dealt with below. Trotsky's major contribution was *Terrorism and Communism: Anti-Kautsky* (1920; rpt. Ann Arbor, 1961) which was a response to Kautsky's *Terrorism and Communism* (1919; rpt. London, 1920). Kautsky responded to Trotsky's book with *Von der Demokratie zur Staats-Sklaverei* (Berlin, 1921). Karl Radek also wrote a response to Kautsky, *Proletarian Dictatorship and Terrorism* (Detroit, 1921). Kautsky wrote two other major attacks on the Bolsheviks, *Die proletarische Revolution und ihr Programm* (Berlin, 1922), translated into English, less the first 63 pages, as *The Labour Revolution* (London, 1925) and *Bolshevism at a Deadlock* (New York, 1931). Kautsky also wrote numerous shorter critiques of the twists and turns of Soviet affairs; these may be found in Blumenberg, pp. 108–33. Of special interest to American readers is one of the shorter critiques which was reprinted in numerous forms in this country, *Communism and Socialism* (New York, 1932), originally published as *Kommunismus und Sozialdemokratie* (Berlin, 1932).

40. *The Dictatorship of the Proletariat* was first published in Vienna in 1918. Large parts of it appeared in Berlin in 1918 under the titles *Volksherrschaft oder Gewaltherrschaft*, *Demokratie oder Diktatur*, and *Der neue Staat*. In 1919, it was reissued, in part, under the title *Gegen die Diktatur*. In addition to the articles in the *Leipziger Volkszeitung* and the

Sozialistische Auslandspolitik, a variation on *Dictatorship* appeared in the Austrian journal *Der Kampf* (8:209-14) in 1920. Lenin's preface and the editor's notes to *The Proletarian Revolution and the Renegade Kautsky* (Peking, 1970) review Lenin's attacks on Kautsky.

41. *The Dictatorship of the Proletariat* (Manchester, 1918), pp. 4-5, 12-15, 27-28, 119-20, 140-41; Kautsky to Pavel Axelrod (16 November 1917), 16:5:88, Nicolaevsky Collection.

42. *Dictatorship,* pp. 19-20, 31-32, 35-38, 42-46, 58, 65-69, 70-71, 73-76, 140-41.

43. Ibid., pp. 15, 24, 27-29, 55-56, 78-81, 88-91, 96-97, 100, 103-04, 108-20, 127, 131-34.

44. Ibid., pp. 12-15, 22, 102-03, 136. I have altered capitalization in this passage.

45. Lenin, *Proletarian Revolution,* pp. 14, 17, 24-25, 32, 38-39, 43-46, 56-62, 65, 99.

46. Ibid., pp. 20, 23, 32, 43-44, 46, 48, 51, 53-54, 65-68, 75, 83, 90-92, 100, 117-18, 120-22. Kautsky remained aloof from the savage moralizing and personal vendettas that increasingly characterized the non-Bolshevik attack on Lenin and the Soviet system. Despite Kautsky's very close relations with the Mensheviks, he did not succumb to the same bitterness that his Russian friends did. When in 1924, at the request of *Izvestia,* he wrote a postmortem evaluation of Lenin, Kautsky praised Lenin's historical role as a leader of the working-class movement, and indulged in no personal recriminations. Apparently the reasoned approach caused many of Kautsky's Menshevik friends to protest, because he had to print an explanation in *Der Kampf* 12 (1924), 176-79. In his justification, Kautsky referred to the need to take into account a person's entire life when making such a postmortem evaluation. He argued that by this standard, Lenin had been a major figure, even though the state he founded continued to be an abomination.

47. Lenin, *Proletarian Revolution,* pp. 121-22.

48. For the German revolution, see A. J. Ryder, *The German Revolution of 1918* (Cambridge, 1967), especially pp. 99-101, 146-49, 171-72, and 180, and Prager, *Geschichte,* pp. 160-71; for the workers' councils, see Eberhard Kolb, *Die Arbeiterräte in der deutschen Innenpolitik, 1918-1919* (Düsseldorf, 1962) and Prager, *Geschichte,* pp. 181-85; for the rejection of the councils as the sole source of the government by the national congress of councils, see "Ein heisser Tag," *Freiheit,* 20 December 1918, no. 20; *Allgemeiner Kongress der Arbeiter- und Soldatenräte Deutschlands, 16-21 Dezember, 1918, Stenographische Berichte* (Berlin, 1919), pp. 141-44, 150, and *Zweite Kongress der Arbeiter-, Bauern- und Soldatenräte Deutschlands, 8-14 April, 1919, Stenographisches Protokoll* (Berlin, 1919), pp. 150-223.

49. "Was will die deutsche socialistische Republik?" handbill (1918), KFA 4; "Über den inneren Gegensatz in der USP," (unpublished article manuscript, KA 83), cited in Kolb, *Arbeiterräte,* p. 207, and Ryder, *German Revolution,* p. 183. Even Kautsky got caught up in the violence in January. On the afternoon of the fifteenth, he was taken prisoner by a group of soldiers and held for a few hours in the barracks of the Fourth Guard regiment. When word of Kautsky's arrest reached the governmental leaders, Ebert was highly distressed. At a joint meeting of the Council of People's Representatives and the *Zentralrat* on 15 January, Ebert said of Kautsky's treatment: "We must find out who was responsible for that, so that he may be properly punished. Kautsky is to be released at once." Soldiers also ransacked the Kautsky's home searching for evidence of a Kautsky-Luxemburg connection. See, "Die Verhaftung Kautskys," *Freiheit,* 16 January 1919, no. 28; Kolb, *Arbeiterräte,* 416 (citing KA, G11); Burdick and Lutz, *Political Institutions,* p. 193.

50. "Das Weitertrieben der Revolution," *Freiheit,* 29 December 1918, no. 79; "Die zweite Phase der Revolution," *Freiheit,* 13 January 1919, no. 23; *Mein Verhältnis,* pp. 11-13. In the latter, written in 1922, Kautsky made the ultimate criticism of Noske, as did many other socialists at that time, by referring to him as the German Gallifet. Gallifet was the commander of the French troops responsible for the massacre of the Communards

in 1871. See also Eberhard Kolb, ed., *Der Zentralrat der deutschen sozialistischen Republik* (Leiden, 1969), p. 240, where an unpublished manuscript by Kautsky ("Die Politik der unabhängigen Sozialdemokratie," KA, 107) is cited for his view that the leftists forced the SPD to the right.

51. Kautsky's fullest discussion of the councils and the constituent assembly was "Nationalversammlung und Räteversammlung," which appeared in the *Freiheit*, 5 and 6 December 1918, nos. 37 and 39, and was reprinted as a pamphlet later in the month. For his view of the councils as revolutionary bodies, see below, and also "Richtlinien für ein sozialistisches Aktions-Programm," a special two-page supplement published by the *Freiheit*, 28 January 1918.

52. Anon., "Deutsche Taktik für die deutsche Revolution!" *Freiheit*, 14 December 1918, no. 54; anon., "Ein heisser Tag," *Freiheit*, 20 December 1918, no. 65; *Mein Verhältnis*, p. 14; USPD, *Protokoll*, March 1919, p. 3; USPD, *Protokoll*, Nov.–Dec. 1919, pp. 3–5.

53. "Kautsky zur Einigungsfrage," and "Einigung," *Freiheit*, 17 May 1919, no. 235, and 13 October 1919, no. 494, respectively.

54. For Kautsky's comments, see USPD, *Protokoll*, March 1919, pp. 123–26, 220–21; for Zetkin's speech, see pp. 128–41, especially, p. 133.

55. USPD, *Protokoll*, March 1919, pp. 117–18; Ryder, *German Revolution*, p. 208. Two months earlier Kautsky had made even more sweeping recommendations for purging the military and bureaucracy in a program proposal. See "Richtlinien," *Freiheit*, 28 January 1919 (special issue). Leftists like Richard Müller, chairman of the executive committee (*Vollzugsrat*) of the Berlin workers' and soldiers' councils, and Emil Barth argued repeatedly for strong measures to reduce the position of the officer corps; see *Vollzugsrat* meeting of 7 December, and cabinet and *Zentralrat* joint meeting of 20 December 1918, in Burdick and Lutz, *Political Institutions*, pp. 88–89, 107–08.

56. Anon., "Die Vorbereitung der Sozialisierung," *Freiheit*, 21 November 1918, no. 12; anon., "Austritt der Unabhängigen aus der Regierung," 29 December 1918, no. 78; Kautsky, *The Guilt of William Hohenzollern* (London, n.d.; translation of *Wie der Weltkrieg entstand*, 1919), pp. 7–8; Ryder, *German Revolution*, pp. 167–68, 188–93; Kolb, *Zentralrat*, p. 316. Though Kautsky officially resigned his office in early January, he continued to work hard to bring the USPD back into the government. On 7 January, as one of the negotiators on the issue, he tried to get a compromise on the SPD's demand that freedom of the press be restored before negotiations began — Spartacists had seized and destroyed 24,000 copies of the *Vorwärts* on the preceding day. Kautsky's proposal that negotiations be reopened on the condition that they lead to restoration of press freedom was rejected, largely because the SPD felt secure in its military position. Kautsky continued through 9 January to try to reopen SPD-USPD negotiations, working through Count Rantzau, the new foreign minister. See conference of the *Zentralrat* and go-betweens, 7 January, and cabinet meeting, 9 January 1919, in Burdick and Lutz, *Political Institutions*, pp. 179–84.

57. *Vom. I. Rätekongress zur Nationalversammlung* (Berlin, 1919), pp. 31–33 (the commission report is reprinted on pp. 32–33); anon., "Die Vorbereitung der Sozialisierung," *Freiheit*, 21 November 1918, no. 12; Kolb, *Zentralrat*, p. 67 n.8; Hermann Müller, *Die November-Revolution* (Berlin, 1928), pp. 197–98; Wolfgang Elben, *Das Problem der Kontinuität in der deutschen Revolution* (Düsseldorf, 1965), p. 82; anon., "Demission der Sozialisierungkommission," *Freiheit*, 9 April 1919, no. 171.

58. "Expropriation und Konfiskation," *Freiheit*, 25 November 1918, no. 19; "Schwierigkeiten der Sozialisierung," *Der Kampf*, 12 (19 July 1919), 469–74.

59. "Expropriation," *Freiheit*, 25 November 1918, no. 19; *Die Sozialisierung und die Arbeiterräte* (Vienna, 1919), pp. 3–7; "Schwierigkeiten," *Der Kampf*, 12 (19 July 1919), 470.

60. "Expropriation," *Freiheit,* 25 November 1918, no. 19; "Richtlinien," *Freiheit,* 28 January 1919 (special issue); *Sozialisierung,* pp. 8-11.

61. "Richtlinien," *Freiheit,* 28 January 1919 (special issue); *Sozialisierung,* pp. 7-8, 11-13.

62. *Sozialisierung,* pp. 15-16; *Zweite Kongress, Protokoll,* p. 243. *Sozialisierung* is the reprinted version of the speech Luise read at the congress, pp. 224-30.

63. Elben, *Problem,* pp. 111-13; *Vollzugsrat* proclamation, 26 November, cabinet meeting, 18 November, *Vollzugsrat* and cabinet meeting, 7 December, cabinet meeting, 9 December, and cabinet meeting, 18 December, in Burdick and Lutz, *Political Institutions,* pp. 62, 72-73, 81, 85-86, 89, 90-92, 99-101; anon., "Spät, aber doch!" *Freiheit,* 12 December 1918, no. 51; anon., "Solfs Rücktritt, *Freiheit,* 18 December 1918, no. 61; anon., "Wechsel im Auswärtigen Amt," *Freiheit,* 21 December 1918, no. 67.

64. Anon., "Ein Skandal," *Freiheit,* 27 November 1918, no. 22; anon., "Das Auswärtige Amt als Friedensstörer," *Freiheit,* 28 November 1918, no. 24; anon., "Die Besetzung des Auswärtige Amtes," *Freiheit,* 29 November 1918, no. 27; Kautsky, "Die Archiv des Auswärtige Amtes, *Freiheit,* 1 December 1918, no. 30; Kautsky, *Guilt,* pp. 7-8.

65. Max Montgelas and Walter Schücking, eds. *Die deutschen Dokumente zum Kriegsausbruch* (1919; rpt. Berlin, 1921); Kautsky, *Guilt,* pp. 8-11. Kautsky received neither pay for his work on the documents from January through November 1919, nor royalties of any sort following publication. Five years later, Kautsky gave his approval to a new edition of the documents, agreed with Schücking and Montgelas that if a private publisher were to reissue the work, the three of them should receive some royalties, but he declined to write a foreword for the new edition. See Schücking to Kautsky (16 May 1924), and Kautsky to Schücking (26 May 1924), KFA 5.

66. *Guilt,* pp. 14, 63-64, 247, 257-69.

67. Hans Delbrück, *Kautsky und Harden* (Berlin, 1920), pp. 6-33; Theodore Schiemann, *Deutschland und Kaiser Wilhelms II. angebliche Schuld am Ausbruch des Weltkrieges.* (Berlin, 1921); Friedrich Freksa, *Menschliche Rechtfertigung Wilhelms II* (Munich, 1920). Hans Helmholt, another prominent historian, also wrote a critique: *Kautsky, der Historiker* (Charlottenburg, 1920). Kautsky wrote a reply to Delbrück: *Delbrück und Wilhelm II* (Berlin, 1920).

68. Kautsky to Benedikt (31 July 1919), Bebel, pp. xxxix-xl. Kautsky's prewar ambiguity on the question of political revolution and its relationship to social revolution is well represented by this passage from his 1902 work, *The Social Revolution:* "The conquest of state power by a previously oppressed class, that is, political revolution, is therefore an essential sign of social revolution in the narrower sense, in contrast to social reform" (p. 6). This view clearly presupposes a much closer temporal relationship between political and social revolution than Kautsky postulated after the war.

69. *Mein Verhältnis,* pp. 14-16; *Georgia: A Social Democratic Republic* (London, 1921). See Robert C. Tucker, *Stalin As Revolutionary, 1879-1929* (New York, 1973), pp. 67-69, for Kautsky's influence on Jordania, Menshevik leader of the Georgian republic, 1918-21.

Chapter Seven: Return to Vienna, 1924-1938

1. Kautsky to Irakli Tseretelli (7 June 1921, 21 October 1927, 20 January 1928, 18 May 1930), Kautsky to Garwy (1 February 1929), 15:3:23, Nicolaevsky Collection; Kautsky to liebe, teure Genossen (circular letter to exiled Georgian Mensheviks, 16 March 1923), KA G17; Kautsky to Theodore Dan (23 April 1929), KFA 8. In what was his strongest denunciation of the Soviet regime to that time, *Die Internationale und Sowjetrussland* (Berlin, 1925), Kautsky discussed the pro- and anti-popular uprising forces at work in

Russia (pp. 18, 20–21, 32–38), renounced armed intervention as too bloody and probably counterproductive (pp. 56–57), but rejected the Bolsheviks as potential comrades because of their slaughter of "brother socialists" and their reliance on brutal suppression at home and conspiracy against foreign socialist parties (p. 6). In this work, he referred to the Bolsheviks as "the most dangerous enemy of the proletariat" (p. 6).

2. Kautsky to Genossen (16 March 1923), KA G17; "Demokratie und Diktatur," *Der Kampf* 26 (1933), 45–58.

3. Kautsky to Garwy (1 February 1929), Kautsky to Tseretelli (18 May, 1 June, 15 June 1930), 15:3:23, Nicolaevsky Collection; Kautsky to Dan (3 June 1929), KFA 8.

4. Kautsky to Garwy (1 February 1929), 15:3:23, Nicolaevsky Collection; Kautsky to Dan (3 June 1929), KFA 8. During the early and mid-1890s, Kautsky had made the same "compromise in practice, but not in theory" distinction while urging the SPD to engage in the Prussian Landtag elections. See above, chap. 4.

5. USPD, *Protokoll*, March 1919, pp. 115–16, 123, 125–26, 220–21; Zetkin's harsh rebuttal to Kautsky is on pp. 136–38. For an account of this Bern conference (there was another in 1920), see Wheeler, "Independent Social Democratic Party," pp. 155–86. Wheeler argues that Kautsky's speech on "democracy and dictatorship" was not entirely hostile to the Bolsheviks (pp. 184–85), and also points out that like many others at the conference, Kautsky wrongly attributed the final resolution on the matter to Kurt Eisner (pp. 177–80).

6. USPD, *Protokoll*, March 1919, p. 221; "Judas in Luzern," *Freiheit*, 20 August 1919, no. 397; *Die Internationale* (Vienna, 1920), pp. 54–59, 65–67, 78–80.

7. Fritz Brügel, *Der Weg der Internationale* (Vienna, 1931), pp. 14–16; Josef Lenz, *Die II. Internationale und ihr Erbe, 1889–1929* (Berlin, 1930), pp. 180–207, 221–29; *Protokoll der internationalen sozialistischen Konferenz in Wien vom 22. bis 27. Februar 1921* (Vienna, 1921), pp. 6–7.

8. Friedrich Adler to Kautsky (9 September 1924, 10 August 1930), KFA 2. An example of Kautsky's differences with the L.S.I. and the Austrian party is the article "Demokratie und Diktatur." It was published in *Der Kampf*, an official journal of the Austrian party, with a note announcing that neither the editorial staff nor the party agreed completely with the views Kautsky expressed. In the same number of *Der Kampf*, the correspondence between Friedrich Adler and Kautsky concerning the latter's article was published. See "Zur Diskussion über Sowjetrussland," *Der Kampf,* 26 (1933), 58–69. Kautsky also took a hard line on the question of a united front. See "Ein Verfechter der Einheitsfront," *Der Kampf,* 21 (1928), 446–52. This, too, was at odds with official L.S.I. policy. There is no survey of the L.S.I.; for its policy positions, see its *Second Congress: Report of the Secretariat,* and *Congress Report* (London, 1926); *Third Congress: Reports and Proceedings* (Brussels, 1928); *Fourth Congress: Reports and Proceedings* (Vienna, 1931); and the *Fifth Congress: Protokoll* (Paris, 1933). Official delegate lists are included at the end of the congress reports. For the delegates at Paris, see *After the German Catastrophe* (Zurich, 1933).

9. L.S.I. fourth congress dossier, Hoover Institution; *Arbeiter-Zeitung* 44:205, 27 July 1931; *Festschrift zur 2. Arbeiter-Olympiade* (Vienna, 1931).

10. Fritz Brügel, "Der Weg der Internationale," *Der Jugendliche Arbeiter* 7 (1931), 9 (later reprinted in longer form as *Der Weg der Internationale* [Vienna, 1931]; see pp. 9–10 for quote on Kautsky); *Die materialistische Geschichtsauffassung,* 2 vols. (Berlin, 1927), p. xii (foreword).

11. Axelrod to Kautsky (5 December 1927), 16:5:84, Nicolaevsky Collection; Garwy to Kautsky (10 November 1927), KFA 3.

12. *Geschichts.*, I, v, 21, 119–27, 140, 197–98, 424–75, II, 630–31; Lenin, *Materialism and*

Empirio-Criticism (1908; rpt. Peking, 1972), p. 420. On pp. 119-27 of his book, Kautsky discussed Ernst Mach's notion of "functional dependence" as an alternative to the cause-and-effect principle. Despite the urgings of Friedrich Adler to the contrary, Kautsky stuck to cause and effect. To substantiate his assertion about the reality of the external world, Kautsky converted Descartes' *cognito, ergo sum* to *ago, ergo sum* ("I act, therefore I am"). He contended that the ability of humans to act, and to perceive the results of their actions, verified not only personal existence, but also the reality of the extrapersonal world (pp. 112-13).

13. Karl Korsch, "Die materialistische Geschichtsauffassung: Eine Auseinandersetzung mit Karl Kautsky," *Archiv für die Geschichte des Sozialismus und der Arbeiterbewegung* 14 (1929), 181, 196-213. Korsch and Kautsky had had previous literary confrontations. See Kautsky's review of Korsch's *Marxismus und Philosophie* (Leipzig, 1923), in *Die Gesellschaft* 1 (1924), 306-14. Here Kautsky took offense at Korsch's observation that the entire second half of the nineteenth century saw a "flattening and impoverishment of the teachings of Marx into vulgar Marxism." For a discussion of Karl Korsch (1886-1961), see Claudio Pozzoli, ed., *Über Karl Korsch* (Frankfurt a.M., 1973).

14. *Geschichts.*, I, vii, 65, 127, 197-98, 791; Kautsky to Dan (23 April 1929), KFA 8.

15. *Geschichts.*, I, 107, 136, 241-306, 570-700, 790, II, passim. In an earlier work devoted to a refutation of Bernstein's insistence on coupling Kantian ethics with Marxism, *Ethics and the Materialist Conception of History* (1906; rpt. Chicago, 1914), Kautsky called changes in techniques of production "the foundation of the entire development of man" (p. 122).

16. "Imperialismus und reaktionäre Masse," *NZ* 35:2 (1916-17), 102-15; *Geschichts.*, I, 1-7, II, 620.

17. *Geschichts.*, I, xv, II, 681. Even after writing *The Materialist Conception*, Kautsky repeated the standard Marxist rejection of absolutes. In "Marxism and Bolshevism," in *Socialism, Fascism, Communism*, ed. Joseph Shaplen and David Shub (New York, 1934), he rejected "doctrinaire fanaticism" as "contrary to Marxist thought, which recognizes no absolute truth but only relative truth" (p. 176).

18. "Hitlerism and Social Democracy," in *Socialism*, ed. Shaplen and Shub, pp. 53-57, 68, 70-71, 86, 92; "Einige Ursachen und Wirkungen des deutschen Nationalsozialismus," *Der Kampf* 26 (1933), 235-45; "Die blutige Revolution," *Der Kampf* 26 (1933), 346-61; Kautsky to Garwy (30 August 1938), KFA 8. The letter to Garwy is reprinted in *Ein Leben für den Sozialismus* (Hanover, 1954), pp. 109-10.

19. "Hitlerism," pp. 73-78, 81, 89, 92, 96, 99-102; "Marxism and Bolshevism," pp. 213-14; Kautsky to Algernon Lee (22 December 1935), KFA 8.

20. Gregory Bienstock to Kautsky (30 December 1933), KFA 2. A portion of this letter is reproduced in *E&E*, p. 7.

21. Kautsky to Bienstock (15 January 1934), KFA 8; "Hitlerism," p. 102. A portion of the letter to Bienstock is reproduced in *E&E*, p. 8.

22. Kautsky to Algernon Lee (7 July 1935), KFA 8; Oscar Pollack to Kautsky (9 March 1933), KFA 8; *Aus der Frühzeit des Marxismus* (Prague, 1935).

23. *Krieg und Demokratie* (Berlin, 1932); *Sozialisten und Krieg* (Prague, 1937). For Kautsky's plans for the four volumes, see *Krieg*, p. vii; for the bizarre fate of the second volume, see *Sozialisten*, pp. v-vi.

24. KFA 118:3 is a collection of letters and clippings concerning Kautsky's nomination for the Nobel peace prize; Paul Olberg, "Karl Kautsky als Kandidat für den Nobel-Friedenspreis 1938," in *Ein Leben für den Sozialismus*, pp. 103-08. Albert Einstein refused to support Kautsky's nomination. See George Garvy, "Albert Einstein and the Nobel Peace Prize for Karl Kautsky," *IRSH* 18 (1973), 107-10.

25. Bruno, review of Karl Kautsky, *Sozialismus* [sic] *und Krieg,* in *Der einzige Weg: Zeitschrift für die Vierte Internationale* 1 (1937), 27-28.

26. *E&E,* pp. 6, 15-16; interviews with Dr, Karl Kautsky, Jr., summer 1972, 1975-76; Benedikt Kautsky to Friedrich Adler (8 June 1945), Benedikt to Felix (24 July 1945), in B. Kautsky, *Luise Kautsky,* pp. 30, 34-40.

27. Interviews with Dr. Kautsky. Benedikt Kautsky wrote an account of the concentration camp experience. *Teufel und Verdammte* (Zurich, 1946).

28. *Luise Kautsky,* pp. 3, 10-12, 17-23, 30.

29. *Bernstein und das sozialdemokratische Programm,* pp. 42-49.

30. "Marxism and Bolshevism," p. 192.

31. Ibid., p. 182.

32. Ibid., p. 181; Rafael Abramowitch to Kautsky (14 October 1930, 5 September 1932), KFA 1:1; Kautsky to Algernon Lee (8 July 1935), KFA 8.

Bibliography

WERNER BLUMENBERG'S *Karl Kautskys literarisches Werk* (The Hague, 1960) is an invaluable catalog of Kautsky's published works. My task would have been immensely more difficult and time-consuming without it. In the list of works that follows, I have not included those items cited in Blumenberg, but have limited myself to works published after his study and to the few items I uncovered that Blumenberg had not listed.

A massive collection of Kautsky's letters and personal papers, over eleven thousand items, is at the International Institute for Social History in Amsterdam. This collection was arranged and cataloged by the Institute with the help of Dr. and Mrs. Karl Kautsky, Jr. The Hoover Institution, Stanford, California, also has many items relating to Kautsky, especially letters to and from Russian socialists in the Nicolaevsky Collection. Kautsky's own memoirs, *Erinnerungen und Erörterungen* (The Hague, 1960), are indispensable for the years up to 1883. Much of Kautsky's correspondence with leading figures of the international socialist movement has been published. The Adler letters appeared in Victor Adler, *Briefwechsel mit August Bebel und Karl Kautsky* (Vienna, 1954), edited by Friedrich Adler. Dr. Kautsky edited the Bebel letters in *August Bebels Briefwechsel mit Karl Kautsky* (Assen, 1971). Kautsky's correspondence with Engels first appeared in an edition done by Kautsky himself, *Aus der Frühzeit des Marxismus* (Prague, 1935), and, following the discovery of Kautsky's letters to Engels, in a more complete edition edited by Kautsky's youngest son, Benedikt, *Friedrich Engels' Briefwechsel mit Karl Kautsky* (Vienna, 1955). Of the major blocks of correspondence, only that between Kautsky and Bernstein and Kautsky and his second wife, Luise Ronsperger, remain to be published. In addition, the published correspondence of other leading figures of social democracy, listed below, contains references to and occasional letters from Kautsky.

Abendroth, Wolfgang. *Aufstieg und Krise der deutschen Sozialdemokratie.* Frankfurt, 1964.
Adamiak, Richard. "Marx, Engels, and Dühring." *Journal of the History of Ideas* 35 (January–March, 1974), 98–112.
After the German Catastrophe. Zurich, 1933.
Allgemeiner Kongress der Arbeiter- und Soldatenräte Deutschlands, 16–21 Dezember 1918. Stenographische Berichte. Berlin, 1919.
Anders, Karl. *Die ersten hundert Jahre.* Hanover, 1963.
Antrick, Otto, Jr. "Karl Kautsky und der Balkenkrieg, 1912." *Gesellschaft, Recht und Politik. W. Abendroth z. 60. Geb.* Edited by H. Maus. Neuwied, 1968.

Ascher, Abraham. "Axelrod and Kautsky." *Slavic Review* 26 (1967), 94–112.

———. "Imperialists Within German Social Democracy Prior to 1914." *Journal of Central European Affairs* 20 (1961), 397–422.

———. " 'Radical' Imperialists Within German Social Democracy, 1912–1918." *Political Science Quarterly* 76 (1961), 555–75.

Ashley, William J. *The Progress of the German Working Class in the Last Quarter of a Century.* London, 1904.

Balfour, Michael. *The Kaiser and His Times.* Boston, 1964.

Barkin, Kenneth D. *The Controversy Over German Industrialization, 1890–1902.* Chicago, 1970.

———. "Conflict and Concord in Wilhelmian Social Thought." *Central European History* 3 (March 1972), 55–71.

Baron, Samuel H. *Plekhanov: The Father of Russian Marxism.* Stanford, 1963.

Bartel, Horst. "Zur Politik und zum Kampf der deutschen Sozialdemokratie gegen die Bismarcksche Sozialpolitik und gegen den Rechtopportunismus in den Jahren 1881–84." *Zeitschrift für Geschichtswissenschaft* 6 (1958), 1089–1106.

Bartel, Walter. *Die Linken in der deutschen Sozialdemokratie im Kampf gegen Militarismus und Krieg.* Berlin, 1958.

Bauer, Otto. "Karl Kautsky und der Bolshevismus." *Der Kampf* 12 (1919), 661–67.

Bebel, August. *Aus meinen Leben.* 3 vols. Stuttgart, 1910–14.

———. *Die Sozialdemokratie im deutschen Reichstage.* Berlin, 1909.

Bechtel, Heinrich. *Wirtschaftsgeschichte Deutschlands im 19. und 20. Jahrhundert.* Munich, 1956.

———. *Wirtschafts- und Sozialgeschichte Deutschlands.* Munich, 1967.

Bergsträsser, Ludwig. *Die Entwicklung des Parlamentarismus in Deutschland.* Laupheim, 1954.

———. *Geschichte der politischen Parteien in Deutschland.* Berlin, 1924.

Berlau, Abraham. *The German Social Democratic Party, 1914–1921.* New York, 1949.

Bernstein, Eduard. *Die deutsche Revolution.* Berlin, 1921.

———. *Eduard Bernsteins Briefwechsel mit Friedrich Engels.* Edited by Helmut Hirsch. Assen, 1970.

———. "The German Elections and the Social Democrats." *Contemporary Review,* April 1907, pp. 479–92.

———. *My Years of Exile: Reminiscences of a Socialist.* London, 1921.

———. *Die Voraussetzungen des Sozialismus und die Aufgaben der Sozialdemokratie.* Berlin, 1899.

Bernstein, Eduard, ed. *Die Briefe von Friedrich Engels an Eduard Bernstein mit Briefen von Karl Kautsky an ebendenselben.* Berlin, 1925.

Bertram, Jürgen. *Die Wahlen zum Deutschen Reichstag vom Jahre 1912: Parteien und Verbände in der Innenpolitik des Wilhelminischen Reiches.* Düsseldorf, 1964.

Bevan, Edwyn. *German Social Democracy During the War.* London, 1918.

Biehahn, Walter. "Die Kautsky-Legende." *Internationale* 7:23/24 (1924), 700–07.

Blank, Robert. "Die soziale Zusammensetzung der sozialdemokratischen Wählerschaft Deutschlands." *Archiv für Sozialwissenschaft und Sozialpolitik* 20 (1905), 507–53.

Blos, Wilhelm. *Denkwurdigkeiten eines Sozialdemokraten.* 2 vols. Munich, 1914–19.

Blumenberg, Werner, ed. *August Bebels Briefwechsel mit Friedrich Engels.* The Hague, 1965.

Böttcher, Ulrich. *Anfänge und Entwicklung der Arbeiterbewegung in Bremen.* Bremen, 1953.

Bolle, Fritz. "Darwinismus und Zeitgeist." *Zeitschrift für Religion und Geistesgeschichte* 14 (1962), 143–78.

Born, Karl E. *Moderne Deutsche Wirtschaftsgeschichte.* Berlin, 1966.

————. *Staat und Sozialpolitik seit Bismarcks Sturz: Ein Beitrag zur Geschichte der innenpolitischen Entwicklung des deutschen Reiches, 1890–1914.* Wiesbaden, 1957.

Braunthal, Julius. *History of the International, 1864–1914.* 2 vols. New York, 1967.

————. *Victor and Friedrich Adler: Zwei Generationen Arbeiterbewegung.* Vienna, 1965.

Brill, Hermann. "Karl Kautsky." *Zeitschrift für Politik* 3 (September 1954), 211–40.

Brügel, Fritz. *Der Weg der Internationale.* Vienna, 1931.

Brügel, Ludwig. *Geschichte der österreichischen Sozialdemokratie.* 4 vols. Vienna, 1922–23.

Bry, Gerhard. *Wages in Germany, 1871–1945.* Princeton, 1960.

Buckle, Thomas Henry. *History of Civilization in England.* 2 vols. New York, 1939.

Buchheim, Karl. *Das deutsche Kaiserreich, 1871–1918: Vorgeschichte, Aufstieg und Niedergang.* Munich, 1969.

Büchner, Ludwig. *Force and Matter.* New York, 1891.

Bukharin, Nikolai. *La bourgeoisie internationale et son apôtre Karl Kautsky.* Paris, 1925.

Burdick, Charles B., and Lutz, Ralph H., eds. *The Political Institutions of the German Revolution, 1918–1919.* New York, 1966.

Butschek, Felix. "Die Geburt des modern Sozialismus." *Zukunft* 2:48–51, 3:82–87.

Calkins, Kenneth R. "The Election of Hugo Haase to the Co-chairmanship of the SPD and the Crisis of Prewar German Social Democracy." *International Review of Social History* 13 (1968), 174–88.

Cecil, Lamar. *Albert Ballin: Business and Politics in Imperial Germany, 1888–1918.* Princeton, 1967.

Chalmers, Douglas A. *The Social Democratic Party of Germany.* New Haven, 1964.

Chickering, Roger. *Imperial Germany and a World Without War.* Princeton, 1975.

Clapham, John H. *The Economic Development of France and Germany, 1815–1914.* Cambridge, 1936.

Cohen, Stephen F. *Bukharin and the Bolshevik Revolution: A Political Biography, 1888–1938.* New York, 1973.

Compte rendu sténographique non officiel du cinquième Congrès socialiste international tenu à Paris du 23 au 27 septembre 1900. Paris, n.d.

Conrad-Martius, Hedwig. *Utopien der Menschenzüchtung: Der Sozialdarwinismus und seine Folgen.* Munich, 1954.

Cornu, Auguste. *The Origins of Marxian Thought.* Springfield, Ill., 1957.

Crothers, George D. *The German Elections of 1907.* New York, 1941.

Cunow, Heinrich. *Partei-zusammenbruch? Ein offenes Wort zum inneren Parteistreit.* Berlin, 1915.

Dade, Heinrich. *Die landwirtschaftliche Bevölkerung des deutschen Reichs um die Wende des 19. Jahrhunderts.* Berlin, 1903.

Dahrendorf, Ralf. *Society and Democracy in Germany.* Garden City, N.Y., 1967.

David, Eduard. *Sozialismus und Landwirtschaft.* Berlin, 1903.

Dawson, William H. *The Evolution of Modern Germany.* New York, 1919.

Deak, Istvan. *Weimar Germany's Left-Wing Intellectuals.* Berkeley, 1968.

Delbrück, Hans. *Kautsky und Harden.* Berlin, 1920.

Denis, Ernest. *Kautsky et la Serbie.* Paris, 1918.

Deutscher Sozialistentag: Protokoll der Konferenz für Einigung der Sozialdemokratie. Berlin, 1919.

Deville, Gabriel. *The People's Marx.* Translated by Robert R. La Monte. New York, 1900.

Dokumente und Materialien zur Geschichte der deutschen Arbeiterbewegung. Vol. 4, 1898 bis 1914. Berlin, 1967.

Domann, Peter. *Sozialdemokratie und Kaisertum unter Wilhelm II.* Wiesbaden, 1974.

Dornemann, Louise. *Clara Zetkin*. Berlin, 1957.

Eckert, Georg. *Wilhelm Bracke und die Anfänge der Braunschweiger Arbeiterbewegung*. Brunswick, 1957.

Eckert, Georg, ed. *Wilhelm Liebknechts Briefwechsel mit deutschen Sozialdemokraten*. Vol. 1, *1862-1878*. Assen, 1973.

Eichler, Willi. *Hundert Jahre Sozialdemokratie*. Bonn, 1962.

Eisner, Kurt. *Gesammelte Schriften*. Berlin, 1919.

Elben, Wolfgang. *Das Problem der Kontinuität in der deutschen Revolution*. Düsseldorf, 1965.

Engelberg, Ernst. *Deutschland von 1871 bis 1897: Deutschland in der Übergangsperiode zum Imperialismus*. Berlin, 1965.

Engels, Friedrich. *Anti-Dühring*. London, 1943.

———. *The Condition of the Working Class in England*. London, 1844.

Engels, Friedrich, and Lafargue, Paul and Laura. *Correspondence*. Translated by Yvonne Kapp. 3 vols. Moscow, 1960.

Ensor, Robert C. K. *Modern Socialism*. London, 1904.

Erdmann, August. *Die Sozialdemokratie im Urteile ihrer Gegner*. Berlin, 1911.

Erenyi, Tibor. "The Activities of the Social Democratic Party of Hungary During the First Decade of the Century." In *Studies on the History of the Hungarian Working-Class Movement, 1867-1966*, ed. Henrik Vass, pp. 55–88. Budapest, 1975.

Fetscher, Iring. *Marxistische Porträts*. Vol. 1., *Politiker*. Stuttgart, 1975.

———. "Das Verhältnis der Marxismus zu Hegel." *Marxismusstudien* 3 (1960), 66–169.

———. "Von der Philosophie des Proletariats zur proletarischer Weltanschauung." *Marxismusstudien* 2 (1957), 26–60.

Finck von Finckenstein, Hans Wolfram. *Die Entwicklung der Landwirtschaft in Preussen und Deutschland, 1800-1930*. Würzburg, 1960.

Fischer, Fritz. *World Power or Decline*. New York, 1974.

Frauendienst, Werner. *Das Deutsche Reich, 1890-1914*. Konstanz, 1959.

Freksa, Friedrich. *Menschliche Rechtfertigung Wilhelms II: Gegen die Kautsky Mache*. Munich, 1920.

Fricke, Dieter. *Bismarcks Prätorianer: Die Berliner politische Polizei im Kampf gegen die deutsche Arbeiter, 1871-1898*. Berlin, 1962.

———. *Die deutsche Arbeiterbewegung, 1869-1890*. Leipzig, 1964.

———. "Der Reichsverband gegen die Sozialdemokratie von seiner Gründung bis zu den Reichstagwahlen von 1907." *Zeitschrift für Geschichtswissenschaft* 7 (1959), 237–80.

Friesen, Abraham. "The Marxist Interpretation of the Reformation." Ph.D. diss., Stanford University, 1967.

Fröhlich, Paul. *Rosa Luxemburg; Gedanke und Tat*. Hamburg, 1949.

Garvy, George. "Albert Einstein and the Nobel Peace Prize for Karl Kautsky." *International Review of Social History* 18 (1973), 107–10.

Gasman, Daniel. *The Scientific Origins of National Socialism: Social Darwinism in Ernst Haeckel and the German Monist League*. London, 1971.

Gay, Peter. *The Dilemma of Democratic Socialism: Eduard Bernstein's Challenge to Marx*. New York, 1962.

Geyer, Dietrich. "Die russische Parteispaltung im Urteil der deutschen Sozialdemokratie, 1903-1905." *International Review of Social History* 3 (1958), 195–219, 418–44.

Gilg, Peter. *Die Erneuerung des demokratischen Denkens im wilhelminischen Deutschland*. Wiesbaden, 1965.

Groh, Dieter. "Marx, Engels und Darwin: Naturgesetzliche Entwicklung oder Revolution?" *Politische Vierteljahresschrift* 8 (1967), 544–59.

――――. *Negative Integration und revolutionärer Attentismus: Die deutsche Sozialdemokratie am Vorabend des I. Weltkrieges 1909–1914*. Frankfurt, 1973.

Grunenberg, Antonia, ed. *Die Massenstreikdebatte: Beiträge von Parvus, Rosa Luxemburg, Karl Kautsky and Anton Pannekoek*. Frankfurt, 1970.

Gulick, Charles A. *Austria from Habsburg to Hitler*. Berkeley, 1948.

Haeckel, Ernst. *The History of Creation*. 2 vols. London, 1876.

Hammann, Otto. *Was nun? Zur Geschichte der Socialistischen Arbeiterpartei in Deutschland*. Berlin, 1889.

Harcave, Sidney. *First Blood: The Russian Revolution of 1905*. New York, 1964.

Haushofer, Heinz. *Die deutsche Landwirtschaft im technischen Zeitalter*. Stuttgart, 1963.

Hautmann, Hans, and Kropf, Rudolph. *Die österreichische Arbeiterbewegung vom Vormärz bis 1945*. Vienna, 1974.

Havranek, Jan. "The Development of Czech Nationalism." *Austrian History Yearbook* 3 (1967), 223–60.

Heidegger, H. *Die deutsche Sozialdemokratie und der nationale Staat: 1879–1920*. Göttingen, 1956.

Helfferich, Karl. *Germany's Economic Progress and National Wealth, 1888–1913*. New York, 1914.

Helmholt, Hans. *Kautsky, der Historiker*. Charlottenburg, 1920.

Hesselbarth, Hellmut. "Der aufkommende Revisionismus in der Bauernfrage und Karl Kautsky," *Marxismus und deutsche Arbeiterbewegung* (Berlin, 1970), pp. 365–97.

Hilferding, Rudolf. *Das Finanzkapital*. Frankfurt, 1968.

Hirsch, Paul. *Der preussische Landtag: Handbuch für sozialdemokratische Landtagswählen*. Berlin, 1908.

Hobsbawn, E. J. *The Age of Revolution, 1789–1848*. Cleveland, 1962.

Hobson, John A. *Imperialism*. London, 1940.

Hodges, Donald C. "Engels' Contribution to Marxism." *The Socialist Register 1965* (New York, 1965), pp. 297–310.

Holzheuer, Walter. *Karl Kautskys Werk als Weltanschauung*. Munich, 1972.

Howard, Earl D. *The Cause and Extent of the Recent Industrial Progress of Germany*. New York, 1907.

Hunt, Richard N. *German Social Democracy, 1918–1933*. New Haven, 1964.

Institut für Marxismus-Leninismus. *Geschichte der deutschen arbeiter Bewegung*. Vol. 2, *Vom Ausgang des 19. Jahrhunderts bis 1917*. Berlin, 1966.

――――. *Geschichte der deutschen Arbeiterbewegung: Chronik*. Pt. 1, *Von den Anfängen bis 1917*. Berlin, 1965.

L'Internationale socialiste a cent ans, 1864–1964. Brussels, 1964.

Internationaler Sozialisten-Kongress, Stuttgart, 1907. Berlin, 1907.

Jansen, Reinhard. *Georg von Vollmar: Eine politische Biographie*. Düsseldorf, 1958.

Jarausch, Konrad H. *The Enigmatic Chancellor: Bethmann Hollweg and the Hubris of Imperial Germany*. New Haven, 1973.

Jenssen, Otto. "Kautsky als Historiker." *Der Kampf* 12 (1919), 690–92.

Johnston, William M. *The Austrian Mind: An Intellectual and Social History, 1848–1938*. Berkeley, 1973.

Joll, James. *The Second International*. New York, 1960.

Jordan, Z. A. *The Evolution of Dialectical Materialism*. New York, 1967.

Kantorowicz, Ludwig. *Die sozialdemokratische Presse Deutschlands*. Tübingen, 1922.

Kapp, Yvonne. *Eleanor Marx*. London, 1972.

Karl Kautsky: Der Denker und Kämpfer. Vienna, 1924.

Kautsky, Benedikt. "Karl Kautsky: Persönliche Erinnerungen an meinen Vater." *Arbeiterkalender, 1954* (Vienna), pp. 102–22.

———. *Teufel und Verdammte: Erfahrungen und Erkenntnisse aus sieben Jahre in deutschen Konzentrationslage.* Zurich, 1946.

Kautsky, Benedikt, ed. *Luise Kautsky zum Gedenken.* New York, 1945.

Kautsky, John H. "J. A. Schumpeter and Karl Kautsky: Parallel Theories of Imperialism." *Midwest Journal of Political Science* 5:2 (May 1961), 101–28.

———. "The Political Thoughts of Karl Kautsky." Ph.D. diss., Harvard University, 1951.

Kautsky, Karl. "Aus der Partei: Bernstein und Kautsky über ihren Aufruf." *Vorwärts,* 11 July 1915.

———. "Hitlerism and Social Democracy." In *Socialism, Fascism, Communism,* ed. Joseph Shaplen and David Shub, pp. 53–102. New York, 1934.

———. "Marxism and Bolshevism—Democracy and Dictatorship." In *Socialism, Fascism, Communism,* ed. Joseph Shaplen and David Shub, pp. 174–215. New York, 1934.

———. *Les trois sources du marxisme; l'oeuvre historique de Marx. Reproduction d'une conference faite en 1907 à Breme.* Paris, 1947.

Kautsky, Luise. *Rosa Luxemburg: Ein Gedenkbuch.* Berlin, 1929.

Kessler, Gerhard. *Die deutschen Arbeitgeberverbände.* Leipzig, 1907.

Kirschner, Lawrence B. "The Bernstein Debate: The Opposition to Revisionism in German Social Democracy, 1898–1903." MA diss., New York University, 1963.

Kohn, Hans. *The Hapsburg Empire, 1804–1918.* Princeton, 1961.

———. *Not by Arms Alone.* Cambridge, Mass., 1940.

Kolb, Eberhard. *Die Arbeiterräte in der deutschen Innenpolitik, 1918–1919.* Düsseldorf, 1962.

Kolb, Eberhard, ed. *Der Zentralrat der deutschen sozialistischen Republik, 19.12. 1918–8.4.1919.* Leiden, 1969.

Korsch, Karl. "Die materialistische Geschichtsauffassung: Eine Auseinandersetzung mit Karl Kautsky." *Archiv für die Geschichte des Sozialismus und der Arbeiterbewegung* 14:2 (1929), 179–279.

Kuczynski, Jürgen. *A Short History of Labour Conditions Under Industrial Capitalism in Germany: 1800 to the Present Day.* London, 1945.

Kuhn, Axel, ed. *Deutsche Parlamentsdebatten.* Vol. 1, *1871–1918.* Frankfurt a.M., 1970.

Labour and Socialist International. *Second Congress: Report of the Secretariat. Congress Report.* London, 1926.

———. *Third Congress. Reports and Proceedings.* Brussels, 1928.

———. *Fourth Congress. Reports and Proceedings.* Vienna, 1931.

———. *Fifth Congress. Protokoll.* Paris, 1933.

Lademacher, Horst. "Zu den Anfängen der deutschen Sozialdemokratie, 1863–1878." *International Review of Social History* 4 (1959), 239–60, 367–93.

Lahdiri, Tayeb. *Lenins Revolutionstheorie und Kautskys Kritik an der bolschewistichen Revolution.* Frankfurt, 1965.

Laschitza, Annelies. "Karl Kautsky und der Zentrismus." *Beiträge zur Geschichte der deutschen Arbeiterbewegung* 5 (1968), 798–832.

Laufenberg, Heinrich. *Geschichte der Arbeiterbewegung in Hamburg, Altona and Umgegend.* 2 vols. Hamburg, 1911–31.

Ledebour, Minna, ed. *Georg Ledebour, Mensch und Kämpfer.* Zurich, 1947.

Lehmann, Hans G. *Die Argarfrage in der Theorie und Praxis der deutschen und internationalen Sozialdemokratie.* Tübingen, 1970.

Lenin, V. I. *Imperialism, the Highest Stage of Capitalism.* New York, 1933.

——. *Materialism and Empirio-Criticism.* Peking, 1972.
——. *The Proletarian Revolution and the Renegade Kautsky.* Peking, 1970.
——. *What is to Be Done?.* Moscow, 1947.
Lensch, Paul. *Die deutsche Sozialdemokratie und der Weltkrieg.* Berlin, 1915.
Lenz, Josef. *Die II. Internationale und ihr Erbe, 1889–1929.* Berlin, 1930.
Lerner, Warren. *Karl Radek: The Last Internationalist.* Stanford, 1970.
Leser, Norbert. *Zwischen Reformismus und Bolshewismus: Der Austromarxismus als Theorie und Praxis.* Vienna, 1968.
Lichtheim, George. *Marxism: An Historical and Critical Study.* New York, 1961.
——. *The Origins of Socialism.* New York, 1969.
Lidtke, Vernon L. "German Social Democracy and German State Socialism, 1876–1884." *International Review of Social History* 9 (1964), 202–25.
——. *The Outlawed Party: Social Democracy in Germany, 1878–1890.* Princeton, 1966.
Liebknecht, Wilhelm. *Briefwechsel mit Karl Marx und Friedrich Engels.* Edited by Georg Eckert. The Hague, 1963.
Lösche, Peter. *Der Bolshewismus im Urteil der deutschen Sozialdemokratie, 1903–1920.* Berlin, 1967.
Lucas, Erhard. "Marx' und Engels' Auseinandersetzung mit Darwin: Zur Differenz zwischen Marx und Engels." *International Review of Social History* 9 (1964), 433–69.
Luxemburg, Rosa. *Briefe an Freunde.* Edited by Benedikt Kautsky. Hamburg, 1950.
——. *Gesammelte Werke.* Edited by Paul Fröhlich. 6 vols. Berlin, 1923–28.
——. *Letters to Karl and Luise Kautsky from 1896 to 1918.* Edited by Luise Kautsky. Translated by Louis P. Lochner. New York, 1925.
Macartney, Carlile. *The Habsburg Empire, 1790–1918.* London, 1968.
Maehl, William H. *German Militarism and Socialism.* Lincoln, Neb., 1968.
Mandelbaum, Kurt. *Die Erörterungen innerhalb der deutschen Sozialdemokratie über das Problem des Imperialismus, 1895–1914.* Frankfurt, 1927.
Marcuse, Herbert. *Reason and Revolution.* Boston, 1960.
Marks, Harry J. "Movements of Reform and Revolution in Germany from 1890 to 1913." Ph.D. diss., Harvard University, 1937.
——. "The Sources of Reformism in the Social Democratic Party of Germany, 1890–1914." *Journal of Modern History* 11:3 (September 1939), 334–56.
Marx, Karl, and Engels, Friedrich. *Selected Correspondence.* New York, 1942.
——. *Selected Correspondence.* Moscow, 1960.
Marxismus und deutsche Arbeiterbewegung. Berlin, 1970.
Matthias, Erich, "Kautsky und der Kautskyanismus: Die Funktion der Ideologie in der deutschen Sozialdemokratie vor dem ersten Weltkriege." *Marxismusstudien,* 2nd ser. (1957), pp. 151–97.
Matthias, Erich, and Pikart, Eberhard, eds. *Die Reichstagfraktion der deutschen Sozialdemokratie 1898 bis 1918.* Düsseldorf, 1966.
May, Arthur J. *The Hapsburg Monarchy, 1867–1914.* Cambridge, Mass., 1960.
McLellan, David. *Karl Marx: His Life and Thought.* New York, 1973.
Mehring, Franz. *Geschichte der deutschen Sozialdemokratie.* Stuttgart, 1919.
Merker, Paul. *Sozialdemokratie und Gewerkschaften, 1890–1920.* Berlin, 1949.
Michels, Robert. "Die deutsche Sozialdemokratie im internationalen Verbände." *Archiv für Sozialwissenschaft und Sozialpolitik* 26 (1907), 148–231.
——. "Die deutsche Sozialdemokratie: Parteimitgliedschaft und soziale Zusammensetzung." *Archiv für Sozialwissenschaft und Sozialpolitik* 23 (1906), 471–556.
——. *Political Parties.* Glencoe, Ill., 1958.

———. *Zur Soziologie der Parteiwesens in der modernen Demokratie.* Leipzig, 1911.

Miersch, Klausjürgen. *Die Arbeiterpresse der Jahre 1869 bis 1889 als Kampfmittel der österreichischen Sozialdemokratie.* Vienna, 1969.

Miller, Susanne. *Das Problem der Freiheit in Sozialismus.* Frankfurt, a.M., 1964.

———. *Burgfrieden und Klassenkampf.* Düsseldorf, 1974.

Mommsen, Wolfgang J. "Domestic Factors in German Foreign Policy Before 1914." *Central European History* 6:1 (March 1973), 3–43.

Montgelas, Max, and Schücking, Walter, eds. *Die deutschen Dokumente zum Kriegsausbruch.* Berlin, 1921.

Moorhus, Roger, ed. *European Socialism and the Problem of Internationalism Before World War One.* New York, 1972.

Morgan, David W. *The Socialist Left and the German Revolution.* Ithaca, N.Y., 1975.

Morgan, Roger P. *The German Social Democrats and the First International, 1864–1872.* Cambridge, 1965.

Moring, Karl-Ernst. *Die sozialdemokratische Partei in Bremen 1890–1914.* Hanover, 1968.

Müller, Hermann. *Die November-Revolution: Erinnerungen.* Berlin, 1928.

Muss, Max Ludwig A. *Das deutsche Wirtschaftsleben seit Beginn des 19. Jahrhunderts.* Leipzig, 1930.

Nettl, John P. *Rosa Luxemburg.* 2 vols. London, 1966.

Neumann-Hofer, Adolf. *Die Entwicklung der Sozialdemokratie bei den Wahlen zum deutschen Reichstage 1871–1903.* Berlin, 1903.

Nicholas, J. A. *Germany After Bismarck: The Caprivi Era, 1890–1894.* Cambridge, Mass., 1958.

Nipperday, Thomas. *Die Organization der deutschen Parteien vor 1918.* Düsseldorf, 1961.

Osterroth, Franz. *Biographisches Lexikon des Sozialismus.* Hanover, 1960.

Pack, Wolfgang. *Das parlemantarische Ringen und das Sozialistengesetz Bismarcks, 1878–1890.* Düsseldorf, 1961.

Paulmann, Christian. *Die Sozialdemokratie in Bremen, 1864–1964.* Bremen, 1964.

Pech, Stanley. "F. L. Rieger: The Road from Liberalism to Conservatism." *Journal of Central European Affairs* 17 (1957), 3–24.

Pierson, Stanley. *Marxism and the Origins of British Socialism: The Struggle for a New Consciousness.* Ithaca, N.Y., 1973.

Pikart, Eberhard. "Der deutschen Reichstag und der Ausbruch des Ersten Weltkrieges." *Der Staat* 5 (1966), 47–70.

———. "Die Rolle der Parteien im deutschen konstitutionellen System vor 1914." *Zeitschrift für Politik* 9:1 (1962), 12–32.

Plener, Ulla. "Karl Kautskys Opportunismus in Organisationsfrage (1900–1914): Zur Entstehung des Zentrismus in der deutschen Sozialdemokratie." *Beitrag zur Geschichte der deutschen Arbeiterbewegung* 2 (1961), 349–70.

Pozzoli, Claudio, ed. *Uber Karl Korsch.* Frankfurt a.M., 1973.

Prager, Eugen. *Geschichte der U.S.P.D.* Berlin, 1922.

Protokoll der internationalen sozialistischen Konferenz in Wien vom 22. bis 27. Februar 1921. Vienna, 1921.

Protokoll des internationalen sozialistischen Arbeiterkongress, 1893. Zurich, 1894.

Puhle, Hans-Jürgen. *Agrarische Interessenpolitik und preussischer Konservatismus.* Hanover, 1966.

Radek, Karl. *Proletarian Dictatorship and Terrorism.* Translated by P. Lavin. Detroit, 1921.

Rappoport, Charles. *Idees et faits socialistes: La discussion Bernstein, Kautsky et Bebel.* Paris, 1899.

Ratz, Ursula. "Karl Kautsky und die Abrüstungskontroverse in der deutschen Sozial-demokratie, 1911–12." *International Review of Social History* 11 (1966), 197–227.

Ratz, Ursula, ed. "Briefe zum Erscheinen von Karl Kautskys 'Weg zur Macht.'" *International Review of Social History* 12:3 (1967), 432–77.

Reichard, Richard W. *Crippled from Birth: German Social Democracy, 1844–1870.* Ames, Iowa, 1969.

———. "The German Working Class and the Russian Revolution of 1905." *Journal of Central European Affairs* 13 (1953), 136–53.

———. "Karl Kautsky and the German Social Democratic Party, 1863–1914." Ph.D. diss., Harvard University, 1951.

Renner, Karl. *Karl Kautsky.* Berlin, 1929.

Ritter, Gerhard. *Staatskunst und Kriegshandwerk: Das Problem des "Militarismus" in Deutschland.* 4 vols. Munich, 1954–68.

Ritter, Gerhard A. *Die Arbeiterbewegung im Wilhelminischen Reich, 1890–1900.* Berlin, 1963.

Roehl, John C. *Germany Without Bismarck: The Crisis of Government in the Second Reich, 1890–1900.* Berkeley, 1967.

Roland-Holst, Henriette. *Generalstreik und Sozialdemokratie.* 1905. Reprint. Dresden, 1906.

Rosenberg, Arthur. *The Birth of the German Republic, 1871–1918.* Translated by Ian Morrow. London, 1931.

Rosenberg, Hans. "Political and Social Consequences of the Great Depression, 1873–1896." *Economic History Review* 13 (1943), 58–73.

Roth, Guenther. *The Social Democrats in Imperial Germany.* Totowa, N.J., 1963.

Rothfels, Hans. "Bismarck's Social Policy and the Problem of State Socialism in Germany." *Sociological Review* 20 (January–July 1938), 81–94, 288–302.

Rubel, M., "Le magnum opus de Karl Kautsky." *La Revue Socialiste* 83 (1955), 4–14, and 85 (1955), 275–91.

Ryder, A. J. *The German Revolution of 1918: A Study of German Socialism in War and Revolt.* Cambridge, 1967.

Sand, George. *The Sin of M. Antoine. Leone Leoni.* Philadelphia, 1900.

Sandkühler, Hans-Jörg, and Vega, Rafael de la. *Austromarxismus.* Frankfurt, 1970.

Sartorius von Walterhausen, August. *Deutsche Wirtschaftsgeschichte, 1815–1914.* Jena, 1923.

Schadt, Jörg. *Die sozialdemokratische Partei in Baden, 1868–1900.* Hanover, 1971.

Scheider, Theodor. *Das deutsche Kaiserreich von 1871 als Nationalstaat.* Cologne, 1961.

Schiefel, Werner. *Bernhard Dernburg, 1865–1937.* Zurich, 1974.

Schiemann, Theodor. *Deutschland und Kaiser Wilhelms II. angebliche Schuld am Ausbruch des Weltkrieges: Eine Entgegnung an Karl Kautsky.* Berlin, 1921.

Schleifstein, Josef. *Franz Mehring: Sein marxistisches Schaffen, 1891–1919.* Berlin, 1959.

Schmidt, Alfred. *The Concept of Nature in Marx.* London, 1971.

Schorske, Carl E. *German Social Democracy, 1905–1917: The Development of the Great Schism.* New York, 1955.

Schräpler, Ernst. *August Bebel: Sozialdemokrat im Kaiserreich.* Göttingen, 1966.

Schröder, Hans-Christoph. *Sozialismus und Imperialismus.* Hanover, 1968.

Schröder, Wilhelm. *Geschichte der sozialdemokratischen Parteiorganisation in Deutschland.* Dresden, 1912.

Schröder, Wilhelm, ed. *Handbuch der sozialdemokratischen Parteitage, 1863–1913.* Munich, 1910–1915.

Schröder, Wolfgang. *Partei und Gewerkschaften: Die Gewerkschaftsbewegung in der Konzeption der revolutionären Sozialdemokratie 1868–69 bis 1893.* Berlin, 1975.

Schult, Johannes. *Geschichte der Hamburger Arbeiter 1890–1919.* Hanover, 1967.

Schulthess' Europäischer Geschichtskalender. Munich, 1885–1914.

Schwarz, Max. *MdR: Biographisches Handbuch der Reichstage.* Hanover, 1965.

Seeber, Gustav. *Die deutsche Sozialdemokratie und die Entwicklung ihrer revolutionären Parlamentstaktik von 1867 bis 1893.* Berlin, 1966.

Shaplen, Joseph, and Shub, David, eds. *Socialism, Fascism, Communism.* New York, 1934.

Sheehan, James J. *The Career of Lujo Brentano: A Study of Liberalism and Social Reform in Imperial Germany.* Chicago, 1966.

Shell, Kurt L. *The Transformation of Austrian Socialism.* New York, 1962.

Sixième congrès socialiste international: Compte rendu analytique. Brussels, 1904.

Simon, Walter M. *European Positivism in the Nineteenth Century.* Ithaca, N.Y., 1963.

―――. *Germany in the Age of Bismarck.* London, 1968.

Simpson, George E. "Darwin and 'Social Darwinism.' " *Antioch Review* 19 (1959), 33–45.

Snell, John L. "The German Socialists in the Last Imperial Reichstag, 1912–1918." *Bulletin of the International Institute for Social History* 7 (1952), 196–205.

―――. "The Russian Revolution and the German Social Democratic Party in 1917." *Slavic Review* 15 (1956), 339–50.

Sombart, Werner. *Die deutsche Volkswirtschaft im neunzehnten Jahrhundert.* Berlin, 1903.

Sozialdemokratische Arbeiterpartei Deutschösterreichs. *Protokoll des sozialdemokratischen Parteitages.* Vienna, 1888/89–1932.

Sozialdemokratische Partei Deutschlands. *Protokoll über die Verhandlungen des Parteitages.* Berlin, 1891–1925.

Sozialdemokratischen Parteivorstand, ed. *Handbuch für sozialdemokratische Wähler: Der Reichstag, 1893–1898.* Berlin, 1898.

Spalcke, Karl E. *Die Diktatur des Proletariats bei Kautsky und Lenin.* Tübingen, 1930.

Statistisches Jahrbuch für das deutsche Reich, 1880–1914. Berlin, 1880–1914.

Stein, Lorenz von. *Sozialismus und Kommunismus in heutigen Frankreich.* 1842.

Steinberg, Hans-Joseph. *Sozialismus und deutsche Sozialdemokratie: Zur Ideologie der Partei vor dem I. Weltkrieg.* Hanover, 1967.

Steiner, Herbert. *Die Arbeiterbewegung Österreichs, 1867–1889.* Vienna, 1964.

―――. *Die Gebrüder Scheu.* Vienna, 1968.

Stern, Leo, ed. *Der Kampf der deutschen Sozialdemokratie in der Zeit des Sozialistengesetzes, 1878–1890.* Berlin, 1956.

Ströbel, Heinrich. "Kautsky als Politiker." *Der Kampf* 12 (1919), 687–90.

Struve, Walter. *Elites Against Democracy: Leadership Ideals in Bourgeois Political Thought in Germany, 1890–1933.* Princeton, 1973.

Stürmer, Michael, ed. *Das kaiserliche Deutschland: Politik und Gesellschaft 1870–1918.* Düsseldorf, 1970.

Thompson, S. Harrison. "The Czechs As Integrating and Disintegrating Factors in the Habsburg Empire." *Austrian History Yearbook* 3 (1967), 203–22.

Tirrell, Sarah R. *German Agrarian Politics After Bismarck's Fall.* New York, 1951.

Tormin, Walter. *Zwischen Rätediktatur und sozialer Demokratie.* Düsseldorf, 1954.

Trotsky, Leon. *Terrorismus und Communismus: Anti-Kautsky.* Vienna, 1920.

Tsuzuki, Chushichi. *The Life of Eleanor Marx, 1855–1898: A Socialist Tragedy.* Oxford, 1967.

Tucker, Robert C. *Stalin As Revolutionary, 1879–1929.* New York, 1973.

U.S.P.D. *Protokoll über die Verhandlungen des ausserordentlichen Parteitages.* Berlin, 1917–22.

Varain, Heinz J. *Freie Gewerkschaften, Sozialdemokratie und Staat.* Düsseldorf, 1956.

Vom I. Rätekongress zur Nationalversammlung: Die Tätigkeit des Zentralrates der sozialistischen Republik Deutschlands. Berlin, 1919.

Wachenheim, Hedwig. *Die deutsche Arbeiterbewegung, 1844 bis 1914.* Cologne, 1967.

Waldenberg, Marek. *Mysl polityczna Karola Kautsky'ego w okresie spou z rewizjonizmem, 1898–1909.* Cracow, 1970.

———. *Wzlot i upadek Karola Kautsky'ego: Studium z historii mysli spolecznej poli ycznej.* Cracow, 1972.

Waldschmidt, Hans J. *Lenin und Kautsky: Verschiedene Wege der Weiterentwicklung des Marxismus.* Wurzburg, 1966.

Walton, Paul, and Gamble, Andrew. *From Alienation to Surplus Value.* London, 1972.

Wehler, Hans-Ulrich. *Moderne deutsche Sozialgeschichte.* Cologne, 1966.

———. *Sozialdemokratie und Nationalstaat.* Wurzburg, 1962.

Wette, Wolfram. *Kriegstheorien deutscher Sozialisten.* Stuttgart, 1971.

Wheeler, Robert F., "The Independent Social Democratic Party and the Internationals: An Examination of Socialist Internationalism in Germany, 1915 to 1923." Ph.D. diss., University of Pittsburgh, 1970.

Whiteside, Andrew G. *The Socialism of Fools: Georg Ritter von Schönerer and Austrian Pan-Germanism.* Berkeley, 1975.

Williamson, John G. *Karl Helfferich, 1872–1924.* Princeton, 1971.

Zacek, Joseph F. *Palacky: The Historian as Scholar and Nationalist.* The Hague, 1970.

Zeman, Z. A. B., and Scherlau, W. B. *The Merchant of Revolution: The Life of Alexander Israel Helphand (Parvus).* Oxford, 1965.

Zmarlik, Hans-Günter. "Der Sozialdarwinismus in Deutschland als geschichtliches Problem." *Vierteljahrshefte für Zeitgeschichte* 11 (July 1963), 246–73.

Zweite Kongress der Arbeiter-, Bauern- und Soldatenräte Deutschlands, 8–14 April 1919, Stenographisches Protokoll. Berlin, 1919.

Index

Braun, Heinrich, 27, 50, 57, 86, 92
Braun, Otto, 189
Breitscheid, Rudolf, 195
Brockdorff-Rantzau, Count Ulrich, 224
Brügel, Fritz, 236
Buchenwald, 244
Büchner, Ludwig: *Force and Matter,*
  24–29 passim; mentioned, 19, 70
Buckle, Thomas Henry: *The History of
  Civilization in England,* 24, 29–30; in-
  fluence on Kautsky of, 29–30, 34;
  Kautsky rejects, 65
Bukharin, Nikolai, 206, 236
Bülow, Bernhard von, 130, 161, 165–66
Bund der Landwirte, 104
Burgfrieden, 179, 185
Byr, Robert: *Der Kampf ums Dasein,* 31

Capital (Marx), 33, 60, 83, 101
Center party, 160–61
"Centrism," 140–41, 168–74, 183–84,
  187–88. *See also* Kautsky, Karl
Chlumsky, Adolph, 13, 17
*Class Struggles in the Age of the French
  Revolution,* 80–82 passim, 133
Commune, Paris: influence on Kautsky
  of, 14, 20–21; mentioned, 208, 259*n19*
Communist Manifesto (Marx and Engels),
  182
Council of People's Representatives, 220
Cunow, Heinrich, 155, 158, 187, 220

Dan, Theodore, 231, 238
Darwin, Charles: influence on Kautsky,
  5–6, 18, 24–25, 65, 237. Works: *Origin
  of Species,* 24; *The Descent of Man,* 24
David, Eduard: *Socialism and Agriculture,*
  111; mentioned, 117, 148, 179, 183
Delbrück, Hans, 226
Deutsche Tageszeitung, 224
Deville, Gabriel, 66
The Dictatorship of the Proletariat, 201, 207
Diefenbach, Hans, 171
Dietz, J. H. W.: on *The Critique of the
  Gotha Program,* 95; and the *Neue Zeit,*
  50, 62, 87; mentioned, 88, 101, 124,
  247
Dittmann, Wilhelm, 198, 220, 282*n26*
Dreyfus affair, 114–15
Duma, 132

Ebert, Friedrich, 198, 214, 220, 284*n49*
Eckstein, Gustav, 155, 158
The Economic Doctrines of Karl Marx, 3,
  66–67, 100, 133
Der einzige Weg, 243
Eisner, Kurt, 144
Emden, Walter, 57
Engels, Friedrich: compares Kautsky and
  Bernstein, 48; contribution to the Er-
  furt program, 99; critique of Wilhelm
  Liebknecht, 269*n35;* death of, 13, 90;
  and dialectical materialism, 63–64; and
  Kautsky, 5, 13, 15–16, 34–35, 46–47,
  48, 50, 59–62, 66, 80–81; literary estate
  of, 62; and Louise (Strasser) Kautsky,
  61; on the *Neue Zeit,* 55–56, 94; on
  Polish nationalism, 137; mentioned, 3,
  43, 73, 75, 141, 155, 163, 171, 208,
  236, 242, 245, 250. Works: *Anti-
  Dühring (Herr Eugen Dühring's Revolution in Science),* 34–35, 45, 63–64, 237;
  Origins of the Family, 237
Das Erfurter Programm, 99–101, 136,
  273*n4*

Fascism, 240, 243. *See also* Hitler
Ferri, Enrico, 116
Feuerbach, Ludwig, 24
First International, 236
Fischer, Richard, 144
Foundations of Christianity, 164–65, 277*n53*
Fourth International, 243
Fränkische Tagespost, 106
Franz Ferdinand, Archduke, 179, 225
Freiheit, 200–01, 220, 224
Freikorps, 215
Freksa, Friedrich, 224
French Socialist Party (SFIO), 233, 242
Freyberger, Ludwig, 61
Frohme, Karl, 98

Gallifet, General, 115, 284*n50*
Gapon, Father, 132
Garwy, Peter, 236
Geiser, Bruno, 34, 50, 52, 54, 110
General strike. *See* Mass strike
Georgia: A Social Democratic Republic, 227
*The German Documents on the Outbreak of
  War, 1914* (Montgelas and Schücking),
  225, 286*n65*